D0553824

The
Gay
Academic

THE GAY ACADEMIC

Edited by
Louie Crew

Edited by Louie Crew

Written by
Ellen M. Barrett
James E. Brogan
Louie Crew
Louis Crompton
John P. De Cecco
Ara Dostourian
S. James Elliott
Byrne R. S. Fone
Stephen W. Foster
Bernhard Frank
Mark Freedman
Edgar Z. Friedenberg
Barbara Gittings
Karla Jay
Clinton R. Jones
John Kyper
John A. Lee
J. Lee Lehman
Michael Lynch
Norman Pittenger
Stephen Risch
Laurence J. Rosán
Michael Shively
James W. F. Somerville
Julia P. Stanley
Jacob Stockinger
Hunce Voelcker

C P

Library of Congress Cataloging in Publication Data

Main entry under title:

The Gay Academic.

  Bibliography: pp. 314, 326, 333-334, 413-414
  Includes index, pp. 426-444
  1. Gay liberation movement — North America — Addresses,
essays, lectures. 2. Educators — North America — Addresses,
essays, lectures. I. Barrett, Ellen M. II. Crew, Louie, 1936-

HQ76.5.G38   301.41'57   75-37780
ISBN 0-88280-036-1

Copyright © 1978 by ETC PUBLICATIONS
Palm Springs
California 92262

Table of Contents

In Memory of All Gay Martyrs

Notes On Contributors To
The Gay Academic

RE: "Gay People and Moral Theology"

ELLEN M. BARRETT (M.A., NYU and M.Div., cum laude, General Theological Seminary) has been a member of the NY Gay Liberation Front, a past co-Chairwoman of NY Daughters of Bilitis, a member of Radicalesbians, a past moderator of the NYU Gay Students Liberation, and a past Executive Secretary of the Homosexual Community Counseling Center in NYC. She was the first co-president of INTEGRITY, the national organization of Gay Episcopalians. In January 1977 she was ordained to the priesthood by the Rt. Rev. Paul Moore, Jr., Bishop of New York. She is the Episcopal's Church's first openly gay person to be ordained a priest. She has actively supported the ordination of all women and of all open gays.

RE: "Teaching Gay Literature in San Francisco"

JAMES E. BROGAN (Ph.D., Yale University) is an associate professor of English at San Francisco State University, where he has taught since 1967. Active during the 1968-1969 strike, Professor Brogan was denied re-appointment by S.I. Hayakawa, but subsequently re-instated. Professor Brogan is interested in contemporary literature. He has taught a course on Doris Lessing's fiction from the perspective of women's liberation, and he has created a course in contemporary American fiction called "Problems in American identity. The latter inspired the anthology *The American's Search for Identity* (HBJ) and an article on American men which will appear in an anthology on changing sex roles edited by Barry and Evelyn Shapiro (Bantam). Professor Brogan began his Gay Literature course in 1972. Currently he is working on a book which focuses on relationships from the perspective of emotional growth, drawing on his relationship with Jack Post, whom he met in 1972.

RE: "Before Emancipation: Gay Persons As Viewed by Chairpersons in English," "The Introduction," and overall editing

LOUIE CREW (Ph.D., University of Alabama) is an associate professor of English at Fort Valley State College in Georgia. With Dr. Rictor Norton he edited the special gay issue of *College English* (Nov., 1974). He is a contributing editor to *Margins: Review of Little Magazines and Small Press Books*, for which he guest edited a special issue on current gay male writing and publishing (May, 1975). He is an editor of *Notes on Teaching English*. In 1974 Professor Crew founded INTEGRITY, the national organization of Gay Episcopalians, and he and his husband Ernest Clay still serve as trustees. Crew edits the organization's *Gay Episcopal Forum*. Dr. Crew turned down a Fulbright lectureship in 1974 to meet commitments to love and research. He has published over 80 items in four years, in *Christian Century, College Composition and Communication, Saturday Review, etc.*; and he was an NEH fellow at Berkeley in 1974. He is a member of the Board of Directors of the National Gay Task Force. For eighteen years he has taught in colleges and boarding schools in Britain and the U.S.A. He is listed in *Leaders of Black America*. His poems *Sunspots* appeared from Lotus Press in Detroit in July 1976. With Dr. Stanley he is co-chair of the National Council of Teachers of English (NCTE) Committee on Concerns of Lesbians and Gay Males in the English Profession.

RE: "Gay Genocide From Leviticus to Hitler"

LOUIS CROMPTON (Ph.D., University of Chicago) is a specialist on Bernard Shaw and nineteenth-century literature. He has published essays on the relation of homosexuality to theology, psychiatry, and the teaching of English. He is on the editorial board of the Arno Press reprint series on "Homosexuality: Lesbians and Gay Men in Society, History, and Literature." He is the co-founder, with Dolores Noll, of the Gay Caucus for the Modern Languages. He has taught at the University of Chicago, the University of California at Berkeley, and now is at the University of Nebraska at Lincoln. He is at work on a book on the status of the homosexual in western civilization. His study, *Shaw the Dramatist*, received the Phi Beta Kappa Christian Gauss award for literary scholarship.

RE: "Conflicts Over Rights and Needs in Homosexual Relationships"

JOHN P. DE CECCO (Ph.D., University of Pennsylvania) is Professor of Psychology at San Francisco State University, where he has taught since 1960. His area of specialization is conflict and conflict resolution. He is principal investigator and director of a project designed to study civil liberty issues that arise in conflicts which homosexual men and women have with officials and personnel in public agencies. He has been awarded a grant for this study by the National Institute of Mental Health. Dr. De Cecco is a founder of Lavender University, a member of the San Francisco Bay Area Gay Academic Union, and the faculty sponsor of the Gay Academic Union at San Francisco State University.

RE: "Gayness: A Radical Christian Approach"

ARA DOSTOURIAN (B.D., Episcopal Divinity School; Ph.D., Rutgers University) is specially trained in medieval history and in Byzantine history. He has been active in the Gay Liberation Front in Atlanta and was advisor to the Gay Liberation group at West Georgia College, where he teaches history. He is active in INTEGRITY, the national organization of Gay Episcopalians.

RE: "Homosexuality in the Crucial Decade: Three Novelists' Views"

S. JAMES ELLIOTT graduated from Princeton in 1972, studied a year in Kiel, Germany, under the auspices of the Fulbright program, and is presently completing a Ph.D. in German at the University of Wisconsin in Madison. He has authored several polemic articles on gay topics and has spoken to the Gay Academic Union and the Modern Language Association on gay themes in literature.

RE: "Sons and Lovers: Three English Portraits"

BYRNE R. S. FONE (Ph.D., New York University) teaches graduate and undergraduate courses in 18th-century English and American literature at City College, CUNY. He has published books and articles in those areas. Since September 1975 he has taught a course in The Homosexual Tradition in Literature. He is presently working on a book about Dr. Johnson and on a critical book about gay literature.

RE: "The Annotated Burton"

STEPHEN W. FOSTER attended Miami-Dade Community College and the University of Miami. He has travelled extensively in his continuing, exhaustive, historical, and cross-cultural study of world homosexuality, gathering notes from more than 1,700 books. He is a former officer of Miami Activists Alliance.

RE: "Homosexual Love in Four Poems by Rilke"

BERNHARD, FRANK (Ph.D., University of Pittsburgh) is Professor of English at State University College at Buffalo, NY. He has published extensively as a fiction writer, a scholar, and a translator, in journals such as *Antigonish Review, Ball State Forum, Canadian Poetry Magazine, CCC, College English, English Journal, Gay Literature, Le Cercle, Mattachine Review, Mouth of the Dragon,* and *Yale Literary Magazine.*

RE: "Towards a Gay Psychology"

MARK FREEDMAN (Ph.D., Western Reserve University) taught at Western Reserve; University of Maryland Far East Division in Japan, Okinawa, and Thailand; the University of Sydney, Australia; California School of Professional Psychology; and San Francisco State University. He was the author of *Homosexuality and Psychological Functioning* (Brooks/Cole, 1971) and a founder of the Association of Gay Psychologists. Dr. Freedman died in San Francisco of hepatitis on July 21, 1976, at the age of 33. His colleagues in psychology are preparing a memorial volume of scholarship.

RE: "Towards a Gay Psychology"

EDGAR Z. FRIEDENBERG was brought up in Shreveport, Louisiana — "at the time, a pretty good place for staying in touch with your feelings." Now 57 years old, he has been a college teacher for more than forty of those years. He is the author of, among other works, *The Vanishing Adolescent, The Dignity of Youth and Other Atavists, R.D. Laing,* and *The Disposal of Liberty and Other Industrial Wastes.*

RE: "Combatting the Lies in the Libraries"

BARBARA GITTINGS is a gay-books buff and a lesbian activist who has worked for 18 years in the movement. Currently she is coordinator of the American Library Association's Task Force on Gay Liberation (Social Responsibilities Round Table), and coordinator of the National Gay Archives and Library Committee. She also serves on the board of directors of the National Gay Task Force. She is a junior editor of the pioneer series for Arno Press (1975) entitled *Homosexuality: Lesbians and Gay Men in Society, History, and Literature.* She lives in Philadelphia where she is active in the Gay Media Project and the Pennsylvania Governor's Task Force on Gay Rights. From 1963-1966, she was editor of the monthly magazine *The Ladder: A Lesbian Review.* She has given speeches at more than 30 colleges and universities, and has addressed the American Psychiatric Association, the Society for the Scientific Study of Sex, the National Association of Women Deans and Counselors, the American College Personnel Association, the Gay Academic Union, and other professional organizations.

RE: "Male Homosexuality and Lesbianism in the Works of Prouse and Gide"

KARLA JAY is co-editor with Allen Young of two anthologies about gay liberation, *Out of the Closets: Voices of Gay Liberation* (Douglas/Links and Pyramid) and *After You're Out* (Links Books). She has been East Coast

Coordinator of The Lesbian Tide and a frequent contributor to such publications as *Win Magazine* and *The Gay Liberator*. She has also written for the L.A. *Free Press, Lavender Woman, Shantih, University Review, Margins,* and other publications. She currently lives in New York.

RE: "Christopher Isherwood and the Religious Quest"

CLINTON R. JONES (M. Div., General Theological Seminary; S.T.M., New York Theological Seminary; D.D.) is Canon of Christ Church Cathedral in Hartford, a member of the Episcopal House of Bishops' Task Force on Homophiles and the Ministry, and a long-time counselor of gay persons. He is the author of *What About Homosexuality?* (Thomas Nelson, Inc.), *Homosexuality and Counseling* (Fortress Press), and *The Way of a Transexual: The Hardest Decisions* (Confide Interview Cassette). The Rev. Dr. Jones has won the Bard Medal for "Outstanding Alumnus," The Silver Beaver (from Boy Scouts of America), and numerous other honors as priest and counselor.

RE: "Coming Out: Towards a Social Anaylsis"

JOHN KYPER is a longtime gay/antiwar activist and a recent graduate in paralegal studies from the University of Massachusetts/Boston. He is a frequent contributor to Boston's *Gay Community News,* and his work has also appeared in the *Vermont Freeman, Win Magazine, Fag Rag, Gay Sunshine,* and *Mouth of the Dragon.* In August, 1974, he was deported for life from Canada as "a member of the prohibited class of persons . . . in that you admit that you are a homosexual." He is a member of the Fort Hill Faggots for Freedom and lives in a gay male collective in Roxbury, MA. He is also a coordinator of the Unitarian-Universalist Gay Caucus.

RE: "Meeting Males by Mail"

JOHN A. LEE (Ph.D., Sussex), Associate Professor of Sociology at the University of Toronto, is author of *Colours of Love* (New Press, 1973), a study of lovers' varying definitions of "being in love," as well as the author of books and articles on faith healing, educational television, gay liberation, ethnic assimilation, medieval "courtly love," etc. He is divorced, the father of two children, 13 and 15; a public gay activist in Toronto and a founder of the Canadian Gay Academic Union.

RE: "Gay Students"

J. LEE LEHMAN is a doctoral candidate in botany at Rutgers University and

Director of the National Gay Student Center (2115 S. Street, NW, Washington, DC 20008). She edits the Center's newsletter *interCHANGE*, and is a co-editor of *The New Jersey Lesbian*. She is also co-coordinator of the Rutgers University Coalition of Lesbians.

RE: "The Life Below the Life"

MICHAEL LYNCH (Ph.D., University of Iowa), attended Oberlin and Goddard as well as the University of Iowa. He is Assistant Professor of English at University of Toronto, where he taught the institution's first gay studies course. He writes regularly for *The Body Politic*, the major gay paper in Canada.

RE: "Evils and God — From a 'Process' Perspective"

NORMAN PITTENGER (S.T.D., Berkeley Divinity School; S.T.M., General Theological Seminary) is a senior member of King's College, Cambridge, and a member of the Faculty of Divinity in the University of Cambridge in England. For many years he taught at the General Theological Seminary in New York, where he was Gomph Professor of Christian Apologetics. He has written some 60 books, several of which deal with a Christian interpretation of sexuality and one, *Time for Consent*, is a discussion of homosexuality. Of Canadian-American family, he was educated at Princeton, Oxford, and the General and Union Seminaries in New York.

RE: "Towards a Gay Analysis of Science and Education"

STEPHEN RISCH (B.S., University of Minnesota), is presently a doctoral candidate in the Department of Zoology, University of Michigan. His current research is in the area of the ecology of agricultural systems in Central America. He is "struggling to develop research methodology and goals, as well as teaching techniques consistent with a gay analysis." He has been active in the publication *Science for the People*.

RE: "Philosophies of Homophobia and Homophilia"

LAURENCE J. ROSÁN (Ph.D., Columbia University) has taught philosophy and the philosophy of religion at Penn State, at Alabama College, and at Queens and Brooklyn Colleges (CUNY). He entered the gay movement when he was pressured to leave Pensacola Junior College, where he taught, upon the discovery that he had been living with his lover for five years. He has written widely for various gay publications; was active very early in the NYC West

Side Discussion Group, GLF, and GAA; was a founder of Miami GAA; is a member and consulting editor of Eulenspiegel Society; and is currently active in the Jacksonville Florida gay movement.

RE: "Conflicts Over Rights and Needs in Homosexual Relationships"

MICHAEL SHIVELY is a graduate student in social psychology at San Francisco State University. His undergraduate studies in psychology at SFSU included a study of the interpersonal conflicts of homosexual men and of homosexual women. He is presently a research associate in the NIMH civil liberties project and a member of the Gay Academic Union at San Francisco State University. With Professor De Cecco he has co-authored "A Study of Perceptions of Needs and Rights in Interpersonal Conflicts in Homosexual Relationships."

RE: "Aesthetic and Sexual Relativity"

JAMES W. F. SOMERVILLE (B.A. — First Class Honors — University of London) has been lecturer in Philosophy at The University of Hull, England, since 1964. Born in Preston, Lancashire, England, in 1941, he was educated at Preston Catholic College and studied philosophy at King's College and Birbeck College, University of London, from 1960 through 1964. He has been a member of The Campaign for Homosexual Equality (CHE) in Britain since 1972, and was the first convenor of the Hull CHE local group. His current research interests are in the field of aesthetics and various problems in epistemology, especially those arising from seventeenth and eighteenth century philosophers. He believes that a discipline like philosophy, which helps in clarifying thought and enables people to see things in differing lights, may be of more service in the fight for gay rights than recondite medical, psychological, or sociological research.

RE: "Lesbian Separatism: The Linguistic and Social Sources of Separatist Politics"

JULIA P. STANLEY (Ph.D., University of Texas) has been a member of The Daughters of Bilitis, a coordinator of the Southeastern Gay Coalition, and a panelist for the first annual conference of The Gay Academic Union. She has written for American Speech, The Bucknell Review, College English, and Foundations of Language. Dr. Stanley says of herself: "Formerly a member of the academic establishment, I have now devoted my energies to creating a community of women, to exploring the politics and perspectives of alternate social structures." Dr. Stanley teaches in the Department of English at the University of Nebraska, Lincoln. With Dr. Crew she is co-chair of the National Council of Teachers of English (NCTE) Committee on Concerns of Lesbians and Gay Males in the English Profession.

RE: "Homotextuality: A Proposal"

JACOB STOCKINGER (M.A., University of Wisconsin) has been a graduate student, Ford Fellow, and Teaching Assistant since 1971 in the Department of French and Italian at the University of Wisconsin in Madison, where he presently is writing a doctoral thesis on contemporary French poetry. Prior to his arrival in Madison, he received his B.A. from Lawrence College, directed the Foreign Book Department at the Yale Co-op in New Haven, and taught French and English at Kailua High School in Kailua, Hawaii. He has addressed the Wisconsin Academy of Science, Arts and Letters, has published critical articles and reviews in *College English* and *Margins* and poetry in *Bloodroot* and *The Madison Review*, and delivered a paper on "Sources of the Homosexual Tradition in French Literature" at the 1975 MLA convention in San Francisco. He has been active in Madison Gay Liberation and is on the board of directors of Gay Renaissance of Madison.

RE: "The Case for Casque"

HUNCE VOELCKER (A.B., Villanova University) is the author of *The Hart Crane Voyages, Logan, Joy Rock Statue Ship, Songs for the Revolution, Parade of Gumdrop, Sillycomb* and most recently, *Within the Rose*. He lives in a house he built himself near Duncans Mills, California, where he has been working for several years on a definitive explication and novel based on Hart Crane's *The Bridge*. "The Case for Casque" is drawn from his notes on this work.

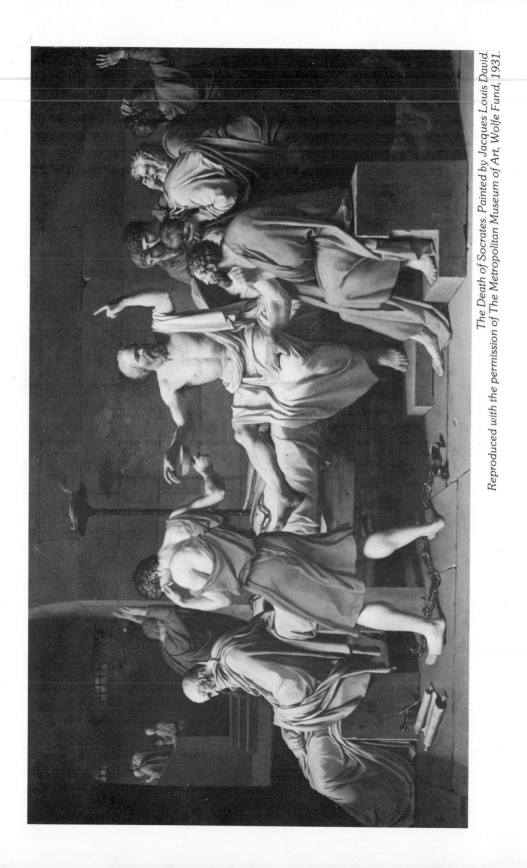

Introduction

AN ANTIDOTE TO HEMLOCK
By Louie Crew

After over 2,000 years of being stigmatized as "corrupters of youth," gay academics are declaring themselves to be what they have always been, viz., an integral part of the academy, serving with distinction in the academy's most celebrated achievements as well as in its more mundane endeavors, certainly with no demonstrable monopoly on corruption, sexual or otherwise.

Before the Stonewall Riots in Greenwich Village in the summer of 1969, it would have been virtually unthinkable for any academic on this side of retirement and on either side of tenure thus to give the truth to that heterosexist calumny about "corruption." While very few academics were with the street queers and drag queens at Stonewall when spontaneously they resisted police brutality and gave birth to the Gay Liberation Movement, even gays in the most isolated library carrels will never be the same again.

This collection makes clear in a small space several truths that could have been discovered by any truth-seekers for the past 20 or so centuries: that gay scholars are not new in any generation; that we come at all times and in all places; that we work in all disciplines; and perhaps most importantly, that we do not speak with one voice or style. Efforts to stigmatize all gay persons, open or closeted, as mindless members of a herd are as false as any dichotomy between "the libbers" and "those who are sensible, like me."

What is new here is the fact that we are all willing to be together in a volume called *The Gay Academic*; we are but a few of the many more gay persons in all professions and stations now seizing our long-denied opportunity to affirm our gay sexuality as of one piece with all that we are.

Many of us discuss herein our uneasiness with gay community. Some of us are more knowledgeable about and more comfortable in the nongay community than we are in the gay community. Our culture has made it very unlikely until quite recently that more than the most furtive communication could exist among those who are gay, particularly those vulnerable enough to be in the professions. Most gay academics still find greater safety in being identified as a part of the nongay world, limiting their communication with gays to those who are not with them in the academy. Often gay space seems more an overlay to a complete picture of our society (as in the kind of body language that occurs without the knowledge of the nonparticipants who are present in the same large room) than a measurable territory that can be located in geographical or temporal terms. Certainly in the academy the gay community is more an idea in the making than an accomplished fact.

In November 1973, 325 gay persons attended the first meeting of the Gay Academic Union at John Jay College (CUNY). Each year since, the GAU has almost doubled membership, with regional meetings often now bringing hundreds. Almost every major academic professional society now has a gay caucus, and many caucuses have influenced their parent organizations to consider resolutions that support gay colleagues. Hardly a campus is without its gay spokespersons, regardless of the success with which they are often silenced. Through all of these efforts gay academics are bidding for the freedom to be self-affirming in a society which continues to deplore us, as in the criminalizing of our sexual behavior in almost 70 percent of the states.

Nongays who oppose gay community as just one more rival dissension are insensitive to the fact that it is the nongays who have created the necessity of gay community. If gay people were not oppressed, there would be little reason for gay community, any more than for blue-eyed community, or freckled community. By law of nature, gay people are born into nongay unions; we are nurtured in institutions controlled by the heterosexual majority. In view of the stigma that gays acquire merely by identifying with other gay people, it seems unlikely that many would do so if our culture provided alternative structures through which we could realize our whole personhood.

Those who control structures, particularly structures designed for their own needs, are not known for their readiness, unasked, to change those structures, or even to provide alternatives. Gay community is being born out of the need to demand such changes.

The "liberal" nongay response to gay openness typically is, "So What? What has private sexuality to do with the public job of teaching?" Only a nongay has the luxury of assuming that she or he has not been "sexual" when routinely appearing as heterosexual, as wife-husband-parent indulging the collectives which do not collect gays (such as "we men know" and "all women know" when followed by heterosexist assumptions).

Contributors to this volume frequently testify to the "academic" effects of our social and political struggles. Several claim that one's sexual orientation can radically affect one's teaching style, and others demonstrate that honesty with sexuality can lead to new dynamics in teaching and research.

Gay academics discussing sexuality are no more overtly "sexual" than are nongay academics discussing marriage, and there is a good chance that the gays will proselytize far less. Few families try to turn nongays into gays, but mothers and fathers usually feel themselves complete failures if they cannot "convert" their gay children into nongays. It is time that all persons respected sexuality of individual persons as holy, complete, and not to be tampered with by any meddling outsider, gay or nongay.

The Gay Academic is not primarily *about* gay academics, but rather *by* academics willing to be identified with the project. It is a multidisciplinary showcase of first time in print works by professionals in our several areas addressing a general academic audience. Most of the contributors focus at least part of the time on sexual questions, but according to no rigid definitions of *sexual*. Part of what gay academics are fighting for is a more universal realization that sexuality has casual registers too, that one is gay or nongay when drinking coffee or grading examinations, even if we have no differentiating or specialized ways that we go about these chores. The "corruption" image would have us gay only when some of us commit crimes or when we are sexually aroused, saying that at other times we are "just persons." By contrast, the majority assures its "just persons" status all the time; and no editor would think to write a headline "Nongay Rapes Little Girl" or "Heterosexual Couple Fined for Beating their Child."

The Gay Academic includes scholars from England, Canada, and all parts of the United States, writing in no fewer than ten disciplines. Intentionally, some of the work is complex and lengthy, some short and expository. The book is intended as a sampler, not a complete text of the volumes of new scholarship spawned in the Gay Liberation Movement. Here we are seen in all of the catholicity of gay life, all of the diversity of our scholarly biases and styles. The book does not yield an abstracted picture of "the" gay academic: part of the purpose of the volume is to demonstrate the absurdity of trying to find a new stereotype (however ameliorated) to replace the old one of the "corrupter." It is time to do away with stereotypes altogether and to respond to each gay person as a full and important individual.

The occasional anger in this volume is the cry of new birth. Far more pervasive still is the sense of joy and excitement, the eureka of self-discovery. From the younger among us, the joy is often communicated as "Yes, I belong!" From some of the old-timers, often it is the wink which says, "Of course; didn't you know? I have been here all along."

Surely nongay outsiders, young and old alike, are not so insecure that they must avoid rejoicing with those who rejoice. The entire culture now has a new and less thwarted access to talent as old as that of Socrates. The only corruption anyone has ever needed to fear is any form of censoring hemlock that would prevent our discovering that the examined life is worth living indeed.

I.
GENERAL ACADEMIC ISSUES

Before Emancipation:
Gay Persons
As Viewed by Chairpersons in English

By Louie Crew

Even to research the status of gay persons is viewed as subversive by many in this country. The following comments come not from the minds of the usual riffraff, but from the graffitic imagination of persons distinguished by being chairpersons of departments of English in colleges and universities across the United States, writing with anonymity in the margins of a questionnaire:

"Gay Persons" — do you mean queers?
This is the damndest thing I have *ever* seen!
Returned with *DISGUST!*
God forbid!
Tell me, Louie, are you a daisy?
Your questionnaire has been posted on our department bulletin
board and has been treated as a joke.

In early February 1975, I purchased from the Modern Language Association (MLA) a mailing list for the Associated Departments of English (ADE). Soon thereafter I posted a questionnaire about attitudes towards gay persons to all 893 U.S. chairpersons on the list. The mailing was funded by the Faculty Research Grants Committee of Fort Valley State College.

The questionnaire brought a sizeable response, particularly in view of its length. Twenty-seven percent of the chairpersons returned something in the envelope provided, some only the blank questionnaires with little or no comment, some with explaining letters, but 24 percent with the completed questionnaires for quantification and analysis. Responses from two of those not completing questionnaires are typical of most: "You are to be honored for your compassion towards teachers who suffer this affliction [sic]"; and "You may be obsessed with the subject of sex, but I have other things to do than pander to this obsession."

Clear Hostility in One out of Four Chairpersons

Based on his/her responses to 29 of the most unequivocal questions, each chairperson was assigned a score on a Hostility-Acceptance Scale.[1] While any prejudice or liberality or whatever is always relative, these individual general measures of hostility or acceptance provide the useful function of making possible a statistical correlation between the hostility-acceptance thus measured and various other chairperson variables.

From a gay point of view there is little comfort in the fact that by this simplest measure 24 percent of all chairpersons proved to be predominately hostile, 32 percent proved to be predominately ambivalent, and only 44 proved to be predominately accepting. In survival terms, these results justify a high degree of professional gay paranoia: one of out every four chairpersons in English is admittedly an anti-gay person, not to mention the many more who like to appear accepting but would capriciously use slight pretexts not even measured here to abandon a gay person under fire.

Tables 1 through 3 scale various chairperson subgroups vertically to show their relative difference in the distribution of themselves as hostile or accepting (as indicated horizontally.) The more divergent a subgroup's distribution from overall chairperson norms (bold face), the greater the influence of the subgroup's distinguishing characteristic is likely to have been in accounting for the divergence; therefore, subgroups at the tops and the bottoms of the tables are those to watch with the greatest concern.

Rightly or wrongly, throughout the interpretation here presented it is assumed that chairpersons in English are a fair index of the colleges where they teach. We allow for some difference between person and institution, but we feel that any radically different professional behavior from that encouraged by the institutions would not allow persons to be chairpersons or to remain chairpersons very long. As one respondent added:

> If we were living in a much more liberated society, many of my answers would be more positive and encouraging to gays. *But*, the southwestern states are not liberated, and Oklahoma in particular is a bastion of sexual bigotry . . . In this state, homosexual activity is a felony, and convicted felons are barred from teaching in our school systems. Thus, a chairman [sic] not only would be justified but would be compelled to not hire or to dismiss a person "convicted for gay sex." Similarly, social pressures in this area are such that an open admission or exhibition of homosexuality — especially by an educator — means instant ruination . . . . Hence, the *reality* of our laws and social pressures dictates some rather negative and dis-

couraging responses: I have answered according not to how things should be but to how they are — Oklahoma is Closet Country.

Institutional Differences

The institutional correlations with hostility and acceptance of Gay persons offer few surprises. Religious colleges lead the way in hostility, reflecting the official religious community which has persisted in its persecution of gay people from the very beginning, as Professor Crompton so tellingly documents elsewhere in this volume. As one chairperson in a Church school in Kansas wrote: "You may wish to recall that all adults, even consenting adults, are responsible to God's laws. The law governing the residents of Sodom has never been changed. In brief, when someone is sick, you help this person. Certainly a help is not a denial of the sickness."

Three other chairpersons wrote similar views with differing tones: "The Church I serve has called homosexuality a reversal of the natural roles of male and female and has condemned it as sin, with a strong emphasis on leading the homosexual away from such behavior." This person went on to give the name of a prominent gay professor whom he had had in graduate school, as if to mitigate some of the indictment by praising the professor personally. A California religious chairperson wrote: "It would be hypocritical of me and the college I teach in to deny the moral values which we subscribe to by allowing homosexuality respectable status on campus, (just as it would be hypocritical of me to hold to no belief that homosexuality is morally wrong and yet deny equal status to the homosexual). At the same time, I do not feel that my judgment that homosexuality is morally wrong means that I condemn the person along with the 'sin.' " The third wrote: "I realize that my responses are highly inconsistent. One problem is that I am tugged in different directions by my own ideas and feelings (negative), my sense of justice (neutral, I hope), and my sense of loyalty to my college, which is committed to the outlook of a fairly conservative Protestant denomination (negative in the extreme)."

Perhaps the most disturbing response of all written in the margins came from a female chairperson at a Southern religious school. At one and the same time she epitomizes the religious judgmentalism and the pious pretention to being genuinely concerned for human beings:

In time perhaps our knowledge will extend to include this group [gays] truly, accurately, fairly. At this time, I can only speak for myself: they are almost invariably known, regardless of efforts to conceal. Further, they are almost all avoided, pitied, regarded as

TABLE 1:
INSTITUTIONAL INFLUENCES ON HOSTILITY-ACCEPTANCE

Distributions on the Hostility-Acceptance Scale are expressed in percentages of the chairperson subgroups.

	INSTITUTIONAL SUBGROUPS OF CHAIRPERSONS IN ENGLISH	HOSTILE	AMBIVALENT	ACCEPTING
INCREASINGLY DANGEROUS FOR GAYS	Private religious schools (†12)	41	28	31
	Southern schools (†67)	39	32	29
	Schools with fewer than 1,000 students (†11)	35	27	38
	Schools with undergraduate programs only (†14)	33	27	40
	South Central schools (†67)	28	41	31
	Western schools (†67)	28	24	48
	Schools with 1,000–2,999 students (†11)	26	32	42
	Schools in towns larger than 15,000 (†13)	25	30	45
	Schools with limited graduate programs (†14)	25	31	44
	ALL CHAIRPERSONS	**24**	**32**	**44**
INCREASINGLY SAFE FOR GAYS	Junior or community colleges (†14)	22	42	36
	Schools in rural communities (†13)	22	39	39
	Schools in small towns, to 15,000 (†13)	21	35	44
	Schools with 15,000 or more students (†11)	21	21	58
	State schools (†12)	20	30	50
	Schools with 5,000–9,999 students (†11)	20	19	61
	Schools with 10,000–14,999 students (†11)	18	45	35
	Schools with 3,000–4,999 students (†11)	17	46	37
	Private nonreligious schools (†12)	17	37	46
	North Central schools (†67)	16	26	58
	Schools with full university programs (†14)	10	32	58
	North East schools (†67)	8	34	58

Numbers following the † correspond with numbers on the questionnaire, reprinted in the Appendix.

definitely abnormal (aberrational), sick *OR* freaks of nature. They arouse snickering and shame. Religiously they are felt unGodly, unBiblical, and definitely inimical to family life — and to the best interests of students. They are regarded as corrupters. Our own campus is very intolerant, though not cruel — the homos usually leave. *One* married, and has caused heartbreak to the girl (all wondered why he married!) — such is much resented. One of our very likable majors left — very torn up (*self*-doubts).

One wishes that this person could get with her colleague at another religious college, who wrote:

Right on, Mr. Crew! Work like this makes all of us reassess our gayness in academia. At a religiously oriented college, it is especially difficult to come out of the closet, even when in all other areas one has made a mature adjustment. The times are a-changing.

Private nonreligious colleges might cite Table 1 in support of their claim that they are important to the nation precisely because they support alternatives the State and the Church will not risk; however, I somehow doubt that they would want to jump at this opportunity to support the claim, even if they were 20 rather than only 3 percentage points less hostile than State institutions.

"Go North, young gay person!"

Geographically the northeastern (postal zips 00001-19999) and north central (zips 40000-59999) states prove to be much safer for gay persons in English than do the homophobic southern (zips 20000-39999), south central (zips 60000-79999), and western (80000-99999) states, in confirmation of the stereotypes of the liberal North and the reactionary South. As one Texas chairperson put it: "I hate to be a mugwump on so many questions, but I am. Generally, in my region of the country the above responses indicate an extremely tolerant attitude."

The size of the institution is a better predictor of hostility or acceptance than is the size of the community. Small colleges as are small departments (cf. Table 2), are clearly unsafe for gay persons, particularly colleges with fewer than 1,000 students, but also colleges with fewer than 3,000. As one chairperson wrote: "I do not have the time or inclination to try to change current attitudes. Obviously a gay *would* desire to change them, but we are too small a school [under 1,000] to afford the luxury of many approaches — we barely manage the mainstream." Another, from a college with 1,000-2999 students, clarified: "My views here reflect the conservative college community where I live and teach. We are not ready for the so-called 'gay revolution.' Although I have some sympathy for gay individuals who wish to be honest and open in their relationships, I personally regard homosexuality as an abnormal condition." One female who teaches in a community college of under 1,000 students in a rural area wrote:

> Personally, I don't care what anyone's sexual preferences are, and I hope I use a positive approach (give a positive attitude) toward homosexuality in my Greek Myth course. But in this community, a gay at the College wouldn't last two minutes. Sorry! Several years ago a few part-time students tried to get a gay organization going but were "laughed" off campus. Then they went to a big city 75 miles away. At that time we had the gay group from that city visit a philosophy class to explain the movement — got quite a hostile reaction from class. I had a lot of explaining to do to administrators that I supported the instructor in having the group in his class.

With above 3,000 students, there is clearly more acceptance, but not in any further progression that correlates with size.

Somewhat contrary to popular mythology, chairpersons from rural communities and small towns (under 15,000) appear to be more accepting than chairpersons overall, though the differences by community size seem too slight for any strong conclusions. The figures suggest that chairpersons respond more to peer prejudice than to town prejudice when reacting to their gay charges.

Full universities are clearly safer places for gay persons in English than are colleges with undergraduate programs only, giving some substance to the claim that in size there is, if not liberality, at least more anonymity and privacy in which to escape censure. Hopefully the more complex the institutional structure the more important the decisions with which chairpersons have to concern themselves, admitting relatively lower priority to sports of witch-hunting or queer-baiting. Chairpersons from community colleges and from colleges with only limited graduate programs show no appreciable difference from overall chairperson norms.

CONCLUSION: Gay job hunters in English would be well advised to qualify themselves for a university post in the Northeast, preferably at a private nonreligious institution, but also allowably at a state one, so long as either has at least 3,000 students. Gay job hunters in English should avoid like the plague any religious institutions, any Southern institutions, and any institutions with fewer than 1,000 students or with limited academic offerings.

Departmental & Curricula Differences

Departmental chairpersons who will not discuss gay writers as such and who will not encourage gay students to tap their gay resources are obviously hostile towards gays, or so it would seem. Some chairpersons disagree. Several emphasized that students are "not encouraged, but are not discouraged either." Another explained an unwillingness to encourage: "Peer pressure [is] too great here." Several said that they did not know whether they even had any gay students and certainly made no effort to identify them. The inclusion of these less generous if not obviously hostile subgroups permits a revealing comparison of their scores on the Scale with the scores of subgroups superficially less perspicuous.

The Size of the Department

The size of the department correlates with hostility towards gay persons most clearly in the cases of chairpersons from the smallest (1-5 persons) and the next smallest (6-10 persons) departments. All English departments with eleven or more members are chaired by persons more accepting of gays than the average chairperson; but after a size of eleven is reached, there is no uniform correlation with bigness and increased liberality, at least on the generalized Scale. However, several specific kinds of acceptance of gays do correlate with bigness. Departments of 25 or more teach 83 percent of all gay literature. (Cf. the chairperson of a department of 6-10 in North Carolina who said that such courses would "never be tolerated — never be dared.") Twelve percent of the chairpersons of the departments of 25 or more persons reported at least some openly gay staff, compared with none reported by chairpersons of smallest departments and compared with 6.5 percent of all chairpersons acknowledging openly gay staff. Departments of 25 or more report even higher percentages of closeted gay staff (30 percent claim to have at least some closeted gays; cf. only 13 percent of all departments); here *closeted* means specifically those staff members who have given their chairpersons only private information about their sexual orientation. Chairpersons from the

TABLE 2:
DEPARTMENTAL & CURRICULA INFLUENCES ON HOSTILITY-ACCEPTANCE

Distributions are expressed in percentages of the chairperson subgroups.

	SUBGROUPS OF CHAIRPERSONS IN ENGLISH	HOSTILE	AMBIVALENT	ACCEPTING
INCREASINGLY DANGEROUS FOR GAYS	Departments of 1-5 persons (†15)	46	31	23
	Departments not offering women's literature (†5)	39	33	28
	Campuses without gay student organizations (†1)	38	31	41
	Departments not offering ethnic literature (†6)	31	36	33
	Departments of 6-10 persons (†15)	31	26	43
	Chairpersons who don't discuss gay writers as such (†4)	29	38	33
	Chairpersons who don't encourage gay students to to use their gay identity as a resource (†7)	26	33	41
	Departments not offering gay literature (†3)	25	32	43
	Departments without open gay faculty (†16)	25	33	42
	ALL CHAIRPERSONS	**24**	**32**	**44**
INCREASINGLY SAFE FOR GAYS	Departments of 25 or more persons (†15)	24	23	53
	Chairpersons who do discuss gay writers as such (†4)	19	26	55
	Department offering ethnic literature (†6)	18	35	47
	Departments of 16-20 persons (†15)	16	48	36
	Departments offering women's literature (†5)	15	31	54
	Chairpersons who do encourage gay students to use their gay identity as a resource (†7)	12	6	82
	Departments of 11-15 persons (†15)	11	39	50
	Campuses with gay student organizations (†1)	10	24	66
	Departments of 21-25 persons (†15)	7	31	62
	Departments with open gay faculty (†16)	7	14	79
	Departments offering gay literature (†3)	0	17	83

Numbers following the † correspond with numbers on the questionnaire, reprinted in the Appendix.

largest departments also are freer to estimate that they have non-disclosed gay staff; 57 percent of the chairpersons in the largest departments estimate they have such undisclosed gay staff, compared with only 15 percent of the chairpersons in the smallest departments thus estimating, and compared with 35 percent of all chairpersons making such estimates.

Presence of Other Minority Interests

Liberality is contagious, it seems.[2] English chairpersons in colleges with women's studies and ethnic studies do express greater acceptance of gay persons than do most other chairpersons. The reverse is even more true, particularly the close correlation between high hostility towards gays by chairpersons at colleges without women's studies. This correlation is ironic when juxtaposed with a comment added by a white chairperson from Mississippi waxing very "liberal" towards those who quite recently were barred from his school:

> Subcultures by accident of birth and voluntary subcultures do not, in my view, enjoy the same status. Ethnic subcultures are entitled to toleration, understanding, and sympathy when their norms confront those of the predominant culture. The cases of voluntary subcultures require only understanding in the academic context. Toleration and sympathy are personal rather than institutional choices and must remain so owing to the nonbinding nature of the collegial relationship.

One wonders whether this self-identified nongay really "volunteers" to turn on to members of the opposite sex? In any event, his "toleration and sympathy" are too smug to seem worth counting. Persons enjoying liberality which costs nothing would be amusing were their opinions not at the expense of others still disenfranchised. Of course, all parallels between the experiences of any two groups are limited. For example, it has never been illegal to be either a practicing female or a practicing black.

With our sample, all of the few departments offering gay literature also offered women's literature, and 83 percent with courses in gay literature also have courses in ethnic literature.

Influence of a Visible Gay Presence

Of chairpersons subgrouped by the four measures of gay presence on their campuses, clearly chairpersons on campuses without gay student organizations proved otherwise most hostile to gay persons generally too. Not enough chairpersons reported faculty gay organizations to make meaningful comparisons, but chairpersons reporting openly gay faculty in their departments were among the least hostile of all subgroups charted on any of the Tables. Such absence of hostility is likely a prerequisite for most gays to be open. Gay courses in the curricula do not appear until ALL of the chairperson's hostility is gone, at least as detected by our admittedly simplistic Scale. Also, the small number of chairpersons (3 percent overall) reporting such courses makes this item a not very ubiquitous barometer. The slighter divergence from overall chairperson norms by those groups who do or do not encourage gay students to be open still follows the pattern: the more visibility to gays on campus, the more accepting English chairpersons are towards gays by other general measures. It is difficult to know which comes first: the visibility of gays or the liberality which makes the visibility less threatening. Given the oppressiveness in most places, it would seem that visibility is usually preceded by at least a few definite signs of liberality, though as an open gay on a rural small Southern campus, I could hardly make a strong case for the universality of such a pattern. Certainly invisibility is not just a metaphor in the gay experience.

CONCLUSION: Gay job hunters who want acceptance in English would be wise to hunt for a department of at least 11 members, in a college that sports an organization of gay students and a variety of curricula in women's and ethnic studies.

Chairperson Personal Differences: Sex and Race

By their own declaration, chairpersons in English are themselves gaier than most estimates for the national population as a whole, which sometimes run as low as 4 or 5 percent. In this study, of all chairpersons willing anonymously to classify themselves on both questions about sexual orientation (27 percent were unwilling), 21 percent are gay or bisexual. Specifically, 8 percent are gay and 13 percent are bisexual. These figures are one index to the frequently heard rumor on campus that disciplines with a high premium on sensitivity attract gay people, a rumor with an ambiguous appeal, as when applied to explain alleged concentration of gays in the fine arts, in fashions, in entertainment . . .

Sociologists routinely rate a chairpersonship of a department in an institution of higher education to be a relatively high status position, the views

TABLE 3:
CHAIRPERSON RACIAL & SEXUAL INFLUENCES ON HOSTILITY-ACCEPTANCE

Distributions are expressed in percentages of the chairperson subgroups.

	SUBGROUPS OF CHAIRPERSONS IN ENGLISH	HOSTILE	AMBIVALENT	ACCEPTING
INCREASINGLY HOSTILE	Female chairpersons (†22)	39	22	39
	Chairpersons not specifying their sexual orientation (†20)	32	27	41
	Nongay chairpersons (†20)	27	32	41
	Chairpersons "preferring" their sexual orientation to be known as "Other" (†19)	27	33	40
	Nonblack chairpersons (†21)	25	30	45
	ALL CHAIRPERSONS	24	32	44
INCREASINGLY SAFE	Chairpersons "preferring" their sexual orientation to be known as "Nongay" (†19)	23	33	44
	Nonfemale chairpersons (†22)	21	31	48
	Chairpersons not specifying their race (†21)	17	50	33
	Black chairpersons (†21)	14	29	57
	Chairpersons "preferring" their sexual orientation to be known as "gay" or "bisexual" (†19)	9	9	82
	Gay and bisexual chairpersons (†20)	8	31	61

Numbers following the † correspond with numbers on the questionnaire, reprinted in the Appendix.

of the chairpersons themselves to the contrary notwithstanding. With high status for gays comes also the fact of being "more worried over exposure and . . . more bothered about being officially labeled homosexual."[3] Hence, it is not surprising that while at least 21 percent of the chairpersons in English are gay or bisexual, only 7 percent of the chairpersons (one-third of all of the gays and bisexuals) "prefer to be [so] identified." *In gay terms, two-thirds of the chairpersons are locked in the closet, a very real measure of the hostility they seek thereby to avoid!* More specifically, 86 percent of the gays are hiding, compared with 41 percent of the bisexuals, who enjoy perhaps a bit more chic these days.[4]

The plight of the gays is best described by one chairperson, who identified himself as preferring to be identified as nongay but really gay: "I had some difficulty in answering all questions because my opinions are colored by the

fact that one's gayness would probably be cause for dismissal at my college."
Another gay chairperson seemed somewhat less threatened: "It depends upon
the person. I would be uncomfortable if my being gay were 'universally' known
at this point. I am becoming less anxious each year."

Many chairpersons resisted being labelled by sexual orientation. An
average of 7.5 percent of all chairpersons omitted altogether the two questions
about their sexual orientation. An additional 24 percent specified "other"
when asked how they "prefer[red] to be identified," compared with 16 percent
who specified "other" when asked their real sexual orientation. Alternate
self-identifications in the spaces provided the following, among others:

unique	Fed up with crap like this
person (5 times)	I don't like to be identified
human (twice)	I dig women! [male]
female	No one asks.
male (twice)	non-practicing gay
who knows?	a human being, a man, a husband,
who cares?	a chairperson, after other tags*
androgynous	celibate
tired	Ukrainian

Five percent objected to *nongay* by writing in *heterosexual* as an equivalent.
As one said, "*Heterosexual* is better than non-*anything*." Several first wrote
"normal," and helpfully appended the necessary clarification, "heterosexual,"
though some put only the ambiguous "normal." One wrote "straight." Some of
these who thus flaunted their heterosexuality later wrote notes objecting only
to gays who flaunt *their* sexuality.

It is clear from Table 3 that those who refuse to identify their sexual
orientation are significantly more hostile towards gays than are chairpersons
overall. In other words, it appears that those who most oppose sexual
polarization into gay and nongay are themselves fairly more hostile towards
gay persons than are most persons willing to be thus polarized, though more
evidence is needed before accepting this as a valid generalization.

The confessed nongays were more hostile than those only "preferring"
nongay, perhaps because gays also often "preferred" *nongay*. Gays and
bisexuals, whether open or closeted, were strong in acceptance. Even most of
the eight percent hostility by gays is accounted for as the expression of hostility
perceived as enforced by virtue of one's rank or of the institutional policy. As

_____

*[This respondent later rated as negative a gay employee's introducing his/her
lover as "my spouse," surely tantamount to labelling oneself as "husband"].

one gay chairperson wrote: "My responses to questions about actions and attitudes of chairpersons and department members reflect the position of the college (as I assess it) rather than my own feelings. All gays and bisexuals among faculty here are closet queens" — from one himself admittedly in the closet.

Thus, while there was often disagreement among gays and bisexuals about some of the complicated questions, those 29 unequivocal items used for the Hostility-Acceptance Scale revealed little evidence of any gay equivalent to Uncle Tomism. Gay persons can routinely expect a fairer shake from all closeted and uncloseted gay chairpersons than from nongay chairpersons. This is not to say, however, that there is the slightest evidence that any one of these chairpersons is willing or even interested in carrying on a crusade against the prevailing attitudes towards all gays at his/her institution. It is still easy to imagine that any gay employee so doing would be considered especially threatening to the security of all other gays around, except perhaps at institutions already with few restrictions. There is no underground railroad for gays in trouble yet, and it will most probably not find many porters among the chairpersons anxious to guard their own threatened positions.

The one chairperson with the highest acceptance score is himself a nongay. He wrote a revealing addendum:

> Sexual preferences, practices and other non-classroom stuff don't count for much in a large urban community college. I'm not gay myself — therefore, I have no insight into how gays are treated [here]. I'm not much concerned so long as folks don't get fucked over for being gay; their decisions to come out are their own. I like to sign my name cause I don't dig anonymous stuff from me. Good luck with your work. It's important. [signed with address]

Females as more hostile than males

Female chairpersons are 18 percent more hostile towards gay persons than are nonfemales. This is the one exception to the pattern of contagious liberality discovered throughout the study. Of course only 15 percent of the chairpersons are females. Why they are more hostile is anyone's guess, but I find persuasive the guess by lesbian Karla Jay (see her essay "Male Homosexuality and Lesbianism in the Works of Proust and Gide" elsewhere in this volume):

> I am not in the least surprised that women are more hostile. It is common that oppressed people become more oppressive than the

"real thing" when they get into power. They work harder, and also take harder lines to show that they belong, that they're just as good. "Just because I am a woman I'm not soft on queers" — Get it? Also, there is the phenomenon which deeply affected victims of concentration camps. Sociology studies have noted how Jewish inmates often identified with their oppressors. It's the old Proustian self-hate perhaps, with also the fact of trying to get yourself up by finding another "lower group."

An interesting side issue is the fact that many chairpersons resented being asked to classify themselves as either "Female" or "Nonfemale," in keeping with the effort throughout to use minority nomenclature instead of the heterosexist terms which pervade most so-called impartial academic writing. One wrote:

> I have a great deal of sympathy with the aims of gay liberation, but I found this questionnaire impossible in its vagueness and imprecision. Repeatedly I found myself answering questions whose meaning I could only guess at. I call your particular attention to the question about "Female" or "Nonfemale." P.S. I am straight, male, and yellow.

Of course, whatever problem this wit had with *nonfemale*, the term is not imprecise. Similarly, one chairperson even objected to the neutral *chairperson*: "Cannot locate any 'chairpersons'! How about Couchperson?" Another male added that *nonfemale* is a ridiculous term, and 6 percent of all males wrote in the word *male* rather than designate themselves *nonfemale* (cf. the 4 percent of nonblacks who wrote in "white" or "Caucasian"). Of course, white males rarely hesitate to order their world and everyone else's with *chairman, nonwhite,* and (less often) *non-male.*

Our black sample is regrettably too small (only seven chairpersons, or 3 percent of total) to be taken very seriously, but that small sample is 11 percent less hostile than the nonblack sample, giving further support to Weinberg and Williams' findings of the adaptations blacks can expect:

> Comparisons between black and white homosexuals in the United States showed that blacks expect less negative reaction to their homosexuality and anticipate less discrimination from other people on account of it . . . It was suggested that this is related to the less puritanical attitudes of blacks and the greater tolerance of homosexuals by the black community.[5]

CONCLUSION: Gay job hunters in English who want acceptance would more likely find it from a black male gay or bisexual chairperson.

Of all chairperson subgroups charted (Tables 1-3) the following 10 are the most accepting of gay persons, in descending order:

1. Chairpersons of departments offering courses in gay literature
2. Chairpersons already reporting open gay faculty
3. Chairpersons of departments with 21-25 members
4. Chairpersons who are gay or bisexual
5. Chairpersons in the Northeast
6. Chairpersons at full universities
7. Chairpersons at institutions with gay student organizations
8. Chairpersons who encourage gay students to tap academic gay resources
9. Chairpersons who are black
10. Chairpersons of departments offering women's studies.

None of these 10 groups registered more than 15 percent hostility, though even so slight an amount may be lethal and is cause for proceding with caution.

Gays in all professional positions who want to *remove* rather than *adjust to* the current patterns of hostility might well consider an altogether different strategy. In the long haul, if not in the short, it might be personally more liberating to forget all the priorities revealed in these charts and to assume courageous responsibility for one's own completeness and oppenness in whatever setting one finds himself. In hiding, we affirm, or at least appear to affirm, the hostile suspicions of which we are the victims. Some of us believe that gay integrity and wholeness is worth far more than the approval of all of these chairpersons put together.[6]

THE SORTING OF SPECIFIC ITEMS
ON THE HOSTILITY-ACCEPTANCE SCALE

Percentages of overall chairperson acceptance or hostility for individual items on the questionnaire give additional measures of what attitudes and behaviors are most or least taboo (Tables 4 and 5). Items are "Gay behaviors and attitudes" only in terms of this study, which cannot thereby speak for all gay persons, many of whom might well consider several of the items either

TABLE 4:

THE TEN MAJOR INSTANCES OF GAY AS TABOO FOR CHAIRPERSONS

(In descending order)

No.	Percentage of all Chairpersons	The Rating	Specific Item from the Hostility-Acceptance Scale
1.	69	Rate negative	A gay person's campus appearances outside class in dress of the opposite sex. (†66)
2.	58	Rate negative	A gay faculty couple's holding hands in public on campus. (†65)
3.	58	Rate negative	A gay faculty member's dating of an upperclassperson or graduate student of the same sex. (†63)
4.	54	Rate negative	Giving a literary reading in class while wearing the clothes of one's opposite sex for purposes related to the reading.(†62)
5.	50	Rate negative	At a campus social function, introducing one's lover as "my lover," "my spouse," "my girl (boy) friend," etc., when the two are of the same sex. (†57)
6.	40	Disagree	A good gay dean or college president should let all who work for her or him know about her/his gayness. (†46)
7.	38	Rate negative	In campus business offices, applying for couple rates on insurance, campus housing, etc., by gay couples. (†58)
8.	35	Agree	In choosing literature for teaching, the instructor can generally assume that students benefit most from works which express heterosexual norms of behavior. (†23)
9.	34	Disagree	Two unmarried employees of the same sex having regular sexual relations are acceptable whether or not they make public this fact. (†53)
10.	34	Disagree	Textbook writers have an intellectual responsibility to note the homosexual contexts of gay writers. (†24)

Numbers following the † correspond with numbers on the questionnaire, reprinted in the Appendix.

nonessential or even irrelevant to their gay experience. All items may loosely be categorized matters of decorum (measuring unwritten laws of social behavior), matters of policy (measuring behaviors seeming to be affected by institutionally defined roles and procedures), and matters of academic substance and opinion.

What is Taboo?

Gay variants of decorum (Taboos 1-2, 4-5, 9) evoke the greatest hostility and the slightest acceptance from the chairpersons. Chairpersons care very much about heterosexist norms of dress, displays of public affection, and simple self-definition of parties to social introductions. While some gay persons may want to take heart that chairpersons after all really object more to superficial variations which are easy to conform to, other gay persons will claim to recognize here the careful functioning of the most powerful weapon of all ruling classes, the power to ostracize into oblivion all and any who, by even the slightest superficial social variation, do not at least appear to confirm the rulers' belief that the world is made in their own image. Just demands by individuals or groups to vary manners are hardly the "mere excuses for indecorum" that the rulers would like to think. Only a member of the ruling class could enjoy the luxury of saying, "I am no more concerned with the sex life of my faculty than I am with what brand of underwear they wear, and I would consider their flaunting of either in equally bad taste." The key here is the word *flaunting*. The heterosexual dictators of our culture have so defined our way of life that heterosexual references to one's wife, husband, children, even in the most academic of settings, are not considered *flaunting*; yet let a gay professor just quietly place a picture of her wife or his husband on the desk in the office like anyone else . . .

Gay culture has long retained a higher tolerance, though not complete approval, of variations from heterosexist norms of dress for females and nonfemales, but clearly gay professors in English must leave these cultural differences to the secrecy of the gay ghetto if they want to thrive in the academy. Of course, historically, even nongay culture has widely varied its norms, which is not to say that each variation was taken lightly. Even today, though, most nongay schoolmasters in England would surely find their American colleagues' disapproval of transvestism rather amusing when the transvesting is in the service of literary texts (Taboo No. 4). Thousands of sexually segregated English schoolboys would still have to concur with Oscar Wilde's celebrated judgment that some male performers still make very impressive Rosalinds!, not to mention the transvestism for Shakespeare's entire original female personae. Yet one chairperson responded: "What? Elizabethan acting customs are *one* thing, but this! Strongly negative"; and another exclaimed, "This is theatre; not education!' — a strange dichotomy for a chairperson in English surely. Only one chairperson had the grace to add: "Everything depends upon the circumstances. I would probably feel uncomfortable about this in most cases."

Outside class, even if on campus, what business is it of chairpersons what *any* professor chooses to wear? Lots according to Taboo No. 1. One female chairperson from the South wrote before registering her "strongly negative" reaction: "[Do you mean women should dress] in the tight, dashing clothes favored by the male homosexuals?" A male chairperson explained his negative reaction: "After all, dress is so flexible today, [campus appearances outside class in the dress of the opposite sex] would be unnecessary, except to affront." Shakepeare's transvested Goneril once noted a similar lack of necessity for Lear to flaunt retainers: Lear replied: "O reason not the *need* . . ./ Why nature *needs* not what thou gorgeous wear'st,/ Which scarcely keeps thee warm" [Italics mine], *King Lear*, II, iv, 267, 272-273.

Even more revealing of powerful though quiet heterosexist controls is the Taboo No. 2, against a gay faculty couple's holding hands in public on campus. Only two respondents proferred comments about this high degree of unanimity:

This is silly. Whatever happened to the concept that relationships are personal? Why all the public stuff?

Negative. The same response I'd give to heterosexual couples.

Apparently those taking this line of defense have not taken much notice of heterosexual campus behavior, which however personal, is *not*, most emphatically not, all that private. A glance through the faculty section of any five alumni publications in the U.S.A. will be sure to turn up pictures sporting heterosexual academic couples displaying some analogous innocuous physical affection. Certainly those who share the views of the second chairperson above (who still maintained a score of "Accepting" on the Scale) have not communicated their restrictions as forcefully to their nongay colleagues as to their gay.

As to the decorum of introducing one's gay lover as "my lover," "my spouse," "my girl [boy] friend," Taboo No. 5, the following explanations were typical:

Neither would I find agreeable introducing "my mistress."
Introductions imply an audience and its sensitivities
are an element in introductions.

I think our sensibilities still require that people of same or opposite sex
not speak of each other as lovers, but the other terms are OK.

I'm ambivalent about this. I like honesty,
but would be suspicious of over dramatization.

Bad taste whatever the sex.

What most of these claiming a single standard ignore is that they have refused to acknowledge gay marriages, only to turn around to say that *lover*, the gay analogue, is tantamount to *mistress*; a nongay can choose to marry his mistress, but not so I my husband. As I stated my own point of view to the College English Association in Atlanta in April 1975:

> I do not normally take it that a nongay has performed a sex act in class when citing her role as mother or father. When I refer to "my husband," I am making a standard reference with no specifically genital or political detail. If you see genitals or hear politics, those are your problems. I simply cannot take responsibility for having named the unspeakable orgies that go on in nongay heads. My husband and I and all of your gay students are going to need to be especially strong to survive such distortions.

Taboo No. 9, opposing even the likelihood of gay employees telling about their gay sex, is the one other Taboo relating mostly to decorum, though some would say it relates more substantially to morality. One dissenter wrote: "I would accept the employees as *people*. No reason to reject the persons though their behavior may be unacceptable." More typically one wrote: "There are better bases of acceptability!" One chairperson did throw in the academic qualification: "[It] depends on the learning in the classroom." (The better the teacher, the more s/he can get away with?) The clearest measure of antigay prejudice, however, is the fact that eleven percent fewer disapproved of the identical behavior when indulged in by unmarried heterosexual employees. Clearly the chairpersons employ different standards.

Taboos relating to policy

Three of the ten most taboo items for chairpersons are principally matters of institutional policy. A chairperson's decision whether it is unprofessional for a gay faculty member to date a same-sex upperclassperson or graduate student (Taboo No. 3) could hinge upon whether any faculty-student dating would be approved. Yet while 58 percent of the chairpersons clearly disapproved of faculty-student same-sex dating, only a small 13 percent of the chairpersons disapproved "A gay faculty member's dating *any* person of the opposite sex." *Any* certainly includes students. In policy as in decorum, then, gay will be much more acceptable if it gives at least the appearance of heterosexual behavior. With this principle clear, it is hard to believe some of the face-saving disclaimers, such as that of one chairperson who explained: "Even if you're normal, this is unacceptable" or that of the woman who said, "As a general rule I think faculty should not date their students, though I don't think it is my, their colleagues', or anyone else's business, really." Another qualified his disapproval: "Tacky behavior." Even one who approved the faculty-student same-sex dating felt obliged to qualify his approval: "if the student is also gay," raising the classic homophobic specter of gay seduction.

Suspicious also is the chairpersons' heterosexist faith in the good effects of heterosexual dating by gay staff. One doubts that nongays would want their *own* children marrying persons whose predominant biological responses are stimulated homosexually. One suspects that really there is more flaunting of a heterosexist sense of superiority than a thoughtful substance to the chairpersons' approval of gays dating nongays.

By hindsight, probably all four questions rating whether and how much a "good gay dean or college president" should disclose her/his sexual orientation are too ambivalent properly to have been included on the Hostility-Acceptance Scale, though in practice the only one of the four to be omitted therefrom was the Super-gay statement that the good gay dean or college president "should make a big public issue of the gay identity."

Still, small measures of hostility towards gays were generated by this series. Three percent of the chairpersons wrote explicit objections to the phrase "good gay dean or college president." Typical of these was one's claim: "You make assumptions that I don't accept." Others circled the item, adding "silly phrasing" and "nonsense." More explicit was the addendum: "Should not hold the position and would probably be fired." Some disclaimed personal hostility: "My response reflects *realpolitik* in the context of this institution" — a private religious community college under 1,000 students with no openly gay English staff; "Here-no!" — a state rural community college under 1,000; "S/he wouldn't stand a chance at our institution" — a private religious college of under 1,000. The more charitable qualifications tended to suggest that the decision should be the dean's or president's private and personal decision. Fifty-nine percent of the chairpersons who feel that openly gay persons are not "highly objectional" still would object to saying that a good gay dean or college president "should let all who work for her or him know." It's one thing to respect candor and quite another to require it.

A gay couple's applying for couple rates on insurance in campus business offices seems a clear issue of civil rights. One chairperson considered such application positive, adding, "if the gay couple is married." Since no gay marriages are legal in the United States as of 1975, he is hardly putting gays on a par with nongays, particularly those gays who cohabit with more commitment to each other than that involved in many instances of nongay shacking. One begs the question to write off a "strongly negative" judgment in one chairperson's terms, as merely a "legal issue"; the real issue is whether chairpersons are prepared to respect as professional behavior a gay colleague's hegemony, whether they will encourage, or at least not discourage, that gay colleague's unpopular efforts to claim as legal those privileges not denied to heterosexuals. As one "accepting" chairperson stated: "That's their business; they should be granted it if they apply."

Only two of the top ten taboos concerned matters of academic opinions, No. 8 and No. 10 on Table 4. The chairpersons (34 percent!) who agree with the hostile assumption that an "institution can generally assume that students benefit most from works which express heterosexual norms of behavior" have prejudged before any tests have been made of the heterosexist assumption. The likely "benefits" of such censorship would be society's continued ignorance of persons unlike the majority. Ignorance is a strange "benefit" for responsible educators to be recommending. One black female chairperson in the South justified her approval of this assumption with the explanation: "Since they [the heterosexuals] are the majority"! What would happen to her black studies and women's studies if feted to the same "logic"? Several explained their "no opinions" here with the view that sexual criteria should play no part in the choice of texts, a view that may be simply antigay quietism or may be genuine aesthetic response which would admit all literature of quality on any sexual subject whatever. Even of all chairpersons who teach gay writers as such in their own classes, only 43 percent clearly disapprove of the assumption of maximum benefit from works which express heterosexual norms. It is little wonder that gay writers wanting an audience feel much pressure to pass in their work.[7]

Taboo No. 10, opposing the idea of an "intellectual responsibility" of textbook writers "to note the homosexual contexts of Gay writers" is a clear

case of censorship, as Dr. Rictor Norton and I have argued extensively elsewhere.[8] This evidence shows to be unfounded the allegations of our critics that
Dr. Norton and I are being paranoid about the censorship of gay materials. Two
chairpersons, one who objected to and one who approved the necessity of
noting homosexual contexts of gay writers, specifically qualified their opinions
by saying that sexual notice should be given "only if relevant." Surely such
qualifications, to be reasonable, should be applied no more nor less
strenuously to homosexual relevance than to heterosexual relevance (as in
determining whether references to a person's wife, husband, etc., are relevant).
In practice, most scholars do not apply equal standards for what is relevant.

What IS Acceptable?

Academic items receive the largest measure of chairperson support from
gay persons, or at least the clearest support, as registered in six of the fourteen
items in Table 5. Of all items, chairpersons rated only one progay response,
Acceptance No. 1, with the support of more than three-quarters of the chairpersons: viz., the statement: "Textbooks which claim a heterosexual context for
the homosexual contexts of Gay writers are intellectually dishonest." Unfortunately this support is vitiated by Taboo No. 8, which affirms the general
superiority of heterosexual texts, and by Taboo No. 10, by which chairpersons
opposed requiring writers of the textbooks "to note the homosexual contexts
of Gay writers." The way is merely opened by Acceptance No. 1 for business
as usual, viz., no textbooks mentioning sexual contexts nongay or gay which
do not affirm heterosexual preferences.

Similarly, Taboo No. 8 and Taboo No. 10 vitiate the academic support
which chairpersons register for giving a broad view of gay persons in any
textbooks which are chosen (Acceptance No. 4). If it is taboo to prefer gay
works and taboo to require textbook writers to note gay contexts of the few
gay works that might have been chosen, *range* becomes a meaningless
concept. These "acceptances" by the chairpersons cost nothing.

Predictably, several chairpersons wrote in a wide range of interesting
clarifications of their registered Acceptance items 1 and 4, as this sample
reveals:

What? I don't expect an instructor to choose works
on the basis of sexual orientation.

If they recognize the context, yes.

TABLE 5:

THE FOURTEEN MAJOR INSTANCES OF CHAIRPERSON ACCEPTANCE OF GAY

(In descending order)

No.	Percentage of all Chairperson	The Rating	Specific Item from the Hostility-Acceptance Scale
1.	79	Agree	Textbooks which claim a heterosexual context for the homosexual contexts of gay writers are intellectually dishonest. (†25)
2.	72	Disagree	A chairperson would be justified in not promoting an employee who had been convicted for gay sex with a consenting adult. (†32)
3.	72	Disagree	A chairperson would be justified in dismissing an employee who had been convicted for gay sex with a consenting adult. (†31)
4.	68	Agree	In choosing the works of gay writers for study, the instructor should include some which give the reader a positive impression of gayness, as well as those which present gay as ill-adjusted, unhappy, or angry. (†26)
5.	68	Disagree	Two unmarried employees of the same sex having regular sexual relations are unacceptable. (†51)
6.	65	Disagree	A chairperson would be justified in not hiring a candidate who had been convicted for gay sex with a consenting adult. (†30)
7.	64	Agree	Gays and nongays alike need to study literature that will increase their understanding of the gay experience as one dimension of our shared culture. (†29)
8.	59	Disagree	Studying gay literature in the open classroom will activate much latent homosexuality. (†28)
9.	57	Agree	Openly gay teachers are on a par with nongays and should have the same privileges of visibility. (†35)
10.	56	Rate positive	Participating in scholarly research to give a positive view of gay people, gay literature, and gay history. (†60)
11.	56	Disagree	Two unmarried employees of the same sex having regular sexual relations are acceptable as long as they do not reveal publicly the nature of their relationship. (†52)
12.	53	Disagree	Openly gay teachers are highly objectionable. (†33)
13.	52	Disagree	Openly gay teachers are tolerable only if they minimize their visibility as gays. (†34)
14.	50	Disagree	Participating in scholarly research to give a negative view of gay people, gay literature, and gay history. (†61)

Numbers following the † correspond with numbers on the questionnaire, reprinted in the Appendix.

He should choose the best books. [a gay chairperson]

In teaching Shakespeare, I do not proselytize.

Obviously this depends on the course, on the whole reading list.
In a course on the American literature of 1920-40,
I don't care whether *Native Son* is balanced by something more euphoric.

Criterion should be excellence!

Agree, though a work can be positive while showing the gay
as angry and unhappy with society's attitudes.

As a measure of my ignorance, I am unaware of the content of the corpus.

One Southern female chairperson spoke about her problems in dealing with such gay materials as manage to get into her texts:

> Only Whitman raises questions and difficulties. I believe that Whitman was homosexual; the best scholarship seems to feel otherwise. I see no marring of this fine literary figure. There is only embarrassment at having to face what Whitman students do broadly feel are accidents of nature and societal misfits.

Chairpersons offering ethnic literature are more concerned (78 percent of them feel) that the ethnic range of positive and negative materials be fair than are chairpersons offering gay literature concerned (only 66 percent of them feel) that the gay range be fair. In black language, black studies are thus much more "together" than gay studies.

The chairpersons' support for the academic opinion that "gays and nongays alike need to study literature that will increase their understanding of the gay experience as one dimension of our shared culture" is promising. With patterns of censorship already demonstrated, however, there will not be any way to fulfill this perceived need without radical revision of current texts and curricula. If chairpersons really believe their response favoring this item, they must be prepared to work for revisions of current offerings. Several disclaimers suggest the rationalizations many will follow:

[The study of experience] is not the purpose of literature.

I like my ivory tower; I will not preach.

"Gay Experience" is jargon:
love is love.

Sharing what!?

Maybe — but [shared cultural experiences]
should happen in sociology and psychology courses.
Literature should mainly be studied aesthetically.

Most chairpersons (59 percent) oppose the old myth that "studying literature in the open classroom will activate much latent homosexuality," Acceptance Item No. 8, though one worries about the 7 percent minority still defending the position. In the words of one chairperson even at a religious college: "How ignorant!" Three who registered "no opinion" added comments:

I'm not a psychologist.

So what if it does? [a bisexual]

Is there any [gay literature] in the field of greatness vying for attention?

One of the seven percent upholding the view questioned the validity of *much*, for which he substituted "will activate *some* latent homosexuality." It seems strange that thousands of years of studying nongay literature have not weighed very successfully in activating in gays any latent nongay sexuality; perhaps the entire question should thus be thrown open for serious investigation.

The majority approval of scholarly research giving a positive view of gays (Acceptance No. 10, Table 5) and the concomitant 50 percent disapproval of research giving a negative view of gays (Acceptance No. 14) predictably brought vivid dissent from several chairpersons, who believe, in the words of one of their spokespersons: "Setting out to *prove* a position is not my idea of 'scholarly' research." The same person earlier had made the "scholarly" judgment that one "can assume that students benefit most from works which express heterosexual norms of behavior"! Clearly what is good for the goose in this case is not good for another goose, only for the gander. The common practice in English departments of dividing the curricula into literatures supporting the various nationalisms (American literature, English literature, Chinese literature, etc.) has rarely been predicated with the demand these literatures be studied as much to reveal the weaknesses as to reveal the positive achievements of these nations. While the critical process inevitably introduces standards of "negative" and "positive" to all study, usually people study their literature because they do have some preconceptions about the worth they hope to discover in it. One would rarely fault a study of Twain, for example, that set out first to discover some of the achievements, unless the study planned thereby to ignore the weaknesses. Many whole schools of criticism suggest that serious study should not be undertaken until one has prejudged the corpus as likely to produce "sweetness and light" and to celebrate "the highest and the best," to borrow spokesperson Matthew Arnold's elitist terms. If applied to all new research areas, this anti-gay notion of what is "scholarly" would be monumentally wasteful and time-consuming. For example, one would have first to analyze completely each metropolitan edition of each telephone directory before saying why such directories should not be a part of all literature departments. Clearly, some preconceptions of the worth of most study are common in scholarship. *Scholarly* should not be allowed to serve as but one more club in the English chairpersons' arsenal for the capricious bludgeoning of gay academics.

Polity items of acceptance

Very important to the job security of gay persons are the three items dealing with chairperson reactions to gay job candidates and employees "who have been convicted for gay sex with a consenting adult" (Acceptances 2, 3, and 6; Table 5). More chairpersons are supportive of gay staff already employed than of job candidates. Unfortunately the phrase "would be justified" in each item encouraged chairpersons to respond with hypothetical moral opinion rather than with commitments about their own behavior to specific employees in view of such convictions. (As an exception, one chairperson did volunteer that another chairperson at her Southern state college had in fact used such grounds for refusing to promote a gay person, an act of which she disapproved, but was powerless to prevent.) It seems unlikely that 72 percent of all chairpersons would really put their own jobs on the line to back up their opinions in behalf of a gay staff member so unfortunate as to be a convicted felon. One indicated that his support is conditional upon the convict's "quality of instruction in the classroom": that is, gay persons, teach especially well, to the approval of your chairperson, and s/he may come to get you out of the clinker. Many of the less "liberal" chairpersons more candidly stated their nonsupport, as in these two samples:

"*Conviction* is the problem, not the sex activities" and "State law prohibits granting of credentials to a felon." From a gay point of view, "the problem" is, of course, not the conviction, but whether or not the chairperson will stand behind the convicted employee in opposition to an unjust law.

Nongays can best see the plight of gays regarding the pervasive sodomy statutes by imagining for a moment a reversal by which heterosexual sexual acts were declared felonies. It would surely not be much support for a chairperson to say, "Oh, it's all right to be *nongay*, but just don't get caught in any nongay behavior!" Yet similar rationalizations from nongays about gays were added on the questionnaires, as in these samples:

I would not be allowed to [hire, retain, or promote gay convicts] here.

As an agent of the institution I would be expected to support these [negative] attitudes" — [this from a closeted bisexual]

These are evasions worthy of an Eichmann, saying, "I am only following orders!" Chairpersons, it turns out, have not much stronger moral fiber than persons do who are less remunerated for their "contributions to society."

The majority of chairpersons *claim* to support openly gay teachers as "on a par with nongays . . . [with rights to] the same privileges of visibility" (cf. Acceptances 9, 12, and 13 on Table 5). Yet, the chairperson Taboos (Table 4) are so repressive that one wonders what chairpersons think "openly gay" could really mean. One who approved of openness qualified the response: "Certain types of behavior polarize students and have resulted in an individual's being less valuable to a department" [as when an individual pushes for higher academic standards?!]. An ambivalent chairperson wrote: "Here I'm not sure about how open your question implies. I would object to any overt gay behavior on campus, even in a secular situation. On our campus it would be cause for dismissal — for students or faculty." Another asserted: "Sexuality is *not* a part of student-teacher relationships, whether gay or nongay." Still another raised specters of gay openness as tantamount to a lurid orgy: "Being a relatively naive nongay, I need a definition of 'openly gay.' Any classroom teacher openly on the make is offensive to me." Of course these respondents forget all of the casual registers of sexuality, such as the flaunting of parental references by nongays in all kinds of professional contexts. No wonder nothing like as many as the 57 percent of the chairpersons who claim to support openly gay teachers have any openly gay teachers to support.

"Come out!" oftens seems tacitly predicated "so I can get you." One

Southern female chairperson objected to the condition in "Openly gay teachers are tolerable *only if they minimize their visibility as gays*": "They never fool anybody." She shares claims to omniscience with an Anglican bishop who recently wrote a parishioner gay psychiatrist: "I am indeed aware of those who are closeted within the Diocese. They may not know it, but the family is small and information is easy to gather" — quoted from the files of *Integrity: Gay Episcopal Forum*. Dare anyone even breathe in such an atmosphere of suspicious unction?

Decorum items of acceptance

Since decorum items dominated the taboo list, it is not surprising that they have a short supply of acceptance. The two items of acceptance (nos. 5 and 11, Table 5) are vitiated by being corollaries to Taboo No. 9, whereby chairpersons opposed such activity "whether or not they make public [their behavior]." By failing to condemn secret gay sex by staff while condemning such behavior the moment it threatens to become known, the majority (68 percent) offers a very mixed blessing, accepting gay sexuality only when it is limited to impersonal genital acts by people willing to seem ashamed to be lovingly associated in a healthy public relationship. Even so, five percent more chairpersons approved secret unmarried sex by nongays than approved the same by gays: thereby the powerful majority claims for itself the best of both the perspicuous and the promiscuous worlds.

CONCLUSION: The chairpersons' ostensibly liberal attitudes towards gay persons are systematically vitiated by the overriding effects of the corollary taboos. At best, the acceptance serves a chairperson's need to feel good about his/her tolerance, but the attitudes do not commit chairpersons to giving visible and tangible support to gays in terms of professional behaviors. The many contradictions in chairperson responses suggest that the chairpersons have not thought very seriously about the consequences of their attitudes in terms of clear dangers to gay students and gay staff.

Major Ambivalence

While ambivalence is a response rich in human appeal, it is virtually worthless as a predictor of behavior, except to warn of possible caprice. Hence, 25 of the 29 items on the Hostility-Acceptance Scale have been discussed in terms of their more forceful polarities of hostility or acceptance. The remaining four (Table 6) scored lesser at the poles than on the high ambivalence.

TABLE 6:

FIVE INSTANCES OF GREAT CHAIRPERSON AMBIVALENCE
OR NON-RESPONSE TOWARDS GAY

By the descending percentages noted, chairpersons registered ratings of "neutral" or "no opinion," or left blank each of the items below.

No.	Percentage of all Chairpersons	Specific Item from the Hostility-Acceptance Scale
1.	55	A good gay dean or college president should let only close friends know about her/his gayness. (†45)
2.	52	Volunteering outside the department to organize or advise student gay groups. (†55)
3.	52	Off campus, participating in gay political activity. (†59)
4.	47	A good gay dean or college president should let no one know about her/his gayness. (†44)
5.	40	Discussing in a Shakespeare class or a freshman survey class as the instructor's own the view that Shakespeare was sexually involved with W.H. (†56)

N.B.   High ambivalence-nonresponse also reinforces Taboo No. 6 (51%) and Taboo No. 7 (44%). See Table 4.

Numbers following the † correspond with numbers on the questionnaire, reprinted in the Appendix.

Ambivalence items 1 and 4 correlate with Taboo No. 6 (see Table 4), concerning the extent to which a "good gay dean or college president" should reveal his/her gayness. While the chairpersons make it taboo to require the gay dean or college president "to let all who work for her or him [to] know," they are reluctant to approve or disapprove "letting only close friends know" (Ambivalence No. 1) or letting "no one know" (Ambivalence No. 4). From the pattern of chairperson quietism towards all gay subjects, as shown earlier, it is predictable that those few chairpersons who do decide clearly more often favor their gay administrators' letting "no one know." Only two persons (one nongay, one gay) of all respondents bit to super-gay bait to approve a fourth item in this series, excluded from the Scale selections as obviously too biased: "A good gay dean or college president should make a big public issue of the gay identity." One California chairperson explained his rating: "This would be the wildest script, but you're really dealing in fantasy here."

Two more ambivalent items also deal with institutional policy, viz., the professional status of staff involved in organizing or advising student gay groups (Ambivalence No. 2) and in off-campus "gay political activity" (Ambivalence No. 3). While 98 percent responded to these two, they responded mainly with "no opinion," and these items evoked only one written explanation, which itself is ambivalent: "Everything depends upon the circumstances." Possibly chairpersons veered away from these items because they are sensitized to the fact that the claims, as worded, sound very like victories already won in familiar AAUP, ACLU, and union cases for other groups. Perhaps, too, the chairpersons merely wanted to avoid involvement in civil rights altogether.

The academic item producing great ambivalence was a staff member's "discussing in a Shakespeare class or a freshman survey class as [his/her] own view that Shakespeare was sexually involved with W.H." In the assorted responses of the ones who wrote explanations (8 percent of total), testiness is more pervasive than scholarly consensus or even basic knowledge of the literature in question (as in response no. 13):

1. I expect the instructor to teach the aesthetic value of literature.
2. This is a scholarly, not a behaviorist question.
3. If pertinent. But what the hell can be conjectured?
4. Irrelevant.
5. He was — it is a public theory.
6. Was he? That would condition the answer.
7. Does it matter?
8. It is questionable scholarship.
9. Not strong evidence for this.
10. If he's fool enough to believe it.
11. If the instructor really believes this to be the case.
12. No problem with Shakespeare class, but question advisability in freshman survey class.
13. Who is W.H.?
14. Damn poor scholarship.
15. I know renaissance scholarship. Position absurd as stated.
16. It depends on how it's discussed.
17. But I would like to know the reasons.
18. Because the sonnets *deny* it flatly.

Purvis E. Boyette's recent brilliant analysis of homophobia in Shakespearean criticism is certainly needed for re-education of our nation's chairpersons. (See "Shakespeare's *Sonnets:* Homosexuality and the Critics," *Tulane Studies in English*, 21 [1974].) Even a look at the many pages on the subject in the *Variorum* is a treasure trove of homophobia, regardless of what one's own personal view is about Shakespeare's personal sexual orientation, much less that of the persona of the *Sonnets*, or of the mysterious W.H.

Miscellaneous Items Not Included on the Scale

Many non-Scale items have already been cited for comparison with the results of relevant Scale items. Two sets of questions remain, one set about gay literature and the other set about general campus attitudes towards gay openness, towards lesbians in comparison with gay males, and towards so-called effeminate gay men. Items in this second set had more than 9 percent nonresponse, about the highest in the entire questionnaire. An average of 40 percent of all chairpersons left blank these three items. Such omission by more than one-third of the nonrespondents was explained with the marginal comment "I don't know."

Since the issues in the second set largely concern in-group facts of campus gay life, it is not surprising that English chairpersons (at least of the nongay variety, who maintained an average of 12 percent more nonresponse than those chairpersons who are gay or bisexual) do not know, though one might question the validity of any chairperson's claim to equal interest in ALL students and staff with so little manifest curiosity about a large minority culture hiding in their very midst. For each of the three items in the set, responses by chairpersons who themselves are gay or bisexual (hence insiders) would seem more knowledgeable. Gay and bisexual chairpersons differ with nongay peers substantially only in assessing whether "so-called masculine gay men [are] respected more than so-called effeminate gay men": of those chairpersons actually answering, 84 percent of the gays and bisexuals said "yes," compared with only 39 percent of the nongays who said "yes." In gay slang, the gay and bisexual chairpersons argue that *butch* is more acceptable than *femme*. Since butch (the so-called masculine gay male) is thought to pass more effectively, perhaps this difference is in part an indirect measure of the pressure gay and bisexual chairpersons feel to pass as nongay? Perhaps nongay chairpersons are simply unaware of this value of their own standards of masculinity for sheer survival by their gay peers? Perhaps they think that the only gays around are the ones that they can readily identify? One nongay Southern female chairperson added to her response: "All gays are rare, inevitably known, and despised. They always leave." One black female Southern chairperson added: "We have no effeminate gay men. We have some very masculine body beautifuls who, I have heard, swing both ways.

Paradoxically, chairpersons on campuses where so-called masculine gay men are respected show 35 percent less disapproval of the so-called feminine behavior, as in reacting to a staff member's "giving a literary reading in class while wearing the clothes of one's opposite sex for purposes related to the reading." Unfavorable response from gay and bisexual chairperson to such readings was only five percent less than that of nongay chairpersons.

Again paradoxically, those who say that openness is more respected are not themselves open. While very few (only seven percent) of all chairpersons who responded say that on their campuses "open gays [are] respected more than gays who successfully hide," twice that percent of the chairpersons who refuse to classify themselves sexually say so. Nongays predictably lead the way in denying respect to gay openness. Only one person reported openly gay persons more respected on his campus and also said that in his own view gays are highly objectionable. Most chairpersons feel themselves more accepting than they estimate their campuses to be, as in the typical liberal pharisaism, "I thank thee Lord, I am not as others are."

Lesbians

Status of lesbians compared with that of gay males is difficult to measure. Forty-one percent of the chairpersons refused to answer, about one-third of these writing in the explanation "I don't know" or "We just hear rumors." A few chairpersons (only one percent) explained nonresponse as the result of being an all-male institution. One bisexual male chairperson said, "Lesbians here are mostly closet gays." One who flaunted himself as a "normal" nonfemale said, "There is no interest in lesbians," and another self-styled "Ukranian Swedish-Irish male" said: "Nobody pays lesbians any attention."

Of the chairpersons who did answer, 84 percent said "Yes, lesbians are equally desirable/undesirable." Seven percent of those so stating explained that *undesirable* was the relevant item in the pair. No one claimed thereby to mean "equally desirable." Three chairpersons helpfully pointed out that *desirable/undesirable* has unfelicitous sexual overtones in this context, further muddling the interpretations possible for the responses.

Of the 16 percent who responded, "No, lesbians are not equally desirable/undesirable," 19 percent of those added that they meant lesbians are "more desirable," including one nongay black male, two gay males, and one nongay woman. One of the gay male chairpersons added: "At a woman's college, female relations are taken for granted." Ten percent of those who disagreed claimed that lesbians are even more undesirable than gay males.

Altogether the respondents seem to be pooling ignorance. The women respondents are more likely to be trusted, particularly since their sample has almost the same proportion of gays and bisexuals as the larger male sample and since their nonresponse rate was only about half that of the males. Fifteen percent fewer female chairpersons than male chairpersons said that lesbians are "equally desirable/undesirable," but they did not say which way the difference goes.

Gay Literature

Questions about gay literature focused on what it includes and where it is best studied. Since several chairpersons admitted complete ignorance of the corpus, it is instructive to compare chairperson overall responses to the response of the various subgroups of chairpersons who through personal gay experience or professional teaching experience likely have more substantial information at their command for use in making these debatable decisions (See Table 7).

Chairpersons experienced with gay persons or literature differ from the inexperienced chairpersons less on notions about where gay literature is to be best taught than on notions about what gay literature includes. Most chairpersons of all sorts prefer standard courses to specialized ones. As one wrote:

> I feel that *any* group that wishes to be accepted and assimilated into the larger group can do itself only a disservice by separating itself in special courses, caucuses, or groups. I have gay friends, although I am not gay, but the gays who hide in gay groups, no matter what they give as a reason, will never be met by me.

Another less charitably said:

> I cannot accept the term "the literature of homosexuality," except insofar as it means clinical reports (as in "the literature of tuberculosis") or propaganda (as in "the literature of socialism"). To me, literature is literature, irrespective of its subject matter or the peculiarities of its creators; and I have always believed that categorizing it artificially (e.g., " 'gay' lit," "women's lit," "black lit") constitutes an affront tó the worth of the art and the dignity of the artist.

Of course, this professor's list of artificial categories did not include "19th-century lit," "English lit," or "dramatic lit," very familiar artifices used in English departments. Some categories are apparently more sacred than others.

Those experienced with gay students or literature show the least clear opposition to specialized courses, especially those with actual experience of offering such courses and those who allow gay students to tap their gay experience as resources for reacting in class and on assignments.

The experienced chairpersons agree with themselves even more in their notions about what gay literature includes. Uniformly their definitions are more catholic, less narrow than are those of their less experienced colleagues, more

TABLE 7:

GAY LITERATURE: WHAT IS IT AND WHERE IS IT BEST TAUGHT?

N.B. Unlike all items on Tables 4 - 6, the items here were not used as a part of the Hostility-Acceptance Scale.

THE SEVEN PROPOSITIONS
1. Gay literature, when studied at all, is best studied in standard courses. (†37)   2. Gay literature, when studied at all, is best studied in specialized courses. (†38)   3. Gay literature includes only literature by homosexuals. (†39)   4. Gay literature includes only literature by open homosexuals. (†40)   5. Gay literature includes all literature by homosexuals. (†41)   6. Gay literature includes only literature about sexuality. (†42)   7. Gay literature includes only literature about homosexuality. (†43)

SUBGROUPS OF CHAIRPERSONS IN ENGLISH		PERCENT DISAGREEING WITH PROPOSITIONS AS NUMBERED						
THE PROPOSITIONS		1	2	3	4	5	6	7
Chairpersons Experienced With gays or gay literature	Chairpersons who themselves are gay or bisexual. (†20)	14	67	86	91	69	82	65
	Chairpersons of departments offering courses in gay literature. (†3)	0	50	66	66	50	80	50
	Chairpersons who do discuss gay writers as such in their own classes. (†4)	8	66	68	78	56	78	56
	Chairpersons who do encourage gay students to use their gay identity as a basis of reacting. (†7)	19	47	65	88	53	94	88
ALL CHAIRPERSONS		7	65	59	69	48	66	50
Chairpersons Not Experienced With gays or gay literature	Nongay chairpersons. (†20)	5	68	54	65	46	61	49
	Chairpersons of departments not offering courses in gay literature. (†3)	7	65	59	70	24	67	53
	Chairpersons who do not discuss gay writers as such in their own classes. (†4)	5	67	52	60	40	60	43
	Chairpersons who do not encourage gay students to use their gay identity as a basis of reacting. (†7)	6	66	58	67	46	63	49

Numbers following the † correspond with numbers on the questionnaire, reprinted in the Appendix.

readily admitting materials by nongays and closeted gays, as well as more readily allowing gay literature to include heterosexual detail and casual non-genital gay experience. Clearly those who want to discuss as gay literature *Moby Dick*, *Leaves of Grass*, or *Remembrance of Things Past* would receive less opposition from chairpersons experienced with gay persons and gay literature. The experienced are more opposed than others to having gay literature include all literature by homosexuals, and would require of literature called gay literature more criteria than the gay sexuality of the author. (After all, is there anything "gay" about a statement by a gay scientist? See Steve Risch's contrary view elsewhere in this volume.)

Gay studies are only beginning, and it would be premature to expect the attitudes even of the experts to remain more than preliminary.

THE LARGER CONTEXT

Gay behavior was a felony in more than forty states when the data in this report was collected in February 1975. No focus on gay status within any one institution, whatever that institution's claims to enlightenment, can afford to de-emphasize for a moment the important reality that *all* gay people walk the streets of the United States as potential felons, whether convicted or not. If we were never "supposed to be" a people or an important minority, that fact alone has served for centuries of oppression to make us a people, a tribe, a force in history. (See Louis Crompton's important historical survey elsewhere in this volume.) The stingiest of nongays estimate that upwards of 20 million Americans indulge in felonious civil disobedience for more than half of their sexual fulfillment. Face to face with the law, gays are all alike, and not one of us can afford to forget that fact very long.

A study of gay status is inevitably a study of caprice. Not even the Nazis murdered all of the gays in their midst, and the most genocidal of establishments will not likely want to arrest 20 million persons. More serious than the slight threat of arrest in the United States is the way the antigay laws legitimize the taboo of the heterosexual majority and thereby give the heterosexual majority myriads of lesser ways randomly to control and restrict the behavior of the gay minority.

Gay status is a survival issue even for the most closeted gay person in higher education. An inordinate amount of professional energy is required to make the vital estimates. How much dare I be open? Does my professor, my chairperson, or my dean know? Would s/he care? Would I be safer in another kind of college, another area, another discipline...? Dare I risk being seen with other gay persons? Dare I risk being discovered by nongay persons? If I declare openly, will my sexuality then become exaggerated into the most important fact about me? Dare I share my professional insights that have come to me specifically through my minority sexual orientation . . .? The law of the jungle requires us to know as precisely as possible when the homophobic tiger hides behind the rock and whether s/he is asleep or awake and hungry.

Nongays too spend much time speculating about the gay world in their midst, not only in idle or malicious gossip, but often in genuine fearful concern about a colleague, a student, or a member of the family.

The law creates an underworld fraught with anxiety, and in that underworld, as accessible as the next whisper, are bred suspicions and myths powerful enough to wreck lives and to warp an entire culture. While a few individual gays and gay couples have discovered for themselves relatively safer corners in the underworld in which to flourish, not much real or lasting relief is likely until the antigay laws are revoked. The gay minority, like any other minority, requires the safety of the Constitution so that we can begin to discover who we are in relationships no longer tyrannized by ignorant and fearful outsiders.

Meanwhile, this study has charted some of the lights and shades of that part of the homophobic jungle which English departments occupy.

NOTES

Special thanks are due to Mr. Louis Adams, director of the computer center at Fort Valley State College, for his valuable aid in the quantification of the data from the questionnaire which generated this study.

Pronouns in this paper are not generic. Chairperson/he and chairperson/she mean precisely that.

1The 29 Scale items are discussed individually as charted later in Tables 4-6. They are marked with an asterisk (*) on the questionnaire itself, reprinted with the overall results in the Appendix.

Each respondent's individual Hostility-Acceptance Scale score was computed as follows: Items 23, 28, 30, 31, 32, 33, 34, 44, 45, 51, 52, and 61 were scored 1 point for strongly positive/strongly agree, 2 points for positive/agree, 3 points for neutral/no opinion . . . Items 24, 25, 26, 29, 35, 46, 53, 55, 56, 57, 58, 59, 60, 62, 63, 65, and 66 were scored in the reverse manner, 1 point for strongly disagree/strongly negative, 2 points for disagree/negative, etc. The highest scores thus represent the most acceptance of gay persons and subjects.

Out of a maximum raw score of 145 (i.e., 29 times 5), 9 groups of 15 points each were used to express individual and group scores, on a scale of 9 (most accepting) to 1 (least accepting). In the distribution tables, 5 was the score for registered "ambivalence" and all other scores went to the more appropriate polarity.

2For additional data supporting this contention, see my similar survey of small press magazine editors in the U.S.: "Editor Responses to Gay Materials," *Margins: Review of Little Magazines and Small Press Books*, No. 20 (May, 1975), 5-9.

3Martin S. Weinberg and Colin J. Williams, *Male Homosexuals: Their Problems and Adaptations* (New York: Oxford University Press, 1974), p. 224.

4See Martin Duberman, "The Bisexual Debate," *New Times*, Vol. 2, No. 13 (June 28, 1974), 34-41.

5*Male Homosexuals: Their Problems and Adaptations* (New York: Oxford University Press, 1974), p. 262.

6Cf. Louie Crew, "The Gay Academic Unmasks," *The Chronicle of Higher Education*, Vol. 8, No. 21 (February 25, 1974), 20.

[7]See "Special Issue Focusing on Gay Male Writing and Publishing," edited by Louie Crew, *Margins: Review of Little Magazines and Small Press Books*, No. 20 (May, 1975).

[8]See our editorial, "The Homophobic Imagination," in the special issue on "The Homosexual Imagination," eds. Rictor Norton and Louie Crew, *College English*, vol. 36, no. 3 (November, 1974), 271-290. See also our contributions to the followup "Comment and Reply," especially our "Replies to Stanley Weintraub," *College English*, vol. 37, no. 1 (September, 1975).

APPENDIX

GAY PERSONS AS VIEWED BY CHAIRPERSONS IN ENGLISH

Dear Department Chairpersons: You are urged to complete the following questionnaire and return it anonymously in the stamped addressed envelope provided. Please feel free to add additional comments on any items. Your cooperation will be greatly appreciated. One use of this study will be in the form of a report to the MLA Committee for Academic Freedom from the Professional Job Security Committee of the Gay Caucus of the MLA.** Thank you. Faithfully yours, Louie Crew, óó, Associate Professor, Department of English, FVSC, Fort Valley, GA 31030.

1. Is there an organization of gay students on your campus? — Yes 38 (18%); No 173 (79%); N.A. 7 (3%)

2. Is there an organization of gay faculty on your campus? — Yes 0 ; No 211 (97%); N.A. 7 (3%)

3. Has your department ever offered any courses in gay literature? — Yes 6 (3%); No 212 (97%); N.A. 0

4. In your own classes, are gay writers ever discussed as such? — Yes 112 (51%); No 99 (46%); N.A. 7 (3%)

5. Do you offer courses in women's literature in your department? — Yes 134 (62%); No 83 (38%); N.A. 1

6. Do you offer courses in ethnic literature in your department? — Yes 165 (76%); No 45 (21%); N.A. 8 (3%)

7. In your own classes, are gay students encouraged to use their gay identity as a basis of reacting to the content of the course? — Yes 17 (8%); No 180 (82%); N.A. 21 (10%)

8. On your campus, are open gays respected more than gays who successfully hide their gayness? — Yes 10 (5%); No 128 (59%); N.A. 80 (36%)

9. On your campus, are so-called masculine gay men respected more than so-called effeminate gay men? — Yes 59 (27%); No 66 (33%); N.A. 93 (43%)

10. On your campus, are lesbians equally desirable/undesirable compared with gay males? If **no**, explain: — Yes 107 (49%); No 21 (10%); N.A. 90 (41%)

11. How large is your student body? Under 1000   37 (17%);   1000-2999   74 (34%);   3000-4999   30 (13%);   5000-9999   41 (19%); 10,000-14,999   17 (8%);   15,000 or more   19 (9%).

12. Characterize your college: state   120 (55%);   private religious   51 (23%);   private other   41 (19%);   N.A.   6 (3%).

13. Characterize your community: rural   26 (12%);   town smaller than 15,000   34 (16%);   15,000 or more   148 (68%);   N.A.   10 (4%).

14. Characterize your curriculum: undergraduate only   60 (28%);   limited graduate programs   81 (38%);   full university   38 (17%); community/junior college only   38 (17%);   N.A.   1.

15. How large is your department?   1-5   26 (12%);   6-10   51 (25%);   11-15   36 (16%);   16-20   31 (14%);   21-25   13 (6%);   Over 25   60 (27%);   N.A.   1.

16. In your department, how many faculty have made their gayness a matter of public record?   Zero   200 (92%);   1-3   13 (6%);   4-6   0;   7-9   0;   10 or more   1 (.5%);   N.A.   4 (1.5%).

17. In your department, how many others have given exclusively private information about their gayness?   Zero   175 (80%);   1-3   32 (15%);   4-6   1 (.5%);   7-9   1 (.5%);   10 or more   0;   N.A.   9 (4%).

18. Exclusive of those in No. 16 and No. 17, how many other members of your department do you estimate to be gay?   Zero   122 (56%);   1-3   64 (29%);   4-6   10 (5%);   7-9   3 (1%);   10 or more   0;   N.A.   19 (9%).

19. How do you prefer to be identified?   nongay   137 (63%);   gay   2 (1%);   bisexual   9 (4%);   other   52 (24%);   N.A.   18 (8%).

20. Which are you?   nongay   133 (61%);   gay   14 (6%);   bisexual   22 (10%);   other   34 (16%);   N.A.   15 (7%).

21. Are you black   7 (3%)   or bonblack   198 (91%)?   N.A.   13 (6%).

22. Are you female   33 (15%)   or nonfemale   172 (79%)?   N.A.   13 (6%).

RATING ATTITUDES

Use the following scale to register your agreement/disagreement with the statements which follow:

A Strongly Agree; B Agree; C No Opinion; D Disagree; E Strongly Disagree

	A	B	C	D	E	N.A.
*23. In choosing literature for teaching, the instructor can generally assume that students benefit most from works which express heterosexual norms of behavior.	22 10%	56 25%	61 27%	62 28%	14 9%	3 1%
*24. Textbook writers have an intellectual responsibility to note the homosexual contexts of gay writers.	27 12%	72 33%	43 20%	51 23%	24 11%	1 1%
*25. Textbooks which claim a heterosexual context for the homosexual contexts of gay writers are intellectually dishonest.	71 33%	100 46%	29 13%	12 5%	2 1%	4 2%
*26. In choosing the works of gay writers for study, the instructor should include some which give the reader a positive impression of gayness, as well as those which present gays as ill-adjusted, unhappy, or angry.	64 30%	83 38%	48 22%	13 6%	4 2%	6 2%
27. In choosing the works of ethnic minority writers for study, the instructor should include some which give the reader a positive impression of the minority ethnic culture, as well as those which present the minority members who are deprived, unhappy and resentful.	86 40%	91 42%	29 13%	7 3%	1 .5%	4 1.5%
*28. Studying gay literature in the open classroom will activate much latent homosexuality.	0	16 7%	73 33%	93 43%	35 16%	1 1%
*29. Gays and nongays alike need to study literature that will increase their understanding of the gay experience as one dimension of our shared culture.	40 18%	100 46%	41 19%	25 12%	9 4%	3 1%
*30. A chairperson would be justified in not hiring a candidate who had been convicted for gay sex with a consenting adult.	19 9%	36 16%	20 9%	84 39%	58 26%	1 1%

	A	B	C	D	E	N.A.
*31. A chairperson would be justified in dismissing an employee who had been convicted for gay sex with a consenting adult.	15 7%	26 12%	17 8%	85 39%	73 33%	2 1%
*32. A chairperson would be justified in not promoting an employee who has been convicted for gay sex with a consenting adult.	15 7%	20 9%	22 10%	92 42%	65 30%	4 2%
*33. Openly gay teachers are highly objectionable.	19 9%	30 14%	47 22%	76 35%	41 18%	5 2%
*34. Openly gay teachers are tolerable only if they minimize their visibility as gays.	5 2%	53 24%	43 20%	70 32%	44 20%	3 2%
*35. Openly gay teachers are on a par with nongays and should have the same privileges of visibility.	42 19%	83 38%	31 14%	33 15%	23 11%	6 3%
36. Openly gay teachers should be given special compensatory privileges and tolerances not allowed nongays.	1 1%	2 1%	10 4%	86 39%	119 55%	0
37. Gay literature, when studied at all, is best studied in standard courses.	31 14%	116 53%	53 24%	13 6%	1 1%	4 2%
38. Gay literature, when studied at all, is best studied in specialized courses.	1 1%	12 5%	60 28%	109 50%	33 15%	3 1%
39. Gay literature includes only literature by homosexuals.	7 3%	18 8%	58 27%	96 44%	33 15%	6 3%
40. Gay literature includes only literature by open homosexuals.	2 1%	3 2%	57 26%	103 47%	47 22%	6 2%
41. Gay literature includes all literature by homosexuals.	9 4%	44 20%	52 24%	74 34%	31 14%	8 4%
42. Gay literature includes only literature about sexuality.	2 1%	10 4%	55 25%	104 48%	38 18%	9 4%

	A	B	C	D	E	N.A.
43. Gay literature includes only literature about homosexuality.	8 / 3%	30 / 14%	56 / 26%	76 / 35%	33 / 15%	15 / 7%
*44. A good gay dean or college president should let no one know about her/his gayness.	12 / 6%	35 / 16%	89 / 41%	62 / 28%	6 / 3%	14 / 6%
*45. A good gay dean or college president should let only close friends know.	3 / 1%	31 / 14%	103 / 47%	57 / 26%	8 / 4%	16 / 8%
*46. A good gay dean or college president should let all who work for her or him know.	3 / 1%	17 / 8%	95 / 43%	60 / 28%	26 / 12%	17 / 8%
47. A good gay dean or college president should make a big public issue of the gay identity.	1 / .5%	1 / .5%	47 / 22%	79 / 36%	80 / 37%	10 / 4%
48. Two unmarried employees of opposite sexes having regular sexual relations are unacceptable.	12 / 5%	22 / 10%	26 / 12%	98 / 45%	56 / 26%	4 / 2%
49. Two unmarried employees of opposite sexes having regular sexual relations are acceptable as long as they do not reveal publicly the nature of their relationship.	9 / 4%	48 / 22%	40 / 18%	82 / 38%	29 / 13%	10 / 5%
50. Two unmarried employees of opposite sexes having regular sexual relations are acceptable whether or not they make public this fact.	37 / 17%	86 / 39%	32 / 15%	36 / 17%	18 / 8%	9 / 4%
*51. Two unmarried employees of the same sex having regular sexual relations are unacceptable.	13 / 6%	20 / 9%	28 / 13%	100 / 46%	49 / 22%	8 / 4%
*52. Two unmarried employees of the same sex having regular sexual relations are acceptable as long as they do not reveal publicly the nature of their relationship.	10 / 5%	53 / 24%	43 / 20%	70 / 32%	31 / 14%	11 / 5%
*53. Two unmarried employees of the same sex having regular sexual relations are acceptable whether or not they make public this fact.	38 / 17%	65 / 30%	33 / 15%	56 / 26%	17 / 8%	9 / 4%

	A	B	C	D	E	N.A.
54. Two gay employees who have announced that they have undergone a gay marriage are more acceptable than unmarried gays in sexual relationships.	0 0%	6 3%	73 34%	83 38%	47 21%	9 4%

RATING BEHAVIORS

Use the following scale to register your rating of the behaviors listed when those behaviors are indulged by potential members of your staff: A Strongly Positive; B Positive; C Neutral; D Negative; E Strongly Negative

	A	B	C	D	E	N.A.
*55. Volunteering outside the department to organize or advise student gay groups.	8 4%	36 17%	109 50%	34 15%	26 12%	5 2%
*56. Discussing in a Shakespeare class or a freshman survey class as the instructor's own the view that Shakespeare was sexually involved with W.H.	16 7%	86 40%	84 39%	22 10%	7 3%	3 1%
*57. At a campus social function, introducing one's lover as "my lover," "my spouse," "my girl (boy) friend," etc., when the two are of the same sex.	6 3%	17 8%	82 37%	76 35%	33 15%	4 2%
*58. In campus business offices, applying for couple rates on insurance, campus housing, etc., by gay couples.	10 5%	29 13%	92 42%	60 28%	23 10%	4 2%
*59. Off campus, participating in gay political activity.	13 6%	51 23%	108 50%	26 12%	16 7%	4 2%
*60. Participating in scholarly research to give a positive view of gay people, gay literature, and gay history.	34 16%	88 40%	65 30%	17 8%	12 5%	2 1%
*61. Participating in scholarly research to give a negative view of gay people, gay literature, and gay history.	11 5%	33 15%	62 29%	71 33%	38 17%	3 1%

	A	B	C	D	E	N.A.
*62. Giving a literary reading in class while wearing the clothes of one's opposite sex for purposes related to the reading.	6 3%	24 11%	65 30%	64 29%	55 25%	4 2%
*63. A gay faculty member's dating of an upperclassperson or graduate student of the same sex.	2 1%	10 5%	75 34%	61 28%	65 30%	5 2%
64. A gay faculty member's dating of any persons of the OPPOSITE sex.	8 4%	29 13%	148 68%	17 8%	12 5%	4 2%
*65. A gay faculty couple's holding hands in public on campus.	4 2%	7 3%	80 36%	82 38%	43 20%	2 1%
*66. A gay person's campus appearances outside class in dress of the opposite sex.	2 1%	8 4%	54 25%	79 36%	73 33%	2 1%

*Marks items which were used in the Hostility-Acceptance Scale. See Note 1 for an explanation of the scoring of each of these items.

TWO ADDITIONAL ITEMS ADDED TO EACH RETURNED QUESTIONNAIRE

Although no question asked persons to specify their geographical location, each of the 168 (77%) envelopes with a postal zip was noted on the appropriate questionnaire, as †67.

Each individual's score on the Hostility-Acceptance Scale was added as †68.

67.		
Persons from Postal Zips 00001-19999	38	(23%)
Persons from Postal Zips 20000-39999	38	(23%)
Persons from Postal Zips 40000-59999	31	(18%)
Persons from Postal Zips 60000-79999	32	(19%)
Persons from Postal Zips 80000-99999	29	(17%)
Persons with no Postal Zips indicated	50	(23% of total)

68. On the Hostility-Acceptance Scale, 1 is the most hostile, 9 the most accepting (See Note 1 for a full explanation):

Persons scoring 9	1	(.5%)
Persons scoring 8	9	(4%)
Persons scoring 7	23	(10.5%)
Persons scoring 6	64	(29%)
Persons scoring 5	69	(32%)
Persons scoring 4	29	(13%)
Persons scoring 3	14	(7%)
Persons scoring 2	7	(3%)
Persons scoring 1	2	(1%)
	218	(100%)

** Improperly named: should be "Gay Caucus for the Modern Languages"

Gaiety and the Laity: Avoiding the Excesses Of Professionalism

By Edgar Z. Friedenberg

In February, 1974, the Canadian Gay Liberation Journal *The Body Politic* published an interview with me by Greg Lehne. Mr. Lehne, a regular contributor to the journal, had heard me speak at Duke University some years ago, but had not seen me until I turned up rather unexpectedly on a panel at a Conference on THE UNIVERSITY AND THE GAY EXPERIENCE in New York in November, 1973. Our interview was recorded during a lengthy break in the proceedings occasioned by a bomb threat; we talked while the police searched the building.

They found nothing; yet, it turned out that a bomb had indeed been present, at least in the making. I found this out when the interview was published. The next issue included, as the lead letter in its "Letters" section a missive about 500 words long headed "No Justification." Four of its eight signers were either members of the collective that publishes *The Body Politic* or, like Mr. Lehne (who was not, of course, among them), listed as regular contributors.

This letter attacked, more in sorrow than in anger, both *The Body Politic* for publishing the interview without identifying "Friedenberg's beliefs for what they are: instruments for the maintenance of gay oppression," and me: "We can only express compassion for this gay scholar, whom sexual oppression has reduced to an embarrassing display of intellectual shallowness on an issue which is so central to his being." "There is no justification," it declaimed, "for the circulation of opinions merely because they are those of an established scholar, that is, a person elevated by the mechanisms of the ruling class to the position of intellectual authority." The writers of the letter did not identify everything I had said that angered them, dismissing much that they found objectionable by asserting: "Friedenberg puts forth many other equally backward notions in the interview, but it is undesirable to give them any more exposure than they have already received in *The Body Politic*." But what especially distressed them was my rather dubious attitude toward sexuality as a generally loving force, rather than a demonic one which may be destructive or humiliating as well as amiable, and a statement in the interview that "All liberation movements, I think, are necessary; and none work. Because politics is politics, and as soon as it becomes politics there's corruption." They were also offended by my asking "Are the laws being changed because the gay liberation movement is getting stronger, or is the gay liberation movement getting stronger because of the social climate which permits the change in the law? I think the latter."

What seemed to annoy them most, however, was the fact that I did not see myself as especially oppressed even though I made it clear in the interview that I was a virgin — there are some secrets still too ugly to reveal. And I suspect that what made the interview truly inexcusable from the writers' point of view was its conclusion, though they did not refer to it specifically.

"(L.) Do you mean that not having sex has not been frustrating in your life?"

"(F.) Not particularly, no. On the whole I'm a pretty happy person."

"(L.) Have you missed having sex?"

"(F.) I'm sure I have, from what I've read, but I can't take it very seriously."

This is hardly the place to reopen a debate with a group of Canadians who published a letter hostile to me in a local journal years ago. I have referred to the incident because it not only raises very real issues about the responsibility gay people owe to the "movement," but it also demonstrates that these issues are in fact a source of conflict among gays. The next issue of _The Body Politic_ included several letters rebutting this one — as well as others which supported a truly coercive attitude against persons, like myself, who do not take their gaiety seriously enough. But I continue to believe very strongly that each individual, whether gay or utterly morose, must determine for himself what aspects of his being are most important to him and what, then, he is obliged to do about them. And what one decides to do about the circumstances, internal or external, of one's life is, of course, both a moral and a political decision. I seem to recall that Paul Goodman, long before he came out in _The New York Times Magazine_, published a review of James Baldwin's _Another Country_ in which he criticized Baldwin for making the sexual predicaments of the characters in that novel the central factor in their lives — a luxury he felt few people, and certainly few people in their position, could afford. Even if I could afford it, it would make me feel rather odd.

As a graduate student at the University of Chicago in the late 1940s, I was privileged to know the distinguished anthropologist, Allison Davis, who was what we would now call a Black man — a designation that I think he would have found distasteful, since he used language very precisely. Davis's attitude would also have distressed present-day militants. We were both railroad buffs, and especially enjoyed riding the *Broadway Limited*, which still exists and at that time was one of the best equipped and well-serviced trains in the world. Professor Davis complained to me, however, that he had recently felt obliged to limit if not forego a pleasure that he had enjoyed for years: that of sitting in the lounge-car and enjoying a few drinks between the time of the *Broadway's* late-afternoon departure and dinner. "Every time I've done that lately," he observed, "within ten minutes somebody has come and sat down in the next seat to talk about 'the Negro question!' I don't *always* want to talk about the Negro question. In fact, I hardly ever want to talk about it when I'm just riding along on a train, enjoying a drink and a little privacy."

Every part of Allison Davis's identity must have been affected by his race. Moreover, as a talented Virginian born at the turn of the century, it must have made him subject to insult and humiliation on many occasions — experiences that were probably responsible for his air of glacial and ironical dignity which did not conceal his warmth but did reveal what it must have cost him to retain it. His *negritude* was not a handicap that he transcended, but, no doubt, the core of the personality that he had elaborated through life. It did not, however, provide him with his profession or his *raison d'être*; and it no longer predominated, if it ever had, in his presentation of self in everyday life. No one but himself could ever have known what being black meant to him; though it must certainly have been essential to his distinction as a person. But we could not have come to know him as a teacher, colleague, and friend, if he had insisted that his race must be the paramount issue in his relationships to us, for that insistence would have falsified the relationship. However important it may have been to him, it wasn't that important to us; and it wasn't as important as what he had become, in which race was hardly the dominant constituent any longer.

The parallel between blackness and gaiety is imperfect, because most blacks, even today — though not the most militant — would maintain that black consciousness is an artefact, though a historical necessity as well. Few would argue that black people have special tastes or special needs except insofar as these have been engendered by racial oppression in the first place; while to argue correspondingly about homosexual desire is to define it as a form of pathology in just the way that gay consciousness finds most offensive. Too much should not be made of these differences, however. Distaste for invidious comparisons among racial groups and the fear of being called racist have forestalled systematic inquiry into the possible distribution of systematic, inherent differences between races; we simply do not know and have not much chance of finding out in the near future what, if any, differences there might be between people who are black — or gay — and their "straight" fellows, if none of the three had been subjected to oppression. The parallels may be closer than we suppose. In any case, gays are oppressed, sometimes lethally; and this is indeed a political fact of first importance. The questions that remain, which I wish to consider here, concern how one should respond to the fact of repression and, especially, whether and how much the oppressed are obligated to center their life around their oppression, and around their membership in the oppressed group.

This is a more difficult question, I think, than it seems. For if a group is defined by its oppressors, as all discriminated groups are, then to center one's life around the consequences of having been assigned to it is to allow the oppressor to dictate the terms of one's life. Nobody should devote his or her life to trying to get other people to change their image of him, whether by submissive wheedling or by forceful political action. Of the two, the latter is of course not only preferable but often essential. But such political action, however militant it may be and however protracted the occasion for it, simply must not be allowed to become the central purpose of life.

We must never allow our adversaries to define our identity for us; it is, after all, as simple as that. Despite a millenium of calumny, culminating in such forgeries as the *Protocols of the Elders of Zion*, Jews, in their praxis as such, never committed atrocities, though we were continually their victims. But the state of Israel — driven, like any other state, by the circumstances of politics and history — does. If the establishment of a Jewish homeland was a victory for Judaism, making us become like *them* in the process was perhaps a profounder victory for anti-semites. Though, of course, the differences were never as great as we like to suppose.

This does not deny the necessity of militant organization to fight our oppressors or the glory victory brings. I, too, think of the battle of Stonewall Inn, or Second Bull Run, as a decisive and joyful historical moment; and I am grateful to those happy few, that little band of brothers, who stood there. But we are not, thank God, yet become a nation; and, as to veteran's organizations, I don't much care for them. Nor do I care for the heightened, but false, sense of mutuality that combat arouses; it is wonderful at the time, but embarrassing in retrospect. How proud we all were of the British carrying on during the Battle of Britain like caricatures of their traditional selves, gathering to listen to Dame Myra Hess in concert while the bombs rained around them! It was magnificent;

it was part of an effort that extended the life of Western civilization by at least 35 years. But if these were indeed representative Britons, not many of them could have liked music as much as all that. A large proportion of this dedicated audience came, I suspect, to lend their friend and countrywoman not their ears but their stiff upper lips.

Inauthenticity is part of the price we pay for devoting ourselves to a common national or tribal purpose that cannot coincide exactly with our own or fully express our feelings. It is a small price when the enemy is Hitler, or even the police. The emotions of the battlefield may be authentic enough; but they seldom last out the war unless they are artificially heightened by exaggerating the terror or oppression that the enemy imposes, and the joys liberation will bring. Life is seldom that simple, it seems to me; and a part of its complexity derives from the fact that it just doesn't turn out to be as joyless as the oppressor would make it; nor does it improve as much as promised when the oppressor is slain or overthrown. The victor establishes his own police; and the victim is seldom wholly deprived of his opportunity to display the talents he has developed for playing that role. Of course, it is better to be the victor and sometimes survival requires it. But victory is an occasion, not a profession; and a satisfactory society cannot be organized around putative military necessity. Even the oppressed need not always feel themselves besieged.

My comments so far are applicable to any kind of group identity, and the costs of committing oneself wholly to it. Anyone who is interested in pursuing this issue to its philosophical foundations will find it discussed *ad nauseam* by Jean-Paul Sartre in his *Critique de la raison dialectique*; and presented in a highly condensed but English version by R.D. Laing in *Reason and Violence*. Vonnegut-readers may condense it still further, without losing the essential point, into the simple admonition: don't give up your *karass* for any *granfalloon*; for gays, like every other group of people held together by a common definition rather than by relationships they have elaborated among themselves, *are* a granfalloon. None of this has anything to do with the fact that the peculiarity that distinguishes gays is sexual. But some important consequences do follow from that fact and create special difficulties for the concept of gay liberation which do not, as I see it, arise in connection with political groups that do not conceive of their consciousness as erotic.

I dislike writing about sex because I know very little about it from personal experience; and I do have a scholar's scruples about publishing on topics I haven't mastered and have few reliable data on. But I do know one thing; I'm damned sick and tired of apologizing for an ignorance that more than forty years after puberty must, after all, be evidence of a certain consistent lack of interest. During these particular forty years, that lack has been treated as the unforgiveable sin — worse, by far, than any inappropriate sexual focus. "Chastity," Anatole France observed, "is the rarest of perversions." Maybe; but it still takes all kinds, doesn't it?

Southern belles, among whom I grew up, do not accept a lack of enthusiasm lightly. But young men still did, then; at least, from other young men. I am quite sure that one reason that I felt free to notice how beautiful they sometimes were and to trust my feeling toward them was precisely because I wasn't expected to *do* anything about it. While I entered a co-educational college at the age of 13 and attended it until I graduated four years later, leading what to me was a satisfactory social life, and receiving a lot of real affection from my peers, nobody ever tried to seduce me. This was perhaps to my discredit; it was certainly not to theirs. The fact that I was so young, of course, made the risks that much greater for anyone who might have tried; but they weren't insuperable — quite a lot of sexual activity could have been fit into the *mores* fairly safely as mere horseplay. One fraternity had in it most of the boys I thought really attractive; and I did wistfully hope they would pledge me after I had become rather famous as a campus intellectual and even had my picture in *Time* magazine, and that some of this would then happen. But they didn't, and it never did. Perhaps they disliked me personally; but some of them are still my friends. Others I still think of from time to time, sometimes quite raunchily. I doubt if they would have lived up to my fantasies about them; we would have embarrassed each other, and I would have been left with less than I have now.

Of course, it seems to me far better that people of the same sex can now express a sexual interest in each other and act on it freely in many communities. But what I can't see is what it is that I should feel aggrieved about. To be denied love or the right to show one's love — that is a grievance indeed, and one that I should think would justify murder. It is not, however, what happened. Conversely, I don't see how anyone that I cared about could have been unaware of my feelings; and few seemed displeased by them. The information that another person finds you sexually attractive, if not conveyed demandingly, is seldom received with acute distress. One of the really curious consequences of my rather curious life, indeed, is that I have never learned how to enter a relationship intended to be temporary; though I have learned how to let people go, in the hope that they will then come back. They usually do; though in any case, whatever erotic scent facilitated the onset of the relationship usually dissipates, leaving the friendship unimpaired if unconsummated.

In truth, there seems to be a great need in this world for affectionate people who try not to demand what their partners cannot afford, and who remain stable over time. Sexual partners are easier to find. And while love can certainly be enhanced by sexual expression, it does not seem to me that in our world sexual relationships are usually intended by either tenderness or stability. Neither Norman Mailer nor William Burroughs has ever written a love story; at least, not about anybody else. Tennessee Williams has, certainly; but they are seldom stories that envisage the possibility of the same people loving one another over a long period of time, to their mutual satisfaction, even though they will assuredly not live happily ever after. E.M. Forster and Henry James, though, did; and though they could not handle fucking as a literary device, they wrote more seriously and perceptively about women than the authors who depend on it for graphic effect. James Joyce is usually held to have successfully rendered both the personalities and the contingent sexuality of his female characters; but I really have no idea what it would be like to spend an afternoon working with Molly Bloom as a colleague; as I certainly do with Isabel Archer or Helen Schlegel.

Now, obviously, the success of militant gay activism has put the possibility of permanent gay households on a firmer basis legally, which seems to me an inestimable contribution to human dignity. Gay marriage is something else again; I feel about that much as I do about trying to build up the enrollment of ethnic minorities and the working class generally in universities. If they want it, fine; but it seems a bit sad for them to be claiming this as a great prize just at the time their social superordinates are abandoning it as worthless — though very convenient, no doubt, for the universities. If I am to applaud, as I do, young men being granted the right to have the state solemnize and thus endorse their household, I must be quick to point out that I am equally pleased that both homo and heterosexual couples now feel free to live together without that support, and that this still seems to me to be the greater freedom. It is true, I believe, that lovers are bound together till death parts them; but not by any oath. This is simply the definition of death, which medical science is having so much trouble formulating on purely empirical grounds. Heart transplants don't work very long, either, Love just is not love which alters when it alteration finds, or bends with the remover to remove, as one of us once observed; and the less the state has to say about it, the better. The great and continuing achievement of gay liberation is to limit the state's ravages and maintain vigilance against it; and for this, all honor to it.

But these are political questions; and politics, though indispensable, is not essential. It is concerned with the conditions of being, not with being itself. Politics must often therefore have first priority; it may require all our attention and energy in order to establish conditions favorable to life or even conditions that will allow life to continue. It is usually unwise to meditate at length upon the possibility of genocide. But politics will certainly take the life of anyone who encourages it to metastasize through his whole being until he judges his every gesture and commitment according to its political, or power-enhancing utility. That is what happens to the people who manage to become Presidents; and though their potency may be enhanced, at least by definition, it is no longer possible to think of them as capable of love. And I doubt that it matters much that one has become a political man in the cause of sexual freedom if one is nevertheless thereby led to assess other persons and respond to them primarily as adversaries or allies rather than as comrades — perhaps in arms, perhaps elsewhere.

Gay Students

By J. Lee Lehman

Whenever the term "academia" comes up, it seems that the speaker is talking about an ivory tower peopled by professors, administrators, and staff (who are kept carefully out of sight, so as not to disturb the sentiments of the keepers of Higher Learning). Judging from the make-up of every institute of higher learning which I've ever seen, there seems to be an element missing, the most populous one, in fact: the student. It seems that many academicians have not abandoned the original concept of what a university is, even though this concept has not been valid for centuries. Universities exist, by the grace of legislators and sponsors, to educate students. I have frequently heard the argument that students, while necessary for such amenities as paying professors' salaries and doing professors' research, need not be taken seriously because they are "transitory." But in these days of budget slashing it would be wrong to assume that professors aren't also transitory. Similarly, there is the argument of the junior faculty member: age or duration does not necessarily imply wisdom.

Since the purpose of this chapter is to discuss gay students, I will dwell no longer on the semantics of academia. I merely want to point out that when faculty get together to discuss academia, they generally mean themselves. I contend that they have no right to assume total claim.

There are many issues which fall under the heading of gay students, but I will discuss only three: coming out on campus, gay student organizations, and gay student-gay faculty relations.

Coming Out

The campus is a popular place for coming out. It is frequently the first chance a student gets to live away from home. It is a time for sexual experimentation, and the university has a more "progressive" (read: bleeding heart liberal) attitude in many cases than what students come to call the "real world." This does not mean that it's easy. Just today a letter came to the National Gay Student Center requesting our list of gay student groups. The address given was a post office box and it was signed "an Indiana college student." Here was somebody so afraid of being discovered that he/she could not even use his/her name in correspondence to a gay group.

Attitudes about gays vary tremendously from campus to campus. At the University of Missouri-Kansas City, students interviewed were split about whether the Gay People's Union should be recognized. Typical comments: "Homosexuality, if given free reign might create unethical acts and hence perpetuate latent homosexuality." "I feel that they create an unnatural influence on campus which is not conducive to the furthering of academic goals. They should either see a psychoanalyst or give it up"[1]. At Temple University the Gay Students set up a "Kiss a Queer" booth at the Student Activities Center on Valentines Day, 1974, with mixed reaction from the student body.[2] At Rutgers University the Homophile League declared the first national Gay Day — "If you're gay, wear blue jeans" ("If you're not gay, and all you got is blue jeans . . . better start streaking, honey!!!").[3] The number of blue jeans on campus, normally about 80-90% of the pants worn, dropped to around 50% (personal observation).

Even in a progressive community, there can be problems with the student's department. Edwin Ellis, a doctoral candidate in psychology at the New Jersey School of Medicine and Dentistry, has noted that many gay medical students fear that coming out would jeopardize their chances of getting through, a fear which Ed feels has some truth to it (personal communication). While graduate schools have their special pitfalls, problems at the undergraduate level are not unheard of. A student at East Tennessee State University wrote the NGSC this spring and said that his school was trying to expel him for being gay.

Although more and more students are emerging publicly from the closet, many are not. They decide to tell only their close friends. They may feel that it's nobody else's business, or that something might get on their record. I have run into this attitude from other gays in my own department. Although they can see that I'm not getting much trouble, they don't want the extra hassle, or they don't feel as strongly as I do.

Even when the student decides to stay at least partly in the closet, there are problems. One of the biggest concerns is that wonderful college institution: the dormitory. In spite of the publicity of the past few years, most dormitories are still same sex institutions. Many of the so-called coed dorms have women and men in different wings, on different floors, or in separate suites. While visitation hours may be abolished, one still finds the same old structure (enterprising heterosexuals were always known to get around the rules). In a same sex environment, it can be very threatening to admit a preference for the same sex. The other occupants suddenly start to fear rape. Friends have told me that people in their dorms stopped talking to them after they came out. Even without coming out there is the necessity of "passing" and enduring that terrible experience: listening to queer jokes and being afraid to say anything.

But the other dorm occupants are no problem at all compared to one special person: the roommate. If the roommate is gay, there's no problem (provided both are out). But otherwise — how do you tell your roommate without making it sound like a proposition? I had to cross that hurdle three different times, but each time I was damn sure what the reaction was going to be before I said anything. And in each case, my roommate took it well, although in one instance my roommate was convinced that I never did "any of those things." I've been lucky, even with two of the three times taking place at a small school in the Midwest (University of Wisconsin-Green Bay). One of my friends was kicked out of her room by her roommate. (Her roommate later came out.) Others have gotten every reaction from "I don't believe it" to threats.

So coming out on campus is not necessarily easy. One has to cope with reactions from professors, administrators, other students, and friends. But at least finding other gays is relatively easy, especially if there is a gay group on campus.

Gay Student Organizations

There are about two hundred gay student organizations in the United States. Most (76%) are mixed (male/female), with a small percentage (20%) of all female groups and an even smaller percentage (6%) of all male groups, according to the 1974 survey of the NGSC).[4] Although most groups are mixed, one third of these groups report a predominantly male membership. Eighty-three percent of the groups were recognized university organizations; a surprising percentage of the recognized groups had been recognized for four or more years (52%). Of course, there was probably some bias built into the questionnaire because the NGSC probably only hears from the more established groups. Of those recognized, 86% had no problems getting recognition. Fifty percent of the unrecognized organizations were in litigation to obtain recognition. One may conclude that most gay student groups are male/female, many are well established on their campuses, and most had few problems getting established.

Gay student groups provide many services for their members and for the campuses they serve. Services for members and for the gay community include coffeehouses and social hours (43% of the groups had these), dances

(31%), counseling (31%), rap groups (23%), referrals (17%), hotlines (14%), newsletters (14%), libraries (14%), drop-in centers (6%), and athletics (3%). Services aimed at the whole university community include speakers' bureaus (66%), political activity (20%), conferences (11%), radio shows (6%), and art shows (3%).

Most groups are primarily concerned with providing services for their members. Social events are a particularly important way of allowing gays to meet other gays in a nonoppressive setting. Most groups also feel a need to educate the rest of the university community. Speakers' bureaus are an essential part of this educational process. An active group will have speaking engagements at a number of universities in the area. Most frequent are classes such as human sexuality, abnormal psychology, social pathology, social psychology, psychology of deviance, and developmental psychology. Dorm speaking engagements are fairly common, and occasionally there are other kinds, including peer counseling orientation sessions. These events provide the major interaction forum for gays and non-gays. Non-gays seldom get the opportunity to explore gay issues in a nonoppressive environment. Although hostile feelings are frequently encountered, they seldom predominate. Many non-gays have told me how important this was for them, their first encounter with people who were not apologetic for being gay. And many gay people have told me how important this was for them, reinforcing their self-concepts and reaffirming that it is possible to be gay and proud. I believe that the impact of speakers' bureaus is grossly underrated. For many people (including some gays) these encounters are the first opportunity to see homosexuality away from the societal myths and to see the real enemy: homophobia. One of the most entertaining bits of consciousness-raising to be had is simply to tell the audience that about one in ten people are gay, then estimate the size of the audience and thereby tell how many gay people there are. As everyone looks around nervously, you may observe that no one in the room has a lavender star on her/his forehead, so they better be careful!

Political activity varies from campus to campus. There are legal restraints at state universities because of the university's own legal status. This usually only precludes lobbying and the endorsement of political candidates. However, there are many other forms of political activity which are perfectly legal: collecting information on candidates' stands on gay issues, talking to or making up packets on gay issues for legislators, or (as individuals) picketing establishments with anti-gay practices. It may or may not be possible for the group to bring suits against individuals or establishments when discrimination is encountered. In the field of political tactics there is much room for creativity, with imaginative picket signs, guerilla theater, or zaps. In many cases one of the most beneficial side-effects of such activity is publicity for the organization. Operating a kissing booth or a gay day as already described is political activity which is also a publicity stunt. It is certainly true in the gay movement that one of the most political things we can do is to make our existence felt.

For other gays on campus, the existence of a gay group can be important. The individual may not feel comfortable being out for many different reasons, and seeing that others are around can reinforce gay pride. At the same time, the up-front gay organization can be a threat, particularly if the individual is ashamed of her/his sexual preference. The individual may have to confront more "flak" directly. For instance, a few years ago the Rutgers University Homophile League was applying for funding from one of the fee boards. The most vocal opposition was from a guy we knew was gay: he'd been seen cruising at all the local men's cruising areas. But what could we do at the meeting — call him out? That would have been to betray the unwritten rules of the gay sub-culture, but there he was, screwing us. Two years later a lesbian was presenting a proposal for a gay studies course. The only opposition came from a professor whom she later met at the local gay bar.

Most people "in the closet" do not try to throw up such barriers. But many people, out or not, have problems which require counseling. Two types are frequent: coming out problems and relationship ones. In both cases the problems are hardly the traditional ones which require psychiatric care. Psychoanalysis can be dangerous for gays because many straight counselors assume that the problem is being gay so that the "cure" is to go straight. For the problems mentioned, it is almost essential that the individual talk to someone else who is gay. That person need not be a professional therapist; in most cases paraprofessional help is in order. Some gay student organizations have set up hotlines or counseling services to fill this need. Since so many gays come out during their college years, the need is often acute. A survey of campus suicides was started by the Student Government Information Service of the National Student Association two years ago. The preliminary results showed that a substantial number of cases involved sexual orientation crises (personal communication). One of the most frequently verbalized fears during crisis counseling is the fear of being alone. With more and more services opening every day, hopefully fewer and fewer people will feel alone.

Gay Student — Gay Faculty Relations

It was encouraging to witness the establishment of the Gay Academic Union several years ago. Gay faculty members have had more problems getting together and organizing than have students. For one thing, there are comparatively few faculty members compared to students. Hence there isn't a large pool of recruits. Furthermore, faculty organizations are not the established tradition that student groups are. And finally, there are additional problems with coming out as a faculty member since the university is one's employer. There are also good reasons why faculty have not simply gone out and joined student groups. Perhaps the foremost reason is the inherent agism in our society. People are simply not that comfortable with people of other ages in a social setting. Faculty members, inevitably the minority, may feel uncomfortable with a bunch of "kids." (I have heard this reaction from graduate students who quit gay student groups too.) Issues are also different: students are generally not concerned with hiring and firing, tenure, promotions, and salary.

The formation of Gay Academic Union chapters has solved these problems. G.A.U. chapters encompassing more than one university thereby increase potential membership. And since the group is one step removed from the campus, members have greater anonymity if they desire it. However, the formation of these groups has not solved one problem: gay student-gay faculty relations.

There are many reasons for promoting good student-faculty relations. Up-front faculty members could be a wonderful role model for emerging gay students. Sharing of experiences would allow insights and might be helpful to younger gays. For faculty members teaching gay studies, gay students represent an important ally. On the other hand, students coming out today are free of many of the pre-1969 guilt-trips, and so their insights may help faculty members (or older students) who came out before them.

But let us face up to the problem: many faculty members are uncomfortable with students in any setting other than the classroom. The fact that both faculty member and student are gay does not ease the problem. Furthermore, this dichotomy infects virtually all faculty members, even the most progressive ones. (I still remember my own reaction the first time I met a former student at a gay dance, and I'm only a teaching assistant! Fortunately, I transcended this feeling by the second time.) The result is that all too frequently the gay students don't know which faculty members are gay and vice versa. This can be tremendously detrimental when it comes to common issues, such as organizing gay studies. The fact that students and faculty members belong to different groups (if they belong to groups at all) aggravates this.

The easing of student-faculty relations will solve this problem. It would be very difficult to expect people to make exceptions to roles on the basis of sexual preference. Unfortunately we are so hung up by our student/faculty roles that it is difficult to get beyond them. The additional bond of being gay is insufficient, particularly since "gay" represents a diversity of lifestyles.

Will we decide to break out of these roles? Gay liberation is yet another example of human liberation; human liberation will not be complete until all arbitrary roles are broken down.

NOTES

1Virgo, Mary. Mixed reaction to gay group. Article in "The University News" (The University of Missouri-Kansas City), February 14, 1974, p. 3.

2Schwartz, Bruce. Gay booth too close to massacre. Article in "The Temple News" (Temple University), February 15, 1974, p. 1.

3Advertisements in "The Targum" (Rutgers University), week of April 15, 1974.

4Lehman, J. L. 1975. National Gay Student Center Gay Student Groups Survey. In: J. L. Lehman, ed., *Gays on Campus*. National Student Association: Washington, D.C. 88 pp.

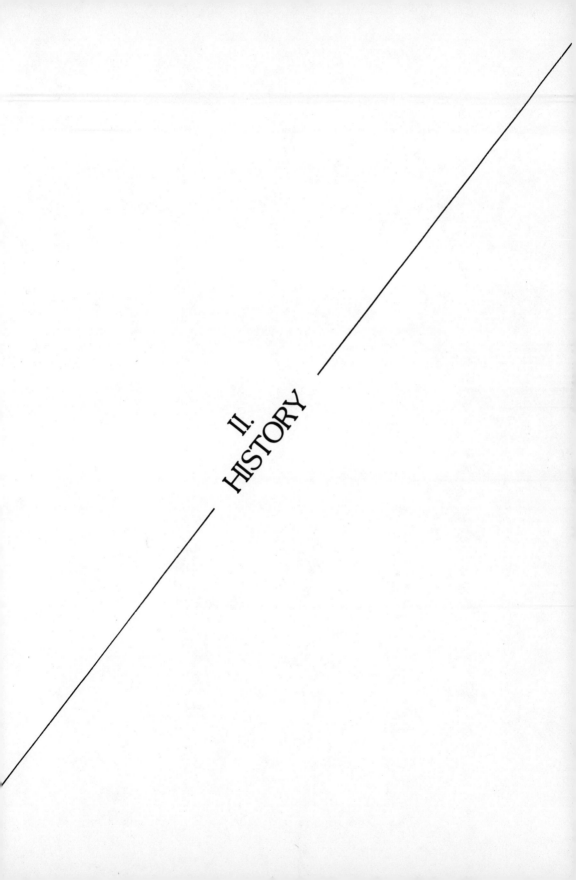

II.
HISTORY

Gay Genocide:
From Leviticus to Hitler

By Louis Crompton

The expression "Gay Genocide" is not in very general use. It sounds dramatic, and I suppose I ought to justify it, so that I will not be accused of trying to exploit people's emotions in an illegitimate way. The 1953 edition of Webster's Collegiate Dictionary — I am deliberately using a dictionary twenty years old — defines *genocide* as "the use of deliberate, systematic measures towards the extermination of a racial, political, or cultural group." Of course, genocide comes to mind when we think of the fate of Jews in Nazi Germany, of the American Indian, of Jesuits in England or Protestants at the St. Bartholomew massacre, or of the losing side in any class war. We have ample records of all of these campaigns of extermination. Why, then, does the word *genocide* strike the ear as novel, or even strained, when applied to homosexuality?

I would like to emphasize immediately that it is not because the facts do not justify the use of the term. The term *genocide* can as properly be applied historically to society's treatment of gay people as to any of these other groups. For a remarkable length of time — not less than 1400 years — homosexual men and women in western society stood under a formal sentence of death, and were, in consequence, systematically killed or mutilated. But there has been no public account of this astonishing crime against humanity, all but unparalleled in its relentless use of sanctified legal traditions, and in its continuance century after century.

This is because there has been no "gay history" as there has been a history of the Jews, of the blacks, of the Indians, and of Christian sects. "Straight" historians have been inhibited from writing on the subject by the taboo which made it "unspeakable," "unmentionable," and "not fit to be named among Christian men." Gay historians, who might have had a greater incentive to record the martyrdom of their sisters and brothers, have been restrained by this convention, and something more: the fear of ceasing to be invisible. Suppose western civilization had killed off its Jews, declared Jewish people to be unmentionables, and discouraged any record from being kept of anti-Jewish pogroms. Suppose the reign of terror had been so complete that Jewish communities and cultures had vanished and no one dared publicly identify himself as Jewish or dared speak, without the most elaborate precautions, to someone he thought might belong to his minority. Suppose, in addition, that Christian scriptures contained an unequivocal law to the effect that all Jews must be killed as practitioners of "abominations." The histories of oppression that today contain chapters on the persecution of Protestants, Catholics, witches, and heretics would no doubt be silent about the Jews, just as they are now silent about homosexuals.

Can this chapter of gay history be written at all, given the centuries' old conspiracy of silence? I would like to suggest that it can, and to make a preliminary effort towards filling in the blank pages in our history books.

First, what have been the laws that have condemned homosexuals to death, and where did they come from? In western Europe they first enter the statute books with the coming to power of Christianity in the fourth century A.D., and they appear to have been inspired by laws adopted by the Jews in Palestine almost a thousand years earlier, probably about 550 B.C. This millennium was, of course, the age in which the civilization of ancient Greece and Rome reached its height. It was also one in which homosexuality, in this classical culture, was tolerated and even honored. In ancient Greece homosexual relations were respected above heterosexual ones: far from being decried, homosexuality was associated with patriotism, with military valor, with opposition of tyrants, and with love, beauty, wisdom, and virtue. It was one of the pieties of the tribe, like football in modern America. Though gay love was already amply celebrated in song and story, it rose to a special height of esteem in Athens in 514 B.C., when the lovers, Harmodius and Aristogeiton, were "canonized" as martyrs in the struggle for democracy. Ironically, at almost the same moment of history the author of the "Holiness Code" in the Book of Leviticus inscribed what was to prove the most fateful statement ever written, anywhere, on the subject of homosexuals. In a bare two dozen words he wrote an edict that was to have immense influence on western law-making in Christian times: "If a male also lie with mankind as he lieth with a woman, both of them have committed an abomination; they shall surely be put to death." [1] The punishment for such an act in Old Testament times was stoning to death. Here is how the Talmud describes the procedure:

> The place of stoning was twice a man's height. One of the witnesses pushed him by the hips, so that he was overturned on his heart. He was then turned on his back. If that caused his death, he had fulfilled his duty. But if not, the second witness took the stone [i.e. a

heavy stone that it took two men to lift] and threw it on his chest. If he died thereby, he had done his duty. But if not he [the criminal] was stoned by all Israel, for it is written: the hand of the witnesses shall be first upon him to put him to death, and afterwards the hand of all the people.[2]

Non-Jews convicted of homosexual offenses under Jewish jurisdiction were also liable to the death penalty.

This was a statutory policy of gay genocide, and following the adoption of Christianity as the official state religion of Rome it became the legal policy of Christian Europe until the French Revolution, and of North and South America as long as they were under European control. Gay culture in Greece, which had celebrated gay love in a thousand poems, dramas, myths, biographies, and epics, vanished, and love between men or between women became what a sixteenth-century Scottish indictment called — "wyild, filthie, execrabill, detestabill, and unnaturall"[3] — an occasion for the death penalty. The cultural shock in the Greek Mediterranean world must have been extreme when we realize that this violent turnabout took place only within the course of two or three generations.

Let me cite an instance. The first Roman imperial edict condemning gay men to "exquisite punishment" was issued in 342 A.D., five years after Constantine's baptism and death, in the name of his sons Constantius and Constans. This law reflected the vehement anti-homosexual policy of Paul and the Church Fathers.[4] Then fifty years later, in 390, Theodosius, the first Christian emperor to decree the death penalty for heretics, passed a law condemning homosexuals to be burnt at the stake. In the same year Theodosius' governor at Thessalonika in Greece arrested a popular charioteer for a minor homosexual offense and jailed him. The Thessalonikans rioted and killed the governor. Theodosius, disguising his wrath, invited the citizens to games in the stadium, hid soldiers in the stands and massacred more than 7,000 of the spectators. For this deed, Theodosius later did penance in Milan Cathedral before St. Ambrose. But gay love was dead, and unrelenting hostility was the policy of Christian Europe from then on.

I have mentioned that Theodosius' edict of 390 condemned homosexuals to be burnt at the stake. This had been the traditional Roman punishment for arson, and was presumably used against homosexuals because of the legend of Sodom and Gomorrah. It was, of course, also the standard punishment for recalcitrant heretics. The so-called *Établissements* of St. Louis, issued about 1270, prescribed that "if anyone be suspected of *bouguerie*, he shall be taken to the Bishop, and if he is proved guilty, he shall be burned."[5]

"Bouguerie" or "buggery" at first meant heresy, then usury, and finally homosexuality. This law was in force in France until the end of the eighteenth century. Justinian's famous edict of 538, which, on the analogy of the Sodom story, blamed homosexuals for the plagues, famines, and earthquakes that had recently beset the Byzantine empire, seems, according to the accounts in Procopius and Theophanes, to have been part of a systematic campaign of terrorism unleashed against homosexuals by the Emperor.[6] Because of the prestige of Justinian's famous code, it also had great influence on later legislation. The earliest English legal treatise that touches on the subject (a work called "Fleta," written about 1300) prescribes an unorthodox penalty: "Those who have connexion with Jews and Jewesses or are guilty of bestiality or sodomy shall be buried alive in the ground."[7] A marginal note in another English treatise of about the same date indicates the role the clergy were to play in identifying gay people for punishment — "The inquirers of Holy Church shall make their inquests of sorcerers, sodomites, renegates and misbelievers; and if they find any such, they shall deliver him to the king's court to be put to death" — in this case by fire.[8] The religious nature of these ordinances is clear enough. But even after Parliament passed a civil statute in 1533 making gay love a felony with hanging as its penalty, commentators like Coke and Blackstone always stressed the religious origin of the law. Coke's *Institutes* tell us the traditional English indictment was "grounded upon the word of God,"[9] and Blackstone, in his *Commentaries* of 1769 says this crime is one which "The voice of nature and of reason, and the express law of God, determine to be capital. Of which we have a single instance . . . by the destruction of two cities by fire from heaven."[10]

On the continent, Spanish law had originally condemned homosexuals to castration and stoning to death. Ferdinand and Isabella, orthodox in all things, changed the penalty to burning. A generation later, Ferdinand's grandson, Charles V, then Holy Roman Emperor, set forth in his Constitutions of 1532 an order that also explicitly condemned not only male homosexuals but also lesbians to the flames: "If a man commit unchastity with a beast or a man, or a woman with a woman, they have forfeited their lives and shall be condemned to death by fire in the usual fashion."[11] According to an eighteenth-century French legal encyclopedia, "The Swiss exercise extraordinary rigors against men guilty of this crime. They cut off one limb after another in the course of several days — first an arm, then a thigh; when the body is a lifeless trunk it is thrown on the fire."[12] These genocidal laws remained in the criminal codes in France till 1791, in England till 1861, and in Scotland as late as 1889.

What of the United States? To what extent were gay people subject to the death penalty in the American colonies? Copies of early American colonial codes are obscure and hard to come by. To date, I have seen nothing about this subject in any book on homosexuality. In 1641, however, Massachusetts Bay colony promulgated its famous "Body of Laws and Liberties," the prototype for much later Puritan legislation. Among the twelve capital crimes — which include idolatry, witchcraft, and blasphemy — is lovemaking between men. The language, however is not that of English law, that is, of Henry VIII's statute of 1533. Instead, the Puritans go "back to the Bible" with a vengeance, and actually legislate Leviticus verbatim: "If any man lyeth with mankinde, as he lyeth with a woeman, both of them have committed abhomination, they both shall surely be put to death."[13] So, with language 2200 years old, America's first settlers condemned their gay sons to death, and in the case of a 1656 New Haven statute, their lesbian daughters.[14] This Old Testament formula was adopted by the colonies of Massachusetts, Connecticut, New Hampshire, New York, New Jersey, and Pennsylvania. Only the Quakers revolted and showed a momentary flash of Christianity. In 1682, William Penn's reform code reduced the penalty for same-sex relations to six months' imprisonment.[15] But in 1700, Pennsylvania re-introduced capital punishment for sodomy in the case of blacks, and eighteen years later, under English pressure, for all men.[16] After the Revolution, Pennsylvania led the way in abolishing the death penalty in 1786 and other states began to follow its example in the next decade.

On the occasion of the Bicentennial of the Declaration of Independence, most Americans are acutely conscious of the fact that the right to "liberty and the pursuit of happiness" did not extend to black slaves in 1776. But how many people are aware that two hundred years ago the law in all the American colonies denied the homosexual an even more basic right, the right to life itself?

This should be ample to suggest the reign of terror gay people faced in Europe and America for almost a millennium and a half. The consequent demoralization, the isolation, the lack of community and common culture can be imagined: we are only beginning to overcome these effects now. Officially, all Christian states were genocidal. In theory at least, the status of a homosexual was even worse than that of a Jew or heretic. Not all Christian countries condemned Jews to death or exile, and a convicted heretic could escape the flames by recanting.

But were gay people actually sentenced to death and killed under these laws? The standard work on the history of such legislation is Derrick Bailey's *Homosexuality and the Western Christian Tradition.* In this book, published in 1955, Bailey notes the severity of the laws passed under Christian influence, but he continually suggests that they were merely moral in intention and rarely applied in their full rigor. In the one hundred and eighty pages of his erudite study, Bailey does not mention a single execution. Clearly, Bailey, who writes as an Anglican theologian, wants to think well of the Church, and wants to soften the reaction that any reader, straight or gay, might have to the harshness of traditional Christian legislation. [17] For many years, lulled by Bailey's optimism, I imagined he was right. I was first jolted out of my complacency by Thomas Szasz's reference to Henry Charles Lea's treatment of the subject in his *History of the Inquisition of Spain*. Lea's monumental work turned out to have what no other standard history known to me contains — a factual account of the actual judicial treatment of homosexuals during a 300-year period in a major European country. According to Lea, Pope Nicholas V empowered the Inquisition in Spain to deal with homosexuality as early as 1451. In 1506, an Inquisitorial tribunal held an investigation in Seville. There were many arrests and many fugitives, and in the end twelve men were convicted and burned. In 1519 plague broke out in Valencia. A friar blamed it on God's wrath against homosexuals. A mob seized four men, who were tried and burned; a fifth was burned without any formalities. In 1562, Pope Pius IV gave the Portuguese Inquisition power to act in homosexual cases, at first only under municipal procedures, later, under the "process for heresy." In Catalonia in 1597 about a quarter of the cases tried by the Inquisition were for sodomy. In the period 1598 to 1602, twenty-seven homosexuals suffered in "autos de fe" — "acts of faith." In all, Lea lists several dozen burnings and more than one hundred other cases. [18]

Information about France proved more difficult to come by since there is a complete break in the French legal tradition with the appearance of the Napoleonic Code, and later legal histories consequently ignore the matter. However, the *Traité de la justice criminelle* of Daniel Jousse, published in 1771, lists nine executions, including the case of a Rector of the University of Paris who was hanged in front of the Louvre in 1584. Others were burned alive; the common sentence was to be "brûlé vif avec son procès" — "burned alive with his trial record." Another French jurist of the same period, Muyart de Vouglans wrote in 1757, "the penalty for so great a crime cannot be less than death. The terrible vengeance which divine justice exacted of the impious cities where this crime was common is enough to show that one cannot punish it with penalties too rigorous. This penalty is set forth expressly in the 20th chapter of Leviticus in these terms: 'If a man lieth with a man, etc.' " [19] Muyart calls it a "shame for our century" that two men had been burned in Paris in 1750 — the "shame" being, not the burning, but that homosexuals still existed to merit this fate. Here I might mention that both Jousse and Muyart state emphatically that women who have relations with women are also liable to the death penalty. One modern French writer mentions an account, by the Renaissance jurist Farinacci, of the execution of a number of women in Rome and Montaigne gives an account of the hanging of a lesbian in 1580.[20]

In one country at least, systematic executions of gay men actually continued into the nineteenth century, and are recorded in government statistical tables. This was England. There are several famous instances of the death penalty being inflicted in England in the seventeenth century. The most amazing document is a pamphlet on the last days of an Anglican bishop who was hanged in the streets of Dublin in 1641.[21] How many men died in the eighteenth century I do not know, though I am aware of at least half a dozen cases.[22] But there is a shocking record, contained in the annual Parliamentary tables on Criminal Offenders of more than fifty hangings from 1806 to 1835.[23] What accounts for this long-lasting British ferocity? No one knows, but French and Italian jurists tell us that men placed in the pillory — not for sodomy but for acts of solicitation — were sometimes stoned to death by London street mobs, and Jeremy Bentham, in an essay he never dared publish, speaks of seeing a judge who had just consigned "two wretches to the gallows," whose face glistened with "delight and exultation."[24] In England in the early nineteenth century, on the average, only one man out of 30 condemned to die was actually hanged, but the majority of the men convicted of sodomy were executed.

How many men were killed in the United States? At present, I know of only three. The trial of William Cornish in Virginia in 1625 is vividly described in H. R. McIlvaine's *The Minutes of the Council and General Court of Colonial Virginia*, and there were two executions under Dutch jurisdiction in New Amsterdam in 1646 and 1660.[25] What other cases exist, only a further search of colonial court records will tell. Obviously, in this sketch I have only touched the top of an enormous iceberg that will take generations of research workers in different countries to uncover. What will the final tally be? My own very cursory searches have so far uncovered over two hundred executions. The total number of executions under Church-inspired laws could easily run into the thousands.

Before turning to the twentieth century, I want to say a word about the most dramatic single episode I have yet come across from the period of capital penal laws. This was a "witch hunt" carried out in Holland in 1730 when men and boys were systematically burned, hanged, beheaded, garrotted, and even judicially drowned as homosexuals. Astonishingly, this drama took place in what has generally been regarded as the most liberal country of Europe in the so-called "Age of Reason." What caused it? The occasion seems to have been

1. *"Temporal Punishments Depicted as a Warning to Godless and Damnable Sinners."* This series of six engravings illustrates the Dutch persecutions of 1730-31. It was published in Amsterdam by Gerrit Bos and Gerrit Bouman with a descriptive poem by G. Tysens. The first scene shows two homosexuals leaving a meeting place during the persecutions. The symbolic figure of the woman with the serpent's tail represents *"abominable sins."*

a wave of religious hysteria strikingly similar to that which had inspired the witch trials at Salem, Massachusetts, a generation before. In April, 1730, some men were arrested at Utrecht; they incriminated others and in July a proclamation was issued by the States of Holland, for posting in every town, announcing that, to avert from Holland the fate that had destroyed Sodom and Gomorrah — "so that God Almighty might not — as he used to threaten at such abominations — punish the iniquity of our land with his terrible judgments, and spew forth the land and its inhabitants," — the crime of sodomy should be punished publicly with whatever form of death the judges

2. *Two men flee their homes during the persecution. The allegorical figure symbolizes despair.*

should decree and the bodies of the executed burned or exposed without burial.[26] The decree also ordered any man who had fled from his home after the beginning of the investigation to come forth and give reasons for his disappearance, under threat of banishment.

An English translation of this decree is printed in full as an appendix to this chapter. It is terroristic in two senses. Its traditional Christian rhetoric reflects the authors' own terror, and it sets forth a program of legal terror against Holland's gay minority, who perhaps not too surprisingly reacted with panic and flight. The hideous consequences of this campaign are dramatically portrayed in a series of contemporary engravings, here reproduced, which show the capture of two victims, and, in a final scene, the various forms of death meted out to them and others. I have also extracted, from a historical

3. The suspects are arrested in the street. The figure stands for fear.

account published in German in 1906, a table of names of those executed throughout Holland with a few details which have survived from contemporary records. These tables tell their own grim tale, with several poignant touches. The full story of these horrors will never be known, but we can imagine some of them from a commentary on Dutch legal procedure that appeared in England during the height of the terror. An article in the *Free Briton* in 1730 noted that Dutch methods of criminal justice approximated those of the Spanish Inquisition. Denunciations were invited from secret informers. Men were not told who their accusers were, nor were they allowed to cross-examine them. They were tortured, and, if they maintained their innocence, ran the risk of serious maiming. If they could not withstand the pain, and guilty or not, confessed to the accusations, they could be put to death.

4. The convicted men await their execution in prison. The figure holds a grid on which their bodies will be burnt.

Records exist of sentences in more than twenty cities and towns. These list thirteen executions in the Hague and five in Amsterdam. All in all we know of at least fifty-nine killings. In most towns one or two men were hanged as a warning and others were banished or imprisoned. The one notable exception was the small village of Zuidhorn — its present population is under 2,000 — where twenty-one victims, including a fifteen- and a fourteen-year-old boy were garroted and burnt on September 24, 1731. The scene of the sentencing comes dramatically to life in the brief recorded reactions of the condemned. The judge for the district of Oosterdeel-Langewoldt who ordered this wholesale slaughter at Zuidhorn was Rudolph de Mepsche, who seems to have proceeded with fanatical bigotry and was later accused of overzealous-

5. and 6. The city square at Amsterdam where homosexuals are being burnt, hanged, drowned, and garrotted. The scroll unrolled by the figure of Death shows ships taking bodies to be thrown into the sea. The seated man holds the flaming sword of Divine Wrath.

ness. The parallels with Salem or the Inquisition are striking. But whereas the persecution of witches or heretics is no longer condoned by modern Christianity, Sodom-mongering is still fully respectable in conservative religious circles which have been prevented by the silence of historians from contemplating the horrors this tradition of hatred and fear has perpetrated. How many Zuidhorns were there? How many town squares in Christendom witnessed scenes like those that took place in that quiet Dutch village attended by the pious formalities of law and religion? We will not know until we have overcome the reign of silence that has outlasted the reign of terror.

I have now to justify my title by bringing my account of gay genocide

down to the twentieth century and Hitler. The Nazi treatment of homosexuals has gone all but unrecorded in standard histories. A number of books in German touch briefly on the subject but until recently the matter had gone unnoticed in English.[27] One ironic consequence of this silence has been the almost universal popular belief that the Nazis tolerated or even promoted homosexuality. This impression is mainly due to the open and well-known homosexuality of Hitler's long-time friend and political supporter, Ernst Röhm, the founder of the Nazi's private army of Brown Shirts.

Hitler himself, of course, had been well aware of Röhm's sexual orientation from the early days of their long association. Nevertheless, in spite of this, the official *public* Nazi party line was implacably hostile to homosexuality. A significant homosexual civil rights movement had existed in Germany since 1897. It was strongly supported both by the Social Democratic and Communist Parties. Led by Magnus Hirschfield, director of the Berlin Institute of Sexual Science, it had worked for abolition of Paragraph 175 of the German Criminal Code, a sodomy statute which had been adopted in 1871 at the time of the creation of the German Empire. The movement was allied with the feminist movement in Germany and with other left-wing causes. Hirschfield himself was a Jew, an anti-militarist, and a socialist. A petition drawn up by Hirschfield's Scientific-Humanitarian Committee was signed by thousands of German writers and intellectuals, including Einstein and Thomas Mann. In the 1920's, during the era of the Weimar Republic, prospects for law reform looked excellent. But in 1928, when letters were sent to German political parties, asking for their position on reform, the Nazi reply was as follows:

Munich, 14 May, 1928

Community before Individual!

It is not necessary that you and I live, but it is necessary that the German people live. And they can live only if they can fight, for life means fighting. And they can fight only if they maintain their masculinity. They can only maintain their masculinity if they exercise discipline, especially in matters of love . . . .

Anyone who even thinks of homosexual love is our enemy. We reject anything which emasculates our people and makes them a plaything for our enemies, for we know that life is a fight, and it is madness to think that men will ever embrace fraternally. Natural history teaches us the opposite. Might makes right. And the stronger will always win over the weak. Let's see to it that we once again become strong! . . . [28]

In 1929, a Reichstag Committee voted 15 to 13 to introduce a Penal Reform bill that would decriminalize private homosexual acts. The crisis provoked by the stock market crash caused the bill to be shelved just when success appeared imminent. Political chaos followed in Germany, and in 1933 Hitler came to power with Rohm at his side as head of the SA. Though some Nazis protested that Röhm was discrediting their party, Hitler continued to ignore Röhm's homosexuality until he was faced with a political crisis a year later. So strong was Röhm that the Wehrmacht was concerned that he might seize control of the army. In 1934, Hitler became fearful that the Wehrmacht was plotting a coup against him to prevent such a takeover. To forestall this danger, Hitler had Röhm and about one thousand other men murdered one weekend in June, 1934, the famous "Night of the Long Knives." Hitler gave as an ostensible reason for the killings his "discovery" that Rohm and the SA were themselves plotting a coup against him, though no one has ever taken this excuse seriously. Later, in justifying his act, Hitler also used the issue of homosexuality against Röhm. Shortly after Röhm's death, he issued an order to the effect that, to preserve "moral purity," homosexuals were to be expelled from the SA and the Nazi Party. He went out of his way to reassure mothers that he was concerned for the moral welfare of their sons. Privately, Hitler was less moralistic. In conversation with Nazi leaders, he took the position that homosexuality was undesirable for eugenic reasons, since it was a contagion that attacked "the best and most manly of characters, solely eliminating from the reproductive process those very men on whose offspring a nation depended."[29]

Röhm was, of course, a brutal Nazi thug. But on June 28, 1935, the anniversary of the Röhm killings, the Nazis began a legal campaign against homosexuals by adding to Paragraph 175 another law, 175a, which created ten new criminal offenses, including kisses between men, embraces, and even homosexual fantasies! Arrests jumped from about 800 to 8,000 a year. More important, the Gestapo entered the picture. In 1936, its leader, Heinrich Himmler, who was violently anti-homosexual, spoke about Röhm's death (which he had planned) and declared: "Just as we today have gone back to the ancient Germanic view on the question of marriage mixing different races, so too in our judgment of homosexuality — a symptom of degeneracy which could destroy our race — we must return to the guiding Nordic principle: extermination of degenerates."[30]

How many perished? We know that more than 50,000 homosexuals were arrested under Paragraphs 175 and 175a during the Nazi terror. In addition, the Gestapo sent many more men to camps without a trial. Homosexuals who had come to the attention of the police prior to the Nazi era were also apprehended and police lists of suspected homosexuals were used. (The Berlin police had an index of 30,000 names.) Homosexuals were also seized in occupied countries such as Holland and Poland and sent to Germany. Reasonable estimates of the number of homosexuals who died from illness, neglect, medical experiments, and the gas chamber have varied from 100,000 to more than 400,000, but no systematic effort has yet been made to determine the facts. Since many Nazi records were destroyed, the total, in all probability, will never be known with any exactitude.

After the war, survivors of Hitler's concentration camps were in the main treated generously by the West German government in the matter of reparations, which amounted to over fifteen billion dollars. Homosexuals, however, were told they were ineligible for compensation since they were technically "criminals." (The Nazi laws were not repealed in West Germany until the Social Democratic Party came to power in 1968.) Most of those who survived kept their experiences secret for fear of further discrimination.

The irony of this situation hardly needs pointing up. It is overwhelming. For fourteen centuries, western civilization, acting in the name of religion and morality, perpetrated a monstrous crime against its homosexual minority. It was in effect the "perfect crime." Death warrants were, so to speak, issued with God's signature attached to them, torture (as Beccaria, Lea, and others tell us) was freely employed to obtain confessions, the victims were labelled "unspeakables" and "unmentionables" and their sufferings were a subject about which silence was rigorously prescribed. Friends, relatives, and lovers who had some insight into these situations were intimidated by what may be called, with exaggeration, an unrelenting reign of terror.

Religion and morality are institutions that have commanded the respect of the world in a way that Hitler has not. Yet Hitler only put into practice what "respectable" Christian society had preached for a thousand years. That the survivors of his campaign of torture and extermination should, by and large, be as silent about their ordeals as the men of the sixth or eighteenth centuries, dramatizes more poignantly the dilemma of the homosexual than any other fact I can think of.

❧

NOTES

[1]Leviticus 20:13

[2]*The Babylonian Talmud: Sanhedrin*, tr. J. Shachter and H. Freedman (London: Soncino Press, 1953), Vol. 1, p. 295.

[3]Robert Pitcairn, *Ancient Criminal Trials in Scotland* (Edinburgh: Bannatyne Club, 1833), Vol. II, Part One, p. 491n.

[4]Cf. Romans 1:27 and St. Basil, Letter 188, VII.

[5]*Code pénal* (Paris: Desaint et Saillant, 1752), p. 255. Translations from French and German sources are my own unless otherwise noted.

6Procopius, *The Anecdota or Secret History* (Cambridge: Harvard University Press, 1935), p. 141; Theophanes, *Chronographia* in *Corpus Scriptorum Historiae Byzantinae* (Bonn: Weber, 1839), Vol. 42, pp. 271-272.

7*Fleta*, tr. H. G. Richardson and G. O. Sayles (London: Quaritch, 1955), p. 90.

8*Britton*, tr. F. M. Nichols (Washington, D.C.: John Byrne, 1901), pp. 35-36n.

9*Institutes of the Laws of England*, Part III, ch. 10 (London: E. and R. Brooke, 1797), p. 59.

10Derrick Sherwin Bailey, *Homosexuality and the Western Christian Tradition* (London: Longmans, Green, 1955), p. 153.

11Article 116; quoted in *Jahrbuch für sexuelle Zwischenstufen*, VIII (1906), p. 376.

12Pierre Jacques Brillon. *Dictionnaire des arrêts, ou jurisprudence universelle* (Paris, 1727), Tome 6, p. 216.

13*The Colonial Laws of Massachusetts, Reprinted from the Edition of 1672 . . . Together with the Body of Liberties of 1641* (Boston: Rockwell and Churchill, 1890), p. 55.

14*The True-Blue Laws of Connecticut and New Haven*, ed. J. H. Trumbull (Hartford: American Publishing Co., 1876), p. 199.

15*Charter to William Penn and Laws of the Province of Pennsylvania*, (Harrisburg: Lane S. Hart, 1879), p. 110.

16*The Statutes at Large of Pennsylvania from 1682 to 1801* (1896), Vol. 2, pp. 79, 202. For early laws see also L. Crompton, "Homosexuals and the Death Penalty in Colonial America," *Journal of Homosexuality*, I (1976), 277-293, where I note a fourth execution.

17Bailey's book, whatever its weaknesses on the historical side, unequivocally supported law reform in England, and helped pave the way for the Wolfenden Report and the positive stand on homosexual law repeal adopted by the Church of England.

[18]"Unnatural Crime," *A History of the Inquisition of Spain* (New York: Macmillan, 1907), Vol. 4, pp. 361-371.

[19]*Institutes au droit criminel*, (Paris: Cellot, 1757), p. 507. Other executions are recorded in Jean Papon, *Recueil d'arrests notables* (Paris: de la Fontaine, 1608), p. 1258.

[20]Raymond de Becker, *The Other Face of Love*, tr. M. Crosland and A. Daventry (New York: Bell, 1969), p. 104: "Clarus and Gomez assert that women were burned alive for this crime, and Farinaccius says that in Rome he saw several women executed in the Campo di Fiori for this reason."

[21]Nicholas Barnard, *The Penitent Death of . . . John Atherton* (Dublin, 1641).

[22]Montgomery Hyde, *The Love That Dared Not Speak Its Name* (Boston: Little, Brown, 1970), chapter 3.

[23]P. E. Coleman, in his essay, "Changing the Law — The English Experience," in *Is Gay Good?*, ed. W. D. Oberholtzer (Philadelphia: Westminster Press, 1971) mentions "two laborers in Bristol whose executions the local newspaper reported in 1860 without further comment," pp. 188-189.

[24]"Offences against Taste," *The Theory of Legislation*, ed. C. K. Ogden (London: Paul, Trench, Trubner, 1931), p. 492.

[25]*Calendar of Dutch Historical Manuscripts in the Office of the Secretary of State, Albany, New York, 1630-1664*, ed. E. B. O'Callaghan (Ridgewood, N.J., 1968), pp. 103, 213.

[26]L. S. A. M. von Römer, "Der Uranismus in den Niederlanden bis zum 19. Jahrhundert, mit besonderer Berücksichtigung der grossen Uranierverfolgung im Jahre 1730," *Jahrbuch für sexuelle Zwischenstufen*, VIII (1906), p. 369. I am indebted to Inge Worth for the translation of the quoted document.

[27]When this address was first delivered in November, 1974, the following account was available only in the form of two newspaper articles by James D. Steakley. It has since been incorporated into his study, *The Homosexual Emancipation Movement in Germany* (New York: Arno Press, 1975). I am

obliged to Mr. Steakley for permission to use this material. His well-documented chapter on the Nazis should be read in full.

28Rudolf Klare, *Homosexualität und Strafrecht* (Hamburg: Hanseatische Verlagsanstalt, 1937), p. 149. Cited by Steakley, p. 84.

29H. P. Bleuel, *Strength Through Joy: Sex and Society in Nazi Germany* (London: Secker & Warburg, 1973), p. 218. See Steakley, p. 109.

30Harry Wilde, *Das Schicksal der Verfemten: Die Verfolgung der Homosexuellen im "Dritte Reich"* (Tübingen: Katzmann, 1969), p. 36. See Steakley, p. 112.

APPENDICES

1. *The Dutch Proclamation of July 21, 1730*

   Several months after the Dutch persecutions began in May, 1730, the following national proclamation was issued. A facsimile of the original was published in the *Jahrbuch für sexuelle Zwischenstufen* in 1906, with a German translation by L.S.A.M. Von Römer. The following is an edited version of an English translation from the German, made for this volume by Inge Worth. I have condensed the legal phraseology and simplified the complicated syntax of the original. Though the "Placat" says no "special" laws had existed in Holland for the punishment of sodomy, Von Römer prints a list of executions dating from as early as 1446. Presumably, the authorities meant that there was no legislation designed to deal with the kind of situation that had developed in 1730. The "Placat" implies that a widespread panic had begun in the Dutch homosexual community. The reference to God's spewing forth "the land and its inhabitants" echoes Leviticus 18:27, where homosexual acts are mentioned as part of the defilement that led God to eject the Canaanites from Palestine in favor of the Jews. The preamble parallels the laws of Justinian, which blamed earthquakes and other natural disasters on God's wrath against homosexuals. The Dutch persecution seems to have had its origin in similar superstitious anxieties, just as the Salem trials were a reflection of the fear that God would punish the community for allowing witches to exist in their midst.

"PLACAT"

The States of Holland and West Friesland, to all who see or hear this proclamation — greetings! Be it known herewith to everyone, that we have perceived, to our most heartfelt grief, that in addition to other transgressions of God's most sacred laws, whereby his just wrath towards our dear Fatherland has been inflamed time and again, some terrible atrocities have been committed for some time past in our dear states of Holland and West Friesland, offending Nature herself, and that many of our subjects have turned so far away from any fear of God as audaciously to commit crimes which should never even be heard of, on account of which God Almighty had in earlier times overturned, destroyed and laid waste Sodom and Gomorrah.

Since we could never imagine that such atrocities could be committed in this land, no special laws have been provided for them. Because we feel a just abhorrence towards this execrable crime of sodomy, and wish to employ our full power and all efficacious means to stamp out, lock, stock, and barrel, this sin that cries to heaven, so that God Almighty might not — as he used to threaten at such abominations — punish the iniquity of our land with his terrible judgments, and spew forth the land and its inhabitants, thus bringing to an end his forbearance to our dear Fatherland, it is decreed after thorough deliberations by the Council and after consultation with the loyal subjects of our President and Council, that, in order to obliterate such a terrible evil from our midst:

First: The above-mentioned crime of sodomy henceforth must always be punished in public, like other crimes, as a deterrent and warning to everyone.

Second: the same crime, according to Divine Scripture, must be punished with death, and the type and manner of death shall be at the discretion of the judge, according to the more or less serious circumstances of this abominable crime.

Third: Everyone who is convicted of having tried repeatedly to debauch others to the crime mentioned, or of having induced others to offer their homes for money for the commission of this crime, shall also be punished with death, even though he has not been convicted of having defiled himself in this manner.

Fourth: The corpse of the executed must, immediately after the execution, be burned to ashes, thrown in the ocean, or exposed as unworthy of burial.

Fifth: The judgments on the above-mentioned crime, with sentences of contempt of court against any fugitives who have been convicted, must be printed and publicly posted in the usual places.

And Sixth: The magistrates, judges, and criminal courts in their respective cities, shall be specially authorized and commanded to investigate thoroughly the reason for the absence of any persons within their jurisdictions, who, since the first of May, when the investigation of those guilty of the above-mentioned crime began, until the first of August next, have secretly, without apparent good cause, absented themselves from their positions, professions, occupations and homes and have thus made themselves extremely suspect of having been guilty of this crime. And if the investigation reveals no reason that would counter the strong suspicion aroused by clandestine departures when they have become matters of common gossip, the authorities shall summon these persons by an explicit edict to give reasons for their suspect absence in person, or through a representative, and those who do not answer after the appearance of the third monthly notice will be exiled under the threat of more severe punishment, should they have the temerity to return to this province.

And in order that the contents of our proclamation shall be visible everywhere so that no one may pretend ignorance of it, we decree that it must be posted in all the usual places used for proclamations. We further command the Representative-General of our Court and all other officers of justice, to proceed against all criminals of this sort without respect to rank, according to the proclamation, without favor or dissimulation, because we think this proper for the good of the country.

Given in the Hague under the Small Seal of the Country, on July 21, 1730.

2. *Executions Resulting from the Dutch Religious Persecutions of 1730-31*
Evidence of the results of the campaign against homosexuals described in the proclamation appear in the twenty-four pages of tables published by L.S.A.M. Von Römer in the *Jahrbuch*. These identify by name and profession over 250 men who were "summoned" by the authorities in the towns listed below and also in the jurisdictions of Leiden, Naarden, Middleburg, Ryswyk, Schieland, Vianen, Voorburg, and Zutphen. Of these, some 91 faced decrees of exile. I have excerpted only the names of those who were sentenced to death and added such information as Von Römer was able to find in contemporary records. In all but four of these cases, Von Römer's source was an account published in 1730 entitled *Schouwtooneel soo der Geexecuteerde als Ingedaagde Over de verfoeielijke Misdaad van Sodomie. Tot waarschouwinge der goede en*

afschrik der booze geopent In de voornaamste Steden van Hollandt en Over-Yssel etc. Anno 1730 (i.e. "Disclosure, literally 'Public Spectacle,' of Those Summoned and Executed for the Detestable Misdeed of Sodomy. Presented as a Warning to the Good and a Deterrent to the Bad in the Most Important Cities of Holland and Over-Yssel etc.") One version of this booklet appeared in 1730 with 64 pages. A longer one with 84 pages bears the same date but includes punishments decreed in 1731. It is not certain if these 60 men represent all those sentenced to die.

Amsterdam

Pieter Marteyn Janes Sohn and Johannes Keep, decorator, strangled and burnt, June 24, 1730.

Maurits van Eeden, house servant, and Cornelis Boes, 18, Keep's servant, each immersed alive in a barrel of water and drowned, June 24, 1730.

Laurens Hospuijn, Chief of Detectives in the Navy, strangled and thrown into the water with a 100-pound weight, Sept. 16, 1730.

Delft

Cornelis Krevel, Jan Woens, and Theys v. d. Meer, hanged and thrown into the sea with 100-pound weights, July 24, 1730.

Groningen

A drummer and an "orphan," names unknown, beheaded, Sept. 22, 1731.

The Hague

Jan Backer, middle man for hiring of house servants, and Jan Schut, hanged and burnt, June 12, 1730.

Frans Verheyden; Cornelis Wassernaar, milkman; Pieter Styn, embroiderer of coats; Dirk van Royen, and Herman Mouilliont, servant, hanged and afterwards thrown into the sea at Scheveningen with 50-pound weights, June 12, 1730.

Pieter van der Hal, grain carrier; Adriaen Kuyleman, glove launderer; David Muntslager, agent; and Willem la Feber, tavern keeper, hanged and thrown into the sea at Scheveningen with 100-pound weights, July 21, 1730.

Antonie Byweegen, fishmonger, hanged, then burnt to ashes, July 21, 1730.

Jan van der Lelie, hanged and thrown into the sea, Sept. 24, 1731.

Haarlem

Jan Claasze van Beveren, collector for an importer, hanged and afterwards thrown into the sea at Zantvoort with a 50-pound weight tied to his body and another tied to his legs, Aug. 1, 1730.

Heusden

Willem Waavre, strangled and burnt to ashes, June 19, 1730.

Cornelis Palamedes, teacher, 56, half strangled, then burnt to ashes, Oct. 19, 1730. For 20 years a teacher in the village of Veen near Heusden. He confessed in prison that 18 years earlier he had seduced Dirk van Rooyen who was executed in the Hague on June 12 and that he had likewise seduced several of his pupils.

Kampen

Jan Westhoff and Steven Klok, soldiers, strangled on the scaffold and buried under the gallows, June 29, 1730.

Abram ten Oosten, old clothes dealer, strangled on the scaffold and buried under the gallows, July 22, 1730.

Leeuwarden

Casper Abrams, gentleman's servant, strangled and burnt, Sept. 30, 1730.

Jurriaan Christiaen, strangled and burnt, Oct. 18, 1730.

Rotterdam

Leendert de Haas, 60, candlemaker; Casper Schroder, distiller; Huibert v. Borselen, gentleman's servant, strangled, burnt, and their ashes carried in an ash cart out of the city and then by a ship to the sea and thrown overboard, July 17, 1730.

Woerden

Pieter Ravensbergen, "Sterf-Heer" of the jurisdiction of Bodegraaf and Zwammerdam, and Kees v. Pinxter, strangled and burnt, Jan. 21, 1731.

Zuidhorn

All the executions in this village were carried out on September 24, 1731.

Gerrit Loer, 48, farmer, scorched while alive and then strangled and burnt to ashes. Had committed the sin often both actively and passively with several persons and in several places, even on the way to church, both before and after the sermon.

Hendrick Berents, 32, scorched while alive and then strangled and burnt to ashes. Had often committed the sin of sodomy actively and passively.

Jan Berents, 19, scorched while alive and then strangled and burnt to ashes. Had often committed the sin actively and passively. Had seduced children of the ages of 10, 11, and 12, and even in the neighborhood of the church during divine service. He uttered lamentations as he was taken to church to hear his sentence.

Asinga Immes, 45, strangled and burnt. Had committed the crime actively and passively.

Eysse Jans, 40, strangled and burnt. Remained silent when sentenced.

Gosen Hendrix, 45, strangled and burnt. Remained silent when sentenced.

Jan Wygers, 45, strangled and burnt. Remained silent when sentenced.

Harmen Arents, 41, farmer, committed the sin with his brother Sikko Arents, a churchwarden. Remained silent when sentenced.

Sikko Arents, 39, churchwarden, died in prison. His body was carried in a cart to the Square of Criminal Justice on the night of September 14 and hanged by the feet from the gallows. On the 24th it was taken down and burnt with the others.

Jan Harms Brakel, 37, strangled and burnt. Remained silent when sentenced.

Mindelt Jansz Rol, 32, strangled and burnt. On hearing the sentence, he swayed back and forth and bowed to those present on departing.

Jan Jacobs van Donderen, 30, strangled and burnt. Cried out, "Oh! oh!" when his sentence was read.

Jan Egberts, 19, strangled and burnt. When the sentence was read in which it was stated that he was 20 years old, he cried out, "That is incorrect, Sir, I am only 19 years old." Bowed his head when going away and said, "It is all right, Sir."

Peter Cornelisz, 20 or 21, strangled and burnt. As the sentence was read he behaved as if he were about to faint, and sighed when leaving.

Hendrik Cornelisz, 21, strangled and burnt. He said, "I forgive you and thank you gentlemen for the sentence which I shall receive."

Hendrick Eeuwes, 19, strangled and burnt. He turned and left abruptly.

Jan Ides, 18, strangled and burnt. He said: "I forgive you for the sin which you have committed against me."

Jan Jansz, 18, strangled and burnt. Remained silent when sentenced.

Cornelis Jansz, 18, strangled and burnt. As the sentence was read to him he looked in all directions and at everyone, and said: "See how you have judged me."

Gerrit Harms, 15, strangled and burnt. Remained silent when sentenced.

Tamme Jansz, 14, strangled and burnt. Remained silent when sentenced.

Thomas Jacobs, 16 strangled and burnt. Remained silent when sentenced.

Zwolle
Gerrit Bauters, coffee and tea dealer, and a button maker named Byleveld,
hanged on the scaffold, dragged through the town, and buried five feet
under the gallows, July 11, 1730.

3. *Executions in England 1806-1835*
The following statistics for executions for sodomy appear in Appendix I,
Table VI, p. 132 of the *Report from the Select Committee on Criminal
Laws* published by the House of Commons in 1819:

1805 – 0	1810 – 4	1815 – 1
1806 – 6	1811 – 2	1816 – 2
1807 – 0	1812 – 1	1817 – 1
1808 – 2	1813 – 1	1818 – 1
1809 – 2	1814 – 5	

The first page of the "Statements on Criminal Law, Prepared by the
Direction of the Secretary of State for the Home Department" published
with the *Tables Showing the Number of Criminal Offenders Committed
for Trial or Bailed . . . in the Year 1836* (1837) gives these figures for the
number of executions for sodomy up till 1836:

1819-25 – 15	1833 – 2
1826-32 – 7	1834 – 4
1831 – 1	1835 – 2
1832 – 0	1836 – 0

*A shorter version of this article was delivered as an address at the second
annual meeting of the Gay Academic Union, New York University,
November 30, 1974.*

The Annotated Burton

By Stephen Wayne Foster

Sir Richard Francis Burton (1821-90) was, among many other things, a pioneering sexologist. He wrote an essay on pederasty which "made a considerable stir upon its first appearance."[1] It has been rumored that Burton was a homosexual, but nothing definite has been proven.[2]

Burton's first study of homosexuality consisted of an official report on male brothels in Karachi in 1845, but this report has disappeared (Brodie, p. 347, n. 29). Outside of a few brief references, the only important mention of homosexuality in his early books is to be found in his *Zanzibar* (London: Tinsley Bros., 1872), I, 380-81.

John Addington Symonds wrote of Burton, "During conversations I had with him less than three months before his death, he told me that he had begun a general history of 'le Vice'; and at my suggestion he studied Ulrichs and Krafft-Ebing" (Symonds, p. 78n). This is a reference to Burton's lengthy annotated translation of *The Scented Garden*. Burton was working on this book on the day of his death, and the manuscript was destroyed by his wife, who insinuated that she had been upset by the homosexual contents of the manuscript (Brodie, pp. 321, 325-29). However, it has been claimed that little of the manuscript dealt with homosexuality (ibid, p. 328). Dr. Grenfell Baker, who saw the manuscript while Burton was working on it, made no mention of homosexuality in his description of its contents.[3]

One of Burton's friends, Henry Spencer Ashbee (1834-1900), preceded Burton in the study of the history of homosexuality with scattered references to this subject in a trilogy which Ashbee wrote under the pen-name of "Pisanus Fraxi."[4] As will be seen, Burton borrowed some information from Ashbee for his own essay.

This essay formed part of the "Terminal Essay" attached to Burton's translation of the *Arabian Nights*.[5] Since this appendix was supposed to provide information about the Muslims, Burton ought to have limited himself to a discussion of pederasty among the Muslims, but he provided information from many cultures and historical periods, paving the way for all future studies of the historical and cross-cultural aspects of homosexuality.

However, his essay on pederasty (and presumably also the rest of his writings) contains many errors of fact and even of spelling. He appears to have written this essay hurriedly, without double-checking his information and spelling. Many of his quotes are actually misquotes. Much of what he writes is obscure to the modern reader, and he makes no attempt at elucidation. He sometimes omits his sources. When he does give a source, it is often some book which has been long since out-of-print, or which is otherwise unavailable to modern readers who might wish to look up his citations.

An annotated edition of Burton's essay is therefore needed in order to overcome all of the faults of the original. Due to limitations of length, the present study can be no more than a preliminary attempt at annotation, and will have to be used in conjunction with a separate edition of Burton's essay. Since the pagination of the original edition has not been used in a reprint since 1912, it will be necessary to cite both the first edition and one of the most recent reprints.[6] In spite of these limitations, this study should fulfill a need for those readers who are unaware of Burton's faults or puzzled by his obscurities. The faults have been itemized for the sake of clarity.

1) Burton quotes one of the *Novelle* of Bandello about a confession made by a "dying fisherman" (Burton, p. 204, n. 2; omitted by Reade). This "fisherman" was actually a poet named Porcellio.[7]

2) Three brothels in Karachi in 1845 had "boys and eunuchs . . . for hire" (Burton, p. 205; Reade, p. 158). These eunuchs were probably *hinjras*, transvestites who were often eunuchs.[8]

3) Burton's famous theory of the "Sotadic Zone" (Burton, p. 206; Reade, p. 159) was named after a poet whom Burton refers to as "Sotades the Mantinaean" (Burton, p. 201, n. 3; omitted by Reade). Actually, Sotades was a native, not of Mantineia in Arcadia, but of Maroneia in Thrace.[9]

4) "But Bernhardy, Bode, Richter, K.O. Müller and esp. Welcker have made Sappho a model of purity . . ." (Burton, p, 208, n. 1; Reade, p. 160, n. 5). This refers to a controversy which began in 1816 when Friedrich Gottlieb Welcker (1784-1868) wrote a pamphlet, *Sappho von einem herrschenden Vorurtheile befreit* (Sappho rescued from a popular misconception), in which he declared that Sappho was not a lesbian.[10] Bishop Connop Thirlwall of St. David's (1797-1875) said that Welcker had rescued Sappho's character "from the unmerited reproach under which it has labored for so many centuries."[11] Welcker's theory was refuted by William Mure in his article, "Sappho, and the Ideal Love of the Greeks" (*Rheinisches Museum für Philologie*, 1857, pp. 564ff.), where he said that the emotion expressed in Sappho's poetry "was not

mere friendship, but irregular passion" (Müller, loc. cit.).

5) Burton's list of sources on ancient Greece includes "Rosenbaum, *Die Lustseuche des Alterthum's*, Halle, 1839" (Burton, p. 210, n. 2; Reade, p. 162, n. 9). This is a misspelled reference to Julius Rosenbaum's *Geschichte der Lustseuche im Alterthum* (Symonds, p. 77).

6) Burton cites Herodotus, II, ch. 80, on "the Orphic and Bacchic rites" (Burton, p. 211; Reade, p. 162). This is a mistake for Herodotus II, ch. 81.

7) "Henry Estienne, Apologie pour Hérodote" (Burton, p. 211, n. 1; Reade, p. 162, n. 11) is discussed by Fraxi (*Centuria*, pp. 157-76).

8) "For the Pederastia of the Gods see Bayle under Chrysippe" (Burton, p. 212, n. 2; Reade, p. 163, n. 13). This refers to the *Dictionnaire historique et critique* (1697) of Pierre Bayle (1647-1706). Looking into Bayle under "Chrysippus" we find information on the Greek gods taken from the writings of Clemens Alexandrinus, Firmicus Maternus, Arnobius, Aelian, Athenaeus, Hyginus, and Pisander. [12]

9) Burton gives us a long footnote on an anonymous Renaissance novel, *Alcibiade Fanciullo a Scola* (Burton, p. 214, n. 1; Reade, p. 164), n. 16). A discussion of this book may be found in Fraxi (*Index*, pp. 23-29). Burton states that Giambattista Baseggio "claims for F. Pallavicini the authorship of *Alcibiades* which the Manuel du Libraire wrongly attributes to M. Girol Adda in 1859" (Burton and Reade, loc. cit.). This seems to mean that Adda was claimed as the author of *Alcibiade*, but Girolamo d'Adda (1815-81) was actually claimed as the originator of the theory that Pallavicino was the author. [13] Brunet's claim is confirmed by Giambattista Passano, who wrote that the *Alcibiade* was an "obscene book attributed by some to Pietro Arentino . . . but my learned and very dear friend Marquis Girolamo d'Adda, tearfully remembered, demonstrated with valid and critical observations (in the *Bulletin du Bibliophile*, 1859, p. 205) that the author was Ferrante Pallavicino." [14]

10) The quote from "Ovid (*Met*. III. 339)" (Burton, p. 215; Reade, p. 165) is actually a quote from lines 353 and 355, the missing line being "Sed fuit in tenera tam dura superbia forma."

11) Burton fails to mention his source for the "individual protests" of Servilianus and Plotius (Burton, p. 218; Reade, p. 167). The source is Valerius Maximus, *De Dictis Factisque Memorabilibus*, Book VI, chs. 5 and 12.

12) Burton quotes "Bayle under 'Anacreon' " (Burton, p. 218; Reade, p. 167) in French. The full passage has been translated thus: "If he is not worthy of that abhorrence which a Christian Poet would well deserve in the like case, because that kind of love was not then branded with infamy, as it is in Christian countries, the wickedness of the age he lived in must suffer for him" (Bayle, I, 637).

13) Martial, cited as "XI.46" (Burton, p. 220; Reade, p. 169), should be XI.45, and Burton's quote, "Sive puer arrisit, sive puella tibi" should read "Seu puer adrisit sive puella tibi."

14) "Martial (X.44)" should be XI.43, and "Mart. XI.71" should be XI.70 (Burton, p. 221; Reade, p. 170).

15) Burton made a mistake in saying that Sonnini visited Egypt in "A.D. 1717" (Burton, p. 225; Reade, p. 172). Actually, Charles-Nicolas-Sigisbert Sonnini de Manoncour (1751-1812) visited Egypt in 1777.[15]

16) Sa'id Pasha, who advised a Dutch diplomat to try sodomy, was the Khedive Sa'id Pasha (1822-63), ruler of Egypt from 1854 to 1863 (Burton, p. 225; Reade, p. 172).[16]

17) "Again, there shall be no whore of the daughters of Israel, nor a sodomite of the sons of Israel (Deut. XXII.5)" (Burton, p. 228; Reade, p. 175). This is actually a quotation of Deuteronomy XXIII, 17.

18) Burton writes, " . . . in the Torah (Deut. XX.5) the sexes are forbidden to change dress" (Burton, p. 230; Reade, p. 175). The correct citation is Deut. XXII, 5.

19) Concerning Rehoboam's reign, Burton quotes a passage which he cites as "I Kings XIV.20" (Burton, p. 231; Reade, p. 177), which is a mistake for I Kings XIV, 24.

20) Burton tells an anecdote about "a certain Mujtahid" (Burton, p. 234; Reade, p. 178). This is not a proper name, but is merely the Persian word for "theologian."[17]

21) Burton tells an anecdote about "Shaykh Nasr, Governor of Bushire" (Burton, p. 235; Reade, p. 179). It is impossible to identify this man, as there were four governors of Bushire named Nasr during the late eighteenth and early nineteenth centuries, all of whom are mentioned in the *Farsnama-ye Naseri* of Hasan ibn Hasan Fasā'i.[18]

22) Burton's information about India is taken in part from the article on "Pédérastie" in Larousse (see my n. 16), although this is not mentioned as his source. In order to back up my contention, I will first quote Burton, and then provide the reader with my own translation of the complete passage in question from Larousse:

"M. Louis Daville describes the infamies of Lahore and Lakhnau where he found men dressed as women, with flowing locks under crowns of flowers, imitating the feminine walk and gestures, voice and fashion of speech, and ogling their admirers with all the coquetry of bayadères. Victor Jacquemont's *Journal de Voyage* describes the pederasty of Ranjit Singh, the 'Lion of the Panjáb', and his pathic Guláb Singh whom the English inflicted upon Cashmir as ruler by way of paying for his treason" (Burton, p. 237; Reade, p. 181).

There exists in the great cities of India houses consecrated to this odious type of prostitution. One meets sometimes in the streets the degraded creatures who are addicted to this infamous profession; habited like women, they allow their hair to grow, destroy their beards, copying the gait, the gestures, the manner of speaking, the sound of the voice, the deportment and the affected manner of prostitutes. It is chiefly in Lucknow and in the Kingdom of Lahore that these impure individuals are numerous. At night they intermingle in holiday processions with coquetries to passers-by, completely like women who exercise an analogous profession. At Sodom, says a traveller, M. Louis Deville (*Excursions dans l'inde*), the immorality was not, it seems, of greater extent than it is today at Lucknow. In many streets, principally at night and in the windows of the houses of bayadères, who have the privilege to attract a numerous crowd, they are noticed mixing in the groups of young persons dressed up ridiculously and adorned like women, with crowns of flowers on their heads. The purpose of this affected coquetry is not very difficult to guess. At Lahore and in other great cities, analogous observations may be made. Anyone who reads the *Journal de Voyage* of Victor Jacquemont, the congenial and intelligent traveller so unfortunately halted in the midst of his courageous career, must remember that the old Runjet-Singh, who occupied at that time the throne of Lahore, indulged without the least scruple in his passion for this type of enjoyment, a passion which seems also to have been shared at all times by all of the Sikhs. It seems that Gulab-singh, who later became Viceroy of the province of Kashmir, by the consent and in the selfish interests of the English, and who obtained a great medal at the first universal Exposition, happened to have served in his youth as catamite (*mignon*) to the old "Lion of the Punjab" (Larousse, XII, 491).

It is to be noticed that Burton misspells "Deville" as "Daville," but his spelling of Indian names may simply be correct but obsolete. "Bayadères" are prostitutes.

23) Burton says that "Orlof Torée(*Voyage en Chine*)" noticed brothels with youths in China (Burton, p. 238; Reade, p. 181). This is a misspelling of Olof Torée, who visited China in 1750, and whose *Voyage en Chine* was published in Milan in 1771.[19]

24) "Mr. Schuyler in his *Turkistan* (I:132) offers an illustration of a 'Batchah' (Pers. bachcheh = catamite), or 'singing-boy surrounded by his admirers' " (Burton, p. 239; Reade, p. 182). This refers to Eugene Schuyler's *Turkistan* (New York: Scribner, Armstrong & Co., 1876), but the illustration faces p. 133 in the second volume. It is drawn by Vasili Vasilievich

Verestchagin (1842-1904). *Batchas* were dancing-boys, not singing-boys.

25) Burton gives H. H. Bancroft's first name as "Herbert" (Burton, p. 240, n. 3; Reade, p. 183, n. 54), but it was actually Hubert.

26) "Even his half-frozen Hyperboreans 'possess all the passions which are supposed to develop most freely under a milder temperature' " (Burton, p. 240; Reade, p. 183). The correct quote from Bancroft is "Nor are those passions which are supposed to develop most fully under a milder temperature wanting in the half-frozen Hyperborean."[20]

27) Burton's quote from "*Martin's Brit. Colonies*" was taken from Bancroft (Burton, pp. 240-41; Reade, p. 183; Bancroft, p. 58, n. 49).

28) Burton's misquote from Bancroft " . . . keeping him at women's work, associating him with women . . . " should read " . . . keeping him at woman's work, associating him only with women . . . " (Burton, p. 241; Reade, p. 183; Bancroft, p. 82).

29) Burton's misquote from Bancroft "these male concubines" should read "these male wives" (Burton, p. 241; Reade, p. 183; Bancroft, p. 82).

30) Burton's misquote from Bancroft "male concubinage obtains throughout, but not to the same extent as amongst the Koniagas" should read "male concubinage obtains throughout the Aleutian Islands, but not to the same extent as among the Koniagas" (Burton, p. 241; Reade, p. 183; Bancroft, p. 92).

31) Burton does not cite the page in Bancroft dealing with "objects of 'unnatural' affection" (Burton, p. 241; Reade, p. 183), which is Bancroft, p. 92, n. 129.

32) "Palon" (Burton, p. 241; Reade, p. 183) is a misspelling of Palou (Bancroft, p. 415, n. 173).

33) Burton's list of Bancroft's sources includes Mofras and Duflot (Burton, p. 241; Reade, p. 184). Actually, these two men were one and the same, Eugène Duflot de Mofras (Bancroft, pp. xxxvii, 415n.).

34) Burton's misquote from Bancroft "In New Mexico according to Arlegui, Ribas, and other authors, males concubinage prevails . . . " should read "According to Arlegui, Ribas, and other authors, among some of these nations male concubinage prevails . . . " (Burton, p. 241; Reade, p. 184, Bancroft, p. 585). In the same passage, Burton's misquote "use of weapons being denied" should read "use of weapons even being denied" (loc. cit.).

35) "Father Pierre de Gand (alias de Musa)" (Burton, pp. 241-42; Reade, p. 184) is a misspelling of de Mura (Bancroft, p. xxix).

36) "History tells us of Zú Shanátir, tyrant of 'Arabia Felix' in 478 A.D. who . . . was at last poniarded by the youth Zerash, known from his long ringlets as 'Zú Nowás' " (Burton, p. 246; Reade, p. 187). This refers to an event

which actually took place between A.D. 500 and 517. The King of Himyar (Yemen) was Khani'ah Yanuf Dhu Shanatir, also known as Ma'di Karib Ya'fur. He was killed by Zur'ah Yusuf ibn Tuban As'ad Abi Karib Dhu Nuwas, also known as Yusuf 'As'ar Yath'ar Dhu Nuwas (Joseph the avenger of the ringlets), who became king.[21]

37) "Yet Joan dos Sanctos found in Cacongo of West Africa certain 'Chibudi' . . . " (Burton, p. 246; Reade, p. 187). This short passage contains four mistakes. Burton misspelled Joanno dos Sanctos and *chibidi*. Burton's quote is not from the *Aethiopia Orientalis* of dos Sanctos, but from a short account written by some Jesuits who visited Angola (not Cacongo) in 1606.[22]

38) "Bayle notices (under 'Vayer') the infamous book of Giovanni della Casa, Archbishop of Benevento, 'De Laudibus Sodomiae,' vulgarly known as 'Capitolo del Forno' " (Burton, p. 247; Reade, p. 188). Actually, *Capitolo del Forno* was the correct name of this poem. Bayle felt "obliged to say" that della Casa "has been wronged by the imputation of being the author of a work entitled *De Laudibus Sodomiae*. This pretended poem is nothing but the *Capitolo del Forno* . . . What is horrible is, that de la Casa having observed, that some lewd youths began to despise that commerce [heterosexuality], adds, that for his own part he was not delicate, and that he seldom looked anywhere else. This was owning, that he sometimes at least was guilty of the sin against Nature" (Bayle, IX, 683).

39) Burton's discussion of Pope Sixtus IV's legalization of sodomy ends with "Hence the Faeda Venus of Battista Mantovano" (Burton, p. 257; Reade, p. 188). Giovanni Battista Spagnoli (Spagnuoli), known as Baptista Mantuanus or Il Mantovano (1447-1516), wrote a poem, *De Calamitatibus Temporum* (1489), which contains passages complaining about the churches having been taken over by catamites.[23] The "Faeda Venus" refers to a phrase ("foeda Venus") in a quote from an unnamed poem by Mantovano (Bayle, IX, 250).

40) Burton mentions "Dr. Gaspar," whose "best known works are (1) *Praktisches Handbuch der Gechtlichener Medecin*, Berlin, 1860; and (2) *Klinische Novellen sur gerechtlichen medicin,* Berlin, 1863" (Burton, p. 248, n. 1; Reade, p. 188, n. 62). This is a misspelled reference to Johann Ludwig Casper (1796-1864), author of *Praktisches Handbuch der gerichtlichen Medizin* and *Klinische Novellen zur gerichtlichen Medizin* (Symonds, p. vii).

41) Burton speaks of Casper's "many interesting cases especially an old Count Cajus and his six accomplices" (Burton, p. 248; Reade, p. 188). Casper was asked by the police to examine the rectums of Cajus and his friends after they had been arrested. Count Cajus was heterosexual until he was thirty-two years old, but was homosexual for the next twenty-six years. He played the

passive role in anal sodomy "at least three or four times a-week," and kept "a written diary containing a daily record of the adventures, amours, and sensations of a *Paederastus*."[24] The remainder of Casper's account of this case deals with rectal examinations of the "accomplices," none of whom are named (Casper, pp. 338-39). This case was part of a chapter on "Disputed Unnatural Lewdness" (ibid., pp. 328-46), a pioneer study of homosexuality.

42) Burton mentions a correspondent of Casper (Burton, p. 248; Reade, p. 188). This correspondent was "a young, very rich, and well-born man" (Casper, p. 330), who wrote to Casper, "We discover each other at once . . . Upon the Righi, at Palermo, in the Louvre, in the Highlands of Scotland, in St. Petersburg, on landing at Barcelona I observed parties whom I had never before seen, and whom I recognised in a second" (ibid., p. 331; cf. Symonds, p. 27).

43) Frederick the Great's advice to his nephew (Burton, p. 248; Reade, p. 188) is taken from Fraxi (*Centuria*, p. 411).

44) Most of Burton's information on France (Burton, pp. 248-52; Reade, pp. 188-91) is taken, as he admits (Burton, p. 251n; Reade, p. 191, n. 68), from Fraxi (*Centuria*, pp. 404-16). Fraxi's text is in French, but an English translation has been made.[25]

45) We now come to Burton's "list of famous pederasts," which was supplied by "a friend learned in these matters" (Burton, p. 252, n. 1; Reade, p. 191, n. 69), namely Fraxi. Of the thirty-six names listed, twenty are to be found in Noel I. Garde's *Jonathan to Gide* (New York: Vantage, 1964), but there are some, omitted by Garde, who are obscure enough to require identification[26]

Charles de Coypeau, Sieur d'Assoucy (c. 1604- c. 1679) was a musician (Fraxi, *Centuria*, p. 411). He escaped fom Montpellier to avoid being burned for sodomy, accompanied by "a pretty page" (Bayle, IV, 522-23). Another source confirms that he was accused of "un crime contre nature."[27]

Charles II of Parma (1799-1883) ruled fom 1847 to 1848 (Fraxi, *Catena*, p. xiv; Larousse, III, 1018-19).

Charles III of Parma (1823-54) ruled from 1848 to 1854 (Fraxi, loc. cit.; Larousse, III, 1019).

Aaron-Louis-Frédéric Regnault, Baron de la Susse (1788-1860), became a vice-admiral in 1844 (Fraxi, loc. cit.; Larousse, X, 226).

"Henne" is a misspelling of Fraxi's "Hume" (Fraxi, loc. cit.), which in turn is a misspelling of Daniel Dunglas Home (1833-86), a famous spiritualist.[28]

Martineau de Soleinne (d. 1842) was a bibliophile (Fraxi, *Centuria*, p. 411).

"Lerminin" is a misspelling of Jean-Louise-Eugène Lerminier (1803-57), "professor of the Collège de France and one of the writers in the *Revue des*

Deux Mondes, etc." (Fraxi, loc. cit.; cf. Larousse, X, 396).

(Fraxi declared, "I know nothing in print concerning de Soleinne and Lerminier, except some offensive allusions in the minor journals of the time to the latter. That they were addicted to the propensity however there can be no doubt, and I have been assured of the fact by one personally acquainted with them both" (Fraxi, loc. cit.)

Joseph Fiévée (1767-1839) was a journalist and secret agent (Fraxi, loc. cit.; Larousse, VIII, 344-45).

Michel-Théodore Leclercq (1777-1851) was a writer whose homosexuality was mentioned in the *Mémoires* of Philarète Chasles (Fraxi, loc. cit.; Larousse, X, 300).

Alfred-Guillaume-Gabriel, Comte d'Orsay (1801-52) was the lover of Lord Blessington.[29]

King William II of Holland (1792-1849) ruled from 1830 to 1840 (Fraxi, *Catena*, p. xiv; Larousse, VIII, 1622).

Comte Horace de Viel-Castel (1798-1864) was a diarist and courtier (Larousse, XV, 1014).

Astolphe-Louis-Léonard, Marquis de Custine (1790-1857), was the author of a notable book on Russia. He was mugged by a hustler in 1824, causing the greatest homosexual scandal of the period.[30] Noel Garde confused him with his grandfather, Count Adam de Custine (Garde, p. 511).

Louis-César de la Baume le Blanc, Duc de la Vallière (1708-80) (Fraxi, *Centuria*, p. 411), was related to another homosexual, the Comte de Vermandois (ibid., p. 412).

Charles, Marquis de Villette (1736-93), was derived by Fraxi from Poulet-Malassis' Preface "to his reprint of *Alcibiade*" (ibid., p. 411).

A fuller study of Burton's writings on homosexuality is needed, but this would require a book instead of an essay. So little study has been done on this subject that Fawn Brodie did not even mention the acquaintanceship between Burton and J.A. Symonds in her biography of Burton. Until a full-length study is written, the present essay will have to serve as an introduction and incentive to such a study.

❧

NOTES

[1]John Addington Symonds, *A Problem in Modern Ethnics* (London: privately printed, 1896), p. 78.

[2]Fawn M. Brodie, *The Devil Drives* (New York: W. W. Norton, 1967), pp. 66, 168-69, 199, 328-29, 335-36.

[3]Norman M. Penzer, *An Annotated Bibliography of Sir Richard Francis Burton* (London: A.M. Philpot, 1923), p. 176.

[4]Pisanus Fraxi, *Index Librorum Prohibitorum* (London: privately printed, 1877); *Centuria Librorum Absconditorum* (1879); *Catena Librorum Tacendorum* (1885).

[5]R.F. Burton, trans., *The Book of the Thousand Nights and a Night* (Benares: Kama Shastra Society, 1885-86), X, 205-54.

[6]Brian Reade, ed., *Sexual Heretics* (New York: Coward-McCann, 1971), pp. 158-93.

[7]Matteo Bandello, *The Novels*, trans. John Payne (London: Villon Society, 1890), I, 99.

[8]G. Morris Carstairs, "Hinjra and Jiryan," *British Journal of Medical Psychology*, 29 (1956), 129-32.

[9]N.G.L. Hammond and H.H. Scullard, eds., *The Oxford Classical Dictionary*, 2nd ed. (Oxford: Clarendon, 1970), p. 1004.

[10]Christian Gottlob Kayser, ed., *Index Locupletissimus Librorum* (Leipzig, 1835), V, 195.

[11]Karl Otfried Müller and John William Donaldson, *A History of the Literature of Ancient Greece*, trans. George Cornewall Lewis (London: J.W. Parker, 1858), III, 443.

[12]Pierre Bayle, *A General Dictionary, Historical and Critical*, trans. J.P. Bernard, T. Birch, J. Lockman and others (London: printed by James Bettenham, 1734-41), IV, 328.

[13]Jacques-Charles Brunet, *Manuel du libraire et de l'amateur de livres* (Paris: Firmin Didot, 1860), I, 150.

[14]Giambattista Passano, *Dizionario di opere anonime e pseudonime* (1887; rpt. New York: Burt Franklin, n.d.), p. 7 (my own trans.).

[15]Edward Godfrey Cox, *A Reference Guide to the Literature of Travel* (Seattle: Univ. of Washington Press, 1935), I, 395.

[16]Pierre Larousse, ed., *Grand dictionnaire universal du XIXe siècle* (Paris: Larousse, 1865-90), XIV, 48.

[17]Jan Rypka and others, *History of Iranian Literature*, ed. Karl Jahn, trans. P. van Popta-Hope (Dordrecht: D. Reidel, 1968), p. 294.

[18]Hasan-e Fāsa'i, *History of Persia under Qajar Rule*, trans. Heribert Busse (New York: Columbia Univ. Press, 1972).

[19]Henri Cordier, *Bibliotheca Sinica* (Paris: Libraire Orientale et Américaine, 1906-07), III, 2097-98.

[20]Hubert Howe Bancroft, *The Works* (San Francisco: A.L. Bancroft, 1883), I, 58.

[21]Maxime Rodinson, *Mohammed*, trans. Anne Carter (New York: Pantheon Books, 1971), p. 30; *Encyclopaedia Judaica* (New York: Macmillan, 1971), XVI, 897-900; *The Jewish Encyclopedia* (New York: Funk & Wagnalls, 1903), IV, 553.

[22]Samuel Purchas, ed., *Purchas his Pilgrimes* (1625; rpt. Glasgow: James MacLehose, 1905-07), IX, 260.

[23]Francesco Arnaldi, L.G. Rosa and L.M. Sabia, eds., *Poeti latini del Quattrocento* (Milan: Riccardo Ricciardi Editore, 1964), p. 928.

[24]J.L. Casper, *A Handbook of the Practice of Forensic Medicine*, trans. George William Balfour (London: the New Sydenham Society, 1861-65), III, 337-38.

[25]Jacobus X. Sutor, *Untrodden Fields of Anthropology*, anon. trans., (1898; rpt. New York: Rarity Press, 1931), pp. 265-79.

[26]The entire list is in Burton, p. 252, n. 1 (Reade, p. 191, n. 69). The citations from Larousse for each name are merely references to general biographical information, and contain no sexual information.

27Dr. Hoefer, ed., *Nouvelle Biographie Générale*, II (Paris: Firmin Didot, 1852), p. 469.

28Nandor Fodor, *Encyclopaedia of Psychic Science* (University Books, n.p., 1966), p. 171.

29Fraxi, *Catena*, xiv; Ellen Moers, *The Dandy* (New York: Viking Press, 1960), pp. 160, 350.

30George F. Kennan, *The Marquis de Custine and his* Russia in 1839 (Princeton, Princeton Univ. Press, 1971), pp. 5-6, 8-9, 24.

III.

LIBRARY SCIENCE

Combatting the Lies
In the Libraries

By Barbara Gittings

I was 17 and a freshman at Northwestern University when the confusion finally cleared and I put the label on and said to myself, "Homosexual — that's what I am, I'm one of those." So what were "those"? What did it mean to be a homosexual? What was in store for me? There wasn't anyone I could ask. So naturally I went to the library for information.

Today when I speak to gay groups and mention "the lies in the libraries," listeners know instantly what I mean. Most gays, it seems, at some point have gone to books in an effort to understand about being gay or get some help in living as gay. What we found was strange to us (I'm the kind of person they're writing about but I'm not like that!) and cruelly clinical (there's nothing about love) and always bad (being this way seems grim and hopeless).

I flunked out at the end of my one year at Northwestern because I had stopped going to classes in order to run around to libraries in Evanston and Chicago and spend my time reading and wondering and worrying. Home in disgrace (home was in a small Eastern city), I couldn't explain to my parents what was wrong, and I still knew no one to approach to talk to — so back to the stacks I went.

This time I was luckier: I found the fiction of homosexuality. In these stories, homosexuality often was an agony and the endings usually were unhappy. Still the characters weren't case histories but people who had feelings and who loved and who even had times of happiness. From Stephen Gordon, the earnest strong dyke, on one hand, to Compton Mackenzie's *Extraordinary Women*, the exotic figures of fun, on the other, they all made me feel much better about being a lesbian.

Soon I had my first reciprocal love affair (we met in an extension course in Abnormal Psychology where I hoped to learn more about myself!), and soon after the end of that I left home and landed in the nearest big city. After seeing to my most urgent needs — food, shelter, and a choral group to sing with — I devoted most of my spare time to my continuing education. I spent hours in the Rare Book Room reading John Addington Symonds and

Havelock Ellis, and even more hours browsing in secondhand bookshops hoping to turn up homosexual novels.

Eventually I read Cory's *The Homosexual In America*, met Cory, and through him found the gay movement which I joined in 1958. I now had less time for reading and collecting. But working in the movement kept reminding me that the written word has such a long-range effect, that the literature on homosexuality is so crucial in shaping the images we and others have of ourselves, that these distorted images we were forced to live with must not be allowed to continue. I knew that the lies in the libraries had to be changed, but I didn't have a clear sense that we gay people could do it.

For a few months in 1970 I was reporting gay news on New York's WBAI-FM. One day, in the station's mail slot for the gay broadcast, I found a news release from the Task Force on Gay Liberation of the American Library Association. A group of gay librarians had formed and was inviting others to join.

Books? Libraries? That rang bells for me!

I went to a meeting of the group. It had been launched by librarians Janet Cooper and Israel Fishman, who met at the 1970 ALA convention. They talked about not running scared anymore, about using their professional skills and about standing openly to influence library holdings on homosexuality. By the time I came along, their small group was ambitiously planning a sizeable annotated bibliography. Meanwhile, a short list of the most positive materials available was wanted for distribution at the mid-year conference of ALA, and I helped put together that first non-fiction bibliography dated January 1971. It had 37 entries — books, pamphlets, and articles — and it featured a GAY IS GOOD logo at the head.

The Task Force on Gay Liberation was the first of its kind, the first time that gay people in any professional association openly banded together to advance the gay cause through that profession. Fortunately, the TFGL did not have to go it alone in ALA. A social activism wing of ALA, the Social Responsibilities Round Table, had been launched in 1969, and under its umbrella the gay group, along with other self-created task forces tackling neglected issues in librarianship, had a semi-official base in ALA and a small share of SRRT's money (derived from dues separate from ALA).

Israel Fishman was the TFGL's first coordinator, and his talent for making a presence helped put the group boldly on the ALA map that first year. For the annual convention in June 1971 in Dallas, the group planned solid, constructive program events: a Gay Book Award, talks by Joan Marshall and Steve Wolf under the joint title "Sex and the Single Cataloguer: New Thoughts on Some Unthinkable Subjects" (about prejudice in subject headings and classification systems), and a talk by Michael McConnell, who had lost a new library job in 1970, after he and his lover Jack Baker applied openly for a marriage license. Michael was fighting his employment case in the federal courts.

But solid, constructive program events need audiences. We needed publicity. At the biggest meetings during the convention, we leafletted with 3,000 copies of a revised edition of the bibliography, by then 48 entries including periodicals. We posted notices of our activities all around the convention premises — and kept replacing them as they disappeared. We had a small hospitality suite in the main convention hotel where we offered free sample copies of gay periodicals and a place to relax and talk. We unobtrusively took over the microphones at a huge meeting of the Intellectual Freedom Committee that was playing fictitious "value games" and claimed the audience's attention with a real example of intellectual freedom abuse: the case of Michael McConnell, whose earlier appeal to the Committee under its own policies clearly applicable to his situation had been brushed aside.

And we learned, with the help of Jack Baker,[1] how to do news releases. Late each night we were in the ALA's on-location offices using the typewriters and xerox machine to produce short write-ups of our past or coming activities, always including not only the main facts but a lively quote or two ("Catalog librarians declare that 15 million gay Americans refuse to be called Sexual Aberations"). Then we went around Dallas hand-delivering the releases to the newspapers, the wire services, and the broadcast stations.

But predictably, it was our gay kissing booth that really threw us into the limelight. All the SSRT task forces had been invited to use a booth in the convention exhibit hall for a couple of hours each during the week. We could have devoted our turn to a nice display of books and periodicals and the Gay Bibliography. But Israel Fishman decided to bypass books and show gay love, live.

We called it Hug-a-Homosexual. The booth was cleared, signs saying Women Only and Men Only were put up at either side, and there we waited, smiling, ready to dispense free (free!) same-sex kisses and hugs.

The aisles were jammed. But no one entered the booth! Hundreds of exhibit visitors crowded around and craned their necks as two Dallas TV stations and a *Life* photographer shot the action in the booth. The eight of us there hugged and kissed each other, called encouragement to the watchers, kissed and hugged each other some more — and between times handed out our bibliography. The TV film was shown twice on the evening news and again the next morning. One librarian was interviewed who said, "I don't know why these people are getting all the attention when we have so many famous authors in town for the conference."

The shock waves from our kissing booth kept our name popping up in the library press for months afterward. One indignant letter in ALA's official magazine probably did us more good than harm. The writer stated reasonably with a rallying call to women, who are 75 percent of the library profession but who seldom have the higher jobs and salaries. But she went on to decry the presence of "the incapable and effeminate man too often entering the library field because he cannot face the rough and tumble competition of male professions." Then she attacked our task force for making gays visible; she was convinced that what we wanted was the freedom to engage in sex in the stacks — and worse, to do it during working hours!

All told, librarians at that 1971 convention learned fast that gay people are here and everywhere, that we won't go away, that we will insist on our rights and recognition. In the last days of the convention, we got both the Council (the elected policy-making body of ALA) and the general membership meeting to pass our pro-gay resolution.[2] Maybe some people voted for it because it seemed innocuously vague, and maybe others voted for it in hopes we wouldn't embarrass ALA with another Hug-a-Homosexual stunt. Still, the resolution did become official policy of ALA.

Our group's aim to change library holdings on homosexuality coincided with a shift in the book business itself. In 1969 even the best non-fiction literature on gays was mostly by non-gay authors and it hedged, sniped, clucked, or dry-dissected. But the Stonewall uprising of 1969 galvanized many gay people to new action. Some produced book manuscripts that caught editors' fancy as the major trade publishers sighted a whole new market. At the time our gay group sprouted in ALA, publishers were processing the first major crop of gay-positive books by gay authors. There were a dozen of them, and they boosted by 50 percent the books section of the June 1972 revision of our bibliography. Now the first title on the list wasn't Atkinson's *Sexual Morality* but Abbott and Love's *Sappho Was a Right-On Woman*.

Our first Gay Book Award also reflected the transition. Isabel Miller, a published author under her own name Alma Routsong, could not, in 1968-69, sell her novel about a lesbian couple homesteading in the early 1800's. So she published it herself in 1970. At the time she came to Dallas in 1971 to receive our Gay Book Award for *A Place For Us*, she was negotiating with McGraw-Hill for a hardcover edition of her novel, to be retitled *Patience and Sarah* — and McGraw-Hill was one of the publishers who had turned it down before. We had found a way to honor our own gay authors just as the wave of general recognition was breaking.

I loved working with the TFGL. So when Israel Fishman said in Dallas that he wanted to step out as coordinator (but stay on as guerrilla theater consultant!), I was delighted to accept the job. I took out membership in ALA (ALA accepts lay members) to facilitate the necessary working through channels within the association.

Since we now had a formula for success at ALA conventions, we used it in Chicago in 1972. Again, posting notices and leafletting large meeting crowds with our bibliography kept people aware of us, and this time our main events were also listed in the official convention program. Michael McConnell brought an overflow audience up to date on his case: a federal appeals court, reversing a lower court's ruling in his favor, had said that while there was no question he was fully qualified for the librarian job he was denied, the university was entitled to refuse him because he demanded "the right to pursue an activist role in *implementing* his unconventional ideas" (court's emphasis). Joan Marshall spoke again on the queer ways gay books are classified and told about one positive change, the Library of Congress's new number for works on "Gay Liberation Movement." The authors of *Lesbian/ Woman* and *The Gay Mystique* were on hand to receive the second Gay Book Award jointly. There were readings from Sappho, Walt Whitman, Constantin Cavafy, and Gertrude Stein, reminding our audience of 250 that these writers whose works they value on the library shelves had a homosexual dimension to their lives and their art. Our hospitality suite that year was large and (thanks to gay friends in Chicago) was kept open 12 hours a day for people to talk, browse through gay books, walk through a display of photos of gay love and gay liberation activities, and examine a set of art works by famous artists (Rodin, Winslow Homer, etc.) showing same-sex couples. When the wife of the ALA president came to look us over (and report back?), we felt we'd really arrived.

But our job is as much to unsettle ALA over gay issues as to settle into the ALA fabric. With good gay reading for adults fairly launched, what about gay reading for kids? In February 1972, *School Library Journal* published an article about our group by member Mary McKenney, who noted that school libraries owe, but rarely give, good service to young gay people or to any students who want sensible information about homosexuality. At the ALA convention in June of that year, we unveiled the first gay primer, *Fun With Our Gay Friends*, featuring Dick and Jane (remember Dick and Jane?) and their playmates meeting same-sex adult couples as a natural, casual part of the world around them. This book was aimed less at youngsters than at grown-ups to show them that we gays have been cut out of the official picture of life presented in kids' books. Frances Hanckel, a non-librarian in the TFGL, insisted the primer deserved more attention than mere display. So, spoofing ALA's famous Newbery-Caldecott Awards for children's books, we created and bestowed the

New Raspberry-Coldcut Award. Alas, there was no rush of publishers to put the winner into mass circulation. But we knew we'd come back to the theme.

We skipped the 1973 convention and the Gay Book Award for that year. None of our core members could get to Las Vegas, and there was no outstanding gay book we wanted to honor. Nonetheless we tried to maintain our presence at ALA by means of a flyer which we asked friends in SRRT to post around the convention and otherwise distribute for us.

We were unmistakably present in New York City in 1974. Our smiling leafletters, all two of them, blitzed the convention in its first three days with 4,000 copies each of our bibliography and a flyer announcing our activities. Almost 300 people turned out to hear "Let's Not Homosexualize the Library Stacks," Michael McConnell's reasoned appeal to move from "Homosexual" to "Gay" in subject headings to spur needed changes in attitudes; and to see two gay playlets by the Oscar Wilde Memorial Players.

Appropriately, our first Gay Book Award recipient, Isabel Miller, presented the 1974 award to *Sex Variant Women in Literature* by Jeannette Foster. Dr. Forster too had had publishing trouble. When in the mid-50's she finished her critical survey of lesbianism and variance in literature from Sappho through 20th-century writings in English, German, and French, no publisher would touch it. She had to go to a vanity press to see it in print, and of course it went out of print soon after.[3]

Dr. Foster, a librarian now retired, couldn't travel but she sent a letter expressing her delight at getting the Gay Book Award and her "happy surprise that my long-respected ALA is willing to admit the existence of Gaiety — and even honor it!" (It was no surprise to us that the library press didn't pick up this statement.)

She also wrote, in answer to our question, "There is little about my personal life I could give you without violating the privacy of persons, some of whom are still living. (You see, our generation grew up concealing our gayness as if it were syphilis!) I can say, however, that I have been deeply attached to a number of women, from the time I was four. Six of these affairs had physical expression."

At our business meeting, a smaller audience enthusiastically tried "The Revolving Closet Door: When to Come Out and When Not to Come Out." This was a series of unscripted role-plays in which the "non-gay" actors are free to make up the situation as they go, after a given start, and the closeted gay person has to decide whether to come out, to avoid the issue, or to lie this time. Examples: You and other library workers are having lunch together and the talk turns to a TV show last night that had a homosexual character . . . In a lounge at library school, Suzy Straight describes in glowing detail her date with

Norman Niceguy, and when conversation moves around the group, eventually someone asks you about your lovelife . . . Each college library staff member at a meeting is being asked to react to the request of the campus gay group for gay books and periodicals in the library, and now it's your turn . . .

"Gay Books Roasted and Toasted" sums up our 1975 convention action. First came the toasting. The 1975 Gay Book Award went to a collection of reprints of gay materials called *Homosexuality: Lesbians and Gay Men in Society, History and Literature.* This series is expected to boost the growth of gay courses around the country. Jonathan Katz, editor of the reprint collection, reminded us in his letter accepting the Gay Book Award that it's because gay people have organized and have created a demand for gay materials that publishers are producing; it didn't happen out of the blue. He also said, about gay studies, "The development of Gay Studies is not a matter of academic interest only. Our rediscovery of our forgotten history, and our new knowledge of ourselves, will provide us with the spiritual nourishment we need for living, loving, and surviving in a genocidal society — for militant struggle against what Christopher Isherwood has aptly called 'the heterosexual dictatorship.' "

And the roasted books? At last Frances Hanckel got to air the issue of gay themes in kids' books. Her forum, called "The Children's Hour: Must Gay be Grim for Jane and Jim?" drew a crowd of nearly 400 people — librarians, editors, and publishers.

Members of our group read plot summaries of the only four teenage novels then available that deal openly with gay experience.[4] We could hardly believe it ourselves: these four stories contain eight central characters with five sets of divorced parents, two of whom are alcoholics, and have plots with three natural deaths and three car crashes resulting in one mutilation, one head injury, and four fatalities, plus two pets' deaths by violence! During the plot narrations, big signs saying "Death" and "Car Crash" were held up at the appropriate moments. Guffaws broke from the audience by the time the signs were hoisted during the final plot summary.

We read letters from all four authors responding to our complaint that in their stories, gayness has no lasting significance and/or it costs someone a terrible price. One author, Lynn Hall, explained that her publisher persuaded her to modify her original pro-gay ending. "One editor wanted me to kill Tom in a car accident (!)," she wrote. "At least I held out for a friendship at the end, one which might or might not develop into something more, depending on the reader's imagination."

Frances Hanckel delivered a devastating critique of the books, but they were defended by our guest speaker, Donald B. Reynolds, Jr., a school librarian who serves on several ALA committees concerned with children's literature, and by a number of other people during spirited audience debate. At the close everyone was happy to learn that several non-grim gay teenage novels are in the works.

"Your program was the hidden gem of the convention!" we were later told by another expert on kids' books.

Our program's success led us to start two more jobs: one, preparing an annotated bibliography of gay fiction and non-fiction for use by youngsters; the other, drawing up Gay Guidelines for writers and publishers of books for kids. The guidelines call for, among other things: more secondary gay characters who aren't 'A Problem' but are just part of the human scenery; no special "explanations" for the gayness of a gay character; depictions of gay affection and falling in love, parallel with straights' experience; illustrations showing same-sex couples; books that tell gay readers they can cope successfully with the problems they'll face and that show non-gays they can appreciate instead of fearing differences in affectional and sexual preference.[5]

The Gay Guidelines have been sent to over a hundred publishers and reviewers of children's books. We hope at least to get dialogue started. McGraw-Hill once adopted anti-sexism guidelines; will they adopt ours aimed at heterosexism?

Our Gay Bibliography continues to be our basic tool for countering the lies in the library. Over 30,000 copies of the 4th edition (January 1974) were distributed on request to libraries of all kinds as well as to teachers, students, researchers, counselors and therapists, lawyers, relatives of gays, gay individuals and groups, church people, public officials, etc. Now the 5th edition is in circulation, with 200 items including an annotated Audio-Visuals section and a section on directories and other bibliographies.[6]

Over the years we've noticed changes in librarians' reactions when we hand out the bibliography at ALA conventions. At first everyone readily accepted a copy. Librarians do love lists. (A few thought they were getting a program for whatever meeting they happened to be entering.) Later a reaction set in and we got some brusque refusals — "I don't need this" or "We already have all that stuff" — usually when the person caught sight of the boldly-lettered GAY on our bibliography and on the badges we wear. But in 1975 we had few demurs and many people even asked for extra copies. By our friendly, persistent presence, we've desensitized crowds at ALA.

We have evidence that libraries are using our bibliography as a guide in ordering. But even in libraries with good collections of gay materials, readers may have trouble finding their way to them. Gay or not, many library users still don't want to announce their interest in this subject matter in order to get help, at least not until they're desperate. (It's that you-are-what-you-read syndrome.)

So you start with the card catalog, under Homosexuality. It may direct you to also see Sexual Deviation or even Sexual Perversion. It will certainly include cards on some of the anti-gay materials that still infest libraries and probably won't be retired for another decade. Also the card catalog leads only to nonfiction; you will need luck and persistence to find gay literature and biography, the flesh-and-blood writing that I, for one, found so nourishing.

When you go to the shelves, hoping no one else is in that aisle, chances are that the more gay-positive items aren't there. Are they checked out? You'll have to either declare your interest by filing a request slip, or else keep haunting the library until the books you want reappear. Have the books been stolen? Library rip-off techniques are always ahead of security measures, and people who want sex-related books are strongly motivated. [7] Sometimes books that are irreplaceable or deemed most-likely-to-disappear are kept in a back room or at the desk, available only through the staff, and while this is a good way to keep the materials on hand for all, many readers are intimidated by having to ask for, say, *Lesbian/Woman.* If you're Sally Sixteen of Smalltown, you simply may not do it.

There are other hurdles for the reader. While much good gay material is in pamphlet or circular form, few libraries keep a pamphlet file on Homosexuality or Gay Liberation or Gay People, and some of those do, neglect to cite it in the card catalog. If the library carries any gay periodicals, the reader has to know specific titles to look for, and the periodicals may also be kept "under the counter" for security, so that one must ask for them. Encyclopedia articles on homosexuality are written by psychiatrists — one wonders in reading them what they'd write if they had to do an equivalent article on Heterosexuality. Moreover, encyclopedia items have a disproportionately bad impact because encyclopedias are the first place many people look for information on homosexuality and because encyclopedias carry authority, especially with school-age readers.

Our TFGL is tackling these problems as best we can. A committee has recommended to the Library of Congress further changes in its subject headings system, including creating a new heading, Gay People, for materials on same-sex affectional ties and lifestyles, and establishing Heterosexuality and Bisexuality as well as Homosexuality as main subject headings. We're encouraging libraries to get quantities of our bibliography and put them where readers who need them can help themselves unnoticed. And our program at the 1976 ALA convention will be on "Serving the Fearful Reader: 'I'm Doing a Term Paper on Homosexuality . . . ' " to show librarians how to be helpful when approached, without being too helpful and thereby overwhelming or scaring the customer.

Our story isn't all successes. We have failed to get ALA to back up librarian Michael McConnell in his gay job-discrimination case. McConnell began in 1971 formally requesting action by ALA to uphold his right to be hired on the basis of his job skills rather than be denied on the basis of his gay lifestyle and activism. His case was shuttled from one committee in ALA to another, and each report has recommended No Action, citing in part such technicalities as the fact that the university that dumped McConnell in 1970 wasn't violating any ALA policy in force at that time. Since ALA did subsequently adopt in 1971 our gay-support resolution (note 2), and in 1974 an equal-employment-opportunity policy including the phrase "regardless of . . . individual lifestyle," it's plain that ALA has violated the spirit if not the letter of its own policies in refusing year after year to go to bat for McConnell.

Also our task force had to shelve plans to issue a booklet for gay groups on how to promote gay materials in their local public and college libraries. And for lack of enough people with the necessary skills and determination, we haven't been able to launch a campaign to influence editors of encyclopedias.

School textbooks too need revamping. Texts on literature do not as yet discuss writers' gayness or gay writings. History and civics texts do not as yet mention the 24-year-old gay movement in the United States. And in those few health/sex education books that include homosexuality, the coverage is brief, is distorted if not downright false, and hardly serves to fortify gay youngsters or enlighten the non-gays who live with them. We've had indications from the Association of American Publishers that they'll discuss gays' demands for changes when gays present solid evidence of schoolbooks' errors and exclusions. One of the TFGL members, librarian John Cunningham, is doing a pilot survey of textbooks used in Philadelphia schools to see how gay-related subjects are treated (if at all) in the curriculum. (Cunningham's survey is under the auspices of the National Gay Task Force.)

We also haven't succeeded in attracting much money. Every donation, even a dollar, cheers us. Since postage outlays and printing bills for the bibliography (running to hundreds of dollars) can't be cut, doing the rest of our work on a shoestring makes us inventive. At the last two conventions we arranged for gay film showings, with co-sponsors who provided the place and equipment free. Our hospitality rooms were financed by having group members sleep in the suite and share the cost. The Gay Book Award mementos — hand-lettered scrolls, mounted enlargements of gay art by famous artists, a lavender mortarboard — cost only a few dollars or were contributed. For products or services we need, we try to find friends in the business who will donate or charge only cost.

Human energy, in fact, is the gasoline we mostly run on. At ALA conventions, local gay people help us get publicity and run the hospitality suite. And since only a dozen or so librarians are active in the TFGL, gays who aren't librarians but who love books, enthusiastically do vital jobs. Lee Lehman, a botany doctoral candidate and director of the National Gay Student Center, helps to locate and judge items for our bibliography. Gay author Kay Tobin works on displays, photos, and publicity. Carolyn Pope, a high school physical education teacher, has been a chief leafletter for two years and took part in "The Children's Hour," along with psychologist Mark Freedman and librarians Jack Latham and John Cunningham. Frances Hanckel is a medical technician and is exporting her talents and TFGL experience by helping to launch the new gay caucus of the American Public Health Association.

We get a great deal of mail from gay people in all kinds of situations. One person wrote, "I am 19 and discovering that all is not heterosexual with me. I need information, more information, and a belief that there are others like me with a need for another kind of love story." What will this reader find, or not find, at the library? Another correspondent wrote, "Although I am comfortable in my gayness and have a beautiful relationship, I am a small-town librarian — and a coward. Good luck to you!" What will help her open her closet door?

My favorite letter hints at a happy ending for all of us. The letter came from the president of the gay group at Northwestern University, the place where I first looked to the library to learn what it means to be gay. He wrote, "As you may know, the Northwestern library has an incredible collection of gay books and periodicals. By the way, they automatically order any book that appears on your list."

For me, that's a very personal triumph.

❖

NOTES

1Jack Baker merits a special place as a gay academic. He was the first openly gay person to be elected and reelected president of a university student body; also he got the National Student Association to establish a gay desk, the National Gay Student Center.

2"The American Library Association recognizes that there exist minorities which are not ethnic in nature but which suffer oppression. The Association recommends that libraries and members strenuously combat discrimination in services to, and employment of, individuals from all minority groups, whether distinguishing characteristics of the minority be ethnic, sexual, religious or any other kind."

3Fortunately, in 1975 Diana Press arranged to repring *Sex Variant Women In Literature.*

4*I'll Get There, It Better Be Worth the Trip* by John Donovan, *Sticks and Stones* by Lynn Hall, *The Man Without a Face* by Isabelle Holland, and *Trying Hard to Hear You* by Sandra Scoppettone.

5The Gay Guidelines are available for a stamped reply envelope, from: Frances Hanckel, 501 S. 44th St., Philadelphia, PA 19104.

6Single copies of Gay Bibliography 25¢ each, 10+ copies 15¢ each, from: Barbara Gittings — TFGL, P.O. Box 2383, Philadelphia, PA 19103.

7Not only in libraries do people get desperate. One young man in Ohio wrote me, "Unfortunately I was forced to shoplift my copy of *The Gay Crusaders* because the clerk in the bookstore knows my mother. But I'm sending a check to XYZ [gay group] and part of it goes, in spirit at least, for *The Gay Crusaders.*"

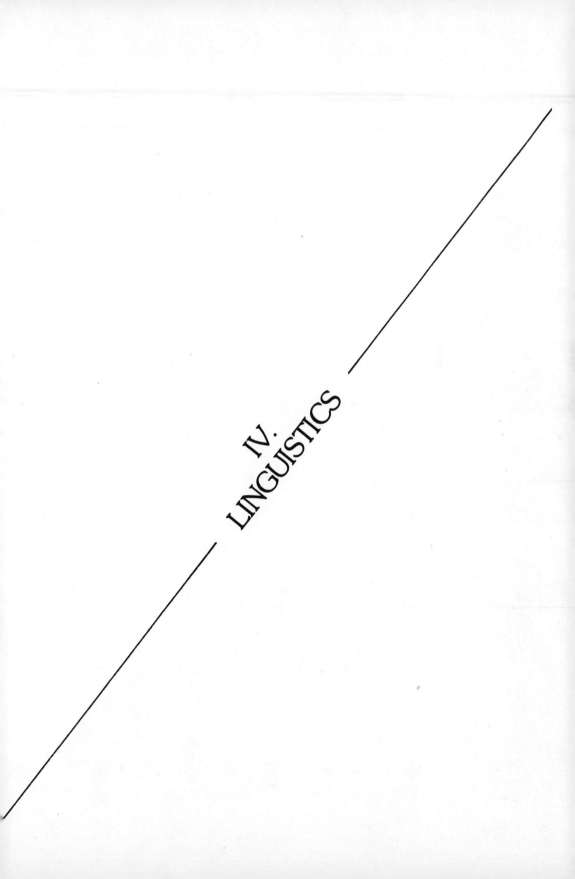

IV.
LINGUISTICS

Lesbian Separatism: The Linguistic and Social Sources Of Separatist Politics

By Julia P. Stanley

This chapter was prepared for a workshop on Lesbian Separatism for the Fourth Annual Conference of the Rutgers Student Homophile League, Rutgers University, April 19-21, 1974.

Separatism as a political stance is certainly not a recent phenomenon, nor is it an issue restricted to the gay liberation movement. For a group of people whose history is one of negative identity, it is probably a necessary first step toward self-respect and self-comprehension. Perhaps because lesbians and gay males have only begun to explore themselves, lesbian separatism has been, and remains, one of the most painful issues within gay liberation organizations. I say "painful" because it is difficult for a lesbian to put aside her neo-humanistic ideal that "we're all human beings, after all," and because gay males have too often interpreted lesbian separatism as a personal rejection rather than seeing it as one part of the generalized anger of women who have to live in a male-dominated culture. In an effort to make clear the political necessity for lesbian separatism, I will present some of the linguistic and personal evidence that moved me into a separatist political position. Comprehension of the sources of separatism may make a painful process less painful for all of us. If we can deal explicitly with the cultural realities that make separatism a necessity, perhaps we can move more quickly to effect social changes.

Lesbian separatism is a subject bound to arouse anger and hostility not only in men but also in women. We are all afraid of it, but for different reasons. Gay men, for some reason, are affronted when lesbians leave their organizations, and I find it unfortunate, though not incomprehensible, that separatism should be taken as singularly antagonistic on the part of lesbians. I've listened to gay men demand "reasons" for the withdrawal of lesbians from the ranks of gay liberation, and they become more angry when lesbians refuse to respond to their demands. Gay men, like men in general, seem to believe that we *owe* them an explanation, and our refusal to offer elaborate justifications is one aspect of our decision not to put our energies into dealing with men. And, as a consequence, there is anger, frustration, and hostility on all sides. As lesbians realize that "Gay Liberation" is "Gay *Male* Liberation," more and more lesbians will gradually drop out of predominantly male organizations, so it is important for us to understand some of the underlying motivations and tensions that make separatism a logical step for lesbians in terms of our own growth.

The withdrawal of lesbians from predominantly gay male organizations is an act necessary for our survival. No, it goes beyond survival. Withdrawal from gay male organizations is the first, most important step we have to take toward establishing our lesbian identity. Hopefully, it will be our first step toward lesbian *community*. I can't begin to define what I mean by "lesbian community," but I want it to come into existence. I cannot conceive what such a sense of community might be like. It's too soon. We are a long way from Lesbian Nation. We don't know *who* we are, and our culture has somehow neglected to provide lesbians with an identity, beyond the traditionally-imposed characteristics of sinfulness, sickness, and illegality. Of course, there are important reasons for this unfortunate oversight on the part of our culture: to name something is to accord it the dignity of recognition. We are "mere obscenities." The only names we have are those men have made for us, and even those names are never heard. For example, the *Random House Dictionary* lists the term *woman-hater* but not its antonym, *man-hater*. Such exclusion is one of those unconscious, unplanned "accidents" that reveal so much. Man-hating is inadmissible in a patriarchal society, woman-hating is a recognized activity. Since lesbians are, by popular definition, man-haters, and since man-hating does not exist, lesbians don't exist. We are syllogistically reduced to zero. No one wants to believe that lesbians exist; no one wants to believe that it's possible for women to love each other. We are the only people who believe in our existence, and it is up to us to define that existence. No one else has a vested interest in it. For once, perhaps, the silence surrounding our lives is to our advantage.

Because our culture has ignored us, we have the unique opportunity few people have: we can set about constructing our lives and deciding who we are. We know that we exist, but even we aren't sure what that *means*. We can't agree among ourselves on what defines a woman as a lesbian, although we are beginning to talk about it. We agree that being a lesbian involves loving other women, but when we try to define what that love entails, our agreement ends.

Can one be a lesbian if she says that her primary love is for other women, or does calling oneself a lesbian depend upon having had *sexual* experiences with another woman? We're arguing not just about labels, but about the concepts behind the labels and their application to ourselves and other women. And, to complicate these discussions, the labels aren't even ours. We didn't make them up, so that the original concept that required the label is not our possession either. As women, specifically as the most despised women, we have no identity, no tradition, no history. We have to begin to create our own traditions and, in order to do this, we have to separate ourselves from gay men and their activities. We have been the small, subordinate subclassification of homosexuality for too long. Without this separation, we will never know who we are or what we might become. We have to discover our meaning of being a lesbian; we can no longer accept the definitions provided *for* us by men. That much is clear.

There is a myth that we have to destroy. The myth, constructed by psychologists and psychiatrists, asserts that there is such a thing as "homosexuality." Those who wish to maintain the myth promote *homosexuality* as a "generic" term for same-sex love, as though there were no qualitative differences. For example, Sheldon Cashdan, in his book *Abnormal Psychology*, defines the term as follows:

> *Homosexuality* is the generic term used to denote sexual responsiveness to members of the same sex. Although more frequently used to describe erotic attachments among men, it also technically encompasses female-female, or *lesbian*, relationships. (p. 44)

In the next two pages, Cashdan goes on to quote a gay male, he cites Humphries' study of tearoom trade, and then he discusses voyeurs. Once you've talked about tearoom activities, any graceful transitions to lesbian life are difficult. The passage from Cashdan exemplifies the traditional treatment of lesbianism, especially in the social sciences. Lesbians don't want to be "technically encompassed" by terms that apply to the lives of men. We want our own identity.

Perhaps a similar quotation from a different field will make my objections even clearer. Rictor Norton, in the March, 1974 issue of *College English*, published an article entitled "The Homosexual Literary Tradition." From the beginning it is clear that the "homosexual literary tradition" belongs to gay men. After he has outlined the first two units of a four-unit course, he suggests that the third unit be devoted to lesbian literature. He justifies such a unit in the following way:

> By now some students may become irritated that only male homo-
> sexual literature has been discussed, so I would devote the third unit
> to lesbian literature. (p. 689)

Norton's primary reason for including lesbian literature in the course he describes is the possible "irritation" of students in the class. (Note also that the students would only be "irritated," not *angry*.) He then goes on to suggest possible inclusions, such as Sappho, the story of Ruth and Naomi, and Pierre Louys' *Songs of Bilitis*. Certainly a "mixed bag." Norton next mentions more contemporary writers, Ann Aldrich and Judy Grahn, and makes the following comment:

> You may also wish to examine how male writers such as Henry
> James, D. H. Lawrence, and Balzac have treated lesbian themes.

Lesbians are reduced to a single unit in a course on the homosexual literary tradition, and our lives become "lesbian themes" in the works of male writers. In any study that assumes that lesbians are "encompassed" by "homosexuality," we are included only as a subordinate clause at the end of a paragraph, or we are left as something to be handled in one unit or one chapter, always at the end.

The course described by Rictor Norton is not one in which many lesbians would have any interest. Quite frankly, as far as I can see, "Gay Studies," should it gain a niche in the academic curriculum, will necessarily remain the preserve of gay men. Whenever lesbians are subsumed under a generic term, whether it is *gay* or *homosexual*, the subject matter has little or nothing to do with our lives. We are trivial marginalia, digressions.

Thus far, I have cited two authors in support of my contention that lesbians have to actively refuse to be included in any discussion that presupposes that the lives of lesbians are covered by the term *homosexuality*. To continue to subsume ourselves uncomfortably under either umbrella term, *gay* or *homosexual*, is to deny the validity of our separate experiences. Worse, as a lesbian, it requires maintaining an uneasy stance in the shadow of the lives of gay men. I'm no longer interested in being defined by comparison *or* contrast with men. What I'm suggesting is something that has been obvious to lesbians and gay men of my acquaintance for a long time: lesbianism and homosexuality are not the same thing. We are dealing with two very different phenomena. The two lifestyles are not identical, however one may wish to construe that fact. There are lesbians, and there are homosexuals, and we need the terminological distinction in order to do justice to the two different kinds of experience. We also need to remember that lesbians and homosexuals did not put ourselves in the same category — the law did, the psychiatrists and the psychologists did. That's the way they classify in the heterosexual world, the better to make generalizations and analyze their statistics, the better to blur the real fear that motivates their classifications and judgments.

Have you ever wondered about the source of the taboos against loving someone of the same sex? Have you ever wondered why, if heterosexuality is, in fact, "natural," it had to be institutionalized? If *everyone* were naturally heterosexual, would it be necessary to buttress this definition of human sexuality with all of the religious, philosophical, political, and legal sanctions our society has formulated? George Weinberg, in *Society and the Healthy Homosexual*, has suggested that the taboos derive from *homophobia*, the fear of homosexuals. But he doesn't ask the next, logical question: What is the source of this fear? I would like to suggest that the fear has a very real cause: If people could be whatever they wanted to be, without all the intense social conditioning, they would be lesbians and homosexuals. *Whoever* set civilization in motion realized something important at an early date: You can't have a society, at least not one like ours, if people are allowed to be whoever they want to be. And if everyone were lesbians and homosexuals, we wouldn't be here, as heterosexuals are fond of reminding us. In short, the taboos against both lesbians and homosexuals are necessary in order to perpetuate society, *as we know it*. From this necessity derive institutionalized heterosexuality, the nuclear family, and the sex-role stereotyping that guarantees the continued existence of our social and economic structure.

I am not concerned here with tracing historical development, chronology, or placing blame. I am not concerned about whether or not it was a patriarchy or a matriarchy that first established the sexual taboos. All of us have to deal with the quality of our life experiences now, today, and tomorrow. We were raised in a society that depends upon sex-role stereotyping for its perpetuation. Because we have all been exposed, are constantly being exposed, to these sex-role stereotypes, lesbianism and homosexuality cannot be the *same* phenomenon. The psychologies of women and men are too different as our society has created them.

In order to make the specific features of the female and male roles more explicit as our culture has defined them, I've copied some definitions of terms from the *Random House Dictionary*. I chose this dictionary as my source because it is recent, and the definitions are those that reflect the cultural belief system with which we were indoctrinated. The terms are *womanly, manly, feminine, masculine, tomboy, sissy,* and the definition of *effeminate* provided under *female*. As you read through these definitions, keep in mind two other terms, *bull-dyke* and *drag queen*, because my later discussion will focus on these terms as representative of the underlying tensions, created by the sex-role stereotypes, that motivate lesbian separatism.

Definitions

manly — having the qualities usually considered desirable in a man; strong, brave; honorable; resolute; virile. Syn. — *Manly* implies possession of the most valuable or desirable qualities a man can have, as dignity, honesty, directness, etc., in opposition to servility, insincerity, underhandedness, etc. It also connotes strength, courage, and fortitude: . . .

mannish — applies to that which resembles man: . . . Applied to a woman, the term is derogatory, suggesting the aberrant possession of masculine characteristics.

(The antonyms listed for *manly* are three: feminine; weak; cowardly.)

womanly — like or befitting a woman; feminine; not masculine or girlish. Syn. — *Womanly* implies resemblance in appropriate, fitting ways: *womanly decorum, modesty. Womanlike*, a neutral synonym, may suggest mild disapproval or, more rarely, disgust. *Womanlike, she (he) burst into tears. Womanish* usually implies an inappropriate resemblance and suggests weakness or effeminacy: *womanish petulance.*

(Under *female* RHD provides the following statement on *effeminate*.)

Effeminate is applied reproachfully or contemptuously to qualities which, although natural in women, are seldom applied to women and are unmanly and weak when possessed by men: *effeminate gestures; an effeminate voice. Feminine*, corresponding to masculine, applies to the attributes particularly appropriate to women, esp. the softer and more delicate qualities. The word is seldom used to denote sex, and, if applied to men, suggests the delicacy and weakness of women: *a feminine figure, point of view, features.*

feminine — 1. pertaining to a woman or girl: *feminine beauty, feminine dress.* 2. like a woman; weak; gentle.

masculine — 1. having the qualities or characteristics of a man; manly; virile;

strong; bold; a deep, *masculine voice.* 2. pertaining to or characteristic of a man or men: *masculine attire.*

tomboy — a carefree, romping, boisterous girl.

sissy — 1. an effeminate boy or man. 2. a timid or cowardly person. 3. a little girl.

If you've read through these definitions carefully, you cannot have missed the reasoning that underlies the exclusion of *man-hater* from this dictionary, the same reasoning that requires the inclusion of *woman-hater.* The existence of these terms in itself demonstrates the basic dichotomy of personality that our culture assumes and perpetuates. The definitions, both in tone and word-choice, reflect the cultural value attached to the cultural roles of women and men, and delineate neatly and unmistakably the sex-role stereotypes with which we grew up. Men can be strong, virile, forthright, honest, and dignified. Women are "naturally" weak, gentle, delicate, cowardly, timid, modest. For women to be honest, dignified, forthright, etc., is regarded as "aberrant." The role of women as our culture defines it is certainly less than fully human, and loaded with negative values, while the role of men is portrayed as positively valued.

With the features and values attached to the sex-role stereotypes explicit, I can now demonstrate the differences between lesbians and homosexuals that necessitate lesbian separatism. From the time we were born, we have been conditioned in terms of our culture's expectations of us. Our conditioning is determined by our biological sex. Somehow, though, some of us escape *total* conditioning and, in varying degrees, some women decide that they can be strong, and some men decide that they can be weak. (Ultimately, we must abandon such adjectives). The lesbian rejects the image and definition of herself as a woman, and the homosexual rejects our culture's definition of him as a man. And within this rejection we can find the origins of the bull-dyke and the drag queen, and the basic differences that distinguish lesbians from homosexuals, as we understand those terms today.

The lesbian rejects the definition of herself as weak, passive, timid, dependent, and instead gravitates toward the male role, which permits her that latitude of self-expression and independence denied to women. It is also the male role that makes it possible for the lesbian to take hold of her anger and act politically in terms of that anger. The homosexual, by rejecting the male stereotype, moves toward the female role, taking on those qualities regarded as characteristic of women — passivity, timidity, and lack of self-assertiveness. (For empirical support of this observation, see the study published by Fred

Myrick, "Attitudinal Differences between Heterosexually and Homosexually Oriented Males and between Covert and Overt Male Homosexuals," *Journal of Abnormal Psychology*, 1974, *83*, 81-86). In addition to his conclusion that homosexuals are lower in self-esteem, personal competence, and self-acceptance than heterosexual males, Myrick also found that covert homosexuals have higher self-esteem and self-acceptance than overt homosexuals. This observation has political implications, which I'll discuss shortly.) The bull-dyke thus represents the lesbian extreme of role-switching, for she may also take on the undesirable features of the male role, violence, woman-hatred (which, for her, involves self-hatred), and a brutal callousness, a refusal to admit to emotions associated with being a woman. In contrast, the drag queen rejects the male role, and acquires the extreme characteristics of the female role, self-trivialization, superficiality, and a refusal to accept responsibility for his actions. The essence of camp is the refusal to take oneself seriously.

As I've indicated, the bull-dyke and the drag queen are extremes, and there are variations in every direction. (For example, the male homosexuals who go to the other extreme with the masculine stereotype.) But I think the consequences of the role dichotomy are evident in all of us to some extent, especially those of us who have been involved in Gay Liberation. Both lesbians and homosexuals are trapped at some point between the female and male roles of our culture. Thus, I may differ only in degree from another woman in the extent to which I can be intimidated by a man. Nevertheless, the tendency to allow myself to be intimidated is always there, and however aggressive and independent I may be I have to constantly monitor my own behavior. Similarly, a gay man differs from a straight man only in the degree of his will to dominate or manipulate others, in particular, women. These are the reasons why it is extremely difficult for lesbians to work politically with gay men. No matter how passive, how inane, how trivialized a gay man has become, he always reserves the right to revert to the male supremacist role. Perhaps an example will demonstrate my point. One night I went with two other lesbians to a gay bar that had a drag show. One of the drag queens, dressed in a tight, red, velvet dress slit up the sides, came out into the audience as part of his performance, doing a "vamp" routine. He was acting out the seductive image of women so popular in our culture. Unfortunately, he chose me as one of his partners in this role fantasy. When he strutted over to me and leaned against me, doing his "come-on," I turned my head and refused to play along. He then leaned over and said, "Aren't we the snotty butch!" I continued to keep my head turned away, until he actually grabbed my chin and jerked my head around, forcing me to look at him. In reply, I shot a bird at him. He stormed off, returned to the stage, grabbed the microphone, and began to insult me. His insults reveal the barriers promoted by sex-role stereotypes. He informed me that no matter how "butch" I thought I was, I was still "just" a woman, and that I would never be "a man." At the end of his tirade, he made one classic statement that is worth repeating verbatim: "Listen, honey! You may think you're as good as a man with those pants on, but let me tell you one thing. Just because I have on a dress and heels doesn't mean I'm not a man, and if you want to find out how much of a man I am, come on outside! We'll see who the man is!"

This was a man who had voluntarily donned women's attire, a man who made some money wearing those clothes that symbolize the female's subordination to the male, the clothes that are designed to make women more available to the male. Of course, he had nothing to lose by wearing women's clothes; biologically, he is still a male and thereby entitled to male prerogatives in our society. This encounter exemplifies the reasons that feminists are opposed to female impersonation. It also foregrounds the psychological differences between homosexuals and lesbians that make political alliances tenuous, at best. Because the female and male roles are polarized in our culture, and because as members of this society we are all thereby polarized, the political goals and the processes leading to self-realization for lesbians and homosexuals cannot be shared.

Many homosexuals have adopted the feminist issue of sex-role stereotyping as a commonly-held problem. They have used this issue to justify female impersonation as a male's way of breaking out of his sex-role. Certainly, in a limited sense, this is true. But as a lesbian, I cannot fight for the right of a man to take on all of the features assigned to women, like passivity and triviality. I cannot support homosexuals who would glorify those characteristics of my sex-role that I detest. While I cannot deny to another human being the right to self-degradation and self-immolation, neither can I be expected to endorse it. As I see it, the personal directions for homosexuals and lesbians take separate paths. While the lesbian's struggle is toward self-confidence, self-assertion, independence, and the ability to express her anger outwardly, the homosexual's struggle is toward realizing his potential for tenderness, reclaiming the emotions he has had to deny as a "man," relinquishing the political power inherent in his biology, and developing his capacity for compassion. But there are serious problems for all of us as we move toward self-integration. As the lesbian acquires strength, dignity, and self-possession, she cannot fall into the trap of also emulating the violence, brutality, and lack of concern for other people that characterize the male sex-role. Nor can the homosexual make the mistake of becoming weak, ineffectual, and the senseless pawn of other people.

Perhaps an example of the consequences of being trapped between the roles will make the dangers explicit. Recently, I went to a party given by a homosexual collective. I arrived late, and most of the other lesbians had already left, although I met a few who were leaving as I was going in the front door. They advised me not to bother going into the house. Once I was inside, I became aware of tension all around me, barely disguised hostility. I could sense the violence around me. A couple of the women who were still at the party came up to me, and told me some stories that confirmed my own initial impressions of the atmosphere. I will give you one example of the overt violence some of the women experienced. One of the women was wearing a purple hardhat with a feminist symbol painted on the front and "Sisterhood is powerful!" painted on the back. A man had asked her why she was wearing the hat. Then he hit her over the head, saying, "Isn't *that* why you're wearing it?" After I'd looked around for myself, and seen all the straight men crowding the dance floor, leaning against the walls staring at the women, and grabbing us as we walked by, I went over and talked to one of the gay men, to find out why all of these straight men were at a party I had believed to be for gay people. He told me that they had crashed the party, but that there was nothing he could do to make them leave. Another gay man told me that another gay man had invited them, but he wasn't going to make them leave either. Although the party was in their home, neither of the gay men, as I was told later, wanted to "get into a macho power trip." For many gay men, asserting one's rights, taking control of one's surroundings, one's home, is a "macho power trip." As all of this translated to me, however, these gay men were saying that they weren't angry about the conduct of these men, they didn't mind the overtly aggressive and hostile behavior, and they weren't going to do anything about it. As one gay man explained it to me later: "We didn't want to discriminate against them because they're heterosexuals." But another gay man admitted that, in fact, *none* of them had been aware that anything was wrong at the party until I mentioned it. It all boils down to the fact that gay men, through their passivity, condone the behavior of other men rather than challenge them. When some of the lesbians took over the dance floor in an effort to dislodge the straight men, the gay men were "shocked" at our "hostile" behavior, and informed me that we had been unduly rude and aggressive. Finally, we decided to leave, and as I was going out the door, one of the gay men came rushing over to me and said, in his thickest back-to-Tara accent: "Why Julia! Why are you leaving?" For me, that capsulized the whole event. It also captures the basic reason for lesbian separatism. If the gay men were appalled by my self-assertion and aggressiveness, I was equally taken aback by their indifference, their lack of concern, their lack of *anger*. Gay men are not angry as I am angry, and if they are angry, it is not at all for the same reasons, because the sources of our anger are different. As a consequence, so are our political goals.

The psychological distance, and the concomitant political estrangement, between lesbians and homosexuals derives from the sex-role stereotypes kept alive within our culture. While gay men are trying to put aside the male stereotype, they tend to discard some of the good features of it along with the bad. In the process of shedding the privileges of male supremacy, it isn't necessary to surrender control over one's life, independence, and the will to assert one's rights. In discarding the negative characteristics of the female role, it shouldn't be necessary for lesbians to give up positive attributes like gentleness and compassion. These are problems that lesbians and homosexuals will have to work through as distinct, self-identified groups. We aren't coming from the same place, and to ignore the real difficulties that set us apart from each other would be to prolong the existence of those differences. I suspect that the sex-role stereotypes, if put back together, would provide us with some idea of what a whole human being might be like. There is no inherent reason why one cannot be both independent and gentle, intuitive and self-assertive, angry and compassionate. Certainly these personality traits are not mutually exclusive, by definition. But lesbians and homosexuals will have to grow toward wholeness in different ways, and we can best help each other by understanding and confronting our differences instead of minimizing them.

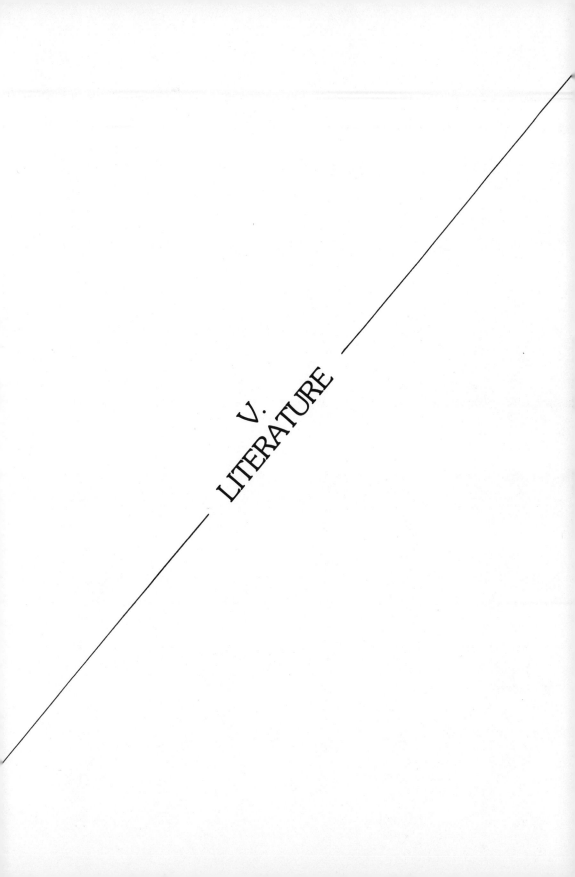

V.
LITERATURE

Homotextuality: A Proposal

By Jacob Stockinger

"To work out: — The sexual bias
in literary criticism . . . "

E.M. Forster's diary, 25 October 1910

I. Minority Criticism and the Formalist Challenge

Whether it appears as Anglo-American "New Criticism," French "Nouvelle critique," structuralism, psycho-criticism, or semiocriticism, the mainstream of literary criticism today is formalist in its perspective. In such a context, the most persistent and damaging accusation leveled against minority criticism is that it cannot directly address a text, that it is not pertinent to literature in a "literary" way. At its worst, which is admittedly too often the reality, minority criticism degenerates into a body of inquisitional attitudes. It elevates or denigrates even the oldest works according to contemporary standards of a "liberated" appreciation. Ignoring historical, social, and artistic realities, this kind of minority criticism ends up being evaluative rather than cognitive and risks turning first-rate authors into second-rate ideologues or vice-versa. At best, many detractors would claim, minority criticism can offer little more than thematic studies and a writer-reader exchange of subjective consciousness. It is true that Northrop Frye and the Geneva School have shown how thematic studies, especially of myths (both external myths incorporated into the literary work and internal myths created by the work itself), and the phenomenological exchange of perceptions are central to the understanding of a work. Yet the most recent exponents of formalism, critics like Ricardou and Kristeva, insist that even these critical techniques are neither sufficiently rigorous nor sufficiently textual.

Conscientious minority critics whose primary concern is the comprehension of literature, and not its ideological annexation, may well be dismayed by their situation. For it is undeniable that few, if any, minority studies have attained the degree of textual precision seen in the best of contemporary criticism. But because of mitigating factors, their distress should be no more than provisional.

It seems only reasonable to assume that fledgling schools of criticism must recapitulate, even if at a more accelerated rate, the development of mature criticisms. Since mainstream literary criticism had to pass through biographical, historical, and thematic studies before arriving at linguistic and semiological analyses, cannot a similar growth pattern be expected from black, feminist, and gay criticism? The theoretical and practical lags of minority criticism compared to mainstream criticism are obvious. But such lags are more the historical effects of past negligence on the part of mainstream criticism toward minority concerns than an indication of permanent incapacities on the part of minority criticism. It is in fact unjust and even oppressive for mainstream cricitism not to recognize the difficulties of minority criticism in simultaneously correcting the past, participating in the present, and positing a future. For mainstream criticism must, after all, bear a good part of the responsibility for the conditions that repressed minority studies until only recently. Louie Crew and Rictor Norton have suggested that "Homosexual literature is not in the mainstream, not because the mainstream is heterosexual, but because the mainstream is homophobic."[1] That statement is as valid for criticism as for literature, and when mainstream critics attack minority critics for immature or inaccurate methods, they are really underscoring their own prejudices and failures.

That minority critics have not yet directly addressed texts in a formalist manner does not lead to the conclusion that they cannot do so. The proposal contained in the following remarks is that minority critics can indeed speak to texts just as directly as mainstream critics do.

II. The "Homotext"

Forster's early realization that sexuality plays a key role in criticism as well as literature is astute and timely. It is nonetheless a simplification of the problem, for there is no single sexual bias to work out in criticism. Rather, there are several.

First, there is the most blatant kind of bias that ignores, belittles, and distorts minority sexuality in literature.[2] It is this kind of criticism that inevitably leads to condemnatory judgments, even if passed in silence, and causes women writers to be excluded from anthologies or authors like Forster himself to withhold manuscripts for posthumous publication. Such a completely uncritical attitude really doesn't warrant further commentary. There remains but one irony to remark: although no one will openly endorse such flagrant sexism, it is nevertheless still the most prevalent form of sexual bias in criticism.[3]

The second kind of sexual bias in criticism is a blend of commendable intentions and questionable methods. Certain critics, amateurs and professionals alike, focus on minority sexuality in literature from the viewpoint of the author, not the text. The notion of the "biographical fallacy" proved long ago that an easy and self-evident proportion cannot necessarily be established between a writer and his writings. There are of course intimate and causal ties between the two, but they are much more subtle and intricate than is usually suggested by critics who treat fictions as merely literary transpositions of biographical facts. This approach can be valuable in that at least it opens up the issue of minority sexuality to critical inquiry; but it fails to the degree it falls into the very traps set out by formalists to demonstrate the textual impertinency of minority criticism. Applied judiciously, the approach certainly merits a place in critical methods — authors like Gide and Genet, who readily admit a close relationship between their works and themselves, seem particularly suited to minimizing the errors of the technique — but even in the most favorable cases, its use must remain as limited as its results.

The third form of sexual bias — "bias" meaning a taking of sides — in criticism is found in the text itself. Although this may seem to be a confusion of literature and criticism, the problem is only apparent and is resolved by recalling the axiom of all contemporary criticism: any text is self-referential, an implicit criticism of itself. The text, then, is the most fertile area for an investigation of the sexual bias in criticism, for it is there that minority sexuality becomes meaningful in a literary, and not merely ideological or biographical way. Before elaborating a critical construct to deal with particular forms of textual sexuality, however, there must be reason to believe that sexuality does in fact enter into the very fabric of the text. In short, before defining "homotextuality" the existence of the "homotext" must be determined.

Even the earliest writers recognized a link between literature and sexuality that went deeper than the presence of erotic topoi; but their insights were more often intuitions than critical concepts. The most convincing proofs of such a link are the modern ones. In an analytic manner, Freud and his heirs, especially Brown, Holland, and Marcuse, have postulated the primacy of sexuality not only in the artistic process but also in the art product. A less systematic, almost mystical view of literature as a privileged field for the transgression of sexual taboos, among which homosexuality must certainly rank high, has been expounded by Georges Bataille in *Death and Sensuality* and *Literature and Evil.* Some critics might willingly grant that sexuality affects the literary work, but only on the level of content. This token acceptance, however, offers no advance from previous and unproductive views of minority sexuality in literature and disregards another tenet of all modern criticism: although form and content are not always identical, they are always inter-related. As one critic states, "form is itself but the working out of content in the realm of super-structure."[4] No less than the author and the critic, then, the text takes sides on sexuality, and subdivisions of sexuality should produce corresponding textual distinctions. The existence of the "homotext" seems probable. To pass from the probability to the certainty of its existence, however, the quantitative and qualitative distinctive features of the "homotext" would have to be delineated in detail. What follows is an attempt to do that.

Before proceeding to the examples which constitute that attempt, a word about the title of this study is in order. The term "homotextuality" may arouse suspicions. It sounds too slick, like a sleight of hand concept. Yet ideas far more deserving of mistrust have been effectively camouflaged by more moderate and impartial sounding titles, especially in the way "scientific" psychoanalytic vocabulary has crossed over into literary analysis. Perhaps the paradigm of words which seem unquestionably denotative but which are nevertheless often connotative is "sexuality."

As an abstract or generic idea, the concept of sexuality is valid. But in specific applications it is unwieldy and uninformative, unless it is reduced to its more precise components such as heterosexuality, homosexuality, bisexuality, and asexuality. These reductions are not always announced; they are in fact most often assumed in silence. No one speaks of "heterotextuality" because there is no need to. The idea of textual sexuality implies textual hetero-sexuality, just as courses in "sex education" could, for the most part, more accurately be called courses in "heterosexual education." What is confronted, in short, is what could be called *the heterosexual assumption*, the same kind of majority assumption that presumes blacks can identify with white values while refusing a reciprocal identification. So it is that the "heterosexual assumption" passes from life into literature and "Virtually all discussions of sexual symbolism in literary works are accompanied by a heterosexually biased innuendo."[5]

The term "homotextuality" will be successful, then, if it is understood within the context of the two goals it is designed to achieve: first, to raise consciousness by contrast about the unspoken assumptions and prejudiced plausibility of mainstream criticism in its dealings with literary sexuality; second, to minimize the abuses of well meaning but misguided apologists for minority sexuality in literature by severing literary homosexuality from exclusively biographical or social sources and allying it at last to the text.

III. Homotextual Structures of Transformational Identity

As a minority group, homosexuals are usually placed in the company of other minorities, chiefly women and blacks. Such comparisons can be productive, but the truly distinctive features of homosexuality would have to be those which distinguish homosexuals from other minority groups as well as from majority groups. One such feature would be the homosexual's ability "to pass." That is, unlike other minority members, homosexuals have the choice of revealing or hiding their stigma. Short of flagrant appearances or mannerisms that fulfill the expectations of heterosexual stereotypes of homosexuals, one's homosexuality is not an *observable* phenomenon.

For the homosexual, then, a dialectical tension with a hostile environment is established, and studies concur that this conflict between self-denial and self-affirmation is the most marked feature of homosexual life in the homophobic Occident.[6] Perhaps this helps to explain Jean-Paul Sartre's fascination with the homosexual as a paradigm of the Self-Other struggle that is at the core of the phenomenological ontology in *Being and Nothingness* and the expansion of his *Saint Genet, Actor and Martyr* from a literary exegesis into a monumental philosophical statement. Having constantly to exercise one's freedom in the choice of an identity is painful and anxiety-provoking, and the homosexual has a special understanding of Sartre's statement that man is *condemned* to freedom. He also has a profoundly personal comprehension of the problems of "authenticity" and "bad faith," for his pain and anxiety are augmented by the fact that it is not only a question of his affirming or denying his homosexual identity to others; it is as much, and maybe even more, a question of his affirming or denying that identity to himself. (To that extent, "passing" is not really an escape from stigma. At best, it is usually a means to contain internally the dilemma of identity conflict. It persists, of course, as an elusive possibility for resolving such conflict, but it is really an impossibility except in a superficial way or for a person who has little or no self-consciousness.) By need and by nature, the psycho-dynamic of the homosexual is fluid and could be called transformational in the sense that it is comparable to transformational grammar: out of an underlying "deep structure" (the homosexual identity) emerge many variations of "surface structure" (either an affirmed or assumed heterosexual identity or, at the very least, modified and repressed forms of a homosexual identity). Given the codeterminative nature of artistic form and content, there is no need not to expect "homotexts" to accommodate this state of constant psychological flux with structures of identity exchange, which in fact they do. And the most frequent and efficacious means — no doubt because it captures all the intricate dimensions of the Self-Other / Self-Self problematic — is that most polyvalent of symbols: the mirror.

Speaking about the most homotextual of authors, Richard N. Coe finds that "the mirror is the most obsessive symbol in Genet's thought . . . the symbol of the whole of Genet's world."[7] Specific examples from Genet's work are too numerous to detail, but one might readily select as a prototype the scene in the *Thief's Journal* where Stilitano literally fights to escape from the Hall of Mirrors at the Fun-Fair in Antwerp. Examples from other authors are no less abundant: the simultaneous attraction to and repulsion by his mirror image on the part of Daniel, the homosexual in Sartre's *The Age of Reason*, matches his inability to accept his deep identity in "good faith" and forshadows his heterosexual marriage in the last volume of *The Roads to Freedom*; certainly Cocteau's fascination with mirrors, especially in *Orpheus*,[8] goes beyond the mere exploitation of stage and cinematic resources; C. P. Cavafy frequently incorporates mirrors into his poetry; and the first verifiable confirmation Michel, the protagonist of Gide's *The Immoralist*, has of his deep homosexual identity is the indirect exchange of mirrored glances with an Arab boy.

The presence of mirrors in "homotexts" becomes especially striking if mirrors are understood in a figurative as well as literal sense. One of the reasons why it is impossible to read Wilde's *The Picture of Dorian Gray* as anything other than a thinly veiled "homotext" is because the structure of identity transformation is so pivotal to its plot. Dorian's portrait stores up his deep identity, from his age to his acts, and allows a surface identity to pass in public. But the climax of the story must necessarily come when the identity exchange breaks down and the surface Dorian is joined to the deep Dorian with the resulting fulfillment of death wishes and self-hatred. A similar use of the painting as a mirror occurs in the episode of Reni's "St. Sebastian" in Mishima's *Confessions of a Mask* where the martyred youth brings the protagonist Kochan to an awareness of his own persecuted deep identity.

Characters can also serve the same function in relationships that make them either mirrors of each other (that is, mirrors of the Self), like in Genet's *The Maids* and *Deathwatch*, or masks for each other (that is, mirrors of the Other), like in *The Blacks*. Of all identity games, however, the most interesting one occurs in the type of character who fabricates a mirror image for himself and exists as both fiction and fact. This self-contained double is the kind of identity mirror emphasized in works like Gautier's *Mademoiselle de Maupin*, Cocteau's *Thomas the Impostor*, Virgina Woolf's *Orlando*, and Mishima's *Forbidden Colors*. Finally, it seems more than coincidental that the young

Rimbaud made his famous observation "I is someone else"[9] shortly before becoming Verlaine's lover.

The ultimate homotextual mirror is of course the text itself. Because of its multiple narrative "Marcel"s and its labyrinthian turning in on its own form and content, Proust's *Remembrance of Things Past* is probably the epitome of possible examples. A much more accessible one, however, is the work of Gide: the "mise-en-abîme," or play-within-a-play, serves as a structural signature to virtually all his works; and two of his most suggestive metaphors — the True Pope-False Pope confusion in *Lafcadio's Adventures* and the true coin-counterfeit coin image in *The Counterfeitors* — are both extensions of the mirror which eventually calls itself, as well as the Self and the Other, into question. For the homosexual, as Gide once remarked to Ramon Fernandez, the lessons of the mirror inevitably lead to the examining and redefining not only of one's personal and social identities but also of one's artistic identity.

> I think it's quite right to say (as you have done so well) that sexual non-conformity is the first key to my works; but I'm particularly grateful to you for already having indicated, after that monster of the flesh, the first sphinx on my way, and the most devouring of them, through what evolution and because of what invitation my mind, its appetite whetted, went even further and attacked all the other sphinxes of conformity, which henceforth it suspected of being the brothers and cousins of the first.[10]

The obsession of "homotexts" with mirrors corresponds, then, to the homosexuals' inescapable awareness of their transformational identity. Unfortunately such mirrors are too often misread as nothing more than symbols of homosexual vanity, a compulsive concern with beauty and youth. Perhaps that is the legacy of psychoanalytic interpretations which emphasize only the self-love aspect of mirrors because it parallels the Freudian view of the homosexual's arrested emotional development and "primary narcissism." There are, to be sure, instances of mirrors which serve such a function, but they are atypical. More often than not, homotextual mirrors elicit responses like the following:

> It was time. As I got up, I stole one more glance toward those chairs in the sun. The group had apparently gone to dance, and the chairs stood empty in the blazing sunshine. Some sort of beverage had been spilled on the table top and was throwing back glittering, threatening reflections.[11]

The homotextual mirror not only provides reflections *of* the disquieting reality of a transformational identity; it also provokes reflections *on* that identity. Far from signaling a superficial vanity, homotextual mirrors signify a profound condition of sexual existence and point the way to a critical rediscovery of the ambiguity latent in the original Narcissus legend.

IV. Homotextual Space

When in 1929 Virginia Woolf discussed the woman writer's need of "a room of one's own," she was obviously referring to the need not only of physical space but also of psychological and social space, ultimately creating and reflected in artistic space.[12] Her comments did not pass into criticism, howerver, until almost thirty years later with the publication of Maurice Blanchot's *Literary Space* (1955) and Gaston Bachelard's *The Poetics of Space* (1957). The two works offer contrasting interpretations of literary space. For Blanchot, the text is essentially steeped in negation and solitude and is autonomous in its separation from non-textual realities.

> The writer's solitude, that condition which makes up his risk, stems from the fact that, in the work, he belongs to what always precedes the work . . . To write is to enter into the affirmation of solitude . . . The work is solitary . . . whoever reads it enters into its affirmation of solitude.[13]

In his work, Bachelard proposes a phenomenological investigation of "topophilia . . . to determine the human value of sorts of space."[14] The reasons for his project were simple enough, based on the primacy of subjective imagination in perception (images are arrived at through deformation, not formation), but far-reaching in their consequences for all architectures, whether of wood or words. What distinguishes his conception of literary space from Blanchot's is its positivity in affirming not solitude from the world but rather individualistic solidarity with it.

> Space that has been seized upon by the imagination cannot remain indifferent space subject to the measures and estimates of the surveyor. It has been lived in, not in its positivity, but with all the partiality of the imagination. Particularly, it nearly always exercises an attraction. For it concentrates being within limits that protect.[15]

Clearly, Blanchot is speaking about the space *of* the text and Bachelard of the space *in* the text. Yet the "homotext" reconciles these two contentions in a unique way.

Blanchot's space of alienation and Bachelard's space of protection are united by the concept of marginality. For the homosexual, marginality is both the price of his stigma and the escape from that stigma; he is both condemned to it and saved by it. Marginal or "homotextual" space should therefore appear in literature with the same significance and patterns it has in the personal experience of homosexuality.

For both authors and characters, the most frequent type of homotextual space is the closed and withdrawn place that is transformed from stigmatizing into redeeming space. The archtypal examples are the persistent dramas of *rooms* in Proust (Proust's own cork-lined room, the bedroom of the young narrative Marcel, and the hotel room at Balbec among others) and the prison cells in Genet's plays and novels and Wilde's *De Profundis*. Yet confinement, whether imposed or chosen, is not the only variety of homotextual space. One can also deliberately flee oppressive space by seeking out the marginal space of the open countryside, which is privileged space for the homosexual because it marks both his ostracism and the chance to recuperate his "unnatural" love in nature. This is the kind of space which Gide experienced in the North African desert (the episode is described in *If It Die*) and which led to an attempt to revitalize the bucolic tradition in his early work (that effort is discussed indirectly in *Corydon*). Perhaps the best explanation of such space is found in E.M. Forster's retrospective comments about his novel *Maurice* (1914) where the writer attributes the somewhat dated quality of the book for the contemporary reader to the following fact:

> . . . it belongs to an England where it was still possible to get lost
> . . . There is not forest or fell to escape to today, no cave in which to
> curl up, no deserted valley for those who wish neither to reform nor
> corrupt society but to be left alone.[16]

Forster's words are especially pertinent to *Maurice* because the polarity he establishes in the novel between London and the countryside parallels his view that oppression and repression stem from the middle and upper classes of society and that liberation necessitates an alliance with the lower classes. His portrayal of the guiltless caretaker may seem naive today, akin to a homosexual version of Rousseau's "noble savage," but it has a certain visionary quality about it. Coming from the European context of homosexual upper class estheticism, the protective social distance that enveloped the Parisian circle of Proust and Gide and the "Bloomsbury Group," Forster nonetheless foresaw the breakdown in class structure that would result from a militant and open sexual liberation (this same insight in Whitman was euphemistically defused by critics who spoke of his "democratic love").

Even from Bachelard's viewpoint, physical space is seen as something essentially static in its objective existence. For all its variables, it shares the concreteness of the Sartrean notion of "situation" or Heidegger's concept of "Dasein." Only our changing perception of that space saves it from absolute immobility. For the marginal figure, however, there exists an additional kind of space, a mediation between presence with and absence from oppressive space. It is the space of the "wandering Jew" and the gypsy: the fluid space of voyage, "Go," writes Vanya to Stroop in Kuzmin's *Wings* (1906) when he finally decides to affirm his homosexual identity, "and take me with you." [17] He is not speaking about flight in the sense of an escape that involves travel only as a means to a specific destination. He is referring instead to travel itself, an external itinerary that corresponds to an internal journey of self-discovery. For the marginal being, mobile displacement is both freedom from condemnation and an impetus to individual, idiosyncratic growth, which explains the persistence of voyage in Gide: Michel's travels in *The Immoralist*, the countless journeys in *The Counterfeitors*, the positive exile in *Fruits of the Earth* and *If It Die*, and the frequent use of the travelog as a literary genre. More recently, marginal movement plays a major role in the novels of Rechy and Burroughs and in the poetry of Ginsberg.

Of course these categories of "homotextual space" are not strict and frequently overlap. In "Calamus," for example, Whitman combines rural retreat and protective mobility into rustic vagabondage.

> We two boys together clinging,
> One the other never leaving,
> Up and down the roads going . . .
> No less law than ourselves . . .
> Fulfilling our foray. [18]

For marginal persons like Whitman, whose secret was such that "I dare not tell it in words, not even in these songs," [19] literary devices other than outright denomination must prevail.

> Here the frailest leaves of me and yet my strongest
>   lasting,
> Here I shade and hide my thoughts, I myself do not
>   expose them,
> And yet they expose me more than all my other poems. [20]

"Homotextual space" is one such device for marking the point where the song of the open road becomes a song of the self and provides additional proof of two coderivative propositions of contemporary criticism: literature does not develop in neutral space and space does not develop neutrally in literature.

V. Homotextual Language and Intertextuality

The limits of the present study obviously preclude an exhaustive examination of all the other directions that research into "homotextuality" could take, but at least two of the more vital ones can be outlined.

Like any subculture, homosexuals have created a minority code out of majority symbols, a minority "speech" within a majority "language." The most evident form of such minority communication is, of course, slang; and an understanding of homosexual slang is often indispensable to a text, as the reader of Genet and Rechy well knows. Curiously, however, there have been few systematic attempts to set down and define collective and individual homosexual slang. The most comprehensive attempt to do so is Bruce Rodgers' *The Queens' Vernacular* (San Francisco: Straight Arrow Books, 1972) but unfortunately it is deficient in both its scope — only rarely does it touch on the literary uses of slang — and its method of gathering data.[21] Since slang reveals much about both the context and the text, there is a pressing need to study it and such an effort should rank high in the priorities of "homotextual" critics.

Slang is certainly the most accessible form of minority language; but it is probably not the only one. Whether there are more subtle and ultimately more significant linguistic properties shared only by "homotexts" will, for the most part, have to be determined by future studies. There are, nevertheless, points of departure presently available to critics. An excellent one is Rictor Norton's comments about "pronoun pathology" and the dynamics of linguistic "passing" in "The Homosexual Literary Tradition."[22] Much suggestive material can also be found in Peter Farb's *Word Play* (New York: Alfred A. Knopf, 1974) and especially in the works by feminist critics, such as Robin Lakoff's *Language and Women's Place* (New York: Harper & Row, 1975), which examine the relationships between language and sexuality. Such research is perhaps the most difficult kind facing minority critics, for it demands highly specialized techniques and promises no positive results. But if Valéry is correct in his assertion that "Literature is, and can be nothing other than, a kind of extension and application of certain properties of Language,"[23] it is imperative to investigate — through syntactic studies and concordances, for example — the ties between sexuality and language not only on the relatively superficial level of slang, but also on the linguistic levels of discourse that are both more concealed and more revealing.

"Intertextuality" is the name given by the "Tel Quel" critics in France to the fact that books beget other books and that literature is a dynamic, self-generating, and unified whole rather than a static accumulation of unrelated works.[24] Within this area of research, one might explore the possibility that homosexual writers and works demonstrate a proclivity for certain genres. Or one might trace the network of allusions among "homotexts," showing how and why they are incorporated into and modified by individual works and whether they contribute to an esthetic self-consciousness that reinforces the widely held myth of a homosexual artistic superiority.

A particularly pertinent problem of intertextuality is the heterosexual appropriation of "Platonic" love in Renaissance and post-Renaissance European literature. To be sure, Socrates and Plato spoke frequently and seriously of spiritual love. But that is not all they spoke of and one can be fairly certain that after the oratorical celebrations of the spiritual love of boys in *The Symposium* had ended, more corporeal celebrations of a physical love of them quickly followed. It seems plausible to consider the development of the conceit of Platonic ideal love as a concession made by a Christian age to its excited but dangerous discovery of pagan thought. Between Athens and Renaissance Rome, the moral atmosphere of Europe had changed, to use Wainwright Churchill's terms, from "sex-positive" to "sex-negative."[25] Renaissance humanists risked heresy and death unless they could transform the open affirmation of the originally homosexual Eros of the Greeks into a form more acceptable to the standards of their own age. First such love was heterosexual-ized, then it was completely idealized. And what emerged was a concept that not only no longer subverted Christian morality, but actually supported the doctrines of symbolic love and the disincarnate union of priests and believers to Christ and the Church, and even strengthened the "sex-negative" environment.

A parallel but inverse process can be seen more recently in Genet's attempt in *The Miracle of the Rose* to appropriate a symbol of heterosexual love running from the Medieval *Romance of the Rose* and the Renaissance Pléiade poets like Ronsard and Du Bellay to the Symbolists and Surrealists of this century. To what extent Genet's effort is a parody — a serious, not comic, one — of heterosexual values and to what extent it is a sincere and positive attempt to forge a personal or collective symbolic tradition for homosexual literature — for he returns time and again to flower imagery — is a valid concern of the intertextualist.

What is most important to see, however, is that the issue at the heart of both these examples goes beyond literary history as it is usually understood. A close examination of the metamorphosis of "homotexts" into "heterotexts" and vice-versa would yield numerous insights that could be applied to the general problems posed by the literary use of literature.

VI. A Prefatory Conclusion

For a proposal to be persuasive, it must anticipate and respond to discouraging or invalidating criticism. This is particularly true in the present case, where space has not allowed for more than a sketch of the subject proposed.

The first objection to "homotextuality" will probably be that it has been treated as if it could develop in total isolation from the general givens of literature when, in fact, it cannot. Mirrors and voyage, to take two examples, are not any more exclusive properties of "homotexts" than is language. That is certainly true, but it does not disprove the possibility that they are quantitatively or qualitatively different when found in "homotexts." The horizon that I have attempted to open is not that certain texts are only "homotexts" but that they are "homotexts" as well as texts and that the failure to appreciate them in that light can be corrected.

There will almost surely be theoretical reservations about this kind of study. But they should really be reservations more about this *kind* of study than about this particular study. Wayne Booth has suggested that "To write one kind of book is always to some extent a repudiation of other kinds."[26] His comment can be extended, I think, to include critical articles which adhere to a certain mode of criticism. The fact that this study has investigated the formal properties of literary homosexuality should not be misconstrued as an endorsement of formalism as the only acceptable critical approach to homosexual literature. As I have said elsewhere,[27] the unstated ideological bases of formalism destroy any possibility of its being an ultimately objective or scientific criticism. The warning made by a famous structuralist about the limits of structuralism might best describe the spirit of the present study.

> . . . structuralism has a comparatively long history, and one lesson to be drawn from this is that structuralism cannot be a particular doctrine or philosophy; had it been, it would have long been left behind. Structuralism is essentially a method . . . Because it is a method, its applicability is limited . . . [28]

"Homotextuality" is not proposed, then, as *the* method of literary analysis for dealing with a specific form of minority sexuality in literature. Rather it is a proposal that should be integrated with other critical methods. It is a supplement to, not a replacement for, other kinds of criticism, and it would be a violation of the very liberation of minority sexuality in life, literature, and criticism to restrict its investigation to a single mode of thought.

Most of all, this proposal is an attempt to resolve the frustration of minority critics. Such critics develop, for the most part, within the academy where formalism has been the official critical voice for the past fifty years. It seems only natural that they should feel frustrated — a feeling that is encouraged by mainstream critics and their *preconceptions* about minority literature and criticism — with non-formalist methods and eventually search for meaning where they have been told it can only be found.

In a recent article, one critic points out that

> Readers over the ages have had to learn this game of literacy, how to conform themselves to the projections of the writers they read, or at least how to operate in terms of these projections. They have had to operate in terms of these projections. They have had to know how to play the game of being a member of an audience that "really" does not exist. And they have had to adjust when the rules change, even though no rules thus far have ever been published and even though the changes in the unpublished rules are themselves for the most part only implied.[29]

Ong's comments apply to the critic's audience as well as to the writer's. And not until only recently have homosexuals realized that, as writers, readers, or critics, they were expected to conform to majority projections of minority sexuality. The rules of that game can now be revised. "Homotextuality" is not so much a way to read texts as a way to reread them and to measure once again the disparity between the reactions that were implied or imposed and the substance that is really there. To that extent, the success of this proposal will not be measured by the acceptance of its title or even its principles but rather by the degree to which it enlightens mainstream and minority critics alike about past critical methods and the textual realities of literature. It does not propose that we fabricate significance where there is none; it seeks rather to lessen the likelihood of fabricating insignificance where there really is significance.

NOTES

[1]"The Homophobic Imagination: An Editorial" in *College English*, Vol. 36, No. 3 (November 1974), p. 280.

[2]Although any number of artists could serve as examples, perhaps the best model for showing how this kind of criticism victimizes the creator is André Gide. From the very beginning of his career, when he was viciously reprimanded by Catholic critics in France and had to publish *Corydon* privately and anonymously in its first edition, until the end of his life, when he was refused admission to the French Academy, was belatedly awarded the Nobel Prize, and had his entire work placed on the Index of Forbidden Books, Gide's sexual preference colored the reception of his works. Such treatment was not uncommon even posthumously, and in the January 1965 issue of *American Opinion* Renato P. Oliver called Gide "a self-confessed pervert" and then dismissed his work as "a superannuated bundle of bunk."

[3]In dealing with minority sexuality, silence is often the liberal's equivalent of the conservative's outspoken indignation. A good example of the persistence of this kind of criticism is provided by two very recent reviews of W. H. Auden's life and work in which Auden's increasing openness about his homosexuality is not even acknowledged. See Howard Moss' review of *Thank You, Fog* in *The New York Times Book Review* of January 12, 1975 and Hannah Arendt's "Reflections" on Auden in *The New Yorker* of January 20, 1975.

[4]Fredric Jameson, *Marxism and Form* (Princeton, New Jersey: Princeton Univ. Press, 1974), p. 329.

[5]Louie Crew and Rictor Norton, "The Homophobic Imagination: An Editorial," p. 286.

[6]See Arno Karlen's *Sexuality and Homosexuality* (New York: W. W. Norton & Co., 1971), Martin Hoffman's *The Gay World* (New York: Basic Books, 1968), Dennis Altman's *Homosexual Oppression and Liberation* (New York: Outerbridge and Lazard, Inc., 1971), Wainwright Churchill's *Homosexual Behavior Among Males: A Cross-cultural and Cross-species Investigation* (Englewood Cliffs, New Jersey: Prentice-Hall, Inc., 1971) and especially the chapters "Self-Other Processes" and "Passing and Being Known About" in Martin S. Weinberg and Colin J. Williams' *Male Homosexuals: Their*

Problems and Adaptations (New York and London: Oxford Univ. Press, 1974).

7*The Vision of Jean Genet* (New York: Grove Press Evergreen Editions, 1969), p. 7.

8Cocteau's choice of Orpheus seems especially significant when we read in Ovid's *Metamorphoses*, X, 79-85, transl. Frank Justus Miller (Loeb Classical Library), Vol. II, p. 71, that " . . . Orpheus had shunned all love of womankind, whether because of his ill success in love, or whether he had given his troth once for all. Still, many women felt a passion for the bard; many grieved for their love repulsed. He set the example for the people of Thrace of giving his love to tender boys, and enjoying the springtime and first flower of their growth."

9"*Je* est un autre," in Rimbaud's letter to Paul Demeny dated May 15, 1871. See *Rimbaud: The Complete Works and Selected Letters* (Chicago & London: Univ. of Chicago Press, 1966), a bilingual edition edited and translated by Wallace Fowlie, pp. 304-5.

10Quoted in Jean Delay's *The Youth of André Gide* (Chicago & London: Univ. of Chicago Press, 1963), p. 438. Other comments pertinent to the role of Gide's homosexuality in the structural aspects of his writings can be found in Germaine Brée's "Beyond Romanticism: Narrative Play in Gidian Fiction" in *Proceedings of the American Philosophical Society*, Vol. 114, No. 3 (June 1970), pp. 163-67.

11Yukio Mishima, *Confessions of a Mask* (New York: New Directions Publishing Corporation, 1958), p. 254.

12Virginia Woolf, *A Room of One's Own* (New York: Harcourt, Brace & World, Inc., 1929).

13Maurice Blanchot, *L'Espace littéraire* (Paris: Gallimard "Idées," 1955), pp. 14, 27, and 11.

14Gaston Bachelard, *The Poetics of Space* (Boston: Beacon Press, 1969), p. xxxi.

15Bachelard, p. xxxii.

[16]E.M. Forster, *Maurice* (New York: New American Library, 1973), p. 250.

[17]Mikhail Kuzmin, *Wings: Prose and Poetry* (Ann Arbor, Michigan: Ardis Publishers, 1972), p. 110.

[18]Walt Whitman, *Leaves of Grass* (New York: W. W. Norton & Co., 1965), ed. Harold W. Blodgett and Sculley Bradley, p. 130.

[19]Whitman, p. 132.

[20]Whitman, p. 131.

[21]For a critique of Rodger's research techniques see Jim Kepner's "Homosexual Imagination" in *The Advocate*, No. 155 (January 15, 1975), pp. 26-7.

[22]"The Homosexual Literary Tradition" in *College English*, Vol. 35, No. 6 (March 1974), pp. 674-92 and especially p. 687.

[23]Quoted in Tzvetan Todorov's "Language and Literature" in *The Structuralist Controversy* (Baltimore & London: The Johns Hopkins Press, 1972), ed. Richard Macksey and Eugenio Donato, p. 125.

[24]For the clearest and most concise exposition of this concept and others of the "Tel Quel" group, see Jean Ricardou's "Rethinking Literature Today" in *Sub-Stance*, Vol. 4 (Fall 1972), pp. 65-72.

[25]*Homosexual Behavior Among Males: A Cross-cultural and Cross-species Investigation* (Englewood Cliffs, New Jersey: Prentice-Hall, Inc., 1971). See especially chapters VII, VIII, and IX.

[26]*The Rhetoric of Fiction* (Chicago & London: Univ. of Chicago Press Phoenix Edition, 1967), p. 136.

[27]"Toward a Gay Criticism" in *College English*, Vol. 36, No. 3 (November 1974), pp. 303-10. See especially pp. 306-7.

[28]Jean Piaget, *Structuralism* (New York: Harper & Row Torchbooks, 1971), pp. 136 and 142.

[29]Walter J. Ong, S.J., "The Writer's Audience Is Always a Fiction" in *PMLA*, Vol. 90, No. 1 (January 1975), p. 12.

Teaching Gay Literature
In San Francisco

By James E. Brogan

From the time I first arrived at San Francisco State from Yale Graduate School in 1967, I always wanted to teach a course in gay literature. I even went so far as to ask my now-retired chairperson for such a course in my second year. I suspect she was against teaching the course at that time primarily because of the political climate; 1968-1969 was the year of the big strike and as a faculty participant, I was particularly vulnerable to the whims of the administration, or at least that is what she told me. She later told me that she had really wanted me to teach the course, but she thought I ought to have tenure first, so I would be protected. She also suggested that it might be too emotionally dangerous to teach, that students between the ages of eighteen and twenty-five often had too confused and tenuous a sense of sexual identity for such a course. This advice activated some deep fear within me. Of what? Student nervous breakdowns and attempted suicides?

She certainly proved correct on the nature of the political climate. About a year later seven young English professors who had been active in the strike, including myself, were provisionally and personally fired by President S. I. Hayakawa, even though they had been supported for retention by the English Department and the Dean of the School of Humanities. No reasons were given. Subsequently some of us were re-instated the following year and I went on to get tenure in 1970-1971. But since no reasons were given for firing us, all of us were free to invoke any kind of personal paranoia available to explain our bad fates. Even though I was the only one of the seven who was gay, I certainly wondered more than once whether or not they *knew* — and were out to get me. In my mind I made an implicit connection between homosexuality and being fired, even though there was no rational justification for such a connection.

By Spring 1972 most of the hopes of the striking teachers and students had long since been broken and we were forced to return to the dreary "business as usual" principle which attempted to reduce us to intellectualizing zombies. Once again I decided to set out on my adventure. I soon discovered I had chosen the right time to do so. It is hard to say why a particular culture reaches a point when it can tolerate something that was previously inconceivable, but it was clear that the time had come. Perhaps enough Gay Liberation had filtered into the consciousness of most of our faculty so that the appropriate analogies were tacitly made with other minority groups without our having to overcome months of the usual ambivalence to new ideas. In any case several faculty members, gay and non-gay, made suggestions to the proper committees for a gay lit course and the course was approved on an experimental basis. And even though several faculty members had indicated that they might be interested in teaching such a course, it took only some gentle politicking on my part to assure my getting it, for I knew that most academics at that time would shy away from the real-life pressures of such a course. Even so I was extremely grateful to all who suggested and defended it.

Spring 1972 was my own personal "spring training." As far as I knew (I know now that I was simply ignorant), there were no such accredited courses at that time, no precedents by which to justify myself. Then there was also the issue of *how* it was to be taught. I was already teaching a contemporary fiction course called "Problems in American Identity" in which, except for explicitly revealing my homosexuality, I discussed many aspects of my personal life and encouraged students to do the same in class and in their writing. Would the system tolerate this degree of frankness on the subject of homosexuality in class? I knew that many of our gay students would insist on open, honest class discussions and would not be satisfied with just a historical survey of gay literature. But was there any line I should fear crossing between personal expression and professional misconduct? Who would judge such distinctions? Would I be accused of trying to "convert" students? What about all those fears which society had put into me about students "freaking out?" What about scandal — what kind of trouble could there be?

The truth is that I decided to make a concentrated effort to understand my irrational paranoic side because I was very eager to grow beyond it *before* beginning the class. Fortunately for me from the time I was fifteen I had been able to talk to two of my high school teachers about my homosexuality. Since then I have always accepted it and have judged myself on my capacity to love, not on which sex I loved. So when I was about to teach this course, I was overwhelmed by a wonderful release of creative energy. I immediately researched and compiled an anthology of gay literature, both out of intellectual curiosity and a desire to "know my field" a little better. If anything, I had delusions of power — and much guilt for feeling this new power. Society's aversion to homosexuality has always been so strong that unconsciously I began to feel I had immense potential to threaten people. On the other hand I was greatly relieved that I at least was going to be one teacher who might break through the academic mystique about homosexuality, a mystique that seemed composed of both intellectual toleration and prurient curiosity, and that seemed to allow only for its underground existence. (Strangely enough, even though I am now into my tenth semester of teaching this course, this mystique is still extremely strong. Not one colleague over thirty-five, heterosexual or homosexual, has asked me a direct question about the course.)

My "spring training" sessions of inner conflict and dialogue were dramatized in psychotherapy. My therapist, whatever his opinions, played the part of my internal hysterical parent (whom I was all too good at repressing in myself) and constantly tried to show me how frightened I really was. "You've been fired once in the strike with a union supposedly protecting you; who will protect you when you're out on a limb by yourself?" He also suggested I wanted to teach the class possibly out of destructive motives. "You are increasingly isolating yourself in your risks so that when disaster strikes you can have revenge on those who let you down in the past." I'll probably never know what degree of truth such suggestions contained, but one result they did have was to break down the facade of my militancy. My repressed fear soon erupted. I wrote in my journal in March, "Will I become a marked man, a followed man, a bugged man, someone whom the system would be out to 'get,' given the least provocation for doing so." I discovered it was very hard to distinguish between irrational paranoia and "rational" political fears. Just three days before I received final approval for the course, my therapist suggested I could be putting myself in a politically dangerous situation that had nothing to do with me. Such a "logical" argument evoked a great deal of fear, especially when he suggested our having an extra session if I needed it — at 6:45 P.M. Friday night! Even though *he* now seemed like the hysterical parent, I did get in touch with a great deal of repressed fear in myself. I declined his offer and "toughed it out" myself. For about a day I even watched in amazement as a self-hating part of me hoped the course proposal would be turned down. But by the next day I had the final approval of the department and I was ready to disclose to all my classes what my teaching schedule for the Fall Semester would be. The step had been taken. Thus six months before the course I had thoroughly examined my feelings and assessed the risks. I decided I was strong enough to confront whatever situation might develop, even a lengthy courtroom trial.

I guess it's clear from this brief account of my feelings how the social oppression of homosexuals creates great barriers to personal liberation in the form of both rational and irrational fears. Inside all gay academics is a voice which warns, "Who is to say the pendulum won't swing back to the 'dark ages' of mysterious and secret firings?" At this point, even though I looked forward to the excitement of this adventure, I still felt very much isolated.

II

My sense of isolation decreased over the course of the summer of 1972 when I met three other English professors who planned to teach gay literature courses in September. The most positive re-assurance came from Sacramento State, another member of the California State College system, which was reported to have a series of courses which comprised a Gay Studies program. (If I had only known this during the Spring — or was it really ultimately beneficial to have lived through all that fear?) I met Charles Moore, who taught the gay literature course there, and we greatly reinforced each other. The cautious side in me was appeased. Faced with an already established group of gay courses at one school, surely the Chancellor or the Trustees wouldn't pick insignificant me as the object of their first attack.

Another development in my life which greatly relaxed me that summer was the beginning of a relationship, the quality of which allowed me for the first time in my life to feel personally content. Much has been said about the difficulties gay people have in meeting each other. Certainly the classroom has the potential to bring gay people together in a much more positive context than bars or other ghetto institutions. This is an opportunity I wanted to give gay students, but I was relieved when it no longer became something I needed for myself. There have been countless marriages and affairs between hetero- sexual teachers and their students, but I was glad not to have to battle the added internal conflicts which would necessarily result from feeling that my classes were perhaps the best source of meeting someone, even though I would vigorously defend the personal rights of any two adults to begin a relationship, no matter what the context of their meeting. (How ironic that I might feel guilty for having this social advantage over other gay people when heterosexuals have the chance of meeting each other virtually anywhere.)

I had decided that in order to protect myself from criticism, I should emphasize the historical development of the literature in my first attempt. But I could not quite hold to this resolution; I finally offered the somewhat more thematic design of my anthology, which uses the literature to develop a pattern of personal liberation. In this way I figured I could anticipate the one great complaint which students might have, namely that the level of gay conscious- ness in practically all the literature was far behind their own 1972 San

Francisco awareness, that in fact they really couldn't *learn* anything from gay literature except historical content. This fear has been justified, but I have been partially successful in trying to use our perceptions about the literature as a springboard to evoke the issues and problems that everyone really wanted to discuss. These early cases did suffer from a feeling of disjunction when we jumped from talking about current ideas to "irrelevant" literature, no matter what its quality. Nevertheless, at that time, it was important to me to give a "legitimate" English department course.

My first weeks of teaching the course were filled with tensions and anxiety. I really didn't know what I was in for. And I still can't conceive of teaching a course which has so many profound emotional problems to confront. I knew it took guts on the students' part just to sign up; once enrolled they had no idea what was expected of them or how they should act. At first I assumed *all* the responsibility for the class, since I had been so indoctrinated that students might "freak out" if exposed to ideas of sexuality they could not handle. I was willing to tell everything about myself, but I respected the fears of students who didn't want to speak in class. I left myself starved for feedback and then sought it from them outside of class whenever I could. I almost tried to keep students apart from each other and kept making apologies for one group to another. It was exhausting, but I felt I had an awesome responsibility as a mother-hen teacher to protect everyone from fears. I simply had to pay the price of this pressure until I was sure I knew what I was doing. But, happily, the students had a great deal of constructive energy and seemed ready to take the risk of getting in touch with people "different" from them. And we had an off-campus party very early in the semester at which everyone in the class went around asking each other "What are you?" Silly as that sounds, the party relieved a great deal of the early pressure.

Because of my own emotional needs, it was inevitable that a part of me would be a "gay chauvinist" for at least a semester. Sometimes I even felt that *only* gay people should take the course; after all these years of oppression, didn't we deserve at least one course of our own? I encouraged gay students to enroll and discouraged anyone whom I felt was a mere curiosity seeker, especially heterosexual women. I now realize that this was a foolish mistake of inexperience, and I'll later explain why. I even got annoyed when we started discussing anything not directly related to homosexuality.

This first class had about thirty-five students, about half of whom were gay men. There were a few gay women who were unusually quiet. Of the dozen or so heterosexual students, eight had already taken at least one course from me before and had clearly developed some trust in me as a person. The few heterosexual men remained very quiet throughout the course, but what chance did they have against our sense of oppression and outrage? There was almost no enrollment from outside the department; the gay grapevine I fantasized about never developed at all. Nor was there the slightest bit of publicity.

Even though I had some residual fears about revealing my gayness in class and using explicit language, I did so anyway, and the class responded by developing an atmosphere of openness and ease about homosexual subject matter that somewhat alleviated the tension. We even read (and brought its author to class), an erotic novel so that everyone in the class had to at least confront the idea of physical acts between members of the same sex. In this class, as well as in all the others which followed, the differences in students' worldly experience was staggering — all the way from seventeen-year-old women who had barely begun to experience their sexuality to hearty veterans of life in their forties. It was fascinating to watch the interaction, and I felt very good that I could help people overcome their prejudices.

But my initial chauvinism somewhat backfired. My own high, personal expectations for what all human beings could accomplish were constantly in conflict with the more guarded, skeptical opinions of an informal male gay ghetto that soon developed. I discovered that I was least effective as a teacher with gay male students, most of whom had been kicked around considerably by their families and the world. Their vulnerability to new ideas and experiences was low since most of them had been hurt so much. Most of them didn't believe it was possible to be both gay and happy; mere survival was just about all they asked out of life. Furthermore, try as I might to avoid its happening, many gay men played out the problems they had relating to older, male authority-figures. They resented a "superior" gay man who pretended both to be happy and "know all the answers."

On the positive side, virtually every gay person in the class told or wrote me that he/she now had a better self-image because of the course. This was particularly true of several older men. And just as gratifying was the appreciation I got from heterosexuals. Although quiet for the most part, everyone of them had learned a great deal about homosexuality. Because we emphasized roleless relationships, many of them said they were forced to confront their own sexual feelings from a new perspective which would help them avoid lapsing into unsatisfying roles with the opposite sex. Furthermore, lo and behold, no one seemed to have been adversely affected by the course. Despite my inherited superstitions, the influence the course has had on all people has seemed overwhelmingly positive.

III

Second semester I changed the title of the course from "The

Homosexual in Literature" to "Homosexuality in Contemporary Fiction." Even with this switch of focus most of the writers were still far behind the level of awareness of most students in the course. I dropped the formal study of Greek, Roman, and Renaissance writers, although I occasionally still introduced poetry, short stories, or fictional excerpts from such writers as Dickens, Whitman, Cavafy, and Lawrence. And I continued to stick to my resolution not to study writers such as Rechy, Burroughs, and Genet who tend to deal primarily with the peripheral world of hustlers, drugs, and surrealistic fantasies. Instead we concentrated on more socially grounded writers such as Isherwood, Baldwin, and Mary Renault of *The Charioteer*. More and more helpful books became available; this second class got a boost from Forster's *Maurice*, Isabel Miller's *Patience and Sarah*, and Dennis Altman's *Homosexual Oppression and Liberation* coming out in paperback. Since then we've added Rita Mae Brown's *Rubyfruit Jungle* and Patricia Nell Warren's *The Frontrunner*. I've also tried to get students to give me copies of their books at the end of each semester to start an informal lending library since I've had great problems with some novels going out of print.

This time the course had about thirty students with a lower percentage of gay men and a higher percentage of heterosexual women. The same tensions existed among students during the first weeks as the previous class, but I myself was considerably more relaxed. I also began to trust students' strengths more. After all, their enrolling in the class was meaningful in itself since many students were afraid of having such a course on their transcript. They were ready to learn, ready to look at themselves honestly. There was so much good energy that it became clear they didn't just want to study literature; they wanted to participate in making a new one. And so we wrote poems, accounts of real life experiences, fantasies, and short stories which we shared with each other. When I learned about what my students had done and wanted to do with their lives, my respect for them greatly increased. No gay male ghetto materialized, and I felt the class had been particularly worthwhile for the young gay people as well as all the non-gay students.

Encouraged by the successes of the first year's courses, I decided to try two major experiments during the next school year, 1973-74. The first was to put the course in our department's Pilot Project, an experiment in which we could give courses during the semester for more than the standard three units of credit. This meant the gay literature course had to receive the approval of the School of Humanities Council. Thus for the first time the course had to be officially approved by an authority outside our department. This change meant longer classes, more time to discuss the problems of both life and literature as well as added opportunities for outside speakers and student presentations.

Most important I felt I could spare class time for students to meet with each other in small groups. I had changed my attitudes a great deal in a year; I now felt it was the *responsibility* of each student in the class to be able to communicate with other students and about their reactions to the course. But I still held off from establishing permanent small groups; just as with the class parties, I simply wanted these groups to facilitate good feelings and understanding among students.

The second experiment was to introduce bisexuality as a major theme. I changed the title to "Homosexuality and Bisexuality in Contemporary Literature" and added such works as Isherwood's *A Meeting by the River,* Penelope Gilliatt's *Sunday Bloody Sunday*, and Ingrid Bengis' autobiographical *Combat in the Erogenous Zone*. The purpose of this second experiment was to encourage all kinds of students to enroll, for what I principally meant by "bisexuality" was something spiritual, a feeling of openness in which everyone is invited to explore personal identity as fully as he or she is able and is encouraged to relate as best as he or she can to both sexes. (And I did have more fears to overcome. For example, would I now be accused of trying to "convert" or "corrupt" even heterosexual students?) This inclusive philosophy was at first resented just a bit by some gay students who wanted and needed their own course. But my personal growth was such that I could no longer be spokesperson for any one group. As I became a self-loving gay person, I realized how important it was for someone to try to teach a course from the perspective of human liberation.

In this bisexual course I honestly feel that the books that we read are about people, whether heterosexual or homosexual, whether man or woman. In my first two attempts I felt this spirit was somewhat hindered by a few students who were militant spokespersons for their particular groups, whether that by gay men, lesbians, or women in general. I try not to underestimate the strength of oppression bearing down on any group, but my goal in the classroom is to try to create an environment where such problems can be at least temporarily transcended, where a few students don't victimize other students with their anger, however justified it is. I reached a point then of no longer even being consciously curious about the sexual identity of the students at the beginning of the course — the whole process of discovery of personal labels now seems routine and reductive. This class included a mother and son, as well as four students taking the course a second time to stay in touch with its changes and its reinforcing environment. I was delighted to find that many of the students often met with each other for coffee after class, even the ones who were the most argumentative and proselytizing.

We also had some interesting guests. One was a heterosexual student friend from the East who had just had his first sexual experience with a man; he read his impressions from his diary to get some feedback. Another visitor to San francisco was one of my personal saviours, one of the high school teachers with whom I had discussed my homosexuality. He talked about his own bisexuality and how he handled his homosexual feelings over the years, even though his personal life centered on his wife and two children. The class was especially interested in how and what he taught his children about their own sexuality as they grew up.

Beginning with the Spring Semester 1974, I realized how important an experience it was for all students in the course to meet in regularly scheduled, permanent small groups on their own. I also decided to reserve the first month of the course to thoroughly examine the dynamics of both gay oppression and sex role programming. Thus, along with Altman's book, I added Weinberg's *Society and the Healthy Homosexual*, Abbott and Love's *Sappho Was a Right-On Woman*, and Nichols' *Men's Liberation* to our required reading. After these initial classes in which we all discussed and compared our oppression in relation to the categories we happened to be in, I then strongly encouraged us to concentrate less on the political issues of our particular groups and more on the common emotional problems we all shared, problems which were blocking us from becoming autonomous human beings.

Propelled by an initial outburst of ethusiastic energy concerning our potential for emotional growth, we were able to carry forward with this new focus for a while. But our momentum could not be sustained until the end of the semester. Exam time found most members of the class pretty well able to accept each other as human beings, but not able to accept themselves as potentially happy people who were no longer oppressed and victimized by our society. Certainly the deepening of the recession allowed them to justify the despair and cynicism they felt within their alienated selves. Even so, when I left school at that time for a sabbatical leave, I was disappointed that we had not yet established in class a true community of equals in which the majority of us were able to transcend our sense of sexual labels and to think of ourselves as teammates who were fighting for human liberation in general.

IV

All this changed when I returned to school for the Spring 1975 Semester. It didn't happen immediately. During the first month, we suffered through the usual nervousness, anxiety, and long periods of silence in class. But by midway through the semester it was evident that many students were able to trust both me and each other in a way which students had never been able to do so before. There wasn't much humorous bantering or glibness of any kind, but there definitely was some listening and communication going on. It was evident we were beginning to really respect ourselves as well as respect each other. Nor did anyone ever jump on anyone else for saying something controversial. Soon we were volunteering very important information about our own personal feelings. Clearly a majority of us were letting ourselves become vulnerable to a positive experience. By the end of the semester, it was evident that we had established a human community which had focused not only on the particular problems of homosexuals, but on the problems each of us must resolve in order to become self-loving enough to discover and then obtain our own unique version of our positive fate.

Before I indicate what some of those problems were, I feel I should suggest an answer to the question of why the course was successful in 1975 in a way in which it had never been before. There is no doubt in my mind that I had grown somewhat as a person while being on sabbatical. I returned as a more compassionate, less judgmental teacher who was able to help everyone in the class feel really welcome. But I think an even more important reason for this success concerns major changes that are now beginning to happen in our culture. For example, several heterosexual men, whom I did not know previously, enrolled in the course and a couple of them soon acknowledged their bisexuality. Moreover, many of the heterosexual women in the course were able to participate actively in the class, without feeling guilty about using their intellectual and emotional powers. This honest, active participation by the heterosexuals in the class enabled us all to break down the barriers between heterosexuals and homosexuals by allowing us to see each other as equally damaged, whether by social oppression or sex role programming. When we all realized how self-defeating it was to identify ourselves as members of a particular sex or sexual identity, we all heaved a sigh of relief and then finally began to catch on to the fundamental problems which all of us shared.

What we discovered was that the most important problem which all of us had to face concerned how we could outgrow our self-hating, alienated selves to become more self-loving, autonomous individuals. As a first step we realized that we could all give each other different, helpful perspectives on how to become aware of our self-hate and how its destructive energy works within us to prevent us from being happier. We also caught on to how our self-hate, whether in the guise of insecurity, inferiority, or a thousand other possible shapes, contaminates and often destroys our relationships. Thus, we created our community through the process of our trying to develop a language through which we could communicate to each other about the damage which had been done to all of us which had caused us to become self-hating. By learning to speak the same language, we were soon able to give each other permission to feel more worthy and deserving of love and happiness.

Another positive change now occurring in our culture which helped all of us grow together was our common apprehension of bisexuality as a real, tangible new force in society. When I first began teaching this class over four years ago, I thought of bisexuality only as a theoretical possibility — and so did everyone else. The people I knew who actually did have sexual experiences with both men and women seemed even more confused and alienated from themselves than those of us who limited ourselves to one sex. Right now this whole situation is definitely changing. Beginning from a common acceptance of the bisexual spirit which I discussed earlier, we were able to make the crucial perception that a good deal of the sexual desire which all of us experience comes from our alienated selves, that our society does, in fact, program us not only to pursue people as sexual and romantic objects, but also to pursue conventionally "attractive" people who cannot in any way satisfy our deeper needs. Because almost our entire class was able to agree that these imposed forms of sexuality were self-defeating, we allowed ourselves a rare opportunity to think about what our unalienated, true sexualities might possibly be. One of the conclusions we came to was that our true sexuality would be based on our responsiveness and the sharing of warmth, never on performance. Another conclusion many of us reached was that once we shook off our obsessions about successful performance and also overcame all the many forms of sexual and emotional repression which had been imposed on us, we *would* be bisexual, at least to the extent that we would allow ourselves to discover a secondary, sexual preference within us.

Our acceptance of the bisexual spirit also enabled us to discuss the issue of monogamy in a way which no longer caused a schism between men and women or between the heterosexuals and the homosexuals. Once we shared the bisexual spirit, all of us admitted our need to have emotional intimacy, if not sexual intimacy, with more than one person, thus establishing an ethic of openness for relationships in general. In previous classes this had been a very divisive issue, causing a great amount of insecurity and defensiveness to surface. This time we were able to approach the whole issue of sexual life-styles through the consciousness of how we might have been programmed by our sex roles to be either for or against monogamy. No doubt it was also of at least equal importance that we were all able to agree that jealousy and possessiveness were manifestations of our self-hate. Thus we came to see that the real issue did not have anything to do with an individual's sexual life-style. The real issue became our common need to grow into self-loving autonomy so as to not poison our relationship with what we came to call "the contaminated spirit of monogamy."

All this actually happened in 1975 and all of it happened while we were reading contemporary literature about gay and bisexual people in a cooperative spirit of trying to respond to it in such a way as to help each other grow in a rapidly changing world. All of us were aware that at this time the community we created within the tolerant, frontier spirit of San Francisco was something that we would have difficulty duplicating in our own lives in the outside world. But once we had actually established this environment of mutual understanding, reinforcement, and affection in the sanctuary of a particular classroom, all of us finished the school year much more predisposed towards acknowledging the possibility of our creating such an environment for our own everyday lives.

Homosexuality in the Crucial Decade
Three Novelists' Views

By S. James Elliott

When the Second World War ended on August 14, 1945, Americans entered an era which one historian has characterized as the Crucial Decade.[1] The years from 1945 to 1955 were crucial for two reasons. First of all, America was involved in an intense ideological conflict. No sooner had the fight against Fascism ended than the new ideological threat of Communism emerged. A hot war in Korea, a cold war with the Soviet Union, and a dirty war with so-called Communists at home flared up simultaneously. In all of these conflicts, America's own ideology, that of the capitalist nation, became more and more clearly defined.

Secondly, Americans were confronted with both economic and social changes on the home front. In the fifty years preceding the Second World War, the simple agrarian economy of the 1800s had grown cancerously into the complex industrial capitalism of the twentieth century, and this change had brought prosperity to the nation. With the prosperity came social liberation. Many women found jobs and left the home. Among the nascent urban intellectual class, Sigmund Freud's work opened a new era of free discussion in sexual matters. And in the big cities, sexual tolerance grew and a gay sub-culture was beginning to form. A feeling of optimism prevailed; greater prosperity was expected and with it more liberation. But when the prosperity came to a sudden end in 1929, and shortly thereafter Americans were marched into an unwanted war, the optimism turned sour. As America emerged from the Second World War to head on a new path of prosperity, critics questioned: Would this prosperity last and bring needed change to the nation? Or would it, shortlived as the preceding boom, lead only to economic crash and another, perhaps even more terrible war?

Homosexuality became a national issue just at the moment of political crisis, when the twin issues of ideological conflict and the merits of prosperity had sparked off a bitter political debate. To be sure, homosexuality had always been present in America, both as a reality and as a literary theme. But only after the Second World War did the major American news magazines begin to print articles on homosexuality, and the *Reader's Guide to Periodical Literature* listed homosexuality as a separate category only after 1955. No doubt, homosexuality owed much of its new position in the public eye to the *Kinsey Report* (1948), a survey of American male sexual behavior which documented, among other findings, a large incidence of homosexual activity.[2] The *Kinsey Report* was reviewed in most major American newspapers and magazines, and though many critics were harsh, especially in regard to the chapter on homosexuality, the Kinsey collective had nevertheless succeeded in bringing the gay issue to the public attention. From now on, homosexuality would take its place among other national controversies.

It took its place too in the political novels of the Crucial Decade. The left-wing and liberatarian authors who began to write after the Second World War were concerned first and foremost with the issues of ideology and prosperity; but, open to new ideas, most were aware of homosexuality, and some included it as a minor theme in their works. Ultimately, of course, this minor theme of homosexuality was colored by the major themes of ideology and prosperity. By looking at three post-war authors, this chapter attempts to show how.

I

Perhaps the brightest and most talented writer to emerge among the left-wing literary lights after the Second World War was Norman Mailer. At the time of the publication of his first novel, Mailer was a Communist sympathiser, who campaigned vigorously for Henry Wallace. Even when the shock of Stalinism rocked the radical camp, Mailer remained true to his Marxist convictions, finding a new home in Trotskyism. Most recently he has defined himself as a liberatarian socialist. Mailer's war novel *The Naked and the Dead* (1948) used the image of the United States Army in World War II to present a cross-section of American social types. A platoon of enlisted men displayed the spectrum of the American lower class; the officer corps represented the upper class. The war itself was seen as a pointless and degrading venture, the burden of whose cruelty fell primarily upon the lower class. That Mailer lashed out with such vindictiveness against the inequalities and inhumanities embodied in the American Army and by implication in the American ideology is all the more startling when one thinks that Mailer was writing at a time when most Americans were basking in self-righteous patriotism. Mailer's strong social analysis of the American class system and his tough criticism of the inhumanity of this ideology are to be commended.

His treatment of the homosexual is not. The major villain of *The Naked and the Dead* was General Cummings, the son of a Midwestern parvenu and a ruthless career officer. Cummings' father had climbed to the top of the American class ladder in order to gain power over others. Cummings inherited this megalomanic trait and rose in the military to achieve the same power over the underlings of society. That the exercise of his power meant depriving other human beings of their rightful freedoms did not trouble Cummings; instead, he regarded the oppression of men through force and terror as the inevitable result of society's historical process of consolidation. "The machine techniques of this century demand consolidation," Cummings theorized, "and with that you've got to have fear, because the majority of men must be subservient to the machine, and it's not a business they instinctively enjoy." Far from attempting to avoid the Fascism implicit in forced subservience, Cummings saw Fascism as a historical trend and admired Hitler for his ability to capitalize on it. "I tell you," he argued, "that Hitler is not a flash in the pan . . . He has the germ of an idea, and moreover you've got to give him political credit. He plays upon the German people with consummate skill." In the crass figure of General Cummings, Mailer has related the ideology of the American military to that of Fascism.

This critique of personal megalomania, historical consolidation, and a dangerous tendency towards Fascism was justified and aesthetically well-executed. But Mailer could not resist one last touch. In a sketch of Cummings' earlier years, he led the General into a gay bar in Rome and let him find a homosexual contact. Mailer believed, he explained later, "that there was an intrinsic relationship between homosexuality and 'evil'."[3] It seemed to him *symbolically* justified to underline Cummings' evil of fascist ambition with a light brush of the supposed evil of homosexuality. Similarly, a villainous police agent, another representative of an unjust system and the enemy of the Marxist ideology with which Mailer sided, was characterized as a homosexual in Mailer's second novel, *Barbary Shore* (1951).

Mailer's third novel left the criticism of war and the American and Fascist ideologies and took up the second major theme of the era: the prosperous society under boom capitalism. To Mailer, the society that blossomed after the Second World War was only a cover-up for the evils of capitalism, all of which still existed under a veneer of prosperity and liberation. Written in 1955, Mailer's novel bore the title *The Deer Park*, an allusion to the corrupt court of Louis XV. Mailer's modern parallel was a rich California resort town called Desert D'Or. This name already implied the duplicity which Mailer wished to expose: it looked golden, but it was really a desert. The new prosperity was transient and reaped only by vice: the protagonist of the story, Sergius O'Shaugnessey, had won a fourteen thousand dollar fortune through gambling, but later he lost it in the same way. Just as Sergius' prosperity was false, so he too was merely an impersonator. "I have always felt like a spy or a fake," he admitted to himself. Like O'Shaugnessey, virtually all the characters in *The Deer Park* led masquerade existences. Even the radical of the story finally gave up his convictions and disguised himself as an exponent of the American ideology so as to be able to make films and money. Behind the facade of this new prosperous society, all moral values crumbled. Gambling, prostitution, free sex and drugs constituted much of the Desert D'Or's entertainment. The new prosperity, Mailer seemed to insist, was but a trick which brought with it not positive liberation but only moral decadence.

This critique of a phony prosperity, like Mailer's criticism of the capitalist ideology, was well-argued and bore the ring of truth. But once again Mailer could not resist pinpointing the evil in a homosexual character. The homosexual in *The Deer Park* was Teddy Pope, a good-looking film star. Pope's attractive exterior offered film-goers an image of out-going heterosexuality, which, of course, they bought eagerly. But this picture of heterosexuality was only an imitation concocted for the marketplace. Inside, Teddy Pope was a rather pitiful homosexual. Just as the society of *The Deer Park* only masqueraded as prosperity and brought with it in reality nothing but corruption, so Teddy Pope presented himself falsely as a heterosexual, while in fact offering only something that Mailer viewed as a sexual immorality.

Thus, Mailer used homosexuality in two ways. First, in the figure of General Cummings, he employed a homosexual metaphor to underscore the evil of the capitalist ideology. Then, in the figure of Teddy Pope, he used the homosexual image to reveal the duplicity and underlying immorality of the new prosperity. But why? Should not the man who characterized himself as a liberatarian socialist have been the first to recognize the need to vindicate the homosexual from a myth of evil? Was it not politically foolish of Mailer to lay the blame for the wrong-doings of capitalism at the door of a helpless minority, instead of heaping it upon the desks of the ruling class, where it belonged? Why did Mailer take an approach that defamed the homosexual and at the same time eroded the message of his own works?

There is a double answer to these questions. First and most simply, Mailer slandered the homosexual out of ignorance. In a later apologia for the vilification of the homosexual, Mailer claimed that he had known no homosexuals at the time he wrote *The Naked and the Dead* and that his first contact with a homosexual came at the time when *The Deer Park* was virtually finished.[4] Not understanding the homosexual as a human being, Mailer used the homosexual as a symbol in his works.

Secondly, Mailer did have strong prejudice against the homosexual, because he used homosexuality not just as a symbol, but specifically as a symbol of evil. His prejudice had two roots, each of which can be traced through a character in *The Naked and the Dead*. One of the few positive characters in Mailer's war novel was a Brooklyn Jew named Joey Goldstein. Flanked by racial prejudice, Goldstein perceived the racist nature of the war against Japan; a member of an oppressed minority, he objected to the inhumanity of war. But Goldstein was isolated in his discontent with the system and realized that he alone could do nothing to change conditions. Like his grandfather, Goldstein accepted Jewish suffering as fate and sought only to reduce his personal distress. This he did by retreating into the Jewish family, a haven which offered him some pleasure as a drug against the ills he was fated to endure. Of Goldstein's marriage, Mailer told us: "They are content and the habits of marriage lap about them like a warm bath. They never feel great joy but they are rarely depressed, and nothing immediate is ever excessive or cruel." This retreat into an anaesthetic marriage was perhaps a solution for Goldstein the Jewish male, but it was problematic for women and carried serious consequences for gays. For if traditional marriage and family life is the ideal, then women must be forced into the role of a child-bearing servant, and homosexuals, as non-family men, excluded from utopia. Goldstein's retreat resulted in sexist prejudice.

The second positive character in *The Naked and the Dead* was a liberal officer, Lieutenant Hearn. From the start, Hearn rebelled against authority. But Hearn's rebellion remained personal; he was never really part of a protest on a broader level; and standing alone, he was doomed to failure. As a boy, Hearn revolted against the camp counselor who forced him to make his bed; but the young Hearn was too weak to revolutionize the camp. Compelled to obey, he could only restore his hurt ego by lashing out viciously at a boxing opponent later in the afternoon. At Harvard, Hearn protested against the bourgeois ideology, but the Marxist forces rejected him as a bourgeois idealist, and once again Hearn stood alone and powerless. This time he patched up his damaged pride by joining the football team and making crude comments to women. In the Second World War, Hearn revolted against the cruelty of General Cummings, but once more he was defeated and humiliated. He left the officer corps for the platoon, where he hoped to restore his ego by being the order-giver instead of the order-taker. In all of these cases, Hearn's protests against authority failed because he was isolated, and each time Hearn, frustrated by defeat, sought to repair a wounded pride by resorting to such male chauvinist antics as boxing, football, caustic sexism, and war-time heroism. This last-ditch attempt to save one's ego resulted, of course, in a chauvinistic derision of supposedly inferior minorities like women and gays. Hearn made superioristic comments to the "weaker sex" and viewed gays as inferior creatures who had submitted to the society against which he so courageously fought. "When nothing else is left," Hearn mused, "I'm going to become a fairy, not a goddam little nance, you understand, but a nice upright pillar of the community, live on green lawns."

These two types — the traditionalist Jew and the male chauvinist liberal — represented no one more accurately than Norman Mailer himself. For Mailer was a Brooklyn Jew who, in a series of five marriages, looked for some sort of happiness in the family. And he was the frustrated radical from Harvard, who, unable to effect change, vented his feelings of inadequacy in a now historical male chauvinism. Mailer's failings are obvious, but it is important to look back at Goldstein and Hearn to find the reason for his prejudices. Just as Hearn and Goldstein were isolated and never found a movement through which to effect positive change, so Norman Mailer found himself alone and ineffective after the War. The radical movement was dissolving. The working class had been co-opted by unions which promised a bigger slice of a growing prosperity, and the War had convinced many to drop the protest against their native land to crusade against the foreign evil of Fascism. Without a vehicle to express his discontent, Mailer was without protection and personally wounded; like the similarly threatened and humiliated Goldstein and Hearn, he retreated to the family and protected his ego with chauvinistic blasts.

II

But Mailer was not the only man on the retreat in the post-war decade. After the War, liberals found themselves in much the same predicament. The traditional liberal hope lay in the belief that one could reform the system and progressively better the world. A linear development of economic gains, technological advancement and education would lead man into a better state. But after the Second World War, this optimistic view had been shattered. The progress of history, it appeared, was fitful, for the hopes of prosperity and liberty expressed in the twenties had brought only war and Fascism. At the same time the liberal hope of reform collapsed, the radical alternative soured too. The Hitler-Stalin Pact, the bloody purges in the Soviet Union, and the knowledge of the high price Communists had paid for their economic gains had convinced liberals that there was nothing to be hoped for in Marxism either.

Pessimistically, the liberals retreated to the very roots of their thought and found comfort in the belief that man was by nature good, however corrupted he may be by the society around him. The eighteenth century French philosopher Jean Jacques Rousseau had been the first to expound a theory of man's innate goodness and the infectious evil of society. His belief in the goodness of man and the evil of society led him to the call "Back to Nature!" Man was cajoled to redeem his unspoiled innocence by leaving society and going back to nature. Rousseau's idea of natural innocence was, however, colored by his bourgeois ideology. Nature meant to him the relationship of man to woman, the process of reproduction and the family. His own life gave a model for such thought. He lived in a free marriage with Therese Levasseur; but although the pair refused, in protest to the demands of society, to legalize their marriage until 1768, it remained a heterosexual union. They stayed together and produced children. Whereas such a conception of "Back to Nature!" may have offered something to heterosexual man, it was as problematic for women and gays as Mailer's ideal of the Jewish family and male chauvinism. Nature meant that the "nature" of woman was to remain faithful to her mate and bear children; and the homosexual, as the non-reproductive, supposedly anti-family man, was then "unnatural."

One such Rousseauian liberal, with bitterness towards society and a belief in a natural kind of marriage, was Gordon Merrick. Merrick's novels began with the cirticism of ideology and prosperity common to the post-war decade, but instead of offering political alternatives, they posited only an ineffective and sexist utopia of nature in which woman was chained to her man and the homosexual appeared as the vile enemy. Merrick's first novel, *The Strumpet Wind* (1949), dealt with a liberal Army Intelligence officer, Roger Chandler, who was sent to France after the Allied troops had succeeded in pushing the German occupational army out of Marseille. Chandler's duty was to arrest an agent of the Vichy government, a certain Mercanton, who had been radioing information on Allied troop movements to a German spy ring. Chandler was then to stay with Mercanton on the latter's farm, maintaining radio contact with the Germans in hopes of catching bigger fish.

But Merrick's novel did not illustrate the triumph of the American ideology over Fascism; rather, it struck out at both ideologies from the standpoint of humanitarian naturalness. Roger Chandler secretly disliked the ideology he served. A man of great personal charm who peacefully accepted life, he hated intelligence work because it had no respect for humanity. Particularly the pose as a double agent, which he viewed as the exploitation of a personal friendship to serve a cold ideology, offended his sense of the obligation of honesty that each man owed his fellows. For Chandler, people came first and ideology second.

Since Chandler's sympathies lay not with the ideology he was forced to serve but rather with a more general commitment to the preservation of the dignity of man, he ended up becoming friends with his ideological opposite Mercanton. A certain basic human trait in Mercanton appealed to Chandler. Not unexpectedly, this trait rooted in a liberal conception of nature and natural innocence. Mercanton was completely naive and trusting. He lived on a farm, far away from the battles and corruption of Marseille; his wife was devoted to him; and he had several children. During his stay with Mercanton, Chandler grew closer and closer to this idyll of farm and family life. He befriended Mercanton's wife and even took a hand in raising the children.

The enemy of this liberal idyll was seen in ideology, which florished in the corrupt atmosphere of the city. The representative of American ideology, Chandler's superior George Meddling, established his headquarters in an expensive villa near Marseille. Meddling was a distasteful individual whose commitment to personal ambition and consequent devotion to the American ideology led him to enjoy the humiliation of mankind his job entailed. He beat and tortured Mercanton with satisfaction. In a similar way, the representatives of the Nazi ideology were portrayed as corrupt members of the urban society. Mercanton's first contact with a Nazi spy occurred in a vulgar apartment in Paris, and later an ugly Fascist spy convinced Mercanton to work for the Germans out of ideological opposition to the Communists. In both camps, urban corruption, devotion to ideology and inhumanity went hand in hand.

Merrick was quick to add the metaphor of homosexuality as a spice to the stew of evils he had cooked up. George Meddling was an attractive bi-sexual who used sexual attraction to forward his career. The Nazi ideologues too were associated with homosexuality. When Chandler arranged to meet a higher-up in the German spy ring, the Nazi contact led him into a gay bar in Marseille. "Vice hides behind vice," the Nazi explained to Chandler, thus linking the evil of their spying to the supposed moral evil of homosexuality. Finally, Merrick brought all the threatening elements together in a climactic tour-de-force. He had Meddling stumble into the bar at the crucial moment and make a few awkward passes at Chandler. In one compact scene, Chandler faced all the evils that hovered over the liberal idyll: the American and Fascist ideologies, urban corruption, and homosexuality.

The end of the story need not concern us. Suffice it to say that the homosexual ideologues succeeded in destroying the liberal paradise. Mercanton was shot, and Chandler's blossoming love affair with a young French woman ended in her suicide. Throughout the story, the vices of the city, the moral evil of homosexuality, and the threat of ideology stood in tragic opposition to the liberal ideal of simple, apolitical, heterosexual life in nature.

Merrick's second novel, *The Demon of Noon* (1954), turned from the critique of the ideologues to the theme of the prosperous society. The hero of *The Demon of Noon*, Stuart Alsop, was described as a liberal type who left the immoral world of his rich parents and the New York society of the booming twenties to establish his own private utopia of nature and the family on a stretch of land on the southern coast of France. Resolved to wrest his fortune from nature in a clean fight rather than to resort to the dirty exploitation of his fellow men, Alsop became a wine farmer. He brought with him his mistress Marthe, whom he never married out of resentment towards the legalization of what he viewed as a natural relationship, and their son Robbie. For a while, the family lived comfortably in the surroundings of nature.

No sooner had this paradise blossomed, however, than the society of prosperity closed in on it. For the coast of Southern France, of course, was the French Riviera, and Alsop watched silently as the neighboring village expanded violently into a roaring resort. Against his will, Alsop was persuaded to sell part of his land to a real estate speculator, and the bargain brought him millions. Like it or not, Alsop was catapulted out of his rural idyll into the urban society of prosperity.

As much corruption flourished in the resort town of Merrick's *The Demon of Noon* as in Mailer's *The Deer Park*. On the yacht of a British admiral, many times married, sons and daughters cavorted incestuously with one another. Alsop also made the acquaintance of a German playboy with a tainted past, who was later revealed to be a Nazi spy. By showing representatives of both the British and German military, Merrick made the point that prosperity only covered up but did not eliminate the evil of ideology; by demonstrating the sexual frivolity of the new society, he emphasized that prosperity brought with it only immoral entertainment and not true happiness.

This prosperous society against which Merrick moved with such vindictiveness was laced through and through with homosexuality. In the resort town, Alsop stepped mistakenly into a gay bar. Just where the evil was most prevalent, Merrick added a dab of homosexuality. The British admiral's son was gay. And the German playboy was bi-sexual. Once again, Merrick brought his work to a climax by knitting all the supposed evils together: the German playboy seduced first Alsop's wife and then Alsop's son and led them both to Fascist France. Thus, marital infidelity, homosexuality, and Fascism are all lumped together in a tragic culmination of evil.

Merrick's next two novels centered predictably on the twin issues of ideology and prosperity. But in these works the homosexual villain had disappeared and was replaced by a malicious female. In *The Vallency*

Tradition (1955) the hero, Lance Vallency, escaped the immoral world of the New York social elite, which was epitomized in his rich and tyrannical mother. Rejecting the corrupt prosperity, he lived in poverty with his mistress and three children in a Central American country. But just as Vallency's happiness in nature and the family became complete, his mother moved to destroy him. She used her money to bribe officials, implicating him in a murder plot from which only further bribes could free him. Lance Vallency had to concede to his mother's demands to save his own throat; he surrendered and returned to New York.

In *The Hot Season* (1958), a liberal diplomat in a country caught between Soviet and American ideologies sought to support an indigenous revolutionary who would save his country from the demands of the capitalist and communist powers. The diplomat failed in this attempt, and, at the same time, his wife flirted with a journalist who staunchly supported the American intervention. Thus, *The Vallency Tradition* identified the corruptness of prosperity with a rich woman, and *The Hot Season* paralleled the triumph of ideology with the unfaithfulness of a diplomat's wife.

The elimination of the homosexual villain from Merrick's novels hardly constituted progress; it meant only that the author had to find another scapegoat. From the viewpoint of his idyll of nature and family, the homosexual was an ideal symbol of evil, but since the family was involved, an unfaithful woman was equally suitable. Merrick's utopia of nature and the family was simply sexist. In order to write a positive novel, he must seek a political alternative to the ideology and prosperity he criticized, an alternative that is not just a refuge for some, but a valid society for all.

III

In both Mailer's and Merrick's works, the homosexual was vilified in the political fight. Both the radical and the liberal author had retreated into narrow utopias from whose vantage point gays looked like an enemy, and both slandered the homosexual as the representative of the adverse ideology and the false prosperity. In times like these, it was tempting for the homosexual to view the political battle with distaste, since many of the rocks thrown in the ideological debate bounced off onto homosexual heads.

When the homosexual Gore Vidal began to write, then, he strove first of all to put an end to the moralistic rock-throwing. His first novel, *Williwaw* (1946), told the story of a ship's encounter with an Alaskan snow storm while on a routine voyage towards the end of World War II. The novel contained no political comment on the Navy nor on the ideology the American military embodied. The battle is not with an ideology but with the natural phenomenon of the snow storm. Moral tension entered the story only in the squabble of two of the ship's men over the affections of an island prostitute. Their struggle culminated when one of the men watched his rival fall overboard and made no effort to rescue him. The captain became aware of the situation, but he initiated no lengthy investigation, and no one was punished. Just as Gore Vidal refused to damn the American ideology, he also advocated suspension of judgment in moral matters, particularly those arising from sexual disputes.

If *Williwaw* refused to take up arms against the problem of the American ideology and of man's sexual behavior and its results, so Vidal's second novel, *In a Yellow Mood* (1947), abstained from the political criticism of the post-war prosperity it described and pointedly refused to take sides in matters of sexual morality. The central figure of the story, Robert Holton, was a young executive in a brokerage firm. Whereas some authors would have used this vantage point to criticize Wall Street capitalism and the masquerade of prosperity. Vidal remained neutral. Holton neither condemned nor affirmed the system within which he worked; he simply did his job. Similarly, when Holton was wisked away by a homosexual art critic to a gay bar in the Village, where he was shown a series of lewd gay dances, and seduced by the wealthy wife of a famous artist, who would leave her husband for him, Holton did not condemn either the sexual deviance of the man nor the marital unfaithfulness of the woman, though he did not himself desire to follow their way of life. Both the woman and the homosexual were vindicated in this novel, albeit only through a complete suspension of moral values.

Having written against the political and moralistic trends of the post-war period, Vidal set out to eliminate the homosexual stereotypes that had been created. At the age of twenty-one, he published a best-selling gay novel with the title *The City and the Pillar* (1948). "I decided to examine the homosexual underworld," Vidal explained later, "and in the process show the 'naturalness' of homosexual relations, as well as making the point that there is of course no such thing as a homosexual."[5] Vidal's novel related the life of a young Virginian from a middle class family who was not bright but was a good tennis player. In the course of the novel this youth, Jim Williard, experienced all the stereotypes of the gay world. His first lover was a Hollywood film star whose duplicity related him to Mailer's Teddy Pope. Willard's second love, Paul Sullivan, was a frustrated radical writer who represented the stereotype of the homosexual ideologue. But whereas Vidal did show both stereotypes — that of the phony film star and that of the gay ideologue — in these two figures, he also wanted to make the point that there is no causal relation between homosexual behavior and either ideology or pseudo-prosperity. In Jim

Willard, he developed a homosexual character who, by conventional American standards, is "normal" in every respect but his homosexuality. "I set out to shatter the stereotype by taking as my protagonist a completely ordinary boy of the middle class," Vidal explained.[6] It is the possible normalcy of homosexuals that Vidal wished to emphasize.

He used the same technique in a powerful short story written in 1950, "The Zenner Trophy." The protagonist here was another conventional American male. Flynn was the star athlete of his high school and was scheduled to receive the school's highest athletic award, the Zenner Trophy, when a scandal erupted over his affair with a fellow student. The teacher whose duty it was to tell Flynn he would not receive the trophy was surprised at the boys's coolness. Flynn was not vindictive; resolved to remain normal even when the world around him seemed crazy, he maintained an air of balance and good sense.

In two following works, Vidal turned directly to the problem of the vilification of the homosexual in the political debate. His play *The Best Man* (1960) depicted the heart of a political struggle: at a national convention in Philadelphia, two top political candidates, the liberal intellectual William Russell and the Middle American career politician Joe Cantwell, vied for their party's nomination for the Presidency. Russell was the mouthpiece for Vidal's indignant protest against a political system that decided its issues on the basis of mere personal quirks and private moral convictions. "You have to pour God over everything like ketchup," former President Art Hockstader coached Russell, but Russell, who did not believe in God either as the Creator or as a political issue, refused. His opponent Cantwell, on the other hand, was willing to invoke the name of the Almighty at every politically opportune moment. The Voice of the American Woman, Mrs. Gamadge, revelled in the pictures of Cantwell with his wife and two sons at the barbecue, but Russell was too honest to exploit a false image of marital bliss. In every respect, Cantwell played upon the moral feelings of the people, whereas Russell courageously fought according to the issues alone.

The dirtiness of this political fight became more apparent in the second act, when Cantwell revealed that he had secured psychiatric files on Russell which, harmless in their content but frightening to an ignorant public, would put an end to Russell's career. At the same time, Russell received documentation that Cantwell was a homosexual. The ambitious Cantwell released his information, certain that Russell would be too honest to exploit Cantwell's homosexuality. Here he was right. Russell withdrew from the race, throwing his support to a third candidate, who, though unknown, had the advantage of a clean record.

The Best Man was a piece of Vidal's political optimism. The courageous political candidate, through an act of devotion to a higher ethic than personal ambition, had saved the homosexual from slander. In reality, however, Vidal knew that the homosexual could expect no such respite. In 1967 he published a novel which recanted this optimism and revealed the homosexual's dismal position on the political scene. *Washington, D.C.* presented a panorama of political types, and each type finally stooped to some sort of underhanded maneuvering. The central figure in the story was the man who manipulated others most ruthlessly: Clay Overly. He owed his career in part to the clever exploitation of two homosexual figures. First, he attracted the wealthy newspaper magnate Blaise Delacorix Sanford, who used his power to forward Overly's career at every turn. Then he secured the affection of a one-time liberal journalist, Harold Griffiths, who stylized Overly into a great war hero and dedicated politician. Overly's hold on Griffiths improved when the journalist was arrested by two Vice Cops who tried to blackmail him. Overly freed his ally from their clutches, but not out of any devotion to the homosexual cause. Rather, Overly was trying to score points in the political debit system. By helping Griffiths, he could be certain that the journalist would now grant him any favor he might ask.

Of the political writers of the Crucial Decade, Vidal was the only open homosexual, and his works therefore exerted a certain appeal in the way they dealt with homosexuality as an important issue. But the hopes Vidal offered led into blind alleys. His attempts to vindicate the homosexual from slander resulted in a dangerous amoralism. In *Williwaw* he was forced to pass over the whole American military without comment and to pardon an act that amounted to murder. His novel *In A Yellow Wood* left the homosexual and the woman free to follow their own way of life, but it let post-war capitalism free to go its own way too, and it extended blanket amnesty to virtually any kind of sexual behavior. When Vidal tried to extricate the homosexual from politics, he ran into similar contradictions. *The Best Man* could help the homosexual only by fictionalizing an ideal character, but Vidal himself must have realized that men like William Russell were rare in real life. In *Washington, D.C.* he rejected this hope and recognized that politicians were ready to exploit the homosexual ruthlessly when it suited their purposes. It was criminal for the homosexual to withdraw from politics, and it was foolish for him to think he could leave the world of politics.

But this alone is not cause for despair. Neither the radical world of Norman Mailer nor the liberal world of Gordon Merrick is essentially opposed to the homosexual. Mailer later apologized for his vilification of the homosexual, and Merrick wrote two graphic gay novels in the early seventies.

The problem of these political authors was only that they wrote at a time when there was no hope in a broad political front and retreated into narrow ideals of their own. Far from choosing to back away from politics, which will only lead others to retreat further, the homosexual must play an important part, convincing radical and liberal writers of the importance of the homosexual theme and leading them out of their ignorance and narrow moralism by indicating a broader political ideal which offers happiness not just to some, but to all. Only under such a broad political concept can the homosexual join others and fight for change and a better world. And those writers too can gain only from such an ideal.

NOTES

[1]Eric C. Goldman, *The Crucial Decade: America 1945-55* (New York: Alfred Knopf, 1956).

[2]Alfred C. Kinsey, Wardell B. Pomeroy and Clyde E. Martin, *Sexual Behavior in the Human Male* (Philadelphia: W.B. Saunders Co., 1948), esp. pp. 610-66.

[3]Norman Mailer, "The Homosexual Villain," in *Advertisements for Myself* (New York: G.P. Putnam's Sons, 1959), p. 223.

[4]Ibid.

[5]Gore Vidal, "An Afterword," *The City and the Pillar Revised* (New York: E.P. Dutton and Co., 1965), p. 245.

[6]Ibid., p. 246.

The Life
Below The Life

By Michael Lynch

Like the spire of some bright Satanic mill, Richard Howard juts out above the grinding landscape of contemporary American literature, an industrious talent and an industrial power to be reckoned with. He has published five volumes of poems. He has translated just about any bellettrist of modern France you'd care to read, poets excepted, totalling (by his count) around 150 works. His critical essays and reviews seem to appear, as Moby Dick was rumored to do, ubiquitously and simultaneously, and he has brought out two critical anthologies: *Alone With America*, a bouquet of forty-one essays about, and often for, contemporary poets, and *Preferences*, a handsome, original coffee-table ornament designed to popularize "modern" verse by showing its continuity with the pre-"modern." He directs the Braziller poetry series, edits poetry for the *American Review*, and in his spare time teaches a seminar at Yale.

Howard also ranks as a force in our gay consciousness. He has participated in the first two conferences of the Gay Academic Union. He edits poems for *Out*, or did, before that In item went Under. His essays include discussions of Allen Ginsberg (a Columbia elder classmate), Frank O'Hara, Daryl Hine, Thom Gunn, James Merrill, Edward Field, and — perhaps most movingly — of Paul Goodman as "the true heir and disciple of Whitman":

> If he had written only poems, he would I think have held the place
> in American poetry today that sexuality, say, has in our assessment
> of human possibilities — central, flawed, affording occasions for joy
> and fulfillment.[1]

In his own poems Howard has dealt with props of the camp sensibility such as Dietrich and Rossini: with gay (or probably gay) figures such as Crane, Wilde,

LITERATURE

Whitman, James, Tennyson, and Hölderlin; and with the historical milieu that saw the emergence of modern gay liberation in late Victorian and early twentieth century England. Neither has he omitted poems of personal gay intimacy, such as "For S.," nor the mandatory Corydon idyll and Hadrian allusion (though he has yet, to my knowledge, to publish a Ganymede poem), nor the wittily erotic, as his poem spoken by a snake-swallower:

> Straight off, and I was just a boy
>   Before I started in,
> They tasted queer: sticky, tart
>   But sweeter too, like tin
> When you bite on a knife.
>
>   . . .
>   It helps to get there first
> With a finger of gin.

("Richard, May I Ask a Horrible Question? Isn't it Painful When Two Men Make Love Together?" is the title of another poem. Richard's reply: "When / two men make love apart, that is the most painful.")[2]

It is Howard's poetry as gay poetry I consider here. For whatever reason he has not appeared in *Manroot, Sebastian Quill,* or *The Male Muse,* but more than any of those who have he has inquired into the meaning of being a gay poet. He has explored in multiple ways a double answer: it is to be historical, recognizing one's place in a tradition of gay poetry, and it is to be non-historical, here in the everlasting and mysterious present of sexuality and speech. With all the risk of a schema, I'll suggest two: that Howard's historical consciousness has involved an interplay between two traditions, the life of artifice and the life of nature; that issues of sex and issues of poetic speech have come to be seen as one issue, as two manifestations of one event. Howard's first two volumes — *Quantities* (1962) and *The Damages* (1967) — assumed, in brief, one mantle of the camp heritage, that of (in Sontag's phrases) "the consistently aesthetic experience of the world. It incarnates a victory of 'style' over 'content,' 'aesthetics' over 'morality,' of irony over tragedy."[3] *Untitled Subjects* (1969) disclosed the historical roots of this high-gloss aestheticism in Victorian England and glimpsed a more directly sexual, gloss-destructive "force" countering this aestheticism. *Findings* (1971) probed tentatively the common ground of art and sexuality (as in the snake swallower's tinny art), while *Two-Part Inventions* (1974) has dramatically confronted Whitman with Wilde; the visionary naturalist (sporting a red necktie) and the Baudelaire-quoting dandy (sporting a heliotrope buttonhole) find in sexuality itself a common basis for their diverse poetries.

Oscar confronts Walt as pupil to master, a bond appearing in many of Howard's poems. The paradigm seems to be Howard's own view of his link with W.H. Auden (the master poet known to his intimates, according to John Button, as "Miss Master").[4] *Quantities* adopts from Auden not just syllabic verse (the "quantities" which inform all Howard's published poems, even the least Audenesque) but also the tight, formal lyricism, meticulous craftsmanship, and secular intelligence that Auden brought to his urban and urbane subjects. "Lyrics from Gaiety, A Farce," seven vignettes that glimpse the purely human mysteries dimly through the party-wit of the chic, includes both the Audenesque verbal adeptness of, say, "Queer's Song":

> For you the darkness does its part —
> Arms fall, and eyes,
> And the heart proves by its lack an art
> the mouth supplies.

and, in the "Duet for Three Voices," a parody-imitation of Auden's own parody-imitation, "The Three Companions":

> O whom are you fooling
> Said Failure to Phony
> What role do you covet
> You never could play?

Though the constriction of Howard's early Audenism was to relax, Auden remained with him. In his second volume, Howard described an accidental encounter with the master during the arid New York Summer of '63, making this confessional tribute:

> And yet you taught me, taught us all a way
> To speak our minds, and only now, at last,
> Free of you, my old ventriloquist,
> Have I suspected what I have to say
> Without hearing you say it for me first.

If the tone and cadence of this offering temper its claim by recalling, for example, Auden's tribute to Freud —

> But he would have us remember, most of all,
> To be enthusiastic over the night

— they recognize the presence-absence of the teacher in the newly non-dependent pupil:

> Like my old love, I have survived you best
> By leaving you, and so you're here to stay.

More than all the passionate craft, Howard has learned from Auden the place of intelligence, no less frequently moving and fertile than wryly self-humoring, in a poem. What Isherwood said of the early Auden — "he has made a virtue of imitation" — goes for the early Howard.[5] Surely Auden himself would enjoy Howard's poem on him in "Compulsive Qualifications":

> Let it come, not as shock but as a saving grace
> If he should answer our hungry interviewers
>   "My dear, let them eat cock!"
> Poets should be obscene and not stirred.

Auden could even have written these lines. The difference is: he would not have published them.[6]

"To Hephaistos," which described that encounter with Auden, defined 1963 as "a year whose characteristic stamp / Will probably be the admission of 'camp' / Into the Unabridged."[7] It was in 1964 that *Partisan Review* printed Sontag's best-known essay, about which she recently told Chuck Ortleb: "As I sat down to write 'Notes on Camp,' I wondered why Auden hadn't written it."[8] Though Auden's art is too morally serious to be true camp, Howard took from Auden the precocious preciosity without the moralizing and produced, in his earlier poems, poetry close to camp: "decorative art" — again, Sontag is speaking — "emphasizing texture, sensuous surface, and style at the expense of content." His showpiece in this mode is the "Jubilary Ode on the Hundredth Anniversary of the Birth of Marlene Dietrich," where Dietrich — her body, her motion, her personal career — becomes a fabulous artifice before whom the very laws of nature bow.

The Dietrich poem dominates the rest because of its successful fabulating. In the others of the first two volumes Howard shows himself ill at ease with the flesh of natural life. Images of aging, attrition, decay recur, suggesting that the drive for artifice comes from one who, in his thirties yet, was prematurely old at heart. Mortality weighs heavy on him, and even sexual climax is dramatic only when it involves an exchange of myth, as of (in "The Shepherd Corydon") Glaucon or Antinous. "The body / Is sick, by nature." *The Damages* particularly focuses this, and answers the poem to Dietrich by one to a Martha

Graham unsaved by the poet's mythic fabulation; Graham must be seen as "An Old Dancer" hanging amid her props "like stale meat on your dead steel branch." This volume's motto reverses that of *Quantities* by seeing "the mind" as "certain of its meat." Thus the tremendous cost of the campy Dietrich poem, only hinted at in its final lines, becomes clear: the denial of time and of the body's health.

Nevertheless, *The Damages* begins a recovery from this inverted aestheticism by admitting Howard's personal history as a subject. The pure dandy has no room for history, is victimized by it. (Is this not why camp emasculates the past by accepting it only as "old-fashioned," as charmingly historical without a threatening historicity?) His poems of childhood here constantly border on mythmaking, as in the second part of the Seferiades poem, but remain grounded in the recognized actuality of memory: "we are always under house arrest." Despite a thrust towards history as timeless myth in "The Encounter," Howard was on his way to an acceptance of time, nature, and history in *Untitled Subjects*. There he would say that biography is "but / the silver-chased fittings of a coffin," yet see beyond the fittings to the "vital principle" which requires the full admission of our historicity.

In this Pulitzer Prize-winning volume Howard portrays a tradition of decorators and craftsmen, of *faces*, and recognizes there the historical sources of his decorative aestheticism.[9] ("Harry," said Wilde's painter of Dorian Gray, "every portrait that is painted with feeling is a portrait of the artist, not of the sitter.") But he also finds the *Schwung* that both gives rise to and destroys these finishes, a force that he will later link with human sexuality. The first glimmerings of this occur in a poem of particular interest to gay people, "1889." Its speaker — most of the poems in *Subjects* are, tellingly, long Browningesque dramatic or epistolary monologues, much laxer than the earlier lyrics — is an unnamed older homophile who has retired to Alassio, one of those Italian sea resorts which so attracted British and German gay men during the nineteenth century. One recalls, for instance, the Italian sojourns of a Symonds or an Ulrichs, but this speaker combines their sexual activity and inquiry with the reticence and distrust of activity that Mann gave to Gustav (von) Aschenbach. Howard's speaker has his Pippo — "white flesh with green eyes" — whose visit, indeed, interrupts the writing of this letter. He is most alive with Pippo — "my nature must be / At the root male and passionate." But he yields to the routines of the society he loathes and is repelled by the very inquiry into sexuality that Symonds and Havelock Ellis were undertaking. Writing to "Ross" — Wilde's friend Robbie? — he scorns Ellis' request for journal extracts:

I am
resolved to abstain,
without appeal, from any undertaking
in which that Pygmy has any part,
squatting in his cesspool and adding to it.

Recognizing the depth and life of his sexuality, yet resisting any openness about it, he is the prototypical closet queen. He personifies, furthermore, aspects of Howard's own style in this volume, but Howard, who in 1974 capsulized an epoch thus:

> The Bible calls it *knowing*, the Stuarts called it *dying*, the Victorians called it *spending*, we call it *coming*, and a hard look at the crisis in our culture suggests that it will not be long before we have a new word for orgasm — we shall call it *being*. [10]

— Howard treats him with a defenselessness which points toward the more central acceptance of sexuality in *Two-Part Inventions*, and indeed enjoys the fellow's play with a line from Tennyson's *Palace of Art:*

I shall
end in the state described by the Laureate:
'dozing in the vale of Avalon,
and watched by weeping queens.' My dear Ross, good night.
(Remember, Ellis
must be *stopped*. I trust you as I do myself.)

Ellis was not stopped, nor fortunately, was the resistance within Howard himself. Four of the six long duets which make up *Two-Part Inventions* address those radical sexual forces that aesthetics have long resisted addressing, three of them in terms of gay male sexuality. And the fifth may by its context link its concern with naming the gods, indeed with naming this historical poet "Hölderlin" himself, to Ellis' search to name the manifestations of sexuality. *Inventions* takes more "liberties" with factuality than *Untitled Subjects* does, although both books know history to be invention. [11] "Richard, What Do You Mean When You Say You're Writing Two-Part Inventions?" is answered, in "Compulsive Qualifications":

> The sense of invention is a coming-upon,
> A matter of finding matter more than of fact,
>   So that the finding matters.
> And if invention is finding, all finding is
> Choosing, and a choice is something made.

"Something made" is no less than the issue of *poesis*, the poem. This is the sense of invention that makes Howard important for gay people today; his *Inventions* motto comes from Bach, selected to pun suggestively:

> Wherein the lovers of the instrument are shown a way to play clearly in two voices and . . . to arrive at a singing style and at the same time to acquire a strong foretaste of composition.

Invention in history, poetry, music, and eroticism share a common vitality. Howard's history enables us to come upon the lost or hidden past of our sexuality.

"Wildflowers" chooses for its moment the momentous meeting of Walt Whitman, the weakened sexagenarian in Camden, with the young Oscar Wilde, assured but fawning on his 1882 American tour.[12] Howard finds in Whitman a "sick old man on Mickle Street," tired and domesticated yet delighted with this "great manly boy." His dismissal of Oscar's apotheosizing adulation yet affirms with eloquence the vision of *Leaves*: "I am not a holy man; or *all* men are." He rejects Oscar's renaming the *Leaves* as *Spears of Grass*, and in doing so limns the defensiveness of Oscar's more aggressively phallic metaphor:

> *Leaves* is what I wrote
>   and what I wear, if my nakedness
> must be covered. Spears? I want no defences.

Oscar recites — in perhaps Howard's most floral invention — a poem from *Les Fleurs du Mal*, enthused by its "sacred botany" and eager for Walt to share his enthusiasm, but he is reproved: Walt hears "a sickly sensuality in it, the sensuality of convalescence." What Oscar admires, Baudelaire's "getting rid of the real," is abhorrent to Whitman, and Oscar during his interview takes back his own first book which he had brought to altar: "it is not the book I must write / for Walt Whitman — that poem will come, bless me, / and it *will* come, from a deeper place than these."

Oscar Wilde, of course, did not learn Whitman's lesson, did not write that poem (the deeper place would be the *Epistola: Incarcere et Vinculis*, "De Profundis"), and one of the sad proleptic ironies of "Wildflowers" is Oscar's account of seeing a prisoner in Idaho, reading novels, and Whitman's answer:

> It was for just such a man
> I wrote *Leaves of Grass:*
>   a man reading in a jail.

But the greater irony, than that Oscar would have his own day, his own two years, in Reading Gaol, despite Whitman, is this: that Howard gives the profoundest statements about sexuality to a man well past his sexual prime. If we hear in this poem the older Howard speaking to the younger, we must also hear the human loss required for discovery.[13] The poem's relaxed domesticity seems a necessary context for Walt's great claim:

> I got it all said in the *Leaves*, Oscar. Sex
>   is the word when you mean sex,
> discredited here
>   with us, rejected from art, but still
> the root of our life, the life below the life.

Uncovering this root, following this *route*, has required large quasi-narrative contexts that the lyric could not provide, and from the perspective of *Subjects* and *Inventions* the early poems seem unsubtle and defensive in their contraction. To gain the depths of the life below one must grasp the breadth of the life above, and so the Browning of *Subjects* becomes *Inventions'* James. "The Lesson of the Master" — now James, not Auden or Whitman — develops wryly the cultivated use of sex as a weapon in the warfare of the genders. Its plot, in brief: in 1912 Edith Wharton is carrying the ashes of her long-term amour, Gerald Mackenzie, to Versailles for burial.[14] She has asked James "to suggest someone I had not met" to accompany her because "on such a journey one may say anything, / and prefers, of course, to say it to no one in particular." He has suggested one Gerald Roseman, about whom Edith learns, en route, not only that she once met him but also that he has had an intimate friendship with Gerald Mackenzie — indeed, one more intimate than she herself had had:

> We were what you failed to be — to become,
> you and Teddy, you and Gerald: one.

Roseman hints at a gay circle including himself, Mackenzie, James, and "Howard Overton," but she fights back with an unfortunate (in English) metaphor: "Nor am I tempted to put you and Gerald / and Mr. James in the same basket of crabs." Despite, nevertheless, the shock of having to recognize — how many women have been such complicit victims of gay men? — she accepts it and insists that Roseman bury his friend's ashes while she concocts vengeance on a James who has "turned his screw":

Silence, then, for Mr. James: it is the one
telling punishment.

Not the least of the cutting Jamesean edges of this poem is Mackenzie's
picture of Wharton as a "self-made man" and of James himself as a bitchy Miss
Master. Edith sees the circle as composed of "men who do not need women,"
and hears Roseman describing himself as "a woman just / because I am a
man." Almost every line witnesses to the butchery beneath the *politesse*. Her
homophobia upon hearing Gerald *brought out* to her —

> you take Gerald from me
> and replace him with
> a preposterous caricature who behaves
> as people behave in the newspapers,
> *some* newspapers, and Elizabethan plays.

— complies with her hate of her own sexuality. Howard manages, however, as
Henry James never did, to make of this viciousness an act of revealed
kindness. By making the truth apparent, even if only "later, after the subject is
dead and actually inside you," Roseman opens the Wharton world to that of
the two Geralds made one —

> Love, Mrs. Wharton, was in the center
> somewhere, anywhere, between us two.

— and Howard opens it to us.[15] Like Whitman and Wharton, the Auguste
Rodin of "Contra Naturam" meets a stranger who knows him, but in this case
not well enough. The man taps Rodin for an account of the Nijinski episode,
when Diaghilev accused the sculptor of pederasty with his boy-dancer model,
and ultimately invites him to the Marseilles steambath.[16] (Rodin refuses.) The
poem accommodates charming gossip, charmingly pegged as "invisible ink,"
which balances the unmasking of homosexuality in the James circle, but is
important for its brooding insight into sexuality and art. Rodin describes
Nijinski's nude dance during the posing session, then his standing still

> long enough (the young
> are often temporary artists) for me
> to observe how nature constructs her solids
> out of her liquids . . . to observe, Monsieur,
> the identity of the evanescent
> with the enduring.

Is not this erection an utmost finding? That in both eros and art liquids solidify, the evanescent hardens? In such an invention converge Howard's hitherto imprecisely related interests: art and sexuality. Long sensed as related, their kinship emerges in metaphor. The artistic act (like the homosexual according to the perverse tradition of Aquinas) is *contra naturam*, but its basis is the moment of the counterpoint.

Auden once described "the vision of Eros" as one of the two types of natural mystical experiences, the one found in the *Symposium*, in *La Vita Nuova*, in Shakespeare's sonnets.[17] It is not related to the fact of art itself; the sonnets struggle, as art, "to preserve the glory of vision [Shakespeare] had been granted in a relationship." Howard has delved deeper than his mentor and found *au fond* one action, the momentary (and momentous) emergence of form from flux.

But lest this lead to a lapidary or a transcendental sense of form, there remains one paradox. As Rodin's interlocutor says, the sexual is "the identity of fulfillment / with renunciation. It is reality." If this afterthought summons up Whitman's other modern heir, Wallace Stevens, "A Natural Death" even borrows words and (with inversions) scene from Stevens to portray the artist as a creator of form out of nature who, on his deathbed, rejoices to learn that nature has taken it back: "give it all back . . . we must survive what we have made."

Howard's etching of Sandro di Fiore — a synthesized *art nouveau* designer whose name evokes not only Alessandro Sforza but also Howard's lover, the novelist Sandford Friedman, and the "sands" that drift into the Paris garret; not only the ornamental blooms of *art nouveau* but also the varied posies of "Wildflowers" — poses itself in a tradition of the natural visionary. In the tones of "Passage to India" (Whitman's, not Forster's), in the ecstasy of Blake's "Time's Ruins Build Eternity's Mansions," we hear an early Wordsworthian celebration of the mansions time ruins. Fiore's "erections — / what else could you call them?" celebrate in all four elements one phallic energy. The "clump of stakes" in the Scena Marina "makes you want / to have old lovers back." Bussaco was built in a wood,

> a kind of male Mystery Cult, those trees up
> and up, and no hope of lying down

for a "queer count" who intended neither hunting nor lodging there but passion. His Chapel Penitant near Var thrust ten "fingers of the earth" into the air, and the Bloemenwerf Town Hall was destroyed by fire. The decay or destruction of each participates in its own energy.

Cynthia, the poem's correspondent, is *the* art history graduate student out to get her man, and her despair adeptly captures a resistance to this identity of fulfilment with renunciation. The only joy is "by forfeiture, by *losing something*" according to her advisor, but she clings too tightly to her dissertation — yet another version of the younger Howard who remains in the older — to accept this. When finally she finds Sandro on his deathbed, indeed, brings him his dying by her coming (and the erotic puns are intended), she finds an ancient man claiming to have "meant" nothing in his art, at least not money or history or knowledge: "I 'meant' the processes of plants." In this extreme the past does not exist — not Cynthia's "subject," not Hadrian's *aureus*, not the Rome of the Antonines. Failure is "not in the nature of things," it "is the nature of things." We must "choose between time and eternity," and Fiore's costly glory is that he has chosen a time that *is* eternity. Only in this time, which reclaims both, do art and sexuality have their life.

"No purpose but ecstacy." Howard has illuminated in this poem — as much, one feels, for himself as for us — paradoxes in the counterpoint of artifice with time. The poem does not choose between Sandro and Cynthia but apprehends each in an ecstacy which is, because always standing wholly *in* the character, a counter-ecstacy. A backwards glance (one starts to recall that this is Wharton's title as well as Whitman's — such are the mines buried below these leaves) confirms the distance Howard has moved from the finely sculpted lyrics, trying to escape time even as they mastered it, to the dramatic inventions of the recent poems.

And even, of late, into personal autobiography? At the 1974 GAU conference Howard read a new poem called "Decades (for Hart Crane)."[18] Its blank verse, in regularly spaced but unrhymed stanzas, turns from a career of quantities to find, and be bound by, Crane. For all their differences Howard is like Crane in being a scion of Cleveland ("our mother-in-lieu"), an erstwhile resident of Paris and New York, and vigorously gay. The poem's five units enact encounters with Hart's ghost at ten-year intervals during Howard's life: at four, on his "first meal *out*," which happens to be in C.A. Crane's "Canary Cottage" the weekend of Hart's death; at fourteen, discovering *The Bridge* in Richard Laukhuff's Bookstore where both poets ate their "Diet of Words"; at twenty-four *aux Deux Magots*, "coming out" to a disturbed Allen Tate and meeting the Fugitive's wince at the *decadence* of "gayety" *parisienne*; at thirty-four in a bar under the Brooklyn Bridge, cruising; and visiting, at forty-four, Crane's Garretsville, Ohio, birthplace.

The poem is a parental and penile "sacramental feast" —

> Our mothers ate our fathers, what do we
> eat but each other? All the things we take

into our heads to do! and let strange creatures
make our mouths their home.

— embracing mothers, fathers, and lovers of "the opposite sex, my own." The
problems: joining the Fathers without losing "the pride of my 'proclivity' ";
marrying the world without becoming fish food for its dinner. Hart
accomplished the former, and Howard becomes his accomplice, by virtue of
Whitman's extended and life-saving (who can forget the candy that C.A.
Crane invented?) hand:

> We join the Fathers after all, Hart,
> not to repel or repeal or destroy, but to fuse,
> as Walt declared it: wisdom of the shores,
>
> easy to conceive of, hard to come by, to choose
> our fathers and make our history.

Hart failed at the latter, and thus Howard's abrupt and ultimately unsolved, or
un-dissolved, swerve from him at the end:

> Hart, the world you drowned for is your wife:
> a farewell to mortality, not my life.

We have glimpsed much of "my life" in Howard's poetry since the
beginning — "we lose, being born, all we lose by dying: / all — but "Decades"
may begin for Howard a poetry in which his personal presence is more
up-front as he joins the Fathers. The paternity is ambitious — Auden, Crane,
Wilde, Whitman — and Howard's continuing predilection for the Fathers *and*
the publishing establishment will not endear him to those among us for
whom poetry must be propaganda or else capitalism. Let this be. Poetry has a
way of insisting that the world is fuller than *any* philosophy dreams of, and I
suspect that an American poet who can thus apostrophize Crane:

> I press your poems as if they were Wild Flowers
> for a sidelong grammar of paternity.

will be speaking for and to many of us, even if our grammars differ from his.

NOTES

[1]*Alone with America* (New York, 1969), 162. Essays on all but one of the poets listed are collected here; for the review of two Gunn collections, see "Ecstasies and Decorum," *Parnassus: Poetry in Review*, II:ii (Spring/Summer 1974), 213-220.

Howard said in 1972 that the "first critical piece I ever published was about Walt Whitman," and that in his senior year at Columbia he edited the famous *Columbia Review* issue devoted to André Gide. He also spoke of his early enthusiastic reading of Genet's poetry and of Proust. See Sandford Friedman, "An Interview with Richard Howard," *Shenandoah*, XXIV:i (Fall 1972), 5-31.

[2]*Poetry*, CXXII:3 (June 1973), 154-161.

[3]Susan Sontag, *Against Interpretation* (New York, 1966), 275-292.

[4]John Button, "Remembering Auden," *Fag Rag*, (Fall 1974), 14-19.

[5]Christopher Isherwood, "Some Notes on Auden's Early Poetry," in Monroe K. Spears, ed., *Auden, A Collection of Critical Essays* (Englewood Cliffs, New Jersey, 1964), 14.

[6]"When I write a poem for publication — naughty limericks for friends are another matter — I always try to write it in such a way that it makes sense for any reader, whatever his or her sexual tastes." Letter from Auden quoted by Ian Young in *The Body Politic*, no. 10, 19. John Button quotes some of these "naughty limericks."

[7]"Hephaistos" alludes to Auden as author of "The Shield of Achilles" as to his craftsmanship in general. Auden once said that "The only Greek god who does any work is Hephaestus," but added: "and he is a lame cuckold." *The Dyer's Hand* (New York, 1968), 430. An Auden elegy, "Again for Hephaistos, The Last Time: October 1, 1973," appeared in *The Ohio Review*, (Fall 1974), 59-61. It includes two amusing anecdotes about "Wystan" and ends: "After you, because of you, / all songs are possible." Accompanying the poem is "Made Things: An Interview With Richard Howard," recorded shortly after Auden's death, in which Howard speaks generously of the "enormous succor" provided him by Auden's "later voice" (pp. 43-58).

8Chuck Ortleb, "Susan Sontag: After the First Decade," *Out: The Gay Perspective*, I:2 (April 1974), 14.

9Fuller consideration of this tradition in Howard's poetry is given in my essay "Richard Howard's Finishes," *American Poetry Review* IV: 6, 5-11.

10*Preferences* (New York, 1974), 246.

11Compare Gore Vidal's "Afterword" to *Burr*: "the story is history and not invention." Curious that the one wholly "invented" character in the novel is the "sodomite" — "gay" in this period dialect meaning "socially lively" or "licentious" — William de la Touche Clancey, "who could, obviously," as Vidal too coyly puts it, "be based on no one at all." *Burr* (New York, 1973), 564.

12Accounts of this January 19, 1882 visit may be found in Horace Traubel, *With Walt Whitman in Camden* (Philadelphia, 1933), 79; and Lloyd Morris and Henry Justin Smith, *Oscar Wilde Discovers America* (New York, 1936), 63-77. In the *Ohio Review* interview Howard says that Whitman was then "in his seventies," but with 31 May 1819 for a birthday Walt must have been in his sixty-third year.

13I find no indication outside this poem that Oscar introduced Whitman to Baudelaire on this occasion. The invention heightens Oscar's similarity to the young Howard: "I was chiefly interested in French symbolism and French literary modernism," he told Sandford Friedman regarding his years at Columbia.

14Although his name suggests that of Compton Mackenzie, whom James knew both as a boy and as a young novelist, Gerald is based on Walter Berry, whose ashes Wharton buried at Versailles in 1927. Teddy Wharton died in 1924, eleven years after Edith's divorce from him.
Why, then, 1912, a date well before Berry's death? Clearly to weight the poem towards the "fact" of the lesson's master. 1912 was James's last fully active year before his lingering illness and death in early 1916. During 1912 Wharton made her last motoring trip with James, as Leon Edel recounts it in *Henry James: The Master* (Philadelphia, 1972), 460 ff. Berry was in Cairo at the time, and during his absence Edith was seeing Morton Fullerton, an effeminate but apparently heterosexual complement to what Edel calls Wharton's "intellectual masculinity" (412); Fullerton, who, incidentally,

appears in Wilde's letters and Auden's review of the Hart-Davis edition of them, is thus another source for Gerald Mackenzie.

In the last volume of the James biography, Edel recounts James's own infatuations with Hendrik Andersen and Jocelyn Persse, as well as Dr. Joseph Collins's conclusion about the "enormous amalgam of the feminine" in James's "make-up." (453) Most curious is his portrayal of James's close novelist friend Howard ("Howdie") Overing Sturgis, whom George Santayana called "a perfect young lady of the Victorian type" (194). Richard Howard's "Howard Overing" makes clear that his poem is correcting the mildly homophobic distortions of Santayana and Edel.

The circle of young men who gathered around Sturgis in his home, called "Queen's Acre" or "Qu'Acre," included Percy Lubbock, Gaillard Lapsley, Robert Norton, and John Hugh-Smith. Millicent Bell describes the circle in her *Edith Wharton and Henry James: The Story of Their Friendship* (New York, 1965).

15Mackenzie's concealment of this from Edith may be subject to the kind of judgment Auden passed on Wilde for marrying Constance Lloyd: "This was certainly the most immoral and perhaps the only heartless act of Wilde's life." (*Forewords and Afterwords* [New York, 1973], 307). Yet this poem is more concerned with James's "screw" and Wharton's response in kind than with Mackenzie's morality. Roseman's "silent" ending is the poem's most benevolent act; Wharton's "tragedy with a happy ending" continues, in a very different silence, the Jamesian game of defensive domination.

16This account of the episode contains no notable divergencies from David Weiss's in *Naked Came I* (New York, 1963).

17*Forewords and Afterwords*, 101-103.

18Privately published "in an edition of 200 copies to mark the 75th anniversary of the birth of Hart Crane," in Kent, Ohio, on 21 July 1974. The pamphlet does not name the publisher. Subsequently printed in *The American Review*, 22, 27-31.

The Case For Casque

By Hunce Voelcker

" . . . that their Highnesses might be informed that our Lord had granted success to the enterprise in the discovery of the Indies . . . he devised a method of acquainting them with the circumstances of the voyage in case they should perish in the storm; this he performed by writing upon parchment an account of it, as full as possible, and earnestly entreating the finder to carry it to the King and Queen of Spain. The parchment was rolled up in a waxed cloth, and well tied; a large wooden cask being then produced, he placed it within, and threw it into the sea, none of the crew knowing what it was, but all taking it for some act of devotion."   —*Journals of Christopher Columbus,*
First Voyage, 1492

Some testament committed in a cask[1]
　　　　—From Hart Crane's
　　　　"Ave Maria," c. 1926

—All this, -- far more floats written in a cask,
Was tumbled from us under bare poles scudding;[2]
　　　　—From Hart Crane's
　　　　"Ave Maria," January 27, 1927

And lowered. And they came out to us crying,
"The Great White Birds!" (O Madre Maria, still
One ship of these thou grantest safe returning;
Assure us through thy mantle's ageless blue!)
And record of more, floating in a casque,
Was tumbled from us under bare poles scudding;[3]
　　　　—From Hart Crane's
　　　　"Ave Maria," *The Bridge,* 1929

In 1937 Philip Horton wrote: "in recounting the heaving overboard of a wooden cask which contained records of the voyage . . ." Hart Crane "changed the crucial word to 'casque,' doubtless thinking that the word for a metal helmet was simply an archaic and more poetic spelling of the word for barrel."[4]

Eleven years later, Brom Weber, without the usual large and bitter measure of pointless negativity which makes the reading of his book the most painful experience in Crane studies, observed: "Although his manuscripts show that the word was spelled 'cask' in early versions, the final spelling was 'casque,' which denotes a military helmet. Crane may have been led to this change by reading in the dictionary that 'cask' was an obsolete way of referring to 'casque'; this may have induced him to think that 'casque' might just as easily be an obsolete term for 'cask.' But the change was probably not so deliberately planned; he simply liked the look of the word 'casque.' "[5]

By the time of Samuel Hazo (1963) and R.W.B. Lewis (1967) the case of "casque" had been relegated to a footnote, but Lewis, here as elsewhere in his scholarship, has succeeded in lighting a direction: "A certain to-do has been made of Crane's spelling of the word 'casque.' In the worksheet it appears as 'cask' ('some testament committed in a cask'); but in the published text, it was changed to 'casque,' which seems not to be an acceptable spelling for the word as meaning 'small barrel.' 'Casque,' which means a small Spanish helmet, can itself be spelled 'cask.' Crane, who spelled as accurately as the next poet, was probably attempting — in this case unsuccessfully and even pointlessly — a Joycean pun which would fuse the Admiral's helmet (as a symbol of authority) and the little barrel in which he dispatched his all-important record. The cask, by the way and however spelled, was never in historical fact recovered."[6]

My own investigations have led me to believe with growing intensity that the spelling which Hart Crane has given to the word in question is not only proper for its usage in "Ave Maria" (or for its usage in the whole of The Bridge for that matter), but that the spelling which Crane had originally given the word would be by far the inferior spelling in this particular case. The poet is divine. His muse works through the collection (the collection itself is toward divinity) of as many as possible of the different levels of his unconscious and the expression of these levels through his consciousness into a word into the poem. The poet is not always (in fact he is often not) aware of this process, but the completion of the process — which is the *feeling* (more emphatically, the *knowledge*) that the word is *right* — is an expression of that divinity wrought from his Dionysian unconscious depths and fashioned through his conscious fusion with Apollo's will. Certainly a poet who worked over his poems as feverishly as did Hart Crane did not make mistakes. At least it would be more reasonable for us to assume that Hart-Crane-as-poet did not make mistakes, than to assume, as has Brom Weber (who, because of his boundless negativity, epitomizes the first thirty years of Crane scholarship), that Allen-Tate-as-critic did not make mistakes.[7] It is through this more positive approach that we, the more enlightened readers of the post-acid years, will gain an insight not only into the potent meanings of the spelling of the word, but also into the secret strange divinity which Hart Crane attempts to share with us.

We are enveloped in the very heart of Hart's Logic of Metaphor, enveloped, "Nigh surged . . . witless," in the "illogical impingements of the connotations of words on the consciousness (and their combinations and interplay in metaphor on this basis);"[8] we are in the middle of the creation of the new language called for by P.D. Ouspensky in *Tertium Organum*.[9]

To begin with, both words, as was observed by Samuel Hazo, "derive from the same etymological source."[10] cask: "[Spanish *casco* potsherd, skull, helmet, cask . . .]" casque: "[alteration (influenced by French *casque*, from Spanish *casco*) of *cask*]"[11] As skulls were originally used for drinking cups, the word "cask" grew; as helmets were invented to protect these skulls from being turned to drinking cups, the word "casque" grew. I see these words as microcosms of the changing and divided aspects of the world, for in their origins these words were one.

"Ave Maria" opens with Columbus standing on the deck of the *Nina* (the *Pinta* and the *Santa Maria* having been lost) "between two worlds." He is between the Old World and his New discovery; but he is also between the God of Fire, the God of Fear of the Old Testament, and the God of Light, the God of Faith of the New Testament.[12] Thus it was "faith, not fear / Nigh surged" him "witless . . . " but the fear remains. Although the faith is favored, faith *and* fear, the new *and* old, the God of Light *and* the God of Fire all seem equally contained within this poem. For it was fear, not faith, notes L.S. Dembo in his book *Hart Crane's Sanskrit Charge*,[13] from which Columbus acted when he threw the cask/casque to the sea. Spain had just finished slaughtering the Moors for being infidels. "Here waves climb into dusk on gleaming mail!" And there is "here/Bewilderment and mutiny," and there "the Moor's flung scimitar/Found more than flesh to fathom in its fall."

Here images of military uniforms and implements abound: *mail . . . locks . . . tendons* (suggesting tinder and flintlock) *. . . Crested . . . chevron . . . scimitar . . . casque*, etc. For it was the old way, the Christian way, to beat the infidels into the Faith. The new God is a God of Love; the new God is to be found within the individual as seen by Emerson and realized by Whitman. The old was dusk and violence; "Here waves climb into dusk on gleaming mail." The new was dawn's clear light: "Till dawn should clear that dim frontier, first seen . . ." As Columbus had been an exile in Genoa, biding his time until "this truth, now proved" was proved, he found himself "biding the moon" which was the *only* light, save stars, at night, "Till dawn . . ." But the moon was there, in darkness, as the truth was there (in unproved thought at least) in Genoa, and as the new is always present in the old, and as the old is always present in (being the father of) the new.

The progress of "Ave Maria" (indeed, of the entirety of *The Bridge*) is toward unity: a total unity, a unity of objects, images and words through definitions, origins, and use, through sound, and through each word's appearance on the page; unceasing and accreting unity as each new sensitive younger reader reads and adds his feelings, his identities, to the divinity, the whole, the poem. The first words of "Ave Maria" are: "Be with me, Luis de San Angel, now — / Witness . . ." The definitions of the word "witness" involve a direct experience. Columbus is asking his patron to be with him, to be actually united with him at the present moment, on this "doubtful day," at the very peak of this transition from the old into the new frontier which still at the moment of discovery was a "dim frontier" and which will remain a "dim frontier" until he can return to Spain with all "this truth, now proved." The word "gleaming" (suggesting "gleaning") suggests the gathering, the uniting of (the drowned men's) "mail" (within a mailman's bag?). A "tendon" is a connective tissue; the "tendons" are "Crested," which leads to whole new areas of unity within the poem: The suggested soldier, from "gleaming mail" to "crest" (which besides being "the Apex of a helmet" is "a usually ornamental tuft or process on the head of a bird"[14]) becomes the sea. The "scimitar," which is an instrument of violence, is also curved, and therefore it suggests a microcosm of the seagull's "inviolate curve" from the second stanza of "Proem: to Brooklyn Bridge" . . . a microcosm of the Bridge and of *The Bridge* themselves.

Mary, through her "mantle's ageless blue," also has become the sea. The word "mantle" is itself packed with "illogical impingements." In addition to the meaning: "the back, scapulars, and wings of a bird when distinguished from other parts of the plumage by a distinct and uniform color (as in some gulls)," there is the meaning: "CEREBRAL CORTEX!"[15] It is the "mantle's ageless blue" upon which the casque will float, even as "thy mantle's ageless blue" is now contained (casque meaning, after all, a helmet) within the casque.

The definitions of the crucial "casque" itself further the bird imagery of the poem: "the process of the bill of a hornbill . . . the frontal shield of a coot or gallinule."[16] As the bird, the gull, and the "flashing scene" of "Proem," the word itself will flash across our consciousness and there connect, impinge itself into the layers of unconscious where our feelings grow.[17] But it is in the strong, the inescapable suggestions of the Spanish helmet that the potency of the word "casque" lies. For just as poetry, Hart Crane wrote, must "absorb the machine, i.e., *acclimatize* it as naturally and casually as trees, cattle, galleons, castles and all other human associations of the past,"[18] the new must absorb the old, the peaceful must absorb the violent, the good must absorb the evil. Within this casque is the collective consciousness of everybody's skull: of Mary's, of the Admiral's and of his crew, of each and every Spanish soldier who had worn or would wear a casque, and, by extension, all of us, even as, within this cask there is contained this "record of more," this record of "The word I bring."

According to R.M. Bucke's *Cosmic Consciousness*,[19] Walt Whitman's self-consciousness and cosmic-consciousness (which is, among other things, a total realization of the unity, the One) lived together and harmoniously within his evolving microcosmic self ("I believe in you my soul, the other I am must not abase itself to you, / And you must not be abased to the other"[20]). In a letter to Gorham Munson, Hart Crane wrote: "I felt the two worlds. And at once."[21] Both these worlds he has contained within this casque. And though R.W.B. Lewis has written that "The cask, by the way and however spelled, was never in historical fact recovered,"[22] the casque has, by a slightly different reading, actually been recovered, and its contents have been published, and been called *The Bridge*.

NOTES

1Crane, Hart. "Ave Maria," *The Bridge* (manuscript), from Lewis, R.W.B. *The Poetry of Hart Crane: A Critical Study*, Princeton University Press, Princeton, New Jersey, 1967, p. 260n.

2Crane, Hart. "Ave Maria," *The Bridge* (manuscript), from a verson sent to his mother, postmarked January 27, 1927, photo-copied from the original in possession of Columbia University Library, Special Collections.

3Crane, Hart. "Ave Maria," *The Bridge*, Liveright, N.Y., 1970. (First published by Black Sun Press, Paris, 1929).

4Horton, Philip. *Hart Crane: The Life of an American Poet*, Viking Press, N.Y., 1937, pp. 195-96.

[5]Weber, Brom. *Hart Crane: A Biographical and Critical Study*, The Bodley Press, N.Y., 1948, pp. 334-335.

[6]Lewis, loc. cit.

[7]For an account of Hart Crane's methods of composition see: Cowley, Malcolm. "The Leopard in Hart Crane's Brow," *Esquire*, October, 1958. See also: Voelcker, Hunce. *The Hart Crane Voyages*, The Brownstone Press, N.Y., 1967.

However limited-in-vision Allen Tate's early review of *The Bridge* ("A Distinguished Poet," *The Hound and Horn*, 3, July-Summer, 1930, pp. 580-585) may be, it seems to be basically written out of the honest beliefs of the reviewer; further, beyond all the dissent that Tate's more limited aesthetic caused between the two, Tate's friendship for Crane remains obvious between the lines. Unfortunately for all concerned, Brom Weber, on the other hand, remains void of either friendship or of honest sight. For a more detailed account of this writer's views of Crane scholarship, see: "Hunce Voelcker interviewed by Richard Tagett," *Gay Sunshine*, Forthcoming.

[8]Crane, Hart. From a letter to Harriet Monroe: Horton, op. cit., p. 330. See also: Herman, Barbara. "The Language of Hart Crane," *Sewanee Review*, Vol. LVIII, no. 1, Winter, 1950, pp. 52-67; and; Voelcker, Hunce, *The Hart Crane Voyages*, loc. cit.

[9]Ouspensky, P.D. *Tertium Organum*, Alfred A. Knoph, N.Y., 1969. See especially page 73. This book is generally accepted to have been a major influence upon Crane. For a discussion of the origins, the uses and ultimates of this "new language," see "Hunce Voelcker interviewed by Richard Tagett," loc. cit.

[10]Hazo, Samuel. *Hart Crane: An Introduction and Interpretation*, Barnes & Noble, Inc., N.Y., 1963, p. 79n.

[11]*Webster's Third New International Dictionary of the English Language Unabridged*, G. & C. Merriam Company, Springfield, Mass., 1971, p. 347.

[12]Andreach, Robert J. "Hart Crane," *Studies in Structure: The Stages of the Spiritual Life in Four Modern Authors*, Fordham University Press, N.Y., 1964.

13Dembo, L.S. *Hart Crane's Sanskrit Charge: A Study of The Bridge*, Cornell University Press, Ithaca, New York, 1960, pp. 55-56.

14Webster, op. cit. p. 535.

15op. cit., p. 1378

16op. cit., p. 347.

17See John Unterecker's argument for an uninterrupted reading of *The Bridge*: "The Architecture of *The Bridge*,": Clark, David R. *Studies in The Bridge*, A. Bell & Howell Co., Columbus, Ohio, 1970, pp. 87-102.

18Crane, Hart. "Modern Poetry," *The Complete Poems of Hart Crane*, Doubleday Anchor Books, Garden City, N.Y., 1958, p. 181.

19Bucke, Richard Maurice, M.D. *Cosmic Consciousness: A Study in the Evolution of the Human Mind*, E.P. Dutton and Company, Inc., N.Y., 1901.

19Whitman, Walt. "Song of Myself," Part Five.

21Crane, Hart. *The Letters of Hart Crane*, University of California Press, Berkeley and Los Angeles, 1965. Letter 101, p. 91.

22Lewis, loc. cit.

Sons and Lovers:
Three English Portraits

By Byrne R. S. Fone

Christopher Isherwood, in *Kathleen and Frank*, observed that heterosexuality wouldn't have suited him; "it would have fatally cramped his style." [1]
With Isherwood there are two other writers who might have shared this
sentiment. English by birth, contemporaries, members, in different stations, of
the affluent and educated class, all shaped by the last years of a waning
empire, J.R. Ackerley, Vita Sackville-West, and Christopher Isherwood share
not only these accidents of time and place, but the fact of homosexuality as
well.

All three wrote books which explore their lives and in larger or smaller
ways their homosexuality. Ackerley's *My Father and Myself* and Isherwood's
Kathleen and Frank both seek out a lost past and parents imperfectly known,
and succeed in discovering an unexpected present and an identity. Vita
Sackville-West's diary, as it is contained in and commented upon in Nigel
Nicolson's *Portrait of a Marriage* leads the reader not only through the
discovery of a mother by a son, but through the personal account of Vita's
homosexual experiences, both in life and art, with the novelist Violet Keppel
Trefusis, and the genius Virginia Woolf.

These three English portraits comprise three enlightening visions of
homosexuality as uniquely seen by three homosexual writers. Vita
Sackville-West says about this unique vision: "I . . . claim that I am qualified to
speak with the intimacy a professional scientist could acquire only after years
of study and indirect information, because I have the object of study always to
hand, in my own heart, and can gauge the exact truthfulness of what my own
experience tells me. However frank, people would always keep back
something. I can't keep anything from myself." [2]

"I was born in 1896 and my parents were married in 1919."[3] This is perhaps the least startling revelation in the remarkable account which J.R. Ackerley gives of himself and his father, Alfred Roger Ackerley. His memoir is the account of a son's search for a father, and his discovery that the conventional and stereo-typical English *pater familias* who he thought he knew not only kept another household, well stocked with three illegitimate daughters, but, as Ackerley finally speculates, may have been in his youth when a handsome guardsman, the companion for four years to a wealthy and cultivated gentleman in his thirties, and later a companion of perhaps a more intimate nature to a bachelor nobleman, the Count de Gallatin, a peer of the Holy Roman Empire who continued "the educational and refining processes begun upon him" by Alfred Ackerley's first benefactor (p. 26). The early chapters of *My Father and Myself* deal with the relationship between the count and the elder Ackerley, with the bachelor establishment for which the count happily paid, with the count's male friends, with the estrangement of the count and his protégé, and with Alfred Ackerley's marriage to his first wife which ended with her death eighteen months later. The account is sketchy, and as the author admits, speculative and inconclusive, but it is the point from which J.R. Ackerley begins his search, not only for "my father," but for "myself." As such, Ackerley's book must stand as a minor classic in the ranks of revelatory homosexual literature.

We need not here dwell long on the search for a paternal identity, since that is the subject of Ackerley's eloquent book. Nor need we speculate on the implications of his chapter on the brother he never knew. But, in the end, when he has discovered his father's passion for smutty story and sexual innuendo — a passion which Ackerly mistakenly saw as the reminiscent braggadoccio of a man past his sexual prime, when he has revealed that his mother was not the only woman in his father's life nor he and his brother the only children, and even when he begins to suspect that the curiously masculine — or rather, male — dominated past spent with the Count de Gallatin might be but a foreshadowing of his own homosexual present, even then we remain most intrigued with the search for "myself."

My Father and Myself reveals a homosexual writer and illuminates the conflicts attendant upon the formation, discovery, and comprehension of his homosexuality and its effect upon his craft. Out of these conflicts, out of the search for "myself" and, importantly, for the "Ideal Friend" who would share his life, there grew a writer who became in thought, if perhaps not always in action, a confirmed, intellectually celebrative homosexual. He describes his view of this world during his Cambridge years:

I was now on the sexual map and proud of my place on it. I did not care for the word 'homosexual' or any label, but I stood among the men, not the women. Girls I despised; vain, silly creatures, how could their smooth, soft, bulbous bodies compare in attraction with the muscular beauty of men? Their place was in the harem, from which they should never have been released; true love, equal and understanding love, occurred only between men. I saw myself therefore in the tradition of the classic Greeks, surrounded and supported on all sides by all the famous homosexuals of history — one soon sorted them out — and in time I became something of a publicist for the rights of that love that dare not speak its name (p. 118).

Of course, this is sheer, and in a way, adolescently collegiate Platonism, And it would take Ackerley years before he could accept homosexuality as more than an intellectual and spiritual experience, though one ought not sneer at an intellectual and spiritual settlement that many of Ackerley's "famous homosexuals of history" were themselves unable to make. His school years are a record of boyish loves and unconsummated romance — a tale too typical to be further rehearsed. And in common with those who seek an ideal, his sexual life seemed to him somehow unfulfilled: "in retrospect it does not look perfectly satisfactory to me, indeed I regard it with some astonishment. It may be said to have begun with a golliwog [a black doll for which he asked his amazed father] and ended with an Alsatian bitch [his dog Tulip, to whom the book is dedicated]; in between there passed several hundred young men, mostly of the lower orders and often clad in uniforms of one sort or another" (p. 110).

Having decided that the pursuit of sex through platonic love during his school years was unsatisfactory, he "started upon the long quest in pursuit of love through sex" (p. 123). He says: "I was to spend twenty-five years in this search, which began . . . in Picadilly, at No. 11 Half Moon Street . . . where I rented a room for a weekend twice I think, in my Cambridge history. Street prowlers and male prostitutes, not many, were my first prey . . . ." He continues:

However, if I was cheerless then, life brightened for me after I came down. I met socially more and more homosexuals and their boy friends and had an affair with a good natured normal Richmond tradesboy . . . By the time I reached [Paris] with my father I was well into my predatory stride. I had just come up from Ragusa, where I had been idling about with a lisping little artist whose girlishness had ended by sickening me; my homosexual Cambridge friend was now living in Paris and we were exploring the queer bars and

Turkish baths . . . . I was busy making assignations with a Corsican waiter in the Cafe de la Paix under my parents' noses. Later on, when my play was produced in London, actors were added to my social list . . . . Though I can't remember my state of mind at this period, I expect that much of all this seemed fun. It certainly afforded pleasure and amusement, it was physically exciting, and in England it had the additional thrill of risk (pp. 123-124).

Amusement, pleasure, risk: was this all there was? The question is annoyingly prudish. These things *are* justification, and if they provide the material for the writer, justification the more. Ackerley is trying to say, perhaps without realizing it, that for him, homosexuality was an acceptable way of life, that the guilt, and there was much, was imposed from without, and that with the discovery or at least the implication of his father's own past, the guilt was somehow, through the cathartic medium of this memoir, dissipated. He says: "sex was delightful and of prime importance . . . ." Yet for him, as for many in the post-Victorian years, his homosexuality stood in a realm of maddening dichotomy. Of some homoerotic poems he wrote at Cambridge he says: "If this life I am prowling about in were someone else's and I its historian (*which in fact is the way I am trying to see it*), I would rub my hands gleefully over some of the poems I wrote and published in Cambridge. What can these curious productions mean unless that although I regarded myself as free, proud and intellectually unassailable as a homosexual, I was profoundly riddled with guilt?" (p. 211). That Ackerley's life as an active homosexual was not satisfying to him, his book tells us, and we need detail it no further — and yet the book, ironic, powerful, moving, details also the life of a man who found in his homosexuality, as he says, if not sexual satisfaction, then freedom and pride, and who never regrets that special nature. Though his picture of the prowling homosexual, seeking his pleasure with sailors and guardsmen, might not be relished by the contemporary Gay Liberationists who often seem to wish that this quite as liberated side of homosexual life did not exist, yet one must insist that Ackerley's book is all the better for its honesty. It is certainly to his credit that in his play *The Prisoners of War* in which the "emotional feeling is all between men and boys," he has his surrogate self, Captain Conrad say in response to the line: "Captain Conrad, I hear you do not greatly care for the fair sex," "The Fair sex? Which sex is that?" And he goes on to say in the book: "Whatever sexual guilt I had to cope with in my subconscious mind I had none in my intellect; I thought, wrote, and spoke the love of man for man . . ." (p. 144).

What does this memoir tell us? Ackerley died in 1967. The memoir covers the period from 1896 to his father's death in 1929 and its materials were collected in his diaries until 1940. It includes, as we have seen, a sexual profile of Ackerley, coping, honestly in public, often with difficulty in private, with his homosexuality. Yet here is more than a clinical study. Here is more than just the record of an incomplete relationship between father and son. And here is more than the admittedly fascinating tale of an eccentric father whose peccadillos both actual and suspected must have both shocked and perhaps secretly gratified his son. Aside from all this, aside from the invaluable glimpse into homosexual life in the first decades of this century in England, we have that material which a writer, and a homosexual writer, has taken and transmuted into a fascinating chronicle about his own homosexuality, its origins, its nature, and his attitude towards it. The book becomes not only the search for a father but the discovery of a life — a life saved and in Henry James' phrase, a life "felt."

Surely that heterosexual life which Ackerley saw in his father's world turned him toward that freedom which he found in homosexuality. "My father's way of life, the commuting life, the regular habit, the daily papers in the same morning and evening trains, the same 'cherrio' travelling acquaintances, the passing on of the latest smutty story . . . seemed to be contemptible, death in life. No, freedom for me!" (p. 106). That he never really achieved his psychological freedom — a freedom from sexual obsession and uncertainty until he encountered his passion for his Alsatian dog, Tulip, about whom he wrote a book is, in passing, as interesting as the same phenomenon in the life of T. H. White, also homosexual, whose fulfillment was found in his dog, Brownie. Where Ackerley did find freedom was in his art and this book clearly shows it. The volume grows, not only out of his obsessive curiosity about his father and the justifactory parallels he seeks to draw, not only out of his obsessive sexuality, but most importantly out of the honesty and conviction of his commitment to the "intellectually unassailable" position of being homosexual.

It was his homosexual imagination — an imagination necessarily bound up with the flesh and the spirit as all imagination must ultimately be — which created this book. And the creation is shaped by the demands of art. As he says in the Foreword:

The apparently haphazard chronology of this memoir may need excuse. The excuse, I fear, is Art. It contains a number of surprises, perhaps I may call them shocks, which, as history, came to me rather bunched up towards the end of the story. Artistically shocks should never be bunched, they need spacing for maximum indivi-

dual effect. To afford them this I could not tell my story straightfor-
wardly and have therefore disregarded chronology and adopted the
method of ploughing to and fro over my father's life and my own,
turning up a little more subsoil each time as the plough turned.

At the center of the book stands Ackerley, debating his sexuality, proud of his
moral and ethical and intellectual homosexuality, alternately delighting in and
being dissatisfied by its physical manifestations. And at either end of the tale, in
tantalizing polarity, stands the narrative of his father's life: the glimpse given at
the beginning of the handsome guardsman and the clearly homosexual count,
the retreat, if such it were, into the world of heterosexual respectability, but this
within a bizarre frame of a double life, and then at the end a return full circle to
the life his father may have lived. Taking rooms in the home of an aging
homosexual, Ackerley discovers among scores of portraits dustily hanging on
the wall a painting of "a pompous old gentleman dressed in ceremonial attire
and seated on a kind of throne . . . . A pale aristocratic hand, issuing from the
folds of his vice-regal robes, rested on the arm of his throne. How was I to
know that this old gentleman was the Count James Francis de Gallatin, my
father's boyhood friend?" (p. 184). Inquiry of his landlord soon establishes the
identity, and the connection, and Ackerley's diary records the interlude, and
turns fact into art:

> 'I can't get me breath. Isn't it awful to be old? First was Louie, then
> Cis, then Miss Emily, and I shall be the next.'
> 'Arthur dear, do tell me. Did your friend the Count de Gallatin
> ever say anything about having made love to my father?'
> 'Oh, the things you say! I'm as nervous as a kitten, the least thing
> sets me off. I can't even write a cheque now, me hand shakes so.'
> 'Arthur, its important. Do you know about my father and the
> Count?'
> 'Oh, you couldn't ask the Count. But I had my ideas all the same.'
> 'I don't want ideas. I want facts. Did they go to bed together?
> *That* is what I want to know. Did the Count ever tell you anything?'
> 'Oh lord, you'll be the death of me! I think he did once say he'd
> some sport with him. But me memory's like a saucer with the
> bottom out' (pp. 202-203).

In examining his mother's papers after her death — she died a secret
drinker with failing faculties — he discovered "an ancient battered black bag
such as doctors used to carry. It was locked. No key could be found, but the

leather had rotted, the bag was easily torn open. The first thing that met my eye was a page of pencilled writing in my mother's hand: 'Private. Burn without reading.' At last! Beneath were sundry packages tied up in ribbon. They were full of wastepaper. There was nothing else in the bag" (p. 208).

He continues:

> This was my mother's comment on life. It might serve also as a comment on this family memoir, which belongs, I am inclined to think, to her luggage. A good many questions have been asked, few receive answers. Some facts have been established, much else may well be fiction, the rest is silence. Of my father, my mother, myself, I know in the end practically nothing. Nevertheless I preserve it, if only because it offers a friendly, unconditional response to father's plea in his posthumous letter: 'I hope people will generally be kind to my memory' (p. 208).

This account of a writer whose homosexuality so obsessed him that he was finally led to write this book, essentially an account of liberation, demands that we must be kind to his memory, not only out of respect, but as well in gratitude and admiration, for this is the portrait of an artist whose life became the subject of his art, and whose book is the testament to his life.

✌

If Ackerley's hope for revelation was lost when he opened that battered leather bag only to discover wastepaper, Nigel Nicolson was more than rewarded when he discovered his mother's remarkable diary in a locked Gladstone bag in the tower of Sissinghurst Castle. This diary "was an auto-biography written when she was aged twenty-eight, a confession, an attempt to purge her heart and mind of a love that possessed her, a love for another woman . . ." (p. vii).

Readers of *Portrait of a Marriage* and students of that peculiar breed known as the English upper class will not have to be told about the lineage of the Sackville-Wests, nor be reminded of the wonders of Knole, their vast home. Of the three portraits here drawn, Vita Sackville-West's is that of an aristocrat in every way, next to whose aristocracy the middle class affluence of the Ackerleys or the gentility of the Bradshaw-Isherwoods considerably pales. Perhaps this consciousness of being elite — and let no democrat gainsay the inescapable fact that she was — must play an important role in her view of her homosexuality. Within that elite world, central to which was the daily practice and enjoyment of being civilized, Vita was given a chance to live and act in a way not granted to the common, nor to the affluent but middle class Ackerleys or the "imperfectly leisured" and moral Isherwoods.

Yet the freedom which the position of her class gave her did not prevent her from experiencing an agony about her homosexuality. But for her it was not an agony of guilt, but rather an agony occasioned by the intensity of an experience, enhanced by a brilliant imagination, and a deep conviction about the rightness of what she did. Thus, her diary becomes, as Nicolson says, "a document unique in the vast literature of love, and among the most moving pieces that she ever wrote; that far from tarnishing her memory, it burnished it . . ." (p. viii). That her homosexual life was carried on concurrently and successfully while she was married most happily to Harold Nicolson (himself homosexual) enhances this memoir and it becomes thus, as Nicolson describes it "a panygeric of a marriage, although it describes a marriage that was superficially a failure because it was incomplete." Vita and Harold "achieved their ideal companionship only after a long struggle, which was still not ended when Vita Sackville-West wrote the last words of her confession, but once achieved it was unalterable and lifelong, and they made of it . . . the strangest and most successful union that two gifted people have ever enjoyed" (p. ix).

Vita's great love was Violet Keppel Trefusis, herself to become a distinguished writer and the center of a Parisian literary salon. Nicolson describes the depth and extent of their passion:

> When together, their feet barely touched the earth. They were carried on the breezes toward the sun, exultant and ecstatic, breathing the thin air of the empyrean. Violet seemed to her a creature lifted from legend, deriving no parentage, unprecedented, unmatched, pagan. Their bond of flesh was so compelling that it became almost spiritual, not a bodily necessity, exacting so close and tremulous an intimacy that nothing existed for them outside. It swept away their careful training, individual and hereditary, replacing pride by another pride. They loved intensively, with a flame that purged all from their love, but the essential, the ideal, passion (p. 150).

This passion was reflected not only in their lives but in their writings. It appears in Vita's novel *Challenge* (1919) in which Julian, a young Englishman incites the natives of a Greek island, Aphros, to revolt. His cousin, Eve, joins him and they become lovers until his commitment to Aphros leads to her betrayal of him. As Nicolson says: "Eve wants Julian absolutely, and to hell with convention . . .Julian is Vita; Aphros stands for Harold, the rival for Eve's love; Eve is Violet to the very inflection of her voice . . . " (p. 149).

And in fact, Vita and Violet played out in life this adventure. Vita, in her diary for October 5, 1920, tells how she "dressed as a boy . . . . I looked like a rather untidy young man, a sort of undergraduate, about nineteen. It was marvelous fun, all the more so because there was always the risk of being found out." The discovery was, she says, too good to be wasted and "in Paris I practically lived that role. Violet used to call me Julian . . . . I personally never felt so free in my life. Perhaps we have never been so happy since" (pp. 110-111).

Vita's life then, inspired by Violet was lived on "two levels, the actual and the fictional, and as her love for Violet intensified, so did that between the fictional Julian and Eve in her novel, with incidents, conversations and letters lifted in the book from reality" (p. 148). And so, the homosexual imagination, fired by life, created fiction.

If Violet inspired Vita, later in life Vita was to inspire another woman, also homosexual, and the greater artist: Virginia Woolf. Vita fell in love with Virginia Woolf, but she insists in a letter to Harold (August 17, 1926): "I love Virginia — as who wouldn't? But really, my sweet, one's love for Virginia is a very different thing: a mental thing; a spiritual thing, if you like, an intellectual thing . . . ." And she continues: "Also she loves me, which flatters and pleases me . . . . I am scared to death of arousing physical feelings in her, because of the madness" (p. 205). That there was a physical union she does at last admit, but the friendship was ultimately one of depth, not of passion. "Her friendship has enriched me so," she says in a letter to Harold (November 30, 1926). "I don't think I have ever loved anybody so much, in the way of friendship" (p. 207). As Nicolson comments: "The physical element in their friendship was tentative and not very successful, lasing only a few months, a year perhaps. It is a travesty of their relationship to call it an affair" (p. 207).

Though Virginia did not, and probably correctly, admire Vita's writing, it was Vita who inspired Virginia to create the strangest of all her novels: *Orlando*. Nicolson describes the situation best:

But *Orlando!* Imagine those two, seeing each other at least once a week, one writing a book about the other, swooping on Knole to squeeze from it another paragraph, on Long Barn to trap Vita into a new admission about her past (Violet, whom Virginia met once, comes into the book as Sasha, a Russian princess . . .), dragging Vita to a London studio to have her photographed as a Lely, tantalizing her, hinting at the fantasy but never lifting more than a corner of it — until one day before publication, *Orlando* arrived in a brown paper parcel from Hogarth Press, followed a few days later by the author with the manuscript as a present. Vita wrote to Harold: "I am in the middle of reading *Orlando*, in such a turmoil of excitement and confusion that I scarely know where (or who) I am!" She loved it. Naturally, she was flattered, but more than that, the novel identified her with Knole forever. Virginia by her genius had provided Vita with a unique consolation for having been born a girl, for her exclusion from her inheritance, for her father's death earlier that year. The book, for her, was not simply a brilliant masque or pageant. It was a memorial mass (p. 208).

And certainly, in this course of inspiration, in her relationship with Violet and with Virginia, one must not forget her inspiration of Harold, also homosexual, biographer of Verlaine and Swinburne. It may well be said that Vita's homosexuality, its vibrancy and life — *Vita* means life — affected all those who knew her as *Portrait of a Marriage* eloquently shows.

But what did Vita herself think about homosexuality? In her novel, *Grand Canyon* (1942), she expresses her feelings about the "normal" act of love: "One wonders how they ever brought themselves to commit the grotesque act necessary to beget children" (p. 135). And it is true that her sexuality was clearly affected by her mother's fastidiousness and her father's reticence, as Nicolson suggests, but he continues: "She had no concept of any moral distinction between homosexual and heterosexual love, thinking of them both as 'love' without qualification" (p. 135). In 1960, in a letter to Harold, she wrote:

> When we married, you were older than I was, and far better informed. I was very young, and very innocent. I knew nothing about homosexuality. I didn't even know that such a thing existed either between men or between women. You should have told me. You should have warned me. You should have told me about yourself and warned me that the same sort of thing was likely to happen to myself. It would have saved us a lot of trouble and misunderstanding. But I simply didn't know (p. 136).

As Nicolson suggests, she clearly "simply didn't know" how strong such passions could be, but she surely knew — witness Rosamund, her first lover —

that such things existed. But she did not "give it a name," as Nicolson says, "and felt no guilt about it" (p. 137).

And despite her letter of 1960, years earlier, in September 1927, seven years after her marriage to Harold, nine years after her sexual initiation by Rosmund, two years after the beginning of her affair with Violet, and two years before she met Virginia Woolf, she wrote:

> I am not writing this for fun, but for several reasons which I will explain. (1) As I started by saying, because I want to tell the entire truth. (2) Because I know of no truthful record of such a connection — one that is written, I mean, with no desire to appeal to a vicious taste in any possible readers; and (3) because I hold the conviction that as centuries go on, and the sexes become more nearly merged on account of their increasing resemblances, I hold the conviction that such connections will to a very large extent cease to be regarded as merely unnatural, and will be understood far better, at least in their *intellectual* if not in their physical aspect . . . I believe that then the psychology of people like myself will be a matter of interest, and I believe it will be recognized that many more people of my type do exist than under the present-day system of hypocrisy is commonly admitted. I am not saying that such personalities, and the connections which result from them, will not be deplored as they are now; but I do believe that their greater prevalence, and the spirit of candour which one hopes will spread with the progress of the world, will lead to their recognition, if only as an inevitable evil.

The prophetic accuracy of her words is remarkable, both in her hope for progress, understanding and candor, and in her equally candid presumption that homosexuality may, after all, be accepted "only as an inevitable evil," an acceptance too readily accorded still. She continues by asserting that such candor will be facilitated by new attitudes towards marriage, divorce and relationships outside of marriage, and concludes that "such advance must necessarily come from the more educated and liberal classes. Since 'unnatural' means 'removed from nature,' only the most civilized, because the least natural, class of society can be expected to tolerate such a product of civilization."

"I advance, therefore," she continues,

> the perfectly accepted theory that cases of dual personality do exist, in which the feminine and masculine elements alternately preponderate. I advance this in an impersonal and scientific spirit, and

claim that I am qualified to speak with an intimacy a professional scientist could acquire only after years of study and indirect information, because I have the object of study always to hand, in my own heart, and can gauge the exact truthfulness of what my own experience tells me. However frank, people would always keep back something. I can't keep back anything from myself (pp. 105-106).

It is now over forty years since those words were written by a product of that "most civilized, because the least natural, class of society." Yet in her life and art — and the two are inseparable it would appear — there is no fatally cramped style, there is none of the guilt nor agony with which Ackerley had to come to terms. We have instead Vita the Artist and Muse. It was Vita the artist whose imagination was fired by Violet and who thus created "Julian," in life a challenge and transformation for any woman, and in art, a book, *The Challenge*. And it was the Muse who led Virginia to write *Orlando* and give Vita's secret life living and artistic habitation. And finally, and luckily for us, it was Vita whose prepossessing brillance and truly innocent yet convinced and passionate homosexuality led her son to give us this portrait, not only of a remarkable union, but a portrait of a woman for whom homosexuality was no burden, but rather a triumph and a liberation.

My Father and Myself and *Portrait of a Marriage*, are tapestried books which weave and interweave recollection, speculation, biography and autobiography, leaving us with complex and intriguing impressions of their subjects. *Kathleen and Frank* is quite a different book. Its authors, like *Portrait of a Marriage*, are mother and son; its search, like *My Father and Myself*, is for a paternal identity. In a way, its subject, like both books, is liberation and the development of the artist, and, as Isherwood comments, "perhaps on closer examination, this book too may prove to be chiefly about Christopher" (p. 510).

While the other books deal primarily with the homosexuality of their subjects, *Kathleen and Frank* is, as its sub-title says, "The Autobiography of a Family." It consists of the diary of Isherwood's mother extending some eighty-seven years from 1883-1960. It records the story of a marriage and indirectly the growth of Christopher, who appears as narrator, in the third person. Isherwood's mother appears through her diary and her letters, his father through her eyes and some of his letters, and both through Isherwood's connecting narrative. His mother appears as a woman increasingly wedded to a Victorian past, his father as a military man more suited by temperament to be an artist but whom duty constantly called. Both members of that class who were the heart and soul of Victorian England, not aristocracy like Vita, nor merchants like the Ackerleys, but gentry with an ancient family, they were devoted to that morality and that duty which was the backbone of England at the end of empire. And thus Isherwood's mother becomes for him the hagiographer of the heroic saint his father was to become, and his father becomes a mystery to be fathomed, a challenge to be met, and finally, a spirit to be laid.

In *Kathleen and Frank*, though he appears as a minor character, and as third-person narrator in the person of historian, we still catch glimpses, impersonal, almost sly, of Isherwood's development. And so it is, that in the end, he becomes convinced that in seeking out the story of his father and mother, in discovering his past, he

> saw how heredity and kinship create a woven fabric; its patterns vary, but its strands are the same throughout. Impossible to say exactly where Kathleen and Frank end and Richard and Christopher begin; they merge into each other. It is easy to dismiss this as a commonplace literary metaphor; hard to accept it as literal truth in relation to oneself. Christopher has found that he is far more closely interwoven with Kathleen and Frank than he had supposed, or liked to believe (p. 509).

And so he concludes that indeed upon closer examination the book may "prove to be chiefly about Christopher."

There is little in the book, however, as there is in the others, which bears directly on Isherwood's development as a homosexual and as an artist. Of course this unequivocal comment leaves little to be said: "Despite the humiliation of living under a heterosexual dictatorship and the fury he often felt against it, Christopher has never regretted being as he is. He is now quite certain that heterosexuality wouldn't have suited him; it would have fatally cramped his style" (p. 380). Later, in the "Afterword," he speculates on his parent's attitude toward his homosexuality: "At best they might have agreed to differ like gentlemen, after Christopher had wasted years of precious youth-time breaking the dreadful news slowly to Frank about boy-love . . . . It was more likely that Frank would have forgotten he had ever wanted Christopher to 'develop along his own lines'; that he would have ended up by disowning his

Anti-Son " (p. 508). We are, of course, reminded of Ackerley's attempt to break the dreadful news to his father, with as little success.

When he tells his mother that he was homosexual, "she didn't seem at all upset. But this, he suspected, was simply because she simply didn't believe that a relationship without a woman in it could be serious, or indeed anything more than an infantile game. He sensed her assurance that he would one day have children, *her* grandchildren — never mind what became of the wretched cheated wife! This arrogant demand of hers would have been enough to deter Christopher from the cowardly crime of an unnatural respectable-mock marriage, if he had ever felt tempted to commit it" (p. 508).

But what is important in this book, as it is important in the other two, is not the revelation of homosexuality, but the acceptance of it. In searching out his past and father, his Hero-Father created in large part by his mother whom he calls the "Holy Widow," he came to realize that in growing up he was better off without him, and that in a way he had never needed him. But because he was, as he says, a "Sacred Orphan," he was constantly under the obligation to be worthy of his dead father. He began to think of those who forced this obligation upon him as "The Others."

> It was easy for these impressive adults to make a suggestible little boy feel guilty. Yet he soon started to react against his guilt. Timidly and secretly at first, but with a passion, with a rage in his bones, he rejected their Hero-Father. Such a rejection leads to a much larger one. By denying your duty toward your Hero-Father, you deny the authority of the Flag, the Old School Tie, The Unknown Soldier, The Land That Bore You and the God of Battles. Christopher's realization that he had done this — and that he must tell The Others that he had done it — came to him only by degrees and not until he was nearly grown up. The rejection caused him much anxiety at first and some moments of panic; later it gave him immense relief and even a little courage (p. 502).

And so while this book is not passionately revelatory in the way Vita's and Ackerley's books are, it is still a tale of liberation and a more simple kind of revelation: deception would have "cramped his style." Such an easy phrase. Such a triumphant style.

In a *New York Times* interview Isherwood is quoted as saying: "Any sort of concealment that an artist puts up about his life injures him as an artist, just as it injures him as a man."[4] He once said that "I've often wondered what would have happened if I began writing my novels from an avowed homosexual viewpoint. I always felt it was there implicitly . . . . For me, as a writer, its never been a question of sex but of oneness, of being the member of a minority, of seeing things from a slightly different angle. If homosexuality were the norm, it would have nothing to interest me as a writer."[5] In another interview he says, "With me, everything starts out with autobiography . . . ." He later continues: "I have written about homosexuals in my novels, and in taking up the cause of one minority, that of homosexuals against the dictatorship of heterosexuals, I have spoken out for all minorities."[6]

Isherwood, anti-Son, anti-establishment Englishman, rejector of mother and motherland, proudly admitted homosexual, stands, of the three writers, clearly the greatest talent. He is the writer whose imagination can most clearly be said to have been shaped in so large a part by his homosexuality. Isherwood's work, of course, goes beyond sexuality — just as Vita's diary stands above sensationalism. Without that sense of oneness which he so clearly describes in *Kathleen and Frank*, without the rebellion that he details for us as he rejects the Hero-Father and the Holy Widow mother, without the quiet yet positive assertion that heterosexuality would have fatally cramped his style, Isherwood would perhaps not have attained that place which he must now be allowed to hold: an artist who is also homosexual, and an artist whose artistry is further enhanced by that uniqueness of vision which like Vita and Ackerley, he proudly wore as an order of merit and as a controlling definition of his art.

۞

From these three portraits then, we can learn that homosexuality can shape and indeed fire the imagination. Each of these memoirs is the story of a quest, not only for parents and lovers, but for the stability of the artist acting freely and deliberately within the homosexual self. They are chronicles of the revelatory experience of a homosexual writer approaching his themes and assimilating them into the social and literary experience of being homosexual. If indeed the homosexual artist functions in a heterosexual dictatorship, then this search is doubly difficult. A writer ultimately writes about those things to which he responds, and given the taboos which society has erected against homosexuality, and which are now only beginning to crumble, we can, with these three books, celebrate that style which might in each have been fatally cramped by heterosexuality, but which was, because of the liberation of homosexuality, joyously and brilliantly unfettered.

NOTES

1Christopher Isherwood, *Kathleen and Frank* (NY, 1971), p. 380. All later references to Isherwood are to this edition. By permission.

2Nigel Nicolson, *Portrait of a Marriage* (NY, 1973), p. 106. All later references to Nicolson are to this edition. By permission.

3J. R. Ackerley, *My Father and Myself* (NY, 1969), p. 11. All later references to Ackerley are to this edition. By permission.

4*The New York Times Book Review* (25 Mar. 73), pp. 10-14.

5*The National Observer* (19 Feb. 72).

6*The New York Times* (15 Feb. 72), p. 26.

Male Homosexuality and Lesbianism
In the Works
Of
Proust and Gide

By Karla Jay

For Joanette

Introduction

Along with time, memory, truth, art, and jealousy, homosexuality is one of the major themes in *A la Recherche du temps perdu* by Marcel Proust. All the major characters in the *Recherche* except Swann, and possibly the Duc and Duchesse de Guermantes are homosexual, lesbian, or bisexual. The narrator himself is of a dubious sexuality, which will be discussed at the appropriate place in this study. In addition, literally hundreds of pages consist of narratives about homosexuals or homosexuality.

Homosexuality is not as pervasive in the work of André Gide. Except in *Les-Faux-monnayeurs*, where many of the characters are homosexual, the homosexual is the exceptional person in a heterosexual society. Thus there is less material on the homosexual in the works of Gide and fewer observations about the homosexual as a human being can be drawn from the work of Gide. One should not conclude, however, that homosexuality is less important to Gide, and as we shall see, homosexuality is also an integral part of his work.

Despite the extent of the subject in the work of Proust and Gide, homosexuality suffers an equal neglect in the field of literary criticism. Aside from a few pages here and there, there are no books written on the theme of homosexuality in the work of either author. Léon Pierre-Quint calls this a "conspiration du silence [qui] dénote la plus flagrante incompréhension littéraire,"[1] but after making this astute remark, Pierre-Quint, like the others, proceeds to do nothing about the subject.

The few books devoted in general to the study of homosexuality in literature, such as the one by Harvey Wickham, *The Impuritans*,[2] denote by their very titles the heterosexual bias put into the making of these books, which treat homosexuality either by moralizing on the subject or by belittling the homosexual author or character; for example, Wickham denounces Proust as "ridiculous and sentimental — the inevitable penalty for giving honour where no honour is due."[3] Thus, most books are virtually useless for an objective study of homosexuality in Gide and Proust, and therefore my study relies primarily on the works themselves. In the case of Proust, I used the complete text of *A la Recherche du temps perdu*. For Gide, I concentrated primarily on *L'Immoraliste, Les Faux-monnayeurs,* and *Les Caves du vatican.*

To remain objective, I avoided all books on psychology, because again such books are written by heterosexuals (homosexuals are not allowed to become psychiatrists in this country if their homosexuality is known) and because homosexuality is treated by conservatives as a sickness, by behaviorists as an incorrect learning pattern to be corrected by shock therapy, and by "liberals" as an aberration. The approach of this study, therefore, is socio-political rather than medical or psychological; that is, homosexuals are treated as a class or group of people. We are first looked at from the point of view of the heterosexual society in which we live and then from our own point of view.

Society and the Homosexual

There is hardly any homosexuality at the beginning of the *Recherche* (up to *Sodome et Gomorrhe*). The narrator spies upon Mlle. Vinteuil and her friend through a window at Montjouvain, and rumors are heard about Odette and others being lesbian, but homosexuals and lesbians are rare and are presented as outside the pale of society (that is, Mlle. Vinteuil and her friend are, for all purposes, outcasts). The members of society, on the other hand, are seen and presented as heterosexual. For example, the Baron de Charlus is first presented as an extremely virile man violently opposed to anything effeminate and equally enamoured of anything feminine. He is admired by those in and seeking high society, and he is also admired for his virility, his family connections, and his snobbishness. His nephew Saint-Loup is presented as a most sought after man. He too is considered to be a woman-chaser and a keeper of mistresses and is admired for his place in high society.

Yet, despite their masks, these two men are homosexuals. They are not seen as such because society is absolutely and intentionally blind to the homosexuals and lesbians in their midst.

Et pourtant, même sous les couches d'expressions différentes, de fards et d'hypocrisie qui le maquillaient si mal, le visage de M. de Charlus continuait à taire à presque tout le monde le secret qu'il me paraissait crier. J'étais presque gêné par ses yeux où j'avais peur qu'il ne me surprît à le lire à livre ouvert, par sa voix qui me paraissait le répéter sur tous les tons, avec une inlassable indécence. Mais les secrets sont bien gardés par les êtres, car tous ceux qui les approchent sont sourds et aveugles. [4]

Even Charlus' close friends and associates do not want to believe that Charlus is a homosexual, and Swann denies to the narrator that Charlus is homosexual: "C'est un ami délicieux. Mais ai-je besoin d'ajouter que c'est purement platonique. Il est plus sentimental que d'autres, voilà tout; d'autre part, comme il ne va jamais très loin avec les femmes, cela a donné une espèce de credit aux bruits insensés dont vous voulez parler. Charlus aime peut-être beaucoup ses amis, mais dans sa tete et dans son cœur." [5]

This blindness extends even to the family of the homosexual. For example, the family of Nissim Bernard never seem to suspect why he eats lunch every day at the Grand Hotel at Balbac: "Or, ce plaisir était si fort que tous les ans M. Bernard revenait à Balbec et y prenait son déjeuner hors de chez lui, habitudes où M. Bloch voyait, dans la première un goût poétique pour la belle lumière, les couchers de soleil de cette côte préférée à toute autre; dans la seconde, une manie invétérée de vieux célibataire." [6]

The narrator shares the blindness of the rest of society. Like Swann confronted with the possibility of Charlus' homosexuality, the narrator rushes to deny hints that Saint-Loup is a homosexual, even when someone tells him confidently that "Rachel m'a parlé de vous, elle m'a dit que le petit Saint-Loup vous adorait, vous préférait même à elle." [7] Repeatedly, the narrator blindly asserts: "Je pus les démentir de la façon la plus formelle en ce qui concernait Saint-Loup." [8]

The narrator is also blind to the lesbian tendencies of Albertine, even though he fantasized her as immoral when he first noticed her. His perception of her as a lesbian has to be awakened in him by Dr. Cottard, who describes clinically the manner in which Albertine is dancing with Andrée.

Françoise seems to be the only one who perceives people's homosexuality, and she warns the narrator about Albertine very early in his relationship with her: "Monsieur ne devrait pas voir cette demoiselle. Je vois bien le genre de caractère qu'elle a, elle vous fera des chagrins." [9] Throughout the *Recherche*, Françoise continues to be a Cassandra whispering doom on the narrator's love: "Françoise parlait des choses les plus invraisemblables, tellement vagues qu'on pouvait tout au plus y supposer l'insinuation, bien invraisemblable, que la pauvre captive (qui aimait les femmes) préférait un mariage avec quelqu'un qui ne semblait pas être moi. Si cela avait été, malgré ses radiotélépathies, comment Françoise l'aurait-elle su?" [10] Perhaps it is her jealousy (her watchful eye for her master's money) which leads Françoise to suspect or even falsely accuse Albertine, but it is true that Françoise seems to catch on quickly to the ties between Jupien and Charlus, and later between Morel and Charlus.

Nevertheless, there is a point at which society becomes painfully aware of the homosexuality of one or more of its members. Those belonging to the homosexual's immediate family try to appear blind to the homosexual's "peculiarity," but when the homosexuality is obvious and the family is being pressured into honesty, the pose of blindness becomes almost comic. The family still denies the homosexuality, but in the case of the Duchesse de Guermantes, her blush gives her away. [11] In another case, the Duc de Guermantes becomes so overly defensive when it is suggested in passing that Charlus has a "cœur de femme" that one becomes suspicious because the duke protests so much: " 'Ce qui vous dites est absurde,' interrompit vivement M. de Guermantes. 'Mémé n'a rien d'efféminé, personne n'est plus viril que lui.' 'Mais je ne vous dis pas qu'il soit efféminé le moins du monde. Comprenez au moins ce que je dis,' reprit la duchesse. 'Ah! celui-là, dès qu'il croit qu'on veut toucher à son frère.' " [12]

Some members of the family, such as Mme. de Villeparisis, seem to feel that they are obligated to protect others from Charlus and his "illness," and she therefore offers veiled warnings to the narrator when he states his intention of going home with Charlus: "Elle en parut contrariée. S'il ne s'était agi d'une chose qui ne pouvait intéresser un sentiment de cette nature, il m'eût paru que ce qui semblait en alarme à ce moment-là chez Mme. de Villeparisis, c'était la pudeur. 'Vous devez partir avec mon neveu Palamède?' me dit-elle. . . . 'Ne l'attendez pas. . . . Tenez, partez, profitez vite pendant qu'il a le dos tourné." [13]

The reaction of the rest of society is not usually so thoughtful, and the immediate response is to eliminate anything which is radically different (and therefore threatening to the social order). When the sister of Bloch openly caresses an actress in the salon of the Grand Hotel at Balbec, all the heterosexuals are scandalized at this flaunting of lesbianism in public. Needless to say, these same people probably would not have been as perturbed if a man and a woman were caressing one another. Two officers complain to the director and demand that the two criminal women be thrown out. And they would have been, were it not for the fact that Mlle. Bloch's relative Nissim Bernard ate every day at the hotel, which was therefore dependent upon his money. [14]

Therefore, homosexuals are tolerated by society so long as finances or other needs dictate such kindness.

In high society, the same type of hypocrisy occurs, but not for financial reasons. Mme. Verdurin is kind to Charlus, as long as she things it is imperative to have him and Morel among her "faithful." She places Charlus and Morel in adjoining bedrooms and treats them like a couple.[15] Picking up their cues from Mme. Verdurin, the members of the clan, especially Ski and Cottard, are patronizing to Charlus:

> Sans doute en sa présence ils gardaient sans cesse à l'esprit la souvenir des révélations de Ski et l'idée de l'étrangeté sexuelle qui était incluse en leur compagnon de voyage. Mais cette étrangeté même exerçait sur eux une espèce d'attrait . . . . Dès le debut d'ailleurs, on s'était plus à reconnaître qu'il était intelligent. "Le génie peut être voisin de la folie", énonçait la docteur . . . . A cette première période on avait donc fini par trouver M. de Charlus intelligent malgré son vice. Maintenant, c'était, sans s'en rendre compte, à cause de ce vice qu'on le trouvait plus intelligent que les autres.[16]

When Charlus is not present, members of the Verdurin clan speak maliciously about Charlus: "Car les mots qu'on disait en l'absence de M. de Charlus, les 'à peu près' sur Morel, personne n'avait l'âme assez basse pour les lui répéter."[17] Mme. Verdurin disparagingly speaks of Charlus and Morel as the "demoiselles."[18] While it is all right for Charlus to speak of other homosexuals in the feminine (as blacks sometimes call each other "nigger"), it is insulting when a heterosexual refers to a homosexual in feminine terms.

Again, the rest of the clan follows the example of Mme. Verdurin. Cottard wonders if he should let such an immoral man in the presence of Mme. Cottard.[19] And in addition to gossiping about Charlus, Cottard and Ski make distasteful jokes about Charlus' homosexuality, in an attempt to hide how uncomfortable they really feel around Charlus. Cottard remarks that he'll have to watch out for Charlus' feet under the table,[20] and Ski wonders if they will ever advance anywhere on the train while Charlus is busy making eyes at the trainman: "Regardez-moi la manière dont il le regarde, ce n'est plus un petit chemin de fer où nous sommes, c'est un funiculeur."[21]

The thin jokes, however, do not really hide the heterosexual's deep-rooted fear of the homosexual, nor does intimate contact with a homosexual such as Charlus destroy basic myths about homosexuals, myths created and harbored by heterosexual society. This fear and misunderstanding are made clear in the incident in which Charlus automatically strokes Cottard's hand when speaking to him, and Cottard's deep-rooted fears emerge: Charlus

> lui prit la main et la lui caressa un moment avec une bonté de maître flattant le museau de son cheval et lui donnant du sucre. Mais Cottard, qui n'avait jamais laissé voir au baron qu'il eût même entendu courir de vagues mauvais bruits sur ses mœurs, et ne l'en considérait pas moins, dan son for intérieur, comme faisant partie de la classe des "anormaux" . . . personnages dont il avait peu l'expérience, se figura que cette caresse de la main était le prélude immédiat d'un viol, pour l'accomplissement duquel il avait été, le duel n'ayant servi que de prétexte, attiré dans un guet-apens et conduit dans ce salon solitaire ou il allait être pris de force. N'osant quitter sa chaise, où la peur le tenait cloué, il roulait des yeux d'épouvante, comme tombé aux mains d'un sauvage dont il n'était pas bien assuré qu'il ne se nourrit pas de chair humaine.[22]

Even Mme. Verdurin, for all her pseudoliberalism, takes malicious glee in breaking up Charlus and Morel by wounding Charlus in his Achilles heel which is his (and every homosexual's) homosexuality. She takes great joy in finding Morel's tenderest spot — his pride — and in pricking it. Furthermore, by persecuting Charlus, she not only enjoys herself, but she also absolves herself of any contamination of homosexuality (she herself was rumored to be a lesbian) — that is, she proves to the world that although she associates with people like Charlus, she is not one of *those* people.

The narrator manages to sum up society's attitudes nicely when he says that homosexuality is "une vie dont les hommes de l'autre race non seulement ne comprennent pas, n'imaginent pas, haïssent les plaisirs nécessaires, mais encore dont le danger fréquent et la honte permanente leur feraient horreur."[23]

The narrator, of course, is part of the society described above, but he has an entire set of beliefs not attributed to the society in general. For example, he believes that homosexuality is hereditary, that homosexuals are a race, and that homosexual men are in part women. But these beliefs would take another study to describe adequately and these beliefs might be held by any of the other members of society. There are, however, two things which are crucial to the entire *Recherche* and which should be told about the narrator's attitude towards homosexuals. These are his curiosity and his jealousy.

His excessive curiosity about homosexuals and lesbians becomes one of the major preoccupations of the narrator in the *Recherche*, but not of the rest of the society. One can argue that the hero's witnessing of the scene between Mlle. Vinteuil and her friend at Montjouvain in *Du Côté de chez Swann* was purely accidental since he fell asleep outside the Vinteuil's window; but the other incidents of voyeurism are not at all fortuitous. In *Sodome et Gomorrhe*, he goes out of his way and even takes a great risk of being exposed as a voyeur in his attempt to spy upon Charlus and Jupien. In *Le Temps retrouvé*, the hero again spies upon Charlus in the brothel.

The curiosity of the hero/narrator does not end at physical voyeurism. Throughout the *Recherche*, he asks people whether they think that other people are homosexual, and he listens with apparent interest to Charlus' tirades on the subject. His curiosity about and jealousy of Albertine's lesbianism are the focal points of his relationship with her: he is continually questioning her and others about her possible lesbian activities, and his curiosity does not die with Albertine. He sends Aimé to Balbec to investigate her lesbian activities there, and he asks Andrée to reveal all Albertine's sexual secrets and even to recreate a scene of lesbianism for him.

It goes without saying that his curiosity about Albertine's lesbian activities is inspired in part by his jealousy. The narrator knows that he, as a man, can never compete with a woman for Albertine's love because he cannot offer her the same thing, nor can he ever know with certainty what joys Albertine experiences in the arms of a woman, whereas he could understand and even empathize with any man Albertine might choose as a sexual partner. Repeatedly, the narrator contemplates lesbian experiences from which he has been excluded: "Andrée m'a dit en souriant à demi: 'Ah! oui, mais vous êtes un homme. Aussi nous ne pouvons pas faire ensemble tout à fait les mêmes choses que je faisais avec Albertine.' "[24]

He realizes, much to his dismay, that Albertine is seeking the same thing he is — a woman — that he can never fulfill her desires but that there are many women who can: 'Car du moment qu'elle avait ces goûts . . . , combien de fois, dans combien de demeures, de promenades, elle avait dû les satisfaire! Les gomorrhéennes sont à la fois assez rares et assez nombreuses pour que, dans quelque foule que ce soit, l'une ne passe pas inaperçue aux yeux de l'autre. Dès lors le ralliement est facile." [25]

The narrator is conscious of the nature of his jealousy and of his consequent hatred of lesbianism. He says in *La Prisonnière*: "Non, jamais la jalousie que j'avais eue, un jour, de Saint-Loup, si elle avait persisté, ne m'eût donné cette immense inquiétude. Cet amour entre femmes était quelque chose de trop inconnu, dont rien ne permettait d'imaginer avec certitude, avec justesse, les plaisirs, la qualité."[26]

The type of jealousy experienced by the narrator is paralleled in other relationships throughout the *Recherche*. If the narrator is jealous of Albertine's lesbian relations with Andrée, Andrée is in turn jealous of the narrator because she cannot compete with a man and because she is necessarily excluded from Albertine's heterosexual relationships. The narrator notices, but makes no comment on Andrée's jealousy: "Les défauts d'Andrée s'étaient accusés, elle n'était plus aussi agréable que quand je l'avais connue. Il y avait maintenant chez elle à fleur de peau, une sorte d'aigre inquiétude, prête à s'amasser comme à la mer un 'grain', si seulement je venais à parler de quelque chose qui était agréable pour Albertine et pour moi."[27]

It is not enough to point out the excessive curiosity and jealousy of the narrator. One must ask why. It is important to remember that the hero was on the point of breaking up with Albertine, when his vague suspicions of her lesbianism were confirmed for him by Albertine's revelation that Mlle. Vinteuil. and her friend acted as her two big sisters.[28] This revelation leads to an immediate reinterest in Albertine and to an immediate increase in jealousy. The hero even makes Albertine a prisoner in his house. Up to this revelation, the hero thought that he knew everything there was to know about Albertine, that he possessed her in every sense of the word, that he had penetrated all her mysteries. But her seeming confession makes her mysterious and exciting once again.

> La découverte qu'elle était une autre personne, une personne comme elles [Mlle. Vinteuil et son amie], parlant la même langue, ce qui, en la faisant compatriote d'autres, me le rendait encore plus étrangère à moi, prouvait que ce qui j'avais eu d'elle, ce que je portais dans mon cœur, ce n'était qu'un tout petit peu d'elle et que le reste, qui prenait tant d'extension de ne pas être seulement cette chose déjà si mystérieusement importante, un désir individuel, mais de lui être commune avec d'autres, elle me l'avait toujours caché, elle m'en avait tenu à l'écart, comme une femme qui m'eût caché qu'elle était d'un pays ennemi et espionne, bien plus traîtreusement même qu'une espionne, car celle-ci ne trompe que sur sa nationalité, tandis qu'Albertine c'était sur son humanité la plus profonde sur ce qu'elle n'appartenait pas à l'humanité commune, mais à une race étrange qui s'y mêle, s'y cache et ne s'y fond jamais.[29]

The hero seeks further confessions to solve the mystery of Albertine's lesbianism, and he wonders why she does not confess outright her tastes, but after he has told Albertine so many times how much he detests lesbianism, how could he ever have expected her to confess to him? And if she did confess, would he believe her or would he discount her story as additional lies? Even a confession would not ease his mind or lessen the exoticism he finds in lesbians and homosexuals, for his original attraction to Albertine was based on the mysteriousness, wildness, and perhaps the immorality he found in her.

Thus Albertine's mysterious and exotic lesbianism was the original source of the narrator's attraction to her and the cause of the reawakening of his interest in her. The confirmation of her exotic sexuality makes him only more eager to penetrate Albertine's mysterious personality. And yet, his search is futile. He is a man, and he can never penetrate her secret, even after her death. The only way really to understand Albertine, or even Charlus for that matter, is to have a homosexual experience, something the narrator never brings himself to, despite his curiosity, despite his closeness and attraction to Saint-Loup, and despite his compulsive desire to penetrate the mysteries of Albertine's nature and thus to possess her.

The hero does not take the step into homosexuality because he, being different from all the other characters in the *Recherche*, is asexual. He prefers Albertine when she is asleep, and the joys of masturbation outweigh bodily contact with another being. In no place in the *Recherche* does the narrator actually seem to have intercourse with Albertine, and it would be equally difficult for the hero to establish a physical relationship with a man. His asexuality is probably partly behind his attraction to lesbians and bisexual women (Albertine, Odette, and the maid of Mme. Putbus) from whom demands of physical virility are less likely to be forthcoming.

But never becoming homosexual, the hero can never enter the world of homosexuals and lesbians. It is true that as a bourgeois, he became a member of the Faubourg Saint-Germain, as an outsider he was able to enter the band of girls at Balbec, but as a heterosexual, he can never enter the world of homosexuals or understand the mystery behind homosexuality, although he did not have to become a noble in order to understand the Guermantes. The narrator is a participant at the Duchesse de Guermantes and at Mme. Verdurin's, but he can only function as a voyeur in the homosexual world. And so homosexuality becomes the one world to which the narrator cannot enter, the one world which will forever remain exotic for him.

In Gide's novels, it is not so easy to define the ideas of society. For one thing Gide does not (nor did he try to) create a complete society — a total world — in his novels as did Proust, Balzac, and others. In addition, his novels contain more than one society: *L'Immoraliste* takes place in France and North Africa, part of *Les Caves du vatican* takes place in Italy, whereas almost the entirety of *Les Faux-monnayeurs* takes place in France. Finally, Gide's heros, such as Lafcadio and Michel (less so with Edouard) are more isolated people than the homosexuals and lesbians in the *Recherche* and appear less frequently at organized social functions (such as Proust's society soirées) and therefore get less reaction and even feedback from society than the homosexuals in the *Recherche*. Nevertheless, there are some startling similarities and differences between Gide's and Proust's societies.

To begin with, Gide's society is not as blind as Proust's but there is of course, some degree of self-deception. Laura, for example, never seems to realize why Edouard's relation with her remains platonic. Vincent seems unaware of Robert's homosexuality and Lady Griffith has to warn him.[30] We have no indication that Marceline is aware of Michel's penchant for little Arab boys, and she might well have no suspicions, since she herself is in the habit of bringing home stray children. However, Georges Molinier in *Les Faux-monnayeurs* picks up on Edouard's homosexuality immediately and even confronts him with it, by saying: "Dites donc . . . ça vous arrive souvent de reluquer les lycéens?"[31] And later, instead of trying to ignore Edouard's homosexuality, Georges threatens to expose Edouard to others: "Si vous racontez à mes parents l'histoire du livre, je . . . dirai que vous m'avez fait des propositions."[32]

One may argue that Georges has not really noticed Edouard's homosexuality but is merely trying to use the word "homosexual" as a weapon to frighten Edouard into silence and thus to end any accusations against himself; but there can be no doubt that Lady Griffith is always aware of Robert de Passavant's homosexuality and that Protos knows the sexual persuasion of Lafcadio. Even Mme. Molinier is perfectly aware of what is going on between Edouard and her son.

Despite this knowledge of what is going on, these heterosexuals feel no hatred, disdain, or even aversion. Lady Griffith has a kind of bantering relation with Robert de Passavant. They are continually making biting and ironic jokes about one another, but the maliciousness is somewhat friendly. Lady Griffith teases Robert about his balding (a sign of age)[33] and they even exchange comments on their taste in men: Lady Griffith says:

—C'est curiuex que vous ne le trouviez pas intéressant.
—Vous le trouvez intéressant parce que vous êtes amoureuse de lui.
—Ça c'est vrai, mon cher! On peut vous dire ça, à vous . . . .

—Moi, je le trouve rasoir, votre Vincent, reprit Robert.

—Oh! "mon" Vincent! . . . Comme si ça n'était pas vous qui l'aviez amené! Et puis je vous conseille de ne pas répéter partout qu'il vous ennuie. On comprendrait trop vite pourquoi vous le fréquentez.[34]

In the above dialogue, two attitudes become very clear. First that she can talk to him about men — knowing that the subject will interest him. And then, unlike the narrator in Proust she does not look on him as competition (even though they both desire men), and she is not jealous. She even refers to what other people will think of his relationship with Vincent — but again she is teasing him because she knows very well that Vincent is too old for Robert's tastes and that he has really cast his eye on the younger Olivier.

Protos has the same bantering relationship (though a bit condescending) with Lafcadio. He sincerely likes him and can even treat his homosexuality lightly — without the discomfort found in the thin jokes of the heterosexuals in Proust. Protos says: "Savez-vous que je vous ai beaucoup aimé, Cadio? J'ai toujours pensé qu'on ferait quelque chose de vous. Beau comme vous étiez, on aurait fait marcher pour vous toutes les femmes, et chanter, qu'à cela ne tienne, plus d'un homme par-dessus le marché."[35]

Even some of the relatives — usually the last ones to know — are aware of the homosexuality in their families. Some, like M. Molinier, are unaware, but he never seems to be in touch with what is really happening to anyone except himself. His wife, however, is aware of Olivier's proclivities and although she isn't exactly ecstatic about his homosexuality, she is resigned to it. She says "Ce que je vois que je ne puis pas empêcher, je préfère l'accorder de bonne grâce."[36] And later, when Olivier moves in with Edouard, she adds: "Je suis déjà rassurée de savoir Olivier chez vous . . . . Je ne le soignerais pas mieux que vous, car je sens bien que vous l'aimez autant que moi . . . . Votre rongeur est éloquente . . . Mon pauvre ami, n'attendez pas de moi des reproches. Je vous en ferais si vous ne l'aimiez pas."[37]

Marceline, too, however little she may know or not know (it is difficult to tell since the story is told from Michel's point of view), accepts Michel for what he is with resignation: "Marceline m'accueillait toujours de même; sans un mot de reproche ou de doute, et s'efforçant malgré tout de sourire."[38]

There is very little indication of what the Arab society thought of Michel's sitting and waiting for little boys coming out of school. But there are no great outcries, and one might assume that Michel's homosexuality is accepted — especially since in Arabia pederasty is accepted because of the complete inaccessibility of women. In fact, Corydon often approves of homosexuality because it would, he claims, protect women from being used as objects by men.[39]

All this is not to say that Gide's homosexuals live in some sort of Utopia. In *L'Immoraliste* there is one incidence which reveals some of the true viciousness of society towards homosexuals. The incidence is the use of Ménalque's homosexuality to attempt to disgrace him. "Recemment un absurde, un honteux procès à scandale avait été pour les journaux une commode occasion de le salir; ceux que son dédain et sa superiorité blessaient s'emparèrent de ce prétexte à leur vengeance; et ce qui les irritair le plus, c'est qu'il n'en parût pas affecté."[40] And like Proust's society, people are willing to forget his vice, publicly at least, when he is an enormous success. "Divers journaux, rappelant à ce sujet son aventureuse carrière, semblaient oublier leur basses insultes de la veille et ne trouvaient pas de termes assez vifs pour le louer."[41]

It is not difficult to see the vast difference between the heterosexual society of Proust and Gide. I could only sum it up briefly at this point by saying that as a homosexual, I would perfer to live in Gide's world!

The Homosexual

The results of the oppressive views of society in the *Recherche* regarding homosexuals and the outright persecution of homosexuals (such as the ostracism of Charlus) are not without effect on the homosexual and lesbian (although, as it has been pointed out) there are actually very few "pure" homosexuals and lesbians in the *Recherche*.

As with the Jews in the *Recherche*, persecution leads to some sort of unity (as in the cohesion of the Jews during the Dreyfus Affair). Homosexuals in the *Recherche* tend to adhere to other homosexuals despite differences of class, religion, and political views, for homosexuality is universal "comptant des adhérents partout, dans le peuple, dans l'armée, dans le temple, au bagne, sur le trône."[42] Being outside the pale of society and law, only the homosexuals dare to break the cast code inherent in the society of the *Recherche*. Thus, one finds that the Baron de Charlus has the tradesman Jupien for his confident and loves Morel, whose father was a servant. In *Le Temps retrouvé*, Jupien's brothel becomes a sort of mock salon where one finds nobles, bourgeoisie, and even criminal elements mixing together in what Charlus calls a "franc-maçonnerie."[43]

The unity, however, is superficial, for deep down, the homosexual, like the Jew in the *Recherche*, is filled with self-hatred. Knowing the attitude of society towards "perverts," the homosexual wants to be identified as part of the ruling heterosexual class and not as a member of a hated and scorned group.

The self-hatred takes on many forms. Legrandin, for example, spreads vicious rumors about other homosexuals in order to prove that he is not one of them, and he tells someone: "J'ai même voyagé dernièrement avec le frère du duc de Guermantes, M. de Charlus. Il a spontanément engagé la conversation, ce qui est toujours bon signe, car cela prouve que ce n'est ni un sot gourmé, ni un prétentieux. Oh! je sais tout ce qu'on dit de lui. Mais je ne crois jamais ces choses-là. D'ailleurs, la vie privée des autres ne me regarde pas."[44]

But while Legrandin shams indifference, other homosexuals actively ban one another from clubs because they don't want to associate with them: "Quand un sodomiste n'y est pas admis, les boules noires y sont en majorité celles de sodomistes, mais qui ont soin d'incriminer la sodomie, ayant herité le mensonge qui permit à leurs ancêtres de quitter la ville maudite."[45]

M. d'Argencourt, another homosexual, is less liberal than Legrandin, who at least speaks to Charlus. D'Argencourt goes out of his way to avoid meeting Charlus, who is walking home with the narrator: "En nous voyant, le ministre de Belgique parut contrarié, jeta sur moi un regard de méfiance, presque ce regard destiné à un être d'une autre race que Mme. de Guermantes avait eu pour Bloch, et tâcha de nous éviter. Mais on eut dit que M. de Charlus tenait à lui montrer qu'il ne cherchait nullement à ne pas être vu de lui, car il l'appela et pour lui dire une chose fort insignificante."[46]

Even though Charlus seems to go out of his way here to confront M. d'Argencourt with his homosexuality, Charlus too is filled with self-hatred. He will approach men, especially young men, but when he thinks someone is sexually approaching him, he is filled with disgust and loathing.[47] What Charlus hates is the image of himself that he sees in the person propositioning him. Charlus' self-hatred is so extreme that he even has a man who propositions him brutally beaten.[48] Saint-Loup, when propositioned by someone on the street, also violently assaults this would-be lover.[49]

Lesbians are, of course, not exempt from this self-hatred. Albertine hates herself for being a lesbian and looks upon the narrator as the salvation from her sexuality. Andrée says: "Elle esperait que vous la sauveriez, que vous l'épouseriez. Au fond, elle sentait que c'était une espèce de folie criminelle, et je me suis souvent demandé si ce n'était pas après une chose comme cela, ayant amené un suicide dans une famille, qu'elle s'était elle-même tuée."[50]

This self-hatred causes the homosexual and lesbian to do anything to hide the fact that he or she is different from the heterosexual norm. To prevent discovery, the homosexual wears a mask. It is true that most characters in the *Recherche* wears masks (Legrandin, for example, pretends to be a snob), but the mask of the homosexual is deeper than all the other masks, for his mask hides the core of his being — his sexuality. Charlus pretends to be virile and to hate anything effeminate; to the world he shows himself to be an inveterate skirt-chaser; and in the end, with his makeup, he literally wears a mask like a clown. Saint-Loup, like his uncle, hides his homosexual activities with a chain of mistresses and pretends to love his wife. Morel tries to hide his homosexuality with the same disguise, but he also does not really love women, so he abandons them one after the other. In addition, Morel pretends that he is completely heterosexual and therefore treats Charlus scornfully only in the presence of heterosexuals. Morel justifies his homosexuality by accepting money and gifts from Charlus and Saint-Loup, and he probably says to himself that he is engaging in homosexual acts for the money. Yet, there are other ways to make money, and his closest heterosexual relationship is with Léa, a masculine lesbian, who treats him like a woman.

However, the mask turns against the homosexual, for he must always wonder whether someone has seen beyond his mask. Charlus waits to be greeted by other people (instead of greeting them) because he is never sure whether they have found out that he is a homosexual since the last time he has seen them. And in the end, the mask for the homosexual seems to be on everyone else, and life becomes a fearful game of guessing who knows what about whom.

This guessing game is only a sample of the world of fear in which the closeted homosexual lives in Proust's *Recherche*. There is no one a homosexual can trust, not even another homosexual because of the self-hatred already discussed. M. de Châtterault does not dare to give his sexual contact his name because he is afraid of being exposed or perhaps blackmailed: "Il s'était borné à sa faire passer pour un Anglais et à toutes les questions passionnées de l'huissier désireux de retrouver quelqu'un à qui il devait tant de plaisir et de largesses, le duc s'était borné à repondre, tout le long de l'avenue Gabriel: *'I do not speak French.'* "[51] From fear of exposure, Charlus intimidates the hero into silence after the hero fails to respond to Charlus' advances, but the epitome of fear in the homosexual is M. de Vaugoubert, whose entire life is dominated by his fear of being exposed: "Il avait l'air d'une bête en cage, jetant dans tous les sens des regards qui exprimaient la peur, l'appétance, et la stupidité."[52] He is so fearful that he goes to great lengths to fire an employee who shows signs of coldness to him.

Because of all this fear and oppression, the male homosexual not only has no self-esteem in the *Recherche*, but he is also lacking in his ability to communicate meaningfully with other homosexuals. The huissier likes M. de Châtterault but develops no real relationship with him because the latter is too afraid to give his name, probably did not even speak to him (since he pretends not to know French), and thus could only offer the huissier money instead of a relationship (which both might have preferred). Because of fear, therefore, the homosexual relationship remains a sexual encounter, usually in the dark, in utter silence, an encounter in which the sexual partner remains a sex object rather than another human being.[53]

It is true that lesbians seem to fare better. Andrée and Albertine seem to be friends above all else, but even their relationship is overshadowed by Albertine's fear of the narrator.

Some male homosexuals and lesbians in the *Recherche* resent the oppression of society, and refusing to bow to the heterosexuals, they wear their homosexuality in public, despite the repercussions. Thus, Albertine, rebelling against her imprisonment by the narrator, wears male attire when she is away from him (she could have adequately disguised herself while retaining women's clothing). At Balbec, two lesbians caress one another in public, and Léa is known to have accompanied Gilberte in the street in men's clothes.

The homosexuals and lesbians who dare not be as open as Léa still resent the domination of a heterosexual society, which, by an inverse snobbism, the homosexual looks down upon as being inherently inferior. In conversation, they slyly point to all the famous people in history who were homosexual or lesbian. This inverse psychology holds that people were famous because they were homosexual or lesbian and not that they were famous and happened to be homosexual. "Ils les démasquent volontiers, moins pour leur nuire, ce qui'ils ne detestent pas, que pour s'execuser . . . . "[54] If one listens to a Charlus long enough, one begins to wonder whether there were any famous people who were not homosexual!

This self-pride does not stop at historical and literary musings on the part of Charlus and others. Charlus looks upon himself and other homosexuals as the martyrs of heterosexual society, morally superior to heterosexuals: "J'ai eu de grands chagrins, monsieur, et que je vous dirair peut-être un jour . . . . J'ai de jeunes parents qui ne sont pas, je ne dirai pas dignes, mais capables de recevoir l'héritage moral dont je vous parle. Qui sait si vous n'êtes pas celui entre les mains de qui il peut aller?"[55]

Yet, whether or not the homosexual hides or flaunts his sexuality — or does both — or whether or not one is part, three-quarters, or one hundred percent homosexual or lesbian, the homosexuals in the *Recherche* communicate with one another and find one another in a presumably hetero-sexual society. Homosexuals claim they can recognize one another anywhere, and their claim is not without foundation. Morel is sure, he tells Charlus, that he has radar: "Oh! en une seconde je les devine. Si nous nous promenions tous les deux dans une foule, vous verriez que je ne me trompe pas deux fois."[56]

The narrator himself recognizes this magnetism or extra-sensory perception: "Le vice de chacun l'accompagne à la façon de ce génie qui était invisible pour les hommes tant qu'ils ignoraient sa présence . . . . Ulysse lui-même ne reconnaissait pas d'abord Athéné. Mais les dieux sont immédiatement perceptibles aux dieux, le semblable aussi vite au semblable, ainsi encore l'avait été M. de Charlus à Jupien. . . ."[57] It is not enough, however, simply to say that such communication is due to radar, for as Proust has lucidly shown in the *Recherche*, communication among homosexuals is much more complex.

The most obvious means by which homosexuals and lesbians communicate is by language. Homosexuals, like many subcultures, have a special language consisting of a number of slang words, which have no meaning for the heterosexual, but which let one homosexual know immediately that another man is also homosexual. For example, when Charlus, who seems to use homosexual slang more frequently than other homosexuals in the *Recherche*, drops the word "truqueur,"[58] the hero, had he been also homosexual, would have recognized Charlus immediately as another homosexual. Another common trait of homosexual slang is to reverse genders. Charlus speaks of a king as "une sôeur"[59] and of his conquests as "elle."[60] Léa also speaks of male homosexuals like Morel as "elle"[61] and presumably Morel would in turn call Léa "il."

The problem with homosexual slang is that it is such an in-group orally developed and transmitted language that one can never be entirely sure that someone using the slang understands the word in the same sense as the hearer. Since there are no written roots to hold down the language, the meaning of the words is subject to change at any moment. Thus, Charlus feels his entire identity being uprooted and destroyed when he sees the words "en être" being used to mean something other than what he has always taken them to mean.[62]

Fortunately for Charlus and others, it is not only the words themselves which have meaning, but also the manner in which the words are spoken. In his first encounter with Jupien, Charlus seems to be having an ordinary conversation. He merely asks Jupien for a light for his cigar, but his manner implies that tobacco is not the subject at hand. Jupien could have said that he did not have a light, thus ending the conversation abruptly and implying to Charlus that he did not understand or was not available. But like two spies meeting to exchange information, each word is greeted by another password, and the conversation is as unnatural and as heavy as watchwords among sentries.

The communication among homosexuals goes even beyond language. Jupien indicates to Charlus that he is homosexual long before any words pass between them. He walks in a certain manner, poses his hand on his hip, thrusts out his rear end; and Charlus does likewise. Of course, this encounter between Charlus and Jupien is greatly exaggerated; homosexuals need even fewer signs to recognize one another, and it could be a manner of holding a cigarette, of shaking hands or of dressing. Bloch's cousin meets another woman by playing a game of footsy with her.

In fact, the most common way in which homosexuals and lesbians find one another in the *Recherche* is by a simple glance. In the following passage, Saint-Loup's eyes give away the fact that he is a homosexual:

> Il levait rapidement ses yeux clairs et jetait sur lui un regard qui ne durait pas plus de deux secondes, mais dans sa limpide clairvoyance semblait témoigner d'un ordre de curiosité et de recherches entièrement différent de celui qui aurait pu animer n'importe quel client regardant même longtemps un chasseur ou un commis . . . . Ce petit regard court, désintéressait en lui-même, révélait à ceux qui l'eussent observé que cet excellent mari, cet amant jadis passionné de Rachel avait dans sa vie un autre plan.[63]

The narrator is fascinated by this rapid and somehow sure means of communication, and he analyzes the all-important eyes of the homosexual and lesbian time and again. He studies Charlus as Charlus cruises with his eyes the attractive sons of Mme. de Surgis, and he studies Saint-Loup, but he is especially fascinated by the magnetic glance sent from one woman to another, a glance which automatically excludes him. To his horror he watches Albertine watching women and women watching Albertine, such as one woman who "lui faisait des signes comme a l'àide d'un phare."[64] Elsewhere, the narrator speaks of the glance of a lesbian as a "phénomène lumineux, une sorte de traînée phosphorescente allant de l'une à l'autre."[65]

Thus, despite the oppression and the self-hatred, the very nature of homosexual love compels one man to seek out another, and one woman to find another, and to develop a system of signs (as complicated as the "mondain" signs, for example) to facilitate the fulfillment of this need.

The homosexual in Gide is different from and more limited in scope than the homosexual in the *Recherche*. First of all, there are no lesbians (perhaps Gide is either against lesbianism or is one of those people under the delusion that *homo* comes from the latin "man," when in reality it comes from the Greek meaning "same"), and Gide presents only one type of active homosexual or bisexual man: the pederast — that is, the homosexual man who loves children. "He does not seem to advocate seduction, but he fails to recognize the usual legal and moral distinction between homosexual (or other) relations freely entered into by adults and the relations of an adult with a minor." [66]

The homosexuals are all such lucid mirrors of Gide's own taste that the minute one spots a beautiful, young boy, one knows what will happen. In *Les Faux-monnayeurs*, Edouard is interested in Bernard, falls in love with Olivier (who is young enough to be his son), and at the end of the novel begins to have an interest in Bernard's younger brother Caloub. [67] Similarly, Robert prefers Olivier to Vincent because the former is younger; Strouvilhou is Edouard's age and thus does not appeal to Robert's tastes.

In *L'Immoraliste* the youthfulness of Charles appeals to Michel: "C'était un beau gaillard, si riche de santé, si souple, si bien fait, que les affreux habits de ville qu'il avait mis en notre honneur ne parvenaient pas à le rendre trop ridicule." [68] When Charles grows into a man, he immediately displeases Michel: "Je vis entrer, à la place de Charles, un absurde Monsieur, coiffé d'un ridicule chapeau melon. Dieu! qu'il était changé! . . . Quand on apporta la lampe, je vis avec dégoût qu'il avait laissé pousser ses favoris." [69]

The other boys who attract Michel usually fit the same description: young, supple, dark, beautiful but *masculine* (femininity also repels Gide's heros). These boys include the 15-year-old son of Heurtevent, [70] the Arab children, and the young Sicilian coach driver, whom he kisses. [71]

In *Les Caves du vatican*, Lafcadio, who is bisexual, also likes younger boys, such as the one traveling with the curé. "Quels beaux yeux il levait vers moi!" Lafcadio tells himself, "qui cherchaient aussi inquiètement mon regard que mon regard cherchait le sien; mais que je détournais aussitôt . . . . Il n'avait pas cinq ans de moins que moi. Oui: quartorze à seize ans, pas plus." [72]

There is only one instance in which two men of approximately the same age are attracted to one another, and this case is the affection between Bernard and Olivier, but they never consumate their affection. It is interesting, however, that the heterosexuals are attracted to people their own age (like Fleurissoire and Arnica) or as in the case of Jérôme, a woman slightly older (Alissa). [73]

As mentioned earlier, there is only one type of active homosexual, but there are some good portraits of latent homosexuals, not present in the *Recherche*. One is Anthime in *Les Caves du vatican*. Although he never openly expresses his homosexuality he, like the active homosexuals, is attracted to young boys. For Anthime, the boy is Beppo: "Dans sa revêche solitude, le cŏeur d'Anthime battait un peu lorsque approchait le faible claquement des petits pieds nus sur les dalles. Il n'en laissait rien voir." [74]

Another latent couple is Blafaphas and Fleurissoire. How many heterosexual men treasure their best friend more than their wife, as Fleurissoire does Blafaphas? "Il prit Blafaphas dans ses bras (la rue était déserte) et lui jura que, pour grand fût son amour, son amitié l'importait de beaucoup encore, qu'il n'entendait pas que, par son mariage, elle fût en rien diminuée et qu'enfin plûtot que de sentir Blafaphas soufrant de quelque jalousie, il était prêt á lui promettre, sur son bonheur, de ne jamais user de ses droits conjugaux!" [75] Assuredly, a strange vow!

Michel (the hero as opposed to Michel the narrator) is probably latent throughout most of *L'Immoraliste*, and the story is partly one of his self-realization as a homosexual. He hints right from the beginning that he never loved a woman.[76] It is probably because of this latency combined with his marriage that makes Michel the only one of Gide's homosexuals to feel guilt (Fleurissoire, on the other hand, feels guilt at his heterosexual initiation with Carola). Michel feels uncomfortable about Marceline's presence when he is with the Arab children: "Oui, si peu que ce fût, je fus gêné par sa présence . . . . Et puis, parler aux enfants, je ne l'osais pas devant elle."[77] As stated before, Marceline seems to be resigned to whatever Michel does but her mere *presence* is enough to bother him, and that is perhaps part of the reason he subconsciously kills her.

Probably due to the lack of hostility in the society, the other homosexuals do not feel the same degree of self-hatred or shame that we find in the *Recherche* among the homosexuals and lesbians. Edouard does not seem to dislike himself at all, and when Olivier tries to kill himself after finally consumating his love for Edouard, the suicide attempt is from sheer joy à la Dostoyevsky rather than shame. As Olivier says: "Je comprends qu'on se tue; mais ce serait après avoir goûté une joie si forte que toute la vie qui la suive en palisse."[78] And later to Edouard: "Ne va t'imaginer pas que c'est par honte."[79] None of Gide's heros surround themselves with countless mistresses or slander other homosexuals or do the other things Proust's homosexuals do to hide the fact that they are homosexual. Michel openly confesses all his tastes to his friends and continually reveals himself instead of masking his true nature.

However, there is probably some self-hatred expressed in the very fact that Gide's homosexuals are repelled by mature men resembling themselves and attracted by innocent youth, but there is only one exceptionally self-hating character — Robert de Passavant and he is a rather despicable creature to begin with. When his father dies, he is willing to marry Lilian to hide his homosexuality from a suspicious society. He also tries to play the dandy in public with Sarah to dispel rumors about himself: "Averti des bruits désobligeants qui couraient sur ses rapports avec Olivier, il cherchait à donner le change. Et pour s'afficher plus encore, il s'était promis d'amener Sarah à asseoir sur ses genoux

. . . . Cependant Passavant craignait d'aller trop vite. Il manquait de pratique."[80]

Also unlike the others, Robert is terrified of what heterosexuals think of him, and like Charlus, he never knows who knows what: "Il venait de surprendre, à la lueur de la cigarette que fumait Vincent, un étrange pli sur la lèvre de celui-ci, où il crut voir de l'ironie; or, il craignait la moquerie par-dessus tout au monde."[81]

Aside from the case of Robert's self-hatred, there are other ways in which Gide's pederasts are similar to Proust's homosexuals and lesbians. For example, they do not seem to develop lasting relationships. Robert flits from youth to youth. Lafcadio is too entranced with his own destiny to bother with others, and he even ends his relationship with Carola at the first opportunity. Michel desires many of the Arab boys along with Charles and others, but he never seems to develop a relationship with any of them.

It is easier, however, to understand the lack of love among Gide's homosexuals. When a mature man is enamoured of a youth or child, there are few grounds on which to communicate other than sexuality. Even the relationship between Edouard and Olivier — the one homosexual relationship in Gide's novels where love truly exists — is plagued by a lack of communication, probably enhanced by the generation gap. Olivier continually misunderstands Edouard's intentions and vice-versa. A typical example of these hiatuses is the meeting between Olivier and Edouard at the station. Each fears that he is imposing upon the other:

> Scrupuleuse à l'excès, son âme était habile à se persuader que peut-être Edouard trouvait sa présence importune. Il n'eut pas plus tôt menti, qu'il rougit. Edouard surprit cette rougeur et, comme d'abord il avait saisi le bras d'Olivier d'une étreinte passionnée, crut, par scruple également, que c'était là ce qui le faisait rougir.[82]

Such embarrassment would be avoided if Edouard and Olivier used the subcultural homosexual language of a Charlus or if they used Jupien's physical gestures to convey their sexuality. But since Gide seems to detest femininity in homosexuals, Edouard and Olivier cannot communicate in this fashion either. They even lack Saint-Loup's telling glances. The result is that Olivier and Edouard are continually misunderstanding, embarrassing, angering, and even alienating one another.

Michel also has difficulty communicating to Charles and other youth his interest in them, but Gide's other homosexuals seem to communicate better. We have already seen how Lafcadio flashes a glance at the youth in the train. Olivier seems to comprehend from the beginning that Bernard is partly homosexual. He asks Bernard what he will do now that he has left his parents and fears that Bernard will "fera le marlou."[83] Olivier also seems to comprehend that Robert is seeking more than an editor to accompany him, and it is probably the very fact of Robert's homosexuality which precipitates Olivier's decision.

Another way in which Gide's homosexuals resemble those in the *Recherche* is that they are also prone to jealousy. However, in the case of the narrator or Andrée, the jealousy is caused by the opposite sex with whom they cannot compete. In Gide's novels, on the other hand, the jealousy is of the same sex, and the cause of the jealousy is exclusion. Bernard feels this jealousy when, after having read Edouard's diary, he discovers that he has been excluded from a large part of Olivier's life and from the relationship between Edouard and Olivier. "A l'immense curiosité qui précipitait sa lecture, se mêlait un trouble malaise: dégoût ou dépit. Un peu de ce dépit qu'il avait ressenti tout à l'heure à voir Olivier au bras d'Edouard: un dépit de ne pas en être."[84]

As alluded to earlier, the jealousy caused by the exclusion of Olivier from the relationship between Bernard and Edouard precipitates Olivier's decision to join Robert.

> Il se sentait à la fois supplanté dans le cœur de Bernard et dans celui d'Edouard. L'amitié de ses deux amis évinçait la sienne. Une phrase surtout de la lettre de Bernard le torturait, que Bernard n'aurait jamais écrite s'il avait pressenti tout ce qu'Olivier pourrait y voir: "Dans la même chambre", se répétait-il — et l'abominable serpent de la jalousie se déroulait et se tordait en son cœur. "Ils couchent dans la même chambre!" . . . Que n'imaginait-il pas aussitôt? Son cerveau s'emplissait de visions impures qu'il n'essayait même pas de chasser. Il n'était jalous particulièrement ni d'Edouard, ni de Bernard; mais des deux. Il les imaginait tour à tour l'un et l'autre ou simultanément, et les enviait à la fois."[85]

The same jealousy causes Olivier to write his boastful and somewhat obnoxious letter to Bernard.[86]

Conclusions

Having viewed the magnitude of the theme of homosexuality in the *Recherche* and in Gide's novels, one must try to comprehend the meaning of it. One significance of this sexuality is its parallelism to other themes. In Proust, for example, the signs that pass from one homosexual to another within the sodomite culture are parallel to the signs that Gilles Deleuze has noted for the world of love and society.[87]

There is also a parallelism in the *Recherche* and in Gide's novels between heterosexual and homosexual love. Homosexuals experience the same sorts of jealousy and need to possess the loved one as heterosexuals feel as in Proust's narrator's need to possess Albertine. If heterosexual relationships have little chance for success in Proust (Swann, for example, does not have a rainbow path in his love for Odette), then homosexual relationships in Proust and Gide are even shakier. Proust and Gide were probably the first writers to recognize this parallelism between homosexual and heterosexual relationships, and between homosexuals and heterosexuals themselves. Is Edouard's love, for example, that different from Jerome's? These authors were apt to note how thin the line really is between hetero- and homo- sexuality.

There is a further parallelism in the *Recherche:* The growing decadence of society is reflected in the growth of homosexuality. Perhaps the height of the social world is reached during the soirée in the second part of *Le Côté de Guermantes.* The narrator seems to have reached the height of his social ambitions, and the society gathered at the Guermantes' is the "cream" of society. Up to *Sodome et Gomorrhe,* homosexuality is present only below the surface like an ominous iceberg. In and after *Sodome et Gomorrhe,* homosexuality starts to emerge, and society begins its decline. By the time we are at the gathering in *Le Temps retrouve* at the home of the new Princess de Guermantes (the former Mme. Verdurin), society has declined; the cream of society is reduced to decaying and decrepit people wearing death masks, and some newer but lesser people have taken their places. At the same time, homosexuality is still rising and almost all the major characters, including Saint-Loup, have now been unmasked as homosexuals. The brothel of Jupien has replaced the brothel where Rachel used to work. Like the Biblical cities of Sodom and Gomorrha, society is now ready to fall and is falling, but this time the catastrophe comes from within rather than from the vengeance of God. This time the cities will perish of themselves. Perhaps the homosexual's indifference to caste will overthrow the social order Proust holds so dear. Or perhaps it is significant that the only quote starting off any of the novels of the *Recherche* is the one by Alfred de Vigny: "La femme aura Gomorrhe et l'homme Sodome."[88] Perhaps Proust sees the sterility resulting from homosexual and lesbian relationships as a peril to society. If all become homosexual or lesbian, will society split into two opposing groups who will put an end to procreation?

But in spite of homosexuality's apparent dangers, it is not without its fascination. For the hero/narrator, homosexuality — and especially lesbianism — are, as pointed out, the ultimate mystery of the individual. In his stagnant asexuality, the hero sees the blossoming bisexuality of everyone around him, and he perceives people filled with every conceivable type of sexual inclination and desire. And while he is struggling to find some sort — any sort — of sexual being within himself, the society is filling up with people who are not only bisexual but also androgynous or hermaphroditic — that is, containing both sexes within themselves. The word *hermaphrodite* appears often, and bisexuals are viewed as hermaphroditic plants: They are men contained within women and women contained within men — people who are pansexual; and the narrator is the man in the sea, who is surrounded by water but unable to drink. Thus the *Recherche* is, in part, a quest for sexuality, for sexual identity, and the quest is one which must look at homosexuality as well as at heterosexuality in order to be complete.

Although homosexuality is not as prevalent in the works of Gide, homosexuality is an integral part of Gide's novels and philosophy. Gide implies that *l'homme libre* must be free from the norms and confines of sexuality as well as free from the standard ethics of the church, the family and other external sanctions. His free men, those capable of *l'acte gratuit*, are all bisexual. Lafcadio, who commits the gratuitous murder of Fleurissoire, is a bastard (free from family), irreligious, and bisexual in nature. Bernard, who steals Edouard's suitcase, is also a bastard and bisexual. Michel, who witnesses the theft of the scissors by the Arab boy and who has no qualms about the theft, is also a free man, who if he cannot commit the act himself can at least witness it. The heterosexuals, such as Julius de Baraglioul and Jérôme, are closely tied to their families and religion. When Julius is briefly disenchanted with the Church, he can then contemplate the gratuitous murder, but when he is back with his wife, religion, and stagnant heterosexuality, he returns to his dull, religious novels.

Thus, Gide, Proust, and other novelists of the same era made homosexuality an integral part of their work. These novels reveal a fair amount of diversity among homosexuals, as opposed to the stereotypes found in the case studies of homosexuality. They also shed some light on the almost unknown life of the homosexuals at the beginning of the twentieth century. Of course, we surely cannot expect either Proust or Gide to have the liberating self-love of some post-Stonewall gays. In Proust's and Gide's association of homosexuality with decadence they may very well have been indulging in self-persecution in much the way that contemporary closeted gay males and lesbians sometimes adopt the negative attitude of the oppressor towards themselves. To the extent that all change means the fall of old standards, few people of any description are likely to welcome change with open arms. Liberation is a painful passage. Perhaps viewing homosexuality as decadent is the price that Proust and Gide had to pay for the self-acceptance that they did muster: that is, like most homosexuals then and possibly now, they did accept their homosexuality, even when to accept it seemed to require the acceptance of society's devaluation as well. Certainly we can all be grateful that they had the intellectual courage not to cover up the negative things, from whatever source, that homosexuals have felt about themselves. Both homosexuals and heterosexuals owe an enormous debt to them.

NOTES

1Léon Pierre-Quint, *Marcel Proust; sa vie, son oeuvre* (Paris, 1946).

2Harvey Wickham, *The Impuritans* (New York, 1929).

3Ibid., p. 199.

4Marcell Proust, *La Prisonnière.* (Paris, 1967), p. 241. The Livre du Poche edition has been used throughout.

5Ibid., *Sodome et Gomorrhe*, p. 111.

6Ibid., p. 246.

7Ibid., *Le Côtè de Guermantes*, Tome II, p. 301.

8Ibid., p. 147.

9Ibid., *Sodome et Gomorrhe*, p. 191.

10Ibid., *La Prisonnière*, p. 103.

11Ibid., *Le Côté de Guermantes*, Tome II, p. 296.

12Ibid., pp. 298-299.

13Ibid., *Le Côté de Guermantes*, Tome I, pp. 395-396.

[14]Ibid., *Sodome et Gomorrhe*, p. 244.

[15]Ibid., p. 445.

[16]Ibid., pp. 440-441.

[17]Ibid., p. 447.

[18]Ibid., p. 443.

[19]Ibid., p. 438.

[20]Ibid., p. 334.

[21]Ibid., p. 441.

[22]Ibid., pp. 471-472.

[23]Ibid., p. 28.

[24]Ibid., *Albertine disparue*, p. 303.

[25]Ibid., *La Prisonnière*, p. 374.

[26]Ibid., p. 412.

[27]Ibid., *La Prisonnière*, p. 61.

[28]Ibid., *Sodome et Gomorrhe*, p. 514.

[29]Ibid., *Albertine disparue*, pp. 184-185.

[30]André Gide, *Les Faux-monnayeurs* (France, 1925), p. 82.

[31]Ibid., p. 111.

[32]Ibid., p. 114.

[33]Ibid., p. 61.

34Ibid., pp. 60-61.

35Ibid., *Les Caves du vatican* (France, 1922), p. 232.

36Ibid., *Les Faux-monnayeurs*, p. 346.

37Ibid., pp. 396-97.

38Ibid., *L'Immoraliste* (France, 1902), p. 166.

39Ibid., *Corydon* (Paris, 1926).

40Ibid., *L'Immoraliste*, p. 105.

41Ibid., p. 114.

42Proust, *Sodome et Gomorrhe*, p. 21.

43Ibid., *Le Côté de Guermantes*, Tome I, p. 405.

44Ibid., *Albertine disparue*, pp. 412-413.

45Ibid., *Sodome et Gomorrhe*, p. 36.

46Ibid., *Le Côté de Guermantes*, Tome I, p. 407.

47Ibid., *Sodome et Gomorrhe*, p. 320.

48Ibid., *A L'Ombre des jeune filles en fleurs*, p. 340.

49Ibid., *Le Côté de Guermantes*, Tome I, p. 254.

50Ibid., *Albertine disparue*, p. 305.

51Ibid., *Sodome et Gomorrhe*, p. 38.

52Ibid., p. 47.

53Ibid., pp. 28-29.

[54]Ibid., pp. 20-21.

[55]Ibid., *Le Côté de Guermantes*, Tome I, pp. 406-407.

[56]Ibid., *Sodome et Gomorrhe*, p. 408.

[57]Ibid., p. 17.

[58]Ibid., *Le Côté de Guermantes*, Tome I, p. 412.

[59]Ibid., *Le Temps retrouvé*, p. 124.

[60]Ibid., *Sodome et Gomorrhe*, p. 14.

[61]Ibid., *La Prisonnière*, p. 229.

[62]Ibid.

[63]Ibid., *Albertine disparue*, pp. 436-437.

[64]Ibid., *Sodome et Gomorrhe*, p. 253.

[65]Ibid.

[66]Van Meter Ames, *André Gide* (Norfolk, Conn., 1947), p. 74.

[67]Gide, *Les Faux-monnayeurs*, p. 495.

[68]Ibid., *L'Immoraliste*, pp. 83-84.

[69]Ibid., p. 134.

[70]Ibid., p. 137.

[71]Ibid., p. 164.

[72]Ibid., *Les Caves du vatican*, p. 192.

[73]Ibid., *La Porte étroite* (France, 1959).

74Ibid., *Les Caves du vatican*, p. 10.

75Ibid., p. 114.

76Ibid., *L'Immoraliste*, p. 18.

77Ibid., p. 43.

78Ibid., *Les Faux-monnayeurs*, p. 342.

79Ibid., p. 402.

80Ibid., p. 375.

81Ibid., p. 194.

82Ibid., pp. 96-97.

83Ibid., p. 36.

84Ibid., p. 145.

85Ibid., p. 215.

86Ibid., pp. 264-269.

87Gilles Deleuze, *Marcel Proust et les signes* (Vendôme, France, 1964).

88Proust, *Sodome et Gomorrhe*, p. 5.

Homosexual Love
In Four Poems
By Rilke

By Bernhard Frank

By all accounts Rainer Maria Rilke (1875-1926) was not homosexual and his works evince no particular interest in same-sex behavior. Even in his *Sonnets to Orpheus* Rilke employs the Greet poet-singer as a symbol of the creative force without reference to his homosexual leanings.

In his earlier volume, *Neue Gedichte* (*New Poems*, 1907, 1908),[1] Rilke finds his symbols first in "*den Dingen*" (the things, the artifacts) which surround humanity: animals ("The Panther," "The Flamingo," "The Swan"), plant life ("Blue Hortensia," Pink Hortensia," "Persian Heliotrope"), and the inanimate ("The Sundial," "The Bed," "The Ball"); secondly, Rilke employs humanity itself ("The Beggar," "The Blind Man," "The Prisoner"); and thirdly he extends man back to his primordial roots through history, mythology, and religion ("Buddha," "Leda," "St. George"). In this last category occur the only four poems in the volume which deal with homosexual love. All four poems are monologues by speakers divorced from Rilke.

The first monologue is spoken to Sappho, the renowned poet of Lesbos (c. 600 B.C.); the second is Sappho's answer:

ERANNA AN SAPPHO

O du wilde weite Werferin:
Wie ein Speer bei andern Dingen
lag ich bei den Meinen. Dein Erklingen

warf mich weit. Ich weiss nicht *wo* ich bin.
Mich kann keiner wiederbringen.

Meine Schwestern denken mich und weben,
und das Haus ist voll vertrauter Schritte.
Ich allein bin fern und forgegeben,
und ich zittere wie eine Bitte;
denn die schöne Göttin in der Mitte
ihrer Mythen glüht und lebt mein Leben.

(from: *Neue Gedichte*, I)

ERANNA TO SAPPHO

You, O savage long-distance thrower:
Like a spear alongside other artifacts
have I lain beside my kin. Your clang
has cast me far. I don't know *where* I am.
Me no one can bring back.

My sisters picture me and weave
and the house resounds with confidential steps.
Only I am distant and removed
and I tremble like a request;
for the lovely Goddess in the midst
of her myths glows and in my life lives.   (translation mine)

SAPPHO AN ERANNA

Unruh will ich über dich bringen,
schwingen will ich dich, umrankter Stab.
Wie das Sterben will ich dich durchdringen
und dich weitergeben wie das Grab
an das Alles: allen diesen Dingen.

(from: *Neue Gedichte*, I)

SAPPHO TO ERANNA

Let me steep you in unrest,
toss you about, an entwined stave.
Let me penetrate you like death
and remit you like the grave
unto the All: unto all these artifacts.   (translation mine)

Eranna (variously referred to as Irana, Erinna, Gyrinno, or Gyrina) was a young poet from Telos who had received her mother's reluctant permission to join Sappho's entourage in Mytelene, where she was said to have been Sappho's favorite; she died at the age of nineteen. A strong sense of sado-masochism pervades the two women's brief exchange. Thus, Eranna's choice of the spear image makes her a passive (and in this case foil-less) agent in the hands of the beloved. Although "I don't know *where* I am" may be a complaint, there appears to be some exultation in the determined hopelessness of "Me no one can bring back."

Understandably, Eranna feels alienated from her kinfolk; rather than *know* her they *endow* her with their own imaginings; she can no longer be part of the "confidential steps" — *her* confidences now lie elsewhere. Yet she makes no effort to bridge the gap but rather seems *proud* to feel "distant and removed" and in the final lines glories in the Goddess of Love's (presumably Aphrodite's) permeation of her inner life.

If Eranna's masochism is only implicit, Sappho's sadistic edge is unmistakeable: You are suffering? Good. You are a spear (and a confounded, "entwined" one, at that)? I shall take full advantage and cast you about. The sexual sense of "penetration" is cruelly and morbidly coupled with death. Conceivably, Sappho feels threatened by the phallic spear-image and must retaliate in kind.

The last lines would seem to predict a speedy termination of the relation-ship: As the grave remits humankind back unto the All, so shall Sappho return Eranna to the "artifacts" whose loss she mourns; and yet Eranna is believed to have been Sappho's favorite. Rilke, here, may well have followed Sappho's lead:

> Never, Irana, have I met anybody
> More bothersome than you.[2]

After all, the moods of love are rarely static.

In the poem, "Lament for Antinous," the speaker, Hadrian, sounds a note of dominance similar to Sappho's yet his destructiveness is involuntary:

KLAGE UM ANTINOUS

Keiner begriff mir von euch den bithynischen Knaben
(dass ihr den Strom anfasstet und von ihm hübt . . .).
Ich verwöhnte ihn zwar. Und dennoch: wir haben
ihn nur mit Schwere erfüllt und für immer getrübt.

Wer vermag denn zu lieben? Wer kann es? — Noch keiner.
Und so hab ich unendliches Weh getan —
Nun ist er am Nil der stillenden Götter einer,
und ich weiss kaum welcher and kann ihm nicht nahn.

Und ihr warfet ihn noch, Wahnsinnige, bis in die Sterne,
damit ich euch rufe und dränge: meint ihr den?
Was ist er nich einfach ein Toter. Er wäre es gerne.
Und vielleicht wäre ihm nichts geschehn.

(from: *Neue Gidichte*, II)

LAMENT FOR ANTINOUS

Not one among you fathomed the Bithynian youth
(enough to have touched the current and lifted from it . . .)
Of course I spoiled him. And yet: we induced
only heaviness in him and forever clouded his spirit.

Who then succeeds in loving? Who knows how? As yet, none.
And so have I inflicted endless pain — .
Now beside the Nile of the allaying Gods is he one,
yet I don't know which and towards him cannot lean.

And you still toss him, Madmen, to the stars
that I may summon you and urge: What, do you think?
Is he not merely mortal? He gladly would have been.
Perhaps then he'd have been spared.

(translation mine)

Antinous, Emperor Hadrian's legendarily beautiful "favorite" (c. A.D. 110-130) was drowned in the Nile on a visit to Egypt; some say he had committed suicide for the Emperor's sake. Hadrian had the youth deified and founded in his memory the city of Antinoöpolis in Egypt. A cult was inaugurated in Antinous' honor. In the poem Hadrian, addressing his retinue, denounces the deification of both the living and the dead Antinous: The very people who now pretend to worship the boy had not deigned to "weet their cork heeled shoon" to save him from the currents of the Nile. Even Hadrian himself, in idolizing his lover, had merely made him unhappy, conceivably by forcing him to live up to an exalted image. Hadrian now suspects "he gladly would have been" mortal. Ironically, had he *not* deified him, the boy might still be living: in trying to *immortalize* man one merely expedites his *mortality*.

The poem has been considered "yet too experimental to be deeply moving."[3] The criticism *may* apply to the poem as a whole, but the lines depicting Hadrian's despair as he stumbles amid a labyrinth of gods, unable to recognize his deified beloved are truly haunting.

Despite his grief, despite his maniacal attachment to the dead, Hadrian is no fool; he knows the court is manipulating him, tossing Antinous "to the stars" simply so that he would depend on them. Only in the line "Who then succeeds in loving? Who knows how? As yet, none" does he give in to the luxury of self-justification. If he failed it was because *no one* had as yet learned how to love.

The destructive element in the fourth and last poem stems neither deliberately nor involuntarily from the characters themselves; it is imposed by external forces: Jonathan, son of the Israelite King Saul and beloved of David, has been slain by the Philistines. Rilke's inspiration here appears to have been the magnificent Biblical lament ending with the lines.

> Jonathan lies slain upon thy high places.
> I am distressed for you, my brother Jonathan;
> very pleasant have you been to me;
> your love to me was wonderful,
> passing the love of women.

(2 Samuel I:25, 26)

KLAGE UM JONATHAN

Ach sind auch Könige nicht von Bestand
und dürfen hingehn wie gemeine Dinge,
obwohl ihr Druck wie der der Siegelringe
sich widerbildet in das weiche Land.

Wie aber konntest du, so angefangen
mit deines Herzens Initial,
aufhören plötzlich: Wärme meiner Wangen.

O dass dich einer noch einmal
erzeugte, wenn sein Samen in ihm glänzt.

Irgend ein Fremder sollte dich zerstören,
und der dir innig war, ist nichts dabei
und muss sich halten und die Botschaft hören;
wie wunde Tiere auf den Lagern löhren,
möcht ich mich legen mit Geschrei.

denn da und da, an meinen scheusten Orten,
bist du mir ausgerissen wie das Haar,
das in den Achselhöhlen wächst und dorten,
wo ich ein Spiel für Frauen war,

bevor du meine dort verfitzten Sinne
aufsträhntest wie man einen Knaul entflicht;
da sah ich auf und wurde deiner inne: —
Jetzt aber gehst du mir aus dem Gesicht.

(from: *Neue Gedichte*, II)

LAMENT FOR JONATHAN

Why even Kings then are not substantial
and perish may like ordinary things,
although their impress like that of seal-rings
reforms itself in the pliant soil.

Still how could you, having begun thus
with the initial of your heart,
cease suddenly: My cheeks' blush.
Oh that someone once more would
procreate you, when the semen in him flashed.

Ostensibly a stranger has destroyed you
and who was your intimate does not signify
and must contain himself and hear the news;
as wounded beasts upon their lair make moan
so would I lie down and cry:

for here and there, from my most secret parts
have you been plucked like hair
which in the armpits grows and there
where women used me for their sport

before you ravelled my disordered senses
the way a skein of wool's undone;
then I looked up and we were one: —
Yet now you're draining from my face.　　　(translation mine)

More than the preceding ones, this poem presents textual ambiguities and consequent translating difficulties. The first image, of kings being like seal-rings whose impress reforms itself after their death, is metaphysical. Conceivably it is the waves their actions had made that return them to the shore of the living.

"Having begun thus / with the initial of your heart" may draw on lovers' practice of writing their initials inside a heart-shape. The lines further suggest that Jonathan put love first, the heart (like the first letter of a name) being the initial of his personality, of his life. Like initials, too, love was the very essence, the very shorthand of his existence.

David's equation of Jonathan with the blush or warmth of his own cheeks tells us most tenderly that Jonathan had become blood of his blood; with his death, in the ultimate line, it is that life blood which is draining from David's face.

The fourth stanza amplifies and humanizes the Biblical David's preference of Jonathan over womankind. Women have used him; their playing in his pubic region has, for him, a touch of the obscene to it; he seems reproachful of the violation of his modesty, of his shiest, his "most secret parts." Only in the hands of Jonathan does he permit himself to unwind contentedly, passive as Eranna's spear but skeinlike, softer and even more confounded. A fusion of the two souls occurs and in death the blood of the one must drain from the flesh of the other.

Ironically, *homophobia* appears in the very poem in which the lovers have been most fulfilled: In the presence of both messenger and by-standers David feels he "must contain himself and hear the news," when he wants to cry out for all the world to hear.

The homophobia however is *not* Rilke's. Although writing in a homophobic age for a homophobic public, he has given his characters complete *laissez-faire*, letting them act out all the foibles and all the grandeur that come with love.

NOTES

[1]Rainer Maria Rilke, *Neue Gedichte*, Ulm, Germany, 1974.

2Sappho, *Poems and Fragments*, Ann Arbor, 1965, no. 36. For further discussion of Rilke's Sappho poems see Joachim Rosteutscher, "Rilke's Sappho Gedichte," *Acta Germanica* VI (1971); 95-105.

3F.W. Van Heerikhuizen, *Rainer Maria Rilke: His Life and Work*, New York, 1952, p. 217.

VI.
PHILOSOPHY

Philosophies Of
Homophobia and Homophilia

By Laurence J. Rosán

This chapter is an introduction to the meta-philosophy of homosexuality. That is, 1) it is an introduction only, not a final or exhaustive study, and only a limited number of examples purposely have been given; but it can help stimulate other, more detailed investigations. 2) "Meta-philosophy" (a recent term) or "the philosophy of philosophy" means, in this case, an analysis of all fundamental types of philosophy from the outside as it were, with as much objectivity as possible. Though everyone has a philosophy of his own, this writer included, this chapter will try to avoid its intrusion in spite of some inescapable clues. 3) "Homosexuality" has here its usual general meaning. But it will immediately be necessary to scrutinize this word and to replace it frequently with "homophilia," the *self-accepting* desire for others of the same sex. "Homophobia" is a convenient term for opposition to this. And we will also need a word for those who are neither favorable, nor opposed, to homosexuality, neutrally regarding it as equally valid as heterosexuality, and for this attitude the writer suggests the term "homoïsaia."[1]

Materialism, idealism, and solipsism will be the philosophies presented first, and under the heading of "clear-cut cases" because they are comparatively easy to understand both in themselves and in their consequences for homosexuality. The second section of "complex cases" will contain most of the varieties of dualism where apparently no simple conclusions can be drawn. The chapter will end with a summary, and a prognosis both for dealing with homophobic philosophies and for constructing homophilic ones.

I. Clear-cut cases.

Materialism or "naturalism" is one of the simplest philosophies to expound.[2] This is because it is based on what has been called "naive realism" or the belief that all the objects we experience in the external world are truly real — which is the *daily* philosophy of the greatest number of people, even if many of them additionally have a nominal belief in the existence of spiritual beings. Materialism takes this generally accepted "priority of external things" and constructs a rigorously consistent and total philosophy upon it. Traditionally (in the East as well as in the West), this has been accomplished by reducing all things to ultimate material "building blocks," in the Western tradition called "atoms."[3] (The original Greek word meant "uncuttables"; the recent "electrons," "protons," etc. do not represent any shift from this position, although they are the result of "cutting the atom" in the *modern* sense of this word, because they themselves in turn are "uncuttable" building blocks of all things, that is, they also are "atoms" or "atomic particles.") In the rare case of a naturalistic theory of *one* "material substance," the philosophy's vocabulary would initially appear different from what is presented below, but there would be no essential change in its conclusions.

Almost all materialists therefore are "pluralists"; reality consists of a (nearly?) infinite number of nearly infinitesimal particles, either all alike or of a number of types. There is nothing else. There is no God of course, no "guiding intelligence," not even "Mother Nature" or any personification of this sort. And the "scientific laws" that describe the behavior of the atoms are only the patterns that we human beings observe and then codify into a "system of physics"; these laws are not in themselves realities. *Only the atoms are realities.* And since they are material particles, not intelligences, they have no "intentions of doing anything," no goals whatever. Even the ultimate end of the universe — it might be "the thinly dispersed particles of energy, having lost all their organization through entropy, moving extremely slowly at a temperature just above Absolute Zero" — is clearly not the result of any planning by the atoms.

This is important for our understanding of materialism as a homoïsic philosophy. For nothing can be called either "good" or "bad"; everything occurs by the mechanical interaction of atomic particles, and the result is entirely neutral. To be sure, particles combine to form more complex collections, and these collections seem to behave in ways differing from the original atoms themselves; thus "protoplasm," a very complex collection of particles, seems to behave in distinctive ways such as moving, ingesting, excreting, reproducing, etc. And further there are very complex forms of protoplasm, which took eons of time to evolve, called "animals and/or human beings" (i.e., human beings *are* animals), which in turn seem to behave in their own distinctive ways — they appear to move to, or away from, certain things outside them, (knowing these things by "sensation" or the influence of external atoms on the internal ones of their receptive "sense organs"). This movement toward or away from things is named respectively "desire" and "fear"; and whatever is desired is called "good for that animal or human being," whatever is feared is called "bad." But "desire and fear," "good and bad," are value-judgments relative only to those complex arrangements of protoplasm called "animals and/or human beings" which, having evolved into existence over a long period of time, may very well evolve out of existence in some indefinite future; the universe cares nothing about them! The atoms make no value-judgments; no values have any reality. For this philosophy, therefore, only one "ethics" or value-theory is consistently possible; it has been traditionally called "hedonism" or the "pleasure doctrine": If there are no real values, what else can each person seek but whatever he or she desires at the moment? His object or goal at that moment becomes "good" for *him*, and the satisfaction of his desire, the sensation of achieving that object, will bring him a "good sensation" or pleasure. Conversely, avoiding a feared object will save him from a "bad sensation" or pain. So let everyone do exactly as he pleases; *"Fais ce que voudras."*[4]

And what about homosexuality? Well, what about it? What's the question? Homosexuality and heterosexuality, masturbation and zoerasty, sex itself versus chastity — none of these has any difference in value; none of them is either good or bad in itself. It is each person's pleasure that alone determines what he will choose, his disinclination or "pain" that determines what he will avoid. Homosexuality compared to heterosexuality is like a taste for rye bread as compared to white bread: *there is nothing to say about it.* There is no "problem" here, there is no "question" to begin with. Materialism or naturalism's attitude to homosexuality is purely and totally homoïsic.

So far we have been examining traditionally consistent materialism which usually offers no "political doctrine" (or what might be the best society) because all values are relative to the individual only. Just as among animals where what is "good" for the predator will be "bad" for its prey, so also a materialist in a society which values "justice," "honesty," "humanity," etc., will advance his own interests as a predator by pretending to be just, honest, and humane, playing the part like a good actor or "hypocrite" (original Greek meaning), seeking to obtain and remain in power, even dictating the meaning of "justice" itself, which is therefore only the "advantage of the strongest" (Thrasymachus in Plato's *Republic*, Stephanos II, 338). But, understandably, various efforts have been made to "soften" this corollary of naturalistic ethics and to develop some justification for a society in which at least overt violence could be prevented, mutual contracts might be honored, and so on; probably the best-known effort is Thomas Hobbes' *Leviathan* (see below). To consider this "politicized materialism" and its potential attitude to homosexuality, however, we should first ask is it really consistent with the rest of materialism? And this suggests a short analysis of what "consistency" means, and why it is important particularly for us who are gay to examine the consistency of any philosophy.

If a person says, e.g., *"Only* material particles are real; they are the building blocks of the *whole* universe, and God will punish sexual deviation," we can immediately and confidently exclaim, "This is an inconsistent philosophy!" Now if he should remove the words "only" and "whole," and connect or relate the third clause with the first two, the sentence could change into "Material particles are real; they are the building blocks of the material portion of the universe; but God also exists, Who created and supervises these material particles, and He will punish sexual deviation." This is a satisfactory statement of a certain type of dualism. But whatever the philosophy may be, *it should be made clear from the beginning.* Only then can we know exactly what kind of philosophy confronts us and, if it appears homophobic, only then could we be fore-armed in our defense.

Returning to "politicized materialism" (Hobbes's version): A hedonist seeks his own pleasure, yes, but he realizes that other hedonists have the same desire; he knows that just as he has no scruples about using violence or trickery for his own ends, so these others could use violence or trickery upon him. Therefore, gathering together with them, he and they all make a kind of contract, an agreement not to harm or be harmed, giving up their possible use of violence against others in return for the clear benefit of not suffering it themselves. Because such an agreement must be guaranteed by some external *power* (since these materialists are not likely to "take an oath on the Bible"!), they arm and authorize the "state," specifically the police power of the state, to intervene should anyone break the agreement by an act of violence, and thus prevent this crime to begin with or else punish it to deter future crime. [5] But when will this "agreement not to harm or be harmed" be consistent with the rest of naturalism? When, say, fifteen people gather together, make this agreement and arm the police, then this contract will be valid *for these fifteen people only* (since only they voluntarily contracted, nor can they obligate even their own children) — and valid *only for as long as they have contracted*; (it is implausible that they would bind themselves for the rest of their lives; rather they would probably make such a contract for a limited period of time, say ten years, and subject to voluntary renewal). Now an agreement not to harm or be harmed made by fifteen people for ten years is reasonably consistent with naturalism. But if we allow this idea to drift into the usual concept of a "social contract" where not only are all the people of a society bound for life but they are bound to a so-called "contract" they themselves never personally made, we have moved far beyond consistent materialism where the individual alone is the creator of all values.

For the fifteen who made an agreement for ten years, however, the implications of their contract will be as homoïsic as before. The police power they authorized will be concerned only with the prevention of violence and trickery as agreed on; it will have not the slightest interest in whether a person eats rye bread or white bread, or whether he or she is homosexual or heterosexual. Any state in which the police *do* take such an interest has surely broken away from its original naturalistic foundation, more likely was never based on it to begin with. We can repeat therefore that materialism or naturalism is a philosophy of homoïsaia, totally neutral to homosexuals and heterosexuals.

۞

Idealism, although also a simple philosophy in itself, has been much more difficult to explain to the general public than materialism, partly because in America from about the Twenties to the Fifties it was the least prevalent: Transcendentalism had long lost its hold, "Science" and "the Bible" were felt to be the only two alternatives for life, and small idealistic sects like Christian Science were objects of considerable mockery. But in the last decade or so, two seemingly unconnected popular trends, the interest in the power of the mind over the body ("psychosomatic medicine"), and the "beat" and "hip" generations' fascination with Zen, Yoga, and the occult, have now combined to make the explanation of idealism noticeably easier.

Unlike materialism, idealistic philosophy has appeared in various "traditions," reflecting either different psychological emphases and/or national-cultural characteristics. It will be useful to mention these traditions immediately, not only as a basis for later reference to them, but also because they provide an "ostensive definition" of idealism, a "pointing out" just which philosophies are generally accepted in this category. The major traditions are 1) Taoism, the native idealism of China, its earliest writing the *Tao Teh King* by "Lao-tse" (c. 6th Cen. B.C.); and its later descendant Dhyana/Ch'an/Zen Buddhism. 2) "Brahman"-ism, the native idealism of India, found earliest in the (nearly undatable) *Upanishads*, and formalized into both the "pluralistic" Sāṅkhya-Yoga and the monistic (Advaita) Vendanta. 3) The "Platonic tradition" (including predecessors like Parmenides) which as "Neo-Platonism" later absorbed the previously independent "Stoic tradition" and which continued in both Near Eastern (e.g., Sufism) and Western forms to about the Seventeenth Century. 4) The "non-traditional" and individualistic idealists of Western Europe and America from about the Seventeenth Century to the present, including "Cartesians" such as Spinoza, et al., subjective epistemologists like Berkeley, and "Kantians" such as Hegel, et al., whose influence on the American Transcendentalists, strengthened by hypnotism's newly demonstrated power of the mind over the body, resulted in modern "New Thought" (Christian/Religious Science, etc.).[6]

The word "idealism" comes from the Platonic doctrine of "eternal Ideas" ("idea" is the actual Greek word) which precede all material appearances and themselves derive from the highest Idea, "the One" or "the Good." We can explain this philosophy therefore in two ways: On one hand, idealism almost always claims there is only one "Reality" (Tao, Brahman, Absolute Divine Mind, etc.); there is nothing else; even though to the human mind the world seems composed of nearly infinite things. But these are only "appearances," they come and go like dreams, and idealism demonstrates them to be merely expressions of the One Reality by a variety of cosmologies varying from one tradition to another. On the other hand, idealism almost always claims that only *mind* (consciousness, awareness, etc.) is reality and that what seems to be a material world exists only in our own mind, just as dreams seem at the moment to be a world outside us. These two claims converge toward the same intuition: there is only One Reality which is a kind of consciousness or Mind and within Which every other thing (thought) exists, or from Which all other things (thoughts) "emanate" and decline into Appearance.[7]

This One Reality is not alien to human beings. It is the same mind or consciousness that they have, and they are already portions of or emanations from It. When a person knows this unity of himself, or "his self," with the One, he is said to have found his real "Self." But most human beings continue living in the world of appearances, and idealism claims there can be no lasting satisfaction or happiness in the transient and dream-like experiences which constitute this world. True happiness can be found only by knowing one's Self and by communing or uniting with the One Reality. This is a subjective motivation; but there is also a metaphysical one: just as upon finding we are in error we seek to rectify it by discovering the truth, so also universally error tends to move toward truth, not vice versa. The movement from the "error" or unreality of transient appearances to the truth of the real Self is a necessary tendency, and some idealists interpret the efforts of all animals and human beings as simply the subconscious strivings of lesser minds toward the One. The One Reality is the "Good" therefore not only as the highest happiness or bliss but also as the inevitable Goal of all consciousness.[8]

To specify idealism's attitude to homosexuality we must distinguish the movement of the human mind to the One into two seemingly complementary efforts: first there is the *turning away from* the distractions of the world of appearances, and secondly there is the *progress toward* the Goal itself. But there are a limited number of idealistic traditions which have emphasized only the first, the withdrawal from worldly sensations and desires generally called "asceticism," implying that the ascetic achieves a state of consciousness which is already akin to the One Reality. The (Hinayana) Buddhist "Nirvāna/Nibbāna" (desirelessness) and the Stoic "apatheia" (Eng. apathy, or emotionlessness) are examples; (both terms contain a negative prefix in the original languages).[9] But since asceticism recommends as little involvement in worldly affairs, sensual desires, etc. as possible, it is clearly homoïsic; that is, it makes no difference whether we are being urged to give up heterosexual or homosexual attachments. It is as if a vegetarian were asked which he avoided more, beef or pork; he would answer that they are completely equal to him, namely that he avoided both; he might further add that anyone who felt there was a difference between beef and pork was evidently still attracted to one or the other and so not yet completely a vegetarian! Similarly the (e.g.) Buddhist or Stoic devotee would say that anyone distinguishing between heterosexual and homosexual desires was still involved in the distracting appearance of such desires and therefore did not yet understand the meaning of "Nirvāna" or "apatheia."

But what about the majority of idealistic traditions which, in addition to a program of withdrawal from appearances, cultivate positive techniques by which the individual can experience a hint or revelation of, communion or even union with the One Reality? The answer depends on the technique(s) that are advocated, and there are many possibilities, but it seems that they all fall into three categories (and their combinations):

1) The inner-intuitive technique (found, e.g., in Rāja Yoga and Vedanta almost to the exclusion of other methods), where all effort is concentrated within, by closing one's eyes and ears as it were, to attain that highest (or deepest) point of one's self which is the real Self (Yoga's Purusha," Vedanta's "Ātman"), and to grasp this Self intuitively as the only reality, or as the very substance of the One Reality.[10] This technique is a positive and strenuous effort; but because it focusses attention entirely within and totally away from everything else around us, it involves the same "turning away from" worldly affairs and interpersonal relationships, and so the same attitude to homosexuality, as asceticism. That is, insofar as any idealism recommends the inner-intuitive technique of attaining the One as the *only* method, it too will be homoïsic, since any attachment to another person, whether heterosexual or

homosexual, would equally distract from the goal of knowing one's Self or its identity with the One.

2) The aesthetic technique (found, e.g., in Taoism and Zen Buddhism as a primary though not exclusive method), where attention is focussed on all of what appears around us as "Nature" or "the World" in a quietly receptive effort to "feel" Its totality and unity, and our kinship or unity with It, including whatever other personal aesthetic experiences might contribute to this awareness.[11] And 3) the passionate-emotional technique (found, e.g., in Sufism and the "psychedelic mysticism" of the recent "beat/hip" generations), where the whole consciousness is dynamically and aggressively directed toward an ideal or compelling experience, a symbol or even a person, which serves to inspire, enthuse (Gr. "enthousiazein": to be filled with the divine) and instill in the devotee a sense of communing or uniting with it, a foretaste or actual instance of uniting with the One.[12] These two techniques should be considered together because any idealism in which either or both of them enter *even as partial* components will imply a (qualified) homophilia! Let us therefore analyze them carefully: The aesthetic technique claims that any experience enhancing our feeling of kinship or unity with the World is a means of reaching an awareness of our unity with the One. For example, imagine a panoramic landscape (cf. the great Taoist/Zen landscape painters of the Sung and related periods in China and Japan), or any feeling of kinship with Nature, like a "beautiful" (that is, spiritually-aesthetically stimulating) flower, or a "beautiful" *person*. Now this "beautiful person" could be of the same or opposite sex, depending on one's sexual orientation; but whatever this be, only a beautiful person *congenial* to one's orientation can be the appropriately elevating aesthetic object! In an abstract sense this could be called a homoïsic (and heteroïsic) doctrine since "it makes no difference whether a person is straight or gay," he or she has the same potentiality for an aesthetic experience of this kind. But in the concrete, practical sense this philosophy should be considered homophilic (and heterophilic) because it is *a positive spiritual value for a homophile* to have a spiritually elevating *homophilic* aesthetic experience, (and for a heterosexual to have such a heterophilic experience). (To remove any lingering doubt as to the propriety of the "gay life" in idealism, we should repeat that human consciousness is a portion of or emanation from the One Reality; all "sexual-orientations" therefore are already contained in the One, Its "Divine Mind" is "pansexual," i.e. "straight, gay, bi" and so on.) Turning to the passionate-emotional technique, it claims that any object of passionate devotion can offer a revelation of communion or union with the One. This "object," as mentioned, can be an ideal, person, etc., and in the latter

case the person selected must be congenial of course to one's sexual orientation, while "passionate devotion" will become synonymous with words like "erotic-rapture" or "love." Here again this could more abstractly be called a homoïsic and heteroïsic teaching; but insofar as a spiritually-passionate, erotically-rapturous *homophilic love* is hereby *positively recommended to homophiles* as a means of elevating consciousness into the One Reality, this "doctrine of idealistic love" is truly homophilic (i.e., relative to homophiles).

To summarize idealism's two basic attitudes to homosexuality: if the "ethical pattern(s)" are *only* "the turning away from the distractions of appearances" and/or *only* "the inner-intuitive technique of finding the Self or its identity with the One," then the idealism will be purely homoïsic. But if the idealism involves, *even if only partly* and in combination with the other pattern(s), the technique(s) of "aesthetic contemplation that stimulates the feeling of unity with the World" and/or "passionate-emotional devotion as a revelation of communion or union with the One," then it will be an example of (qualified or relative) homophilia.

As in the case of materialism, efforts have been made to "politicize" idealism; but these efforts are even more inconsistent, in spite of some famous names like Plato and Hegel having been involved. [13] The inconsistency of the expression "idealistic government" is revealed by recalling that in this philosophy there is only one human goal: to turn away from appearances and return toward the One Reality. "The State," "society" or any government has no ethical purpose unless it can help its individual members achieve this awareness of the One. But how could any government do this? Only by leaving its people completely alone to discover their own spiritual needs and techniques! By comparison to governments already in existence therefore, idealism's political structure is a non-entity, a *non*-government, i.e., an "anarchy" ("no government" of anyone by anyone else). If, say, fifteen idealists decided to cooperate in matters of food, shelter, etc. so as to have greater freedom for their spiritual pursuits, then this "society" would be in existence for these fifteen people and for as long as any of them continued cooperating. (Nor would they require a "police power" as in Hobbes's example, since there is no need for violence or trickery against others when the goal of life lies only in the Mind.) But any government that might restrict total human liberty is immediately inconsistent with the doctrine that consciousness must be continuously free to move toward the One, so we will not need to discuss a so-called "idealistic government's" implications for homosexuality.

Solipsism (Latin "solus" [only] + "ipse" [oneself] is based on one idea: "Only I exist." Its source is the epistemological intuition that "everything I know is what *I* know," or "for *me* there is nothing that I don't know" (since if I could assert "there is something I don't know" to this extent I would already know it). Called the "egocentric predicament," this problem of knowledge is taken seriously by solipsism and results in the metaphysical conclusion "I ≡ reality," that is, "I am all reality and all reality is me."

No other idea *necessarily* follows. Since the solipsist is all of reality, any other statement he or she makes, no matter how strange it may seem to others, is true for him. He could be a materialist, an idealist, a dualist, or any even seemingly inconsistent combination, simply by the fiat of his decision; and as for homosexuality, he could be homophobic, homophilic, homoïsic, or any combination of these he desires! Solipsism's attitude to homosexuality therefore is "unpredictable."

At this point one might ask, "Why bother to mention solipsism?" to which there are at least two answers: First, this philosophy, although infrequently espoused openly, has been a constant potentiality in Eastern and Western thought, the subject of many efforts at refutation by those who sense its "dangers," and yet is almost impregnable to attack.[14] Secondly, though an extremely homophobic form of solipsism can be imagined and some day may appear in writing, the same holds true for an extremely homophilic form of solipsism. So why not get this going immediately?! It's easy; a solipsist asserts or denies reality as he or she wishes. Start with "other homophiles," particularly "other homophiles congenial to me" (you, the solipsist), and claim them as "the only real creations of my mind, while everything else is comparatively unreal, and some things" (homophobes?) "don't exist at all." In this way a totally, passionately homophilic philosophy can be developed suited to your tastes and unfettered by any of the traditional philosophical requirements because based on nothing but the solipsistic principle "only I am reality."[15]

✥

II. Complex cases (dualisms).

Dualism can be defined as maintaining the ultimate independence of two distinct types of reality, one always being the "material" in the common-sense meaning of the word, the other being called, for convenience, the "non-material," but naturally more difficult to describe. We should in fact distinguish at least three kinds of "non-material realities" (making at least three types of dualism): A. "spirit(s)," a kind of personality that can exist apart from a material body; B. "personalities in bodies," which can exist only within a body;

and C. "formal causes," borrowing the term from Aristotelian philosophy to apply to any non-material essence or quality which usually, though not necessarily, exists in close connection with its individual material expression. Placing dualism under "complex cases" may surprise a person who believes, for instance, in God's creation of the world according to Genesis, for we are so accustomed to this type of doctrine that even non-believers fully understand it. But dualism has a great number of varieties with equally various consequences for homosexuality; on this ground alone it must be separated from the comparatively uniform philosophies already discussed. Moreover it poses several difficult technical problems. Some of these — the metaphysical problem of how the non-material and material can influence each other, the epistemological topic of how the human mind gains knowledge of non-material things, and the psychological problem of how the human body can interact with the mind/soul/spirit — are not directly pertinent to homo-sexuality and will be omitted for reasons of space. But the "ethical problem," namely, *how to determine the goal of life* for a human being within a dualistic world-view, is not only difficult and complex but obviously of crucial importance for clarifying its attitude to homosexuality. Throughout this section therefore we will be *probing and searching* into the difficult question of what are the ethical consequences for homosexuality of this or that dualistic view; the results will be a series of suggested, tentative hypotheses.[16]

❧

A. Belief in some kind of "spirit(s)" has been almost universal. Without implying any theory of derivation, we will start from the "earliest" or simplest cases of spirits and move toward the "later" more complex ones. (The first two types are pre-sexual but are important as a foundation.)[17] 1) Spirits of inanimate objects that are striking (but non-functional for human needs) such as unusually shaped rocks, mountains, etc.: What might be the ethical consequences when a striking rock formation is felt to be inhabited by a spirit? This rock undoubtedly would not be approached like an ordinary rock; rather whoever nears it would feel a special sense of *awe* — the rock itself is in some way *sacred*, in fact its sacredness may be so great that it becomes *taboo* to approach it. 2) Spirits of plants, trees, etc., particularly those used for food: If a plant has its own spirit, the same sense of awe will be felt in its presence. But if a person wants to use this plant for food, tearing off its leaves and fruit, even killing the plant itself, he will experience a conflict between his inner awe of the sacred/taboo spirit of the plant which he is offending by violating, and his clear need to eat. He undoubtedly will feel *guilt*, an unpleasant subjective condition which automatically suggests its removal through an act of *atonement*. His atonement could be a self-punishment unrelated to the plant, but more likely he may wish to appease the angered spirit directly by *propitiation*. (Yet he cannot promise the plant's spirit never to eat this plant or others like it again). So perhaps he will make a (fertilizing?) offering to a still-living plant of the same species; or, knowing the significance of a seed, he may plant it to insure future growth, stimulating the plant's *fertility*, not for his own selfish purpose (the origin of agriculture), but rather in this case as an act of atonement.

3) Spirits of animals, fish, etc., particularly those used for food: This case is similar to the preceding one. Thus a person who, for food, kills an animal he believes has its own spirit, would feel a sense of guilt and need for atoning propitiation; nor could he promise to give up killing these animals in the future. He might therefore make an offering to the animal's spirit, or try to increase that species' fertility. Let's examine the latter case: animals (this would be less true for birds or fish), being structured much like human beings, (and assuming the "facts of reproduction" were already known), would be understood to have "fertility" in their sex organs; "increasing animal fertility" therefore would mean either mating a male and female of the same species, or simply any effort to stimulate their sex organs with this end directly or symbolically in mind. Thus the beginnings of zoerasty! But here this term does not mean the use of animals merely for satisfying one's own urges (which may be a later result), but rather the propitiatory effort to provide the animals with sexual excitement and its associated fertility, motivated by guilt and contrition over the offending of their spirit(s) by their being continuingly killed for food. This is *propitiatory zoerasty*, and it could easily be either heterosexual or homosexual. Thus a contrite, say, male butcher of sheep may try to mate a ewe with a ram as an atoning reparation, or he may propitiatingly stimulate the sex organs of either a *ewe* or a ram, which latter would be a kind of *homosexual zoerasty*. Insofar therefore as the belief in spirits includes only those categories already discussed (inanimate things, plants and/or animals) and not beyond, its attitude to propitiatory zoerasty, it is suggested, will be homoïsic.

4) Spirits of human beings who are currently living (*not* implying continuation after death): The awe and reverence toward these sacred/taboo "human spirits" would be even greater than that for the animals. Yet in almost all societies there has usually been plenty of killing of other human beings, as in warfare, vendetta, cannibalism, etc. The inner conflict between the reverence for the sacred spirit and the clear violation of the taboo by slaying its body often resulted in a very strong, deep-seated guilt in the slayer's heart and a

consequent need for atonement. (Nor in view of the continuing possibility of war, etc. could he promise to abstain from this slaughter.) — But suddenly the analogy with the previous sections disintegrates! For human beings are not felt to be grouped into "species" governed by overall spirits as plants and animals are, but each "living human spirit" is considered autonomous with its own body, and not continuing after death, cannot be propitiated. Is there any other atonement possible? We recall (above, section 2 on plants) that there could be also a "self-punishment" unrelated to the spirit involved. The atonement for killing the body of a "living human spirit" therefore would have to be of this type, a self-punishment or, what is the same thing, a punishment accepted by the guilty party but administered by another person delegated for this purpose. This idea becomes all the more interesting when we reflect that warfare (this would be less true of vendettas, cannibalism, etc.) has been nearly universally waged by males against males, that is, it has been an intra-sexual phenomenon. In the environment of warfare, the reverence for the sacred human spirit, the violation of that spirit by killing its body and the subsequent deep-seated guilt and need for atonement would all have occurred in a psychological ambience that was male intra-sexual (or "homosexual" in the most abstract sense of the word). So if and when the atoning self-punishment was not directly self-inflicted but administered by a delegate, there is the inevitable suggestion here that it would have been courted by a guilty male seeking it to be inflicted at the hands of another male who, temporarily at least, would play the role of the punisher. This would be the foundation for what could easily become a purely voluntary homosexual sado-masochism. And since in this case of warfare the likelihood of a homosexual relationship is very much greater than a heterosexual one, we can suggest that, wherever there is a belief in spirits up to the "living-human" level and not beyond, we can find the possibility of a *sado-masochistic homophilia.*[18]

5) Ancestor spirits: A wholly new attitude seems to develop with the belief in the *continuation* of the "human spirits" after their bodies have died. For reverence to or propitiation of these spirits must now also continue; and although it might seem that any living person could reverence any or all deceased spirits, practically speaking only their direct decendants are specifically required to remember them. They are truly "ancestors" therefore; a so-called "ancestor spirit" who no longer has any descendants us usually a forgotten spirit! Clearly it immediately becomes crucial for each living person to have as many descendants as possible lest, after death, his spirit some day be in the fearful limbo of having no one remember or reverence him. This is a powerful incentive to have many children and so to enter heterosexual marriage. The belief in ancestor spirits therefore is entirely heterosexually

oriented and could very easily regard homosexuality as a waste of reproductive power and an affront to all the possible ancestor spirits whose memory might be blotted out thereby. Although this is our first confrontation with a truly homophobic philosophy, it must be kept in mind from now on. For there is a tendency among the "later" beliefs in spirits to retain characteristics from previous stages, so that all the remaining types of "spirit dualisms" presented below, in spite of their own specific qualities, will continue to be tinged with this apparently fundamental "ancestor-spirit homophobia."

6) Hero(ine) — spirits, i.e., outstanding ancestors: A hero-spirit (according to the belief) was at one time a living person but no longer needs to have descendants because his deeds and charisma are so great that he is reverenced, and his tale is retold by, *all* the people who acknowledge him. Moreover, there are certain isolated examples of homosexual heroes and heroines.[19] But, as mentioned, if this stage of belief is the "latest yet achieved," any possible homophilia stimulated by these would be in conflict with the still overwhelming number of ordinary ancestor spirits and its consequent strong homophobia.

7) Polytheism or "belief in many gods": There is no sharp line between a "great spirit" and a "god"; heroes were already equivalent to "demi-gods," and Euhemerus' theory (c. 300 B.C.) was that all (Greek) gods were only heroes originally. Usually a "god" has a distinct personality of his or her own and may be only casually connected with this or that natural or psychological phenomenon. Furthermore, like heroes, the gods are generally known through stories or "myths" handed down, spoken or written, about them. The number of possible types of gods is therefore very large. For example, a famous world-wide "gestalt" or syndrome is that of the god(s) of agricultural fertility, human fertility, and human immortality; here the story is recurrently told of the god who dies and is reborn, or who alternates between death and life, thus directly symbolizing and guaranteeing in various degrees both agricultural fertility and human immortality (human fertility however somewhat indirectly and more by association with the other two). But this far-flung belief, still very pervasive up to the present, doesn't seem to have any clear implications for homosexuality.[20] And when we turn to the specific gods or symbols of sexuality, such as Dionysus and Priapus in the West, the Lingam and Yoni in India, etc., we find a heterosexual rather than a homosexual interpretation.[21] On the other hand, if we consider the *priests* (witch-doctors, shamans, etc.) of these polytheistic or spirit religions, we discover a converse tendency: here the ordinary worshipper's desire for a human intermediary with the spiritual realm has favored the development of a spirit-oriented personality that is expected to

be "different" — unworldly, even eccentric, given to visions, dramatic pronouncements and so on — an ideal opportunity for both male and female homosexuals![22]

8) Henotheism and monotheism: A transitional doctrine, "henotheism" is a polytheism where one of the gods becomes supreme, or in the reverse direction, a monotheism where the one god develops many divine helpers, which occurred in certain branches of Christianity and in the movement from Hinayana to Mahāyana Buddhism. Monotheism of course is "the belief in the existence of only one (personal) God." In both cases what was previously perhaps oral mythology tended to be written down into "sacred scriptures," sometimes considered "divine revelation." These scriptures are generally very old (even most of the newer ones, such as the Book of Mormon or Bāha'u'llāh's writings, are firmly grounded upon the older ones), and therefore like their linguistic function of preserving old words and forms they conserve older patterns such as (for our topic) the need to perpetuate the memory of ancestors by having as many children as possible in the face of high infant mortality.

For an example of a sacred scripture we may concentrate on the Hebrew-Christian-Muslim tradition's common foundation, the Old Testament. In this scripture there are at least seven sentences (Lev. 18,22; 20,13; Deut. 23,18; I Kings 14,24; 15,12; 22,47; and II Kings 23,7; Masoretic numbering) which specifically, and negatively, refer to male homosexuality. In addition to the general suggestion already made, that this homophobic attitude was based on reverence for ancestor spirits, a more immediate reason is strongly implied in Lev. 18,27: After verse 22 ("You shall not lie with a male as with a woman, it is an abomination"), verse 27 continues, "For all of these abominations the men of the land did, who were before you, so that the land became defiled." That is, homosexuality had been current among the indigenous Canaanites, into whose land the Hebrews were at that time moving, and from whom they were very concerned to differentiate themselves, lest the native culture threaten the survival of their group by infiltrating their own distinctive customs — an infiltration which occurred in part as the four sentences from Kings reveal. Now the Canaanite culture at a very early period had involved fraternal polyandry, or the plurality of brother-husbands to one wife, which made homophilic relations among these brothers living together conveniently easy and as natural as fraternal affection itself. Secondly, Canaanite religion was of the agricultural/animal/human fertility type, with a conspicuous place for the sex goddess Ashtart, also known as "Kadesh" (holy), and a sex or fertility god Lahmu; sexual/fertility rites therefore were naturally part of this religion. The combination of these two factors produced male as well as female "temple courtesans," the Hebrew word for whom was "kādēsh" (masculine singular), that is, "holy or cloistered male," and it is this word which has been so pejoratively translated as "sodomite(s)" by the King James and other Versions.[23] Thus what for the Canaanites was a natural expression of their fertility cult as influenced by an ancient polyandry, became for the Hebrews an "abomination," based (it is suggested) on two needs felt necessary to their nation's existence: the retention of their traditional culture in a new land, and the remembrance of ancestral spirits, the purity of whose geneaological lineage indeed was of utterly absorbing interest to them (cf. Gen. 25, 31-34, Esau's selling Jacob his primogeniture, as an example).

In very recent years there have arisen new "gay churches and synagogues" whose general ethical program remains within the Hebrew-Christian tradition but which refuse to accept the homophobic pronouncements in the Old Testament (and their reflections in the New Testament). Since almost the whole orthodox law of the Old Testament was thoroughly reinterpreted and re-cast by the Talmud, and transformed if not nullified by Christianity (including two of the "most sacred Ten Commandments" — "graven images" and "seventh-day Sabbath"), it shouldn't be difficult for gay Jews or Christians to demonstrate to heterosexual Jews and Christians how the essential teachings of these religions ought to transcend any homophobia. And there are isolated homophilic scriptural passages such as the stories of David and Johnathan (I Sam. 20,41; II Sam. 1,26) or Ruth and Naomi (Ruth 14-17) or even Jesus and his "beloved disciple" John (John 13,23) which should help mollify or neutralize the rage of the homophobes. But, as all know, these gay churches and synagogues are being met with continuing hostility.

B. "Personalities in bodies" is a phrase meant to suggest the very frequent attitude of "taking people seriously," being concerned about their opinions, that is, dealing with human personalities *as if* separate from their bodies but without actually thinking of them as in any way continuing after death. Unlike the "belief in living human spirits" (above, section 4), this philosophy does not involve spirits or any other non-material reality, and may be considered the metaphysically weakest type of dualism. But it is ethically strong: these human personalities are of utmost importance in the business of daily living; their opinions can "make or break" a person, i.e., can bestow on him "high status" or "low status." We might call this philosophy "status dualism" therefore, since the goal of life is to retain or increase one's status (or "honor") by remaining in everyone's good opinion, and to avoid blame, shame or "stigma" by falling into general contempt, very much like the "other-directed" personality-type proposed and analyzed by David Riesman in *The Lonely Crowd* (New Haven, 1950, pp. 22 on), a kind of person who gains his or her values only from the members of his immediate peer-group because of his intense desire to conform to their expectations, avoid their disapproval, and obtain a sense of their support.

Since this is purely imitative of others, status dualism cannot ordinarily *create* an attitude to homosexuality, but it can very tenaciously *maintain* whatever happens to be current. And because most current social attitudes are homophobic (for whatever reason), status dualism and its "other-directed" devotees constitute the major social problem for nearly all gay people, namely, how to avoid "exposure" by staying "in the closet" and so on.[24] On the other hand, the same sense of "support" that is offered by the peer-group in status dualism can be developed among homophiles too; they can support one another, and this would seem to justify every gay effort toward and every successful instance of mutual contact, yea, even the bushes, baths, and tearooms! For no matter how "primitive" or "oppressive" these environments may seem, any such meeting between gay persons, even just a conversation between an openly gay man and gay woman, provides a measure of support which counteracts the current "made in Straightland" stigma. And extending this, increasing the number of gays involved, parlaying the momentum into clubs, "cruising areas," whole neighborhoods, etc., could actually create a new *homophilic* version of status dualism, with the same "personalities in bodies" and "other-directed" individuals, but now operating within a framework of values that are homophilic (or at least homoïsic). The Alpine County project in California (which failed) and the maintenance of Cherry Grove on Fire Island, New York as a gay resort (which has been successful for more than 25 years), are examples of environments for such a homophilic status dualism. This philosophy therefore, though mostly homophobic in historical fact, is not inherently so, and can become homoïsic or even homophilic with proper planning and effort.

✧

C. As noted, the term "formal cause(s)" has been borrowed from Aristotelian metaphysics; it means a characteristic of a thing that is co-existent with and inseparable from its material substance or "material cause" which in turn individualizes it from all other identical examples; (e.g., the identical "form of a dime" exists in every dime but the actual metal is different in each one). A very similar metaphysics existed in the "Li School" of Neo-Confucianism (Eleventh Cen. A.D. and after), where there was the same dualism between the matter (ch'i) and form (li) of every particular thing; this type of philosophy therefore has appeared at many times and places.[25] But for our purposes we must ask, how is the form of any particular thing known or discovered? And in both Aristotelian and Neo-Confucian "formal-cause dualism" the answer is that first we experience individual things, finding the characteristics or forms many of them have in common, and then we isolate these forms in our mind and speak of them as logically independent from the material substance of which the original things are also made. So the theory of knowledge for formal-cause dualism is actually the same kind of "empiricism," or "sense perception leading to inductive generalization," which is so consistent with the philosophy of *materialism*, but which in dualism immediately runs the danger of being overly pretentious, as if some new kind of knowledge is being gained of a realm of truth which is, however, only an abstraction from our own experience. For example, what is the "form or true nature of a cow?" In materialism we understood that nothing has any constant "nature"; there are cows and cows, and animals transitional between cows and something else — there is no such thing as a "normal cow." But in formal-cause dualism we evidently look at familiar cows and, generalizing from our experience, develop the idea of what is the "true form of a normal cow." Clearly nothing comes out of this kind of philosophy that was not already put into it! Therefore, if a formal-cause dualist lives in a society that regards heterosexuality as proper and "normal," he will of course find the "form or true nature of a human being" to be heterosexual, so that homosexuality becomes "deviation from the form or norm." But if that dualist lived his whole life in Cherry Grove on Fire Island, New York, he would undoubtedly have exactly the converse definition! The conclusion is that formal-cause dualism, for all its subtlety and traditional philosophical importance, is like status dualism: it cannot create any attitude to homosexuality; it can only maintain some attitude already in existence for other reasons.

❧

III. Summary and prognosis.

We have found consistent materialism always to be homoïsic; consistent idealism always to be at least homoïsic when involving only its pattern(s) of "turning away from distractions" and/or "inner-intuitive technique for attaining

Self/Reality," but relatively homophilic when involving any element of its "aesthetic" and/or "passionate-emotional" techniques; while solipsism we found to be unpredictable. In the case of dualism our conclusions are more complex; they can be summarized by suggesting that 1) a true homoïsaia is found only in the "earliest" forms of the belief in spirits, where inanimate, plant and/or animal spirits are revered. 2) One stage beyond, the belief in spirits of living human beings, may have generated a type of homophilic "sado-masochistic" (i.e., dominant/submissive) pattern based on male intra-sexual guilt and atonement. 3) With the belief in ancestor spirits a distinctive form of homophobia becomes developed which permeates all "later" stages of spirit-dualism up to the concluding monotheisms. 4) Rare exceptions may be found among these homophobic types, such as homophilic heroes, gods, or isolated passages in scriptures. 5) Philosophies such as "status" and "formal-cause" dualisms have no inherent significance for homosexuality and merely reflect already existing attitudes. 6) Actual homoïsic/homophilic examples of status dualism and even Hebrew-Christian monotheism can be and have been developed by gay people.

What are the chances of reducing or removing the world-wide homophobia based on the feeling that our ancestors depend on direct descendants for remembrance and thus for their happiness in the afterlife? I suggest that the idea of *reincarnation* (in which after death we do not enter a "single place of afterlife" but rather repeatedly return to one life, or "plane of existence," (after another) would have two helpful, intertwining results. First, it would mean that everyone has innumerable parents and other forebears, a different set for each of our past and future lives, thereby greatly reducing the uniqueness of our "obligation" to our forebears of *this* life. Secondly, reincarnation implies that our deceased ancestors are already busily living other lives, and are no more remembering "us, their former descendants," than we are currently remembering "our former descendants in previous lives"; and if they do not remember us, they will not *need* to be remembered by us. I suggest, therefore, that the more a reincarnation doctrine supplants the belief of a "single afterlife," the less emphasis will be placed on the production of descendants via heterosexual marriage, that is, the less homophobia.

For readers who are religiously Hebrew-Christian-Muslim, I offer a second suggestion: the idea of *subjective revelation*. This means that God has been, is, and will continue to be revealing Himself, even if in small ways, to individuals throughout the ages. Any person reflecting on his or her life and finding the "hand of God" in it would be justified in accepting this intuition as "God's voice speaking to him" or a "revelation." On July 2, 1969, a man calling himself "Om" was lecturing in New York City on how God had revealed to him that the purpose of life was to have as much sexual intercourse as possible, as a divine ritual of communion with God; and when I asked him if this applied to homosexuals also, he said "yes." Similarly any gay person who sincerely feels that his or her life as a homophile is rewarding enough to see the "hand of God" in it may accept this as his "subjective revelation." And if increasingly many gay people have this same intuition, these subjective revelations will accumulate into a historically new "objective revelation." Bāha'u'llāh, Joseph Smith, Mary Baker Eddy, et al., all have comparatively recently proclaimed their own "objective revelations." So the time may be approaching for a new, objective Divine Revelation of homophilia.

The two preceding paragraphs have been "coping with homophobia"; but what are the chances for a truly homophilic philosophy, one that asserts *gay superiority?* To construct a consistent homophilia the following seem to be requisites: 1) The keystone must be the "essence of homosexuality," that is, the idea of "identity or great similarity" as compared to the heterosexual "difference." 2) To insure the significant use of this "essence," the importance of interpersonal relationships, where alone this distinction properly applies, must be demonstrated. 3) Any philosophy which is inherently non-committal (homoïsic/unpredictable/imitative) must be rejected as an unsafe foundation; (thus the suggestion made earlier of a solipsistic homophilia is vulnerable to solipsism's unpredictability which could just as well spawn homophobia). For a safe foundation we have discovered apparently only two philosophies that could be called homophilic: certain types of idealism, and the belief in (but not "beyond") "living human spirits." Here I will select only the former as perhaps less hypothetical and more currently possible. The reader will recall that in idealism the "aesthetic" and "passionate-emotional" techniques both placed a *cosmic* value on interpersonal relationships as one means of elevating consciousness toward the One Reality. The first method stresses a quiet, receptive appreciation of a "spiritually-beautiful person" who could induce an inner reverberation of a "beautifully-spiritual experience"; the second stresses a dynamic, aggressive love or erotic-rapture leading to an intimate communion or union with another person as a foretaste or revelation of the One. In both cases there is need for the *deepest* kind of relationship, the innermost sympathetic or empathic stimulation and/or response. Sympathy ("feeling with") and empathy ("feeling inside", i.e., the almost physical sensation that we experience when someone, e.g., cuts his finger) are based on similarity; the more similar any two people are, mentally/emotionally (sympathy) or physically (empathy), the more easily they can reverberate or commune with each other. This is the "essence of homosexuality" of course, identity or great similarity. We can suggest therefore that homophilic relationships are better able to produce "spiritually elevating aesthetic experiences" and/or "erotically rapturous feelings of communion or union" than heterophilic ones. And in the world-view of idealism this means that homophiles are more predisposed to attaining the One Reality than heterophiles, or what is actually the same thing, that the One Reality manifests Itself more immediately and clearly in the gay consciousness than in the straight one. Whatever the reader's opinions of this kind of idealism may be, it is at least an example of a consistently-constructed doctrine of gay superiority!

NOTES

1The word "homosexuality" has two disadvantages: first, it combines the Greek prefix "homo-" (the same, as opposed to "hetero-," other, different) with the Latin root "sexus," a faulty construction to begin with; but more importantly, in our language "sexual" hardly connotes mere anatomical gender (the original intention) but rather stimulation of the sex organs or "sex," and as gay people know, this is only one of the many motivations for homosexuality; but the words "homosexual-ity" will remain useful for a vague, generalized reference. "Homoeroticism," which is purely Greek in derivation, also mostly suggests sexuality; though "erōs" meant love in general, in English "erotic" now implies sex. But "homophilia," from the Gr. verb "philein" (to like, kiss, love), has remained in conformity with its original meaning (helped by the root's continued use as, e.g., the suffix "-phile" as in "Anglophile"); so also the concrete noun "homophile" and the adjective "homophilic." In this chapter these words will have a connotation slightly different from "homosexual-ity"; they will connote a *favorable* attitude to one's own homosexuality as in the popular word "gay(ness)." "Homophobia" is actually an abbreviation for "homophilephobia," since strictly speaking it would mean "dislike for those of one's own sex," clearly not the intention; "male homophobes" do not "dislike other males" but rather "dislike those (male or female) who are attracted to their own sex." For the attitude that is truly neutral about homosexuality, Liddell & Scott's *Greek-English Lexicon* (9th ed., Oxford, 1940; p. 836) gives a somewhat rare but valid noun "isaia" (equality) which has the advantage of only 3 syllables like "philia" and "phobia"; [other, longer possibilities are the 4-syllable "isaxia" (equal worth), and the 5-syllable "isomereia" (equal share), "isonomia" (equal rights) and "isotimia" (equal privilege)]. This gives us the abstract noun "homoïsaia" (spelled with the diaeresis to avoid suggesting the prefix "homoi-," similar to); but notice that this *also* is an abbreviation for "homophileïsaia," since it doesn't mean "neutrality to those of one's own sex" but "neutrality to those who are attracted to their own sex." The adjective "homoïsic" is based on the analogy with "homophilic" and "homophobic"; but the concrete noun should also be "homoïsic" since there is nothing here corresponding to "-phile" or "-phobe"; (nor would "homoïse" be acceptable! and there are many cases in Eng. where the Gr. adjective ending "ikos" serves also as a noun, such as "mystic," etc.).

2Because "materialism" has frequently been used derogatorily by this philosophy's opponents, its adherents have sought other terms, such as "naturalism." Wishing to avoid lurking value-judgments, I will use both words interchangeably as needed, and synonymously.

3For a classic presentation of these ideas see Lucretius, *De Rerum Natura*, Book I, lines 216 f. (basic building blocks of matter); 330 (empty space); 420 f. (nothing but matter and space); 482 f. (solid, eternal atoms); II, 83 (motion of atoms); 402 f. (sensation, pleasure and pain); III, 161 (material nature of mind & "soul"); 417 (mortality of soul). Hedonistic doctrines are found in Epicurus, *Letter to Menoeceus* (e.g., *The Philosophy of Epicurus*, tr. Geo. Strodach; Evanston, Ill., 1963); pp. 178-185.

4"Do as you wish," the only rule in Rabelais' Abbey of Thélème (*Gargantua and Pantagruel*, Book I, Ch. 57).

5"I authorize and give up my right of governing myself to this man or to this assembly of men, on the condition that thou give up thy right to him and authorize all his actions in like manner" (*Leviathan*, p. 132 in orig. 1651 ed., rpt. Oxford, 1909).

6I have omitted the Buddhist tradition because, like the Hebrew-Christian-Muslim tradition, it has been an intermixture of both monistic and dualistic elements, though with greater emphasis on the idealistic/monistic than the H-C-M. Both religions have idealists such as Vasubandhu and Angelus Silesius, but they were more influenced by "Brahman"-ism and Neo-Platonism respectively than by their religions.

7The exposition is naturally abbreviated and some of these generalizations may appear untrue now of this, now of that example. Thus 1) "Tao" was first conceived as the "Essence of Nature" more than a "mind"; but Chuang-tse (only 2 cen. after Lao-tse) already stressed the relativity of waking and dreaming (II, p. 197 in Legge's trans., see note below), the primacy of mind, and Tao more as "Essence of Thought." 2) Sānkhya/Yoga is called "pluralistic" since each person's self (Purusha) is numerically separate from every other, but without *any* further qualitative difference and so hardly distinct from Vedanta which reduces "all selves" to "One Self." 3) Spinoza is sometimes not called an idealist because he makes "mind" and *"extension"* co-equal "attributes of God or Substance"; but since this One Reality is prior to both, It could Itself be grasped only by the highest kind of consciousness or Mind.

8Cf. the Neoplatonist Proclus: "O Absolutely Transcendent . . . all keen desires or lusts, all painful passions are yearnings only for Thee" ("Hymn to God"); and "Therefore the whole of our life is a struggle toward that Vision" (*Commentary on Plato's Parmenides*); both quotes from L. J. Rosán, *The Philosophy of Proclus: the Final Phase of Ancient Thought* (New York, 1949), p. 204.

9"What now is the Noble Truth of the origin of suffering? It is craving . . . What now is the Noble Truth of the extinction of suffering? It is the complete fading away and extinction of this craving . . . wherever in the world there are delightful and pleasurable things, there this craving may vanish" (*Digha Nikaya*, 22, tr. the Bhikkhu Nyanatiloka (1935), found in *A Buddhist Bible*, ed. Dwight Goddard; Dutton: Boston, 1938). And from the Stoic Epictetus, *Discourses*, Book II, Ch. 17 (tr. Geo. Long; Philadelphia, 189_): " 'I desire to be free from passion and perturbation; . . . not only when I am awake, but also when I am asleep . . . filled with wine [or] melancholy.' Man, you are a god."

10Patanjali, *Yoga Sutras*, Bk. I, sutra 51; III, 51,56; IV, 33. Also the Vedantist Śankara's "Blessed am I; I have attained the consummation of my life . . . I am that Self-effulgent, Transcendent Ātman . . . I am verily that Brahman, the One without a second . . . I am the Universal, I am the All . . . " (*Vivekachudāmani*, tr. Swami Madhavananda; Mayavati, India, 1952; slokas 488, 507, 514, 516).

11This 2nd and the 3rd techniques' significance for homophilia suggests somewhat fuller quotation here and in the next quote. The Taoist Chuang-tse (*The Texts of Taoism*, tr. Jas. Legge; Oxford, 1891; rpt. Dover: N.Y., 1962; Book XIV, pp. 348-351) says: "You were celebrating, O Tī, a performance of music . . . in the open country near the Thung-thing Lake . . . The Perfect Music . . . showed the blended distinctions of the four seasons and the grand harmony of all things; . . . the brilliance of the sun and moon . . . like the music of a forest produced by no visible form . . . This is what is called the music of Heaven, delighting the mind without the use of words." In *Zen and the Fine Arts* (Kodansha Ltd., 1971), Shin-ichi Hisamatsu derives all Zen arts from the "Formless Self" and demonstrates how they conversely stimulate awareness of this Self (pp. 51-52 esp.). A western example, Geo. Berkeley (*Principles of Human Knowledge*, Par. 148) writes: "We do at all times and in all places perceive manifest tokens of the Divinity — everything we see, hear, feel, or anywise perceive by Sense being a sign or effect of the power of God."

¹²The Sufi, Jelālu'ddīn Rūmī says, "O lovers, ιι is time to abandon the world: . . . With each moment a soul is setting off into the Void . . . O Soul, seek the Beloved, O friend, seek the Friend" ("Divani Shamsi Tabriz," tr. R.A. Nicholson; p. 55 in F.H. Davis, *Jelālu'ddīn Rūmī*, Sh. Muhammad Ashraf: Lahore, India, 1907). Shamsi Tabriz is said by Davis to have been Jelāl's homosexual lover (pp. 31-32). Another Sufi, Farīd al-Dīn 'Attār (*Readings from the Mystics of Islām*, ed. & tr. Margaret Smith; Luzac: London, 1950 & 1972; Pars. 88, 97) writes: "A third moth rose up, intoxicated with love, and threw himself violently into the candle's flame . . . As he entered completely into its embrace, his members became glowing red like the flame itself . . . In truth, it is the one who has lost . . . all trace of his own existence who has, at the same time, found knowledge of the Beloved . . . Now I am made one with Thee . . . I am Thou and Thou art I — nay, not I . . . I have become altogether Thou." A psychedelic example: "I took my pill [mescaline] at eleven . . . The Beatific Vision, *Sat Chit Ananda*, Being-Awareness-Bliss — for the first time I understood, not on the verbal level . . . but precisely and completely what those prodigious syllables referred to" (Aldous Huxley, *The Doors of Perception;* N.Y., 1954; pp. 16, 18.

¹³In the *Republic* (Stephanos II, 368) Plato slips into his doctrine of the "ideal society" ostensibly to illustrate the relationship of each individual's psychic elements to one another by "magnifying" this into the "larger and more visible picture" of a whole society, though in his philosophy "psyches" are real, mere collections of psyches are not (Hegel (*The phenomenology of Mind*, tr. Baillie, 2nd ed.; Allen & Unwin: London, 1931) clearly says "The goal . . . is Absolute Knowledge or Spirit" (last page, 808), while "state-power" (last mentioned on p. 535) "means nothing else than . . . a moment of self-conscious life, i.e., it *is* only by being sublated [transcended]."

¹⁴A famous presentation is Max Stirner, *Der Einzige und sein Eigenthum* (Leipzig, 1845; Eng. tr. S. Byington, *The Ego and Its Own*; N.Y., 1907 & 1918); also a recent defense by William Todd, *Analytical Solipsism* (Martinus Nijhoff: the Hague, 1968).

15The respective implications of materialism (neutrality), idealism (neutrality/favorability) and solipsism (unpredictability) for homosexuality would seem to be equally applicable to certain more specialized phenomena in the gay life such as transvestitism, pederasty and sado-masochism. Provided that every relationship is purely voluntary, I feel that the three "clear-cut" philosophies would have nothing different to say about these "specialized phenomena." (This will not hold true for the "more complex dualisms" below.)

16Why are dualistic ethics generally more obscure than the other philosophies? In the Fall of 1944, Prof. J. H. Randall, Jr. of Columbia U., himself a kind of Aristotelian dualist, in one of his lectures made a distinction between "holoscopic" and "meroscopic" world-views which contains an implied answer: a "holoscopic" (whole-viewing) system, he said, starts with universal principles, deducing all particulars from them (materialism, idealism, and solipsism are examples); a "meroscopic" (part-viewing) philosophy takes up the many questions of life first, then constructs a total outlook from the various answers found. The dualisms are usually meroscopic, and naturally we cannot swiftly discover a goal of life if we must first respond to the variety of questions that our lives apparently offer.

17See "Animism" in Hastings, *Encyclopedia of Religion and Ethics* (Edinburgh, 1908-22); the arrangement of categories is different from mine; also, the definition of "animism" in the *Schaff-Herzog Encyc. of Religious Knowledge* (N.Y., 1910-12), Vol. III, p. 194.

18To deal with some possibly strong reader resistance at this point, I must mention A) the pansexual (straight/gay/bi) Eulenspiegel Soc. (founded in N.Y.C., 1971), an "S/M Liberation" group whose 4-year program of forums and C.R. sessions has developed the general consensus that i) "S/M" refers to any case of "dominance vs. submission" (the infliction of *pain* implied by the more extreme term "sado-masochism" being only a special instance, and not necessarily involved even in the text's example!); and ii) not only sexual, but emotional and psychic satisfactions justify the seeking of "S/M experience" (the removal of guilt by atonement is a "psychic satisfaction"); and B) "homophilia" here means "a much greater likelihood of homosexual than heterosexual expression," because, occurring at the stage in "spirit-belief" where homophobia has not yet surfaced, this is tantamount to simple acceptance.

19Two examples are Ganymede and Penthesilea. The former name means either "joyful counsel" (medos) or "joyful genitals" (medea), and the story of how Zeus in the form of an eagle abducted him is well-known. See *New Century Classical Handbook* (ed. C.A. Avery; N.Y., 1962) p. 491: " . . . [he] supplanted Hebe in her function as cup-bearer, . . . in Latin the name appears as Catamitus, whence the English term catamite" (i.e., passive partner in anal intercourse). The first clause symbolically suggests the later, more bisexual attitude in Greece. Penthesilea (possibly "gracious [hileos] in mourning [penthesis]" referring to Achilles' being struck by her beauty after killing her) was an Amazon queen, fathered by Ares, god of war; "P. led her 12 princesses into battle . . . slashed about her mightily and the Greeks fled in panic . . . she leaped like a leopard to meet [Achilles]" (*Handbook*, p. 842).

20A) When the transvestite "Galloi," male priests of the Earth Mother Cybele, occasionally castrated themselves in her honor (Hastings, *Encyc.* IV, 377-378) they were indeed ancient analogues of the modern transsexuals; but transsexuality and transvestitism not being limited to homosexuals, this is not "an implication for homosexuality." B) When the "gay churches" maintain "Jesus died for all people, straight and gay," it seems totally consistent with the Christian doctrine that His death guaranteed immortality for all, transcending "moral" distinctions (cf. the thief in Luke 23, 40-43), which is to this extent homoïsic; but the question is whether, once in heaven, these immortal spirits still require remembrance from their descendants on earth.

21"Phallism," Hastings, 'Encyc. The "Dionysian orgies" involved men and women with probably only incidental homosexuality, while Priapus and his phallic symbols (like other cultures' enormous ithyphallic forms) were worshipped mostly by heterosexual women. Similarly the Lingam (penis) and Yoni (vulva) were revered by the opposite sex, and though among the Lingayats (Hastings, VIII, 69 ff.) both men and women wear the lingam amulets and/or caste marks, it is merely a "group identification symbol" of this sect whose purpose was to overcome caste distinctions. In his documentary motion picture "Phantom India" (viewed on T.V., 8/20/74), Louis Mallé suggests that, though surrounded by extreme visual eroticism of temple bas-relief, Hindus are sexually undemonstrative and more concerned with traditional child-bearing marriage.

22"Shamanism," Hastings, *Encyc.* Also the converse long-standing opinion of male and female homosexuals as "wizards," "witches," etc.

23"Canaanites," Hastings, *Encyc.* References to "temple courtesans"

(Revised Standard Version: "cult prostitutes") in the O.T. are associated with the phallic posts called "ashĕrīm" from the Heb. root " ⸴ sḥ ṛ" meaning either "to be erect" or "to be happy."

24A valuable analysis in Laud Humphreys, *Out of the Closets: the Sociology of Homosexual Liberation* (Prentice-Hall, 1972; Ch. 8: "Confronting Stigma") lists 5 stages of coping; (based on ideas from Irving Goffman, *Stigma: Notes on the Management of Spoiled Identity*; Pr-H, 1963).

25"Formal cause" in Greek: "eidos," "logos." "Li": third tone: character formed from the 96th radical and a phonetic which is also the 166th radical, thus not the same as the famous "li" or "ritual." In Fung Yu-lan, *Short History of Chinese Philosophy* (N.Y., 1948), Chu Hsi, major philosopher of the "Li School" of Neo-Confucianism, says "There is no form without matter and no matter without form" (p. 300), and "for the bamboo chair there is the *li* of the bamboo chair" (p. 296), practically identical with Aristotle's "formal cause," though it is true the *li* were also conceived in a realm by themselves (like "Platonic Ideas").

Aesthetic and Sexual Relativity

By James W. F. Somerville

Are matters of taste "no more than matters of taste?" The question is not pleonastic because the expression "people's tastes" is ambiguous: it could mean either their opinions in matters of taste, which are expressed by explicit or implicit aesthetic judgments and appraisals; or merely their likes and dislikes. Some philosophers have argued that aesthetic judgments and appraisals do not concern people's likes and dislikes; otherwise disagreements in matters of taste would, contrary to plain matter of fact, not be possible. G. E. Moore in the following passage is talking about moral judgments, but his argument applies equally to aesthetic ones:

> If, when one man says, "This action is right" and another answers, "No, it is not right," each of them is always merely making an assertion about *his own* feelings, it plainly follows that there is never really any difference of opinion between them: the one of them is never really contradicting what the other is asserting. They are no more contradicting one another than if, when one had said, "I like sugar," the other had answered, "I *don't* like sugar." . . . It is surely a plain matter of fact that when I assert an action to be wrong, and another man asserts it to be right, there sometimes is a real difference of opinion between us: he sometimes is denying the very thing which I am asserting.[1]

Although aesthetic judgments are not *the same as* statements that people have certain likes or dislikes it might still be that such statements are the only reasons which can be given in justification of them; aesthetic judgments would still be "no more than matters of taste." Immanuel Kant strongly rejects such a view: "what has pleased others can never serve as the ground of an aesthetic judgment."[2] His reason is that it is no more than a matter of fact that a thing pleases a person, whereas a judgment that is beautiful — what Kant says "are alone proper judgments of taste" (14) — involves something else: "It is an empirical judgment, that I perceive and judge an object with pleasure. But it is a judgment *a priori* that I find it beautiful" (37). Like Moore, Kant stresses that disagreement in matters of taste must be possible. In the section called "The Antimony of Taste" (56) he picks out what he calls two commonplaces of taste. The first is that *everybody has his own taste*; the second, which, despite Kant, amounts to little more than a re-statement of the first, is that *there is no disputing about taste*. Between the two, Kant says, is a third proposition which has not become a proverb, namely, that *there may be quarreling about taste*. With both disputing and quarreling, Kant thinks, the parties aim ultimately to reconcile their differences and reach agreement; disputing differs from quarreling in that with a dispute there is a hope of bringing agreement about by proof. Kant thinks judgments of taste cannot be proved because they are "subjective." What he means is that the predicate *beautiful* refers not to anything "in" the object judged but to "the feeling of pleasure or displeasure" the person who makes the judgment feels when affected by the object (1). His view seems to be that the judgment, "this flower is beautiful" is not, despite its grammatical form, about the flower but the feeling which is to be had when it is judged to be beautiful;[3] in other words, beauty is a quality relative to those who judge it to apply to things or persons.

Kant produces no argument for the "subjectivity" — in effect, the relativity — of judgments about beauty. Dogmatism will not do: some philosophers have denied that aesthetic qualities are relative. Moore, for example, asks his readers to imagine two worlds: one exceedingly beautiful, the other the ugliest which can be conceived; what they must not imagine is "that any human being . . . can *ever see and enjoy* the beauty of the one or hate the foulness of the other." Moore then asks whether it would not be "better that the beautiful world should exist, than the one which is ugly?" He thinks it would be: "the beautiful world *in itself* is better than the ugly."[4]

There are many judgments, however, where terms are predicated of a thing (or person) in a way which is clearly relative to those who submit it to their judgment. These are affective terms.[5] Examples are: *attractive, exciting, amusing, pleasing, moving, disgusting,* and so forth. What is fascinating to a botanist may be only interesting to a student, and boring to a farmer. Many, though not all, judgments containing affective terms are aesthetic judgments, and the aesthetic qualities they ascribe to things (or persons) are unarguably relative. But Kant does not hold that *beautiful* logically, if not grammatically, behaves like an affective term. "It would," he rightly says " . . . be ridiculous[6] if anybody who prided himself somewhat on his taste were to think of justifying himself by saying: 'This object . . . is beautiful *for me'* " (7). The real reason, which escapes Kant, is that unlike *attractive* or *agreeable*, it makes no sense to say that a thing (or person) is *beautiful* (or *graceful* or *pleasant*) *to* or *for* somebody. Aristotle, while discussing views such as that suggested by the saying of Protagoras that "man is the measure of all things"[7] complains that' their holders "must make everything relative — relative to opinion and perception;" what they should say is not that something is true, "but true for this man."[8] But this does not make sense; if truth is relative, its relativity cannot be stated. Besides, it is a purely empirical judgment that a thing (or person) is attractive to a group of people, since it merely states that it tends to attract them, and Kant thinks judgments of taste are *a priori*. (To say it is attractive to them is not to say it actually attracts them, only that it has the characteristics of so doing, or is apt to.)

Possibly the reason why Kant thinks judgments about beauty are "subjective" is that he holds, circularly, that they cannot be proved. This is a consequence of their being nonempirical and of two other features they possess: their autonomy and their claim to universal validity. Autonomy of judgment is judging for yourself. Kant says: "Taste lays claim simply to autonomy. To make the judgment of others the determining ground of one's own would be heteronomy" (32). A modern philosopher, Frank Sibley, draws a clarificationary analogy: "rather as a color-blind man may infer that something is green without seeing that it is, and rather as a man, without seeing a joke himself, may say that something is funny because others laugh, so someone may attribute balance or gaudiness to a painting, or say that it is too pale, without himself having judged it so."[9] Of the claim to universal validity, Kant says that it "essentially belongs to a judgment by which we declare anything as beautiful" (8). This does not mean that everybody actually agrees about what is beautiful: "the judgment of taste does not postulate everybody's agreement . . . it only *imputes* this agreement to everybody" (8). A person makes a judgment of taste, then, "without the need to grope around, by experience, among the judgments of others and to instruct himself beforehand as to their pleasure or displeasure with the same object" (32). And, "he does not in any way count on the agreement of others with his judgment of pleasure since he has found them many times in agreement with his own; he *demands* it from them" (7). A person passing judgment on a thing's beauty "judges not merely for himself but for everybody" (7) and that "one believes one has a universal voice of one's own" (8). But:

If anybody does not find a building, a view, a poem beautiful, *to begin with* he does not let the approval even of a thousand voices all praising it highly put pressure on him inside. He may indeed pretend that it pleases him also so that he is not regarded as having no taste; he can also even begin to doubt whether he has built his taste on a knowledge of a moderate enough number of objects of a certain sort (as one, who in the distance thinks he recognizes something as a wood what others regard as a town, doubts the judgment of his own sight). But he perceives quite clearly that the approval of others does not afford any valid proof at all of the estimation of beauty .... The unfavorable judgment of others can of course make us rightly scrupulous in respect of our own, but never convince us of its wrongness. (33)

What Kant overlooks is that affective terms can be used according to either a relative or an absolute construction. I can say that a thing is interesting to some person or that it is interesting *tout court*. Kant seems to think that the absolute construction of affective terms is always an ellipsis for the relative one. He says that a person "is quite content that if he says 'Canary wine is agreeable,' another man corrects the expression and reminds him he ought to say 'it is agreeable *to me*' " (7). But when affective terms are used absolutely the judgment is not elliptical.

This mistaken view is part of a larger one which is exemplified by the attempt of David Hume to show that there is no important difference between aesthetic qualities and sensible qualities, such as colors. "If, in the sound state of the organ, there be an entire or a considerable uniformity of sentiment among men, we may thence derive an idea of the perfect beauty; in like manner as the appearance of objects in day-light, to the eye of a man in health, is denominated their true and real color, even while color is allowed to be merely a phantasm of the senses." [10] Hume sees that the uniformity of tastes is no argument against their relativity, though it is left to his modern disciple, Sibley, to see that neither is diversity of tastes an argument *for* their relativity, as Hume supposes. Sibley concedes that in matters of taste "awareness of the alleged properties is relative not just to a certain physical condition, but to a certain mental condition, the result of experience, etc;" [11] he thinks it is odd that "this relevance of one's mental condition should often be cited as a main reason why they cannot be objective matters" (p. 40). Their larger mistake is to suppose that there is a standard — an emotional standard — in matters of taste to appeal to as there is with colors, namely, the color an object looks to normally sighted people under standard conditions. With affective terms there is no such equivalent to the physiological criteria to appeal to as with colors: what offends some people merely makes others laugh. What emotional effect things (or persons) have on people is not to be determined *merely* by experience and observation but also by the exercise of judgment. What I am arguing is that judgments using affective terms according to their absolute construction share with judgments about beauty Kant's three features of being not merely empirical, autonomous and claiming universal validity. (When used relatively judgments containing affective terms are merely empirical).

Since affective terms are used in judgments which are undeniably aesthetic there is a *prima facie* case for arguing that nonaffective terms for aesthetic qualities, such as *beautiful, graceful, pleasant*, behave logically, despite their grammatical form, like affective terms. The case becomes stronger once it is appreciated that affective terms can be used either absolutely or relatively and that the absolute construction is not an ellipsis for the purely empirical, relative one. More weight is still required, however, for the conclusion to carry conviction that the nonaffective aesthetic terms share the relativity of affective terms when used absolutely. If there is an area where everybody agrees, not just certain philosophers, that our aesthetic judgments are relative, and, further, that there is no importance difference between our use of affective terms (according to the absolute construction) and nonaffective terms in this area, the case for the relativity of *all* aesthetic qualities, and, so of all aesthetic judgments, will have been made.

There is one area, often forgotten about, where relativity is both uncontroversial and incontrovertible. This is the area of sexual attractiveness. Judgments that other people are beautiful, pretty, good-looking, "sexy," "gorgeous," (sexually) attractive or interesting, erotic, plain, ugly, repulsive, and so forth. Nobody denies, at least after some thought, that these judgments are relative. What might be in dispute is in what way our sexual or erotic appraisals are relative. Philosophers have rarely expressed themselves on the matter, possibly because they have not given it much thought. One account, which will be familiar enough, would be that these judgments are relative solely to the sex of the person who judges. For example, a man who thinks that a woman is pretty or sexually attractive does so, in part at least, because he is male. The objections to this account are clear.

First, other men, whose heterosexuality has been proved and tested in the eyes of their acquaintances beyond doubt, may not find the particular woman in question either pretty or attractive. Perhaps it is not mere parochialism to argue that the gay liberation movement may also help to liberate heterosexual men and women. The idea that all healthy heterosexual men or women should swoon over and goggle longingly at the popular pin-ups and idols carefully fostered and exhibited by the publicity machines of today is ridiculous. But I rather think it took courage until recently for even heterosexuals to dissent from what they imagined to be the consensus of popular opinion, or to express openly, except for rare moments of candor, belief in the diversity of opinion about which people are sexually attractive or erotic, even within the confines of heterosexuality. Kant remarks that "an obligation to enjoyment is a manifest absurdity" (4 ftn). In this he is right, though probably for the wrong reasons. You cannot choose to enjoy yourself or be pleased by something. Sometimes, however, people *feel* constrained by a bantering conviviality. As gay people, Kant's point that somebody may pretend to be pleased for fear of being thought to have no taste answers our own experience only too well; so much so that it is difficult for us to imagine a generation of gay people who do not have to unlearn concealing their true sexual feelings. For heterosexuals, it need not be the fear of being thought homosexual that may press them to be a party to these polite insincerities but of being thought totally lacking in feelings indulgently looked on as excusable foibles which are thought to be among the more attractive traits of humanity. Still, I doubt if it is merely out of considerations of what Kant calls "sociability" (7, 41) that leads heterosexuals to feign a greater uniformity in erotic appraisals than is the case. In the world of Hollywood the only hint that there might be some diversity is when the wife or woman friend of the hero, seeking his opinion of a flighty bit who she suspects might be a rival for his attentions, receives the reply that the supposed rival is "not my type"; though even here the impression created is that she fails to meet the hero's unqualified approval on grounds of character, not erotic appeal.

Second, how does the wife in the Hollywood set scene arrive at her suspicions that the flighty piece might be a rival for her husband's attentions? By his behavior, perhaps, though as the scene usually runs this is not the grounds of her suspicions. Her grounds are that she judges the flighty piece to be sexually attractive to (heterosexual) males on an appraisal of her looks and figure. It is because she so judges that she fears her husband, being a heterosexual male, will succumb to temptation despite his apparently proven past loyalty. She knows there is no such thing as proven loyalty where sex is concerned; everybody knows that boys will be boys, because that is the way they are made. It would be subversive to suggest that she is able to judge the other woman to be sexually attractive because she is sexually attracted to her herself. To return to real life, if there is considerable diversity of opinion about erotic appraisals, she might be wrong in concluding that the other woman is sexually attractive to her husband, though right in general in thinking that she is sexually attractive to most other male heterosexuals. Does this mean that she cannot say that the other woman is sexually attractive *tout court* unless she herself is sexually attracted to her? If this were so, it would be hard to avoid concluding that she could not, unless she were homosexual, say that the other woman is beautiful or pretty, either. In short, that she could not appraise her sexually or erotically at all. This seems to conflict with common experience; we can know quite well that a person is sexually attractive or good-looking without being attracted to the person ourselves; and we do not acquire this knowledge solely by observing the behavior of others or by conducting a straw poll. We judge for ourselves on the basis of the looks, manner, presence, and so on, of the person that he or she is sexually attractive, though perhaps the person is not sexually attractive to us. I do not deny that there is a puzzle here, but it is not solved by saying that erotic appraisals are relative only to the sex of the persons making them.

Finally, the account assumes that erotic appraisals are all heterosexual. It is not hard to imagine how the account could be amended to accommodate homosexual appraisals. Michael Tanner, replying to a paper of Sibley's writes: "Of course one doesn't expect a child to be moved by the *Grosse Fuge*, a sadist by *King Lear*, or a male homosexual to be excited by the pull-outs in *Playboy*; and if Sibley is right, too, in saying that because these facts are relative more to psychological than to physical conditions, we should not feel the more inclined to say that aesthetic properties aren't objective". [12] Homosexual appraisals on the amended account of the relativity of erotic appraisals, can be explained away easily by such factors as abnormality, disease (physical, mental, endocrinological), immaturity, perversity, depravity, sheer idiosyncrasy or oddity, etc.; factors which need not make you pause and wonder whether a privileged logical status should be given to heterosexual appraisals.

Erotic appraisals make use of terms for aesthetic qualities, including affective terms, so there seems no reason why they should not be counted as aesthetic judgments. Many aestheticians, however, have denied that they are. Clive Bell comments: "When an ordinary man speaks of a beautiful woman he certainly does not mean only that she moves him aesthetically; . . . With the man-in-the-street 'beautiful' is more often than not synonymous with 'desirable,' the word does not necessarily connote any aesthetic reaction whatever, and I am tempted to believe that in the minds of many the sexual flavor of the word is stronger than the aesthetic." [13] R. G. Collingwood goes further. He believes "beautiful" has no aesthetic use at all.

The words "beauty," "beautiful," as actually used, have no aesthetic implications . . . . A beautiful woman ordinarily means one whom we [14] find sexually desirable; . . . Certainly we often call our fellow creatures beautiful by way of saying that we love them, and that not only sexually. The bright eyes of a mouse or the fragile vitality of a flower are things that touch us to the heart, but they touch us with the love that feels life, not with a judgment of their aesthetic excellence . . . . The word "beauty," wherever and however it is used, connotes that in things by virtue of which we love them, admire them, or desire them.[15]

It is the possible involvement of desire and, consequently, of action that is the main argument for excluding erotic appraisals from the domain of aesthetic judgments. Collingwood's remarks on the subject are revealing:

The extent to which this make-believe sexuality has affected modern life can hardly be believed . . . pornography homoeopathically administered in doses too small to shock the desire for respectability, but quite large enough to produce the intended effect . . . . An aphrodisiac is taken with a view to action: photographs of bathing girls are taken as a substitute for it. The truth may rather be that these things reveal a society in which sexual passion has so far decayed as to have become . . . a toy: a society where the instinctive desire to propagate has been weakened by a sense that life, as we have made it, is not worth living, and where our deepest wish is to have no posterity. (pp. 84-5)

And this was in 1938! In discussing what he calls "sexual fantasy" Collingwood is confusing appreciation, judgment, and appraisal with action. The pictures of bathing girls are not substitutes for action as such, though they may assist in the substitution of one sort of action (masturbation) for another (coition); but there is no need to regard them as substitutes, necessarily, at all. Further, if he is discussing the enjoyment or appreciation of *actions* rather than enjoyment or appreciation as such, his contrast between fantasy and life "as we have made it" is difficult to apply in the sexual field: fantasy is a part of sexuality.

Kant argues similarly that where appetite or desire can be involved our pleasure cannot belong to the sphere of taste: "everybody says hunger is the best cook, and people with a healthy appetite relish everything so long as it is edible; and so such a pleasure shows no choice governed by taste. Only when the need is satisfied can one decide who among many has or has not taste" (5). Kant has an analogy with morals in mind. Where your moral duty and what you want to do (inclination) coincide Kant supposes (cynically some might think), that it is not clear from which motive you acted; it is only where duty and inclination are incompatible that it can be seen whether you acted from duty or inclination. In the same way, it is only when an appetite or desire has been satisfied that it becomes clear whether your pleasure is of the sort that belongs to taste. As an argument for the nonaesthetic character of appraisals where appetites for food or sex can be involved, it fails. My motive in seeking out somebody's company may be that I think that I shall enjoy her or his company or it may be that I see the person as a future bed partner, or it may be a bit of both; just as I may buy some strawberries, not because I am particularly hungry but because I enjoy their taste, or it may be a mixture of the two. The presence of an appetite may alter appreciation, indeed, as Kant apparently concedes, it may enhance it, and once satisfied it may diminish appreciation, but this can scarcely be an argument against appraisals made during the appreciation belonging to the sphere of taste, unless you hold, as Kant does not, that judgments of taste can be proved. Since aesthetic judgments cannot be established beyond argument there is no reason why the same person may not make several contrary appraisals, each claiming universal validity, about the same food or person at different times according to whether an appetite is involved, and whether it has been satisfied or not. If Kant's point is that the presence of an unsatisfied appetite makes us less discriminating, that is, less fussy or selective, this may be true but the knowledge or memory that at a different time we would not be so pleased or pleased at all cannot affect the claim to universal validity of the judgment we pass now: what has pleased ourselves at another time can never serve as the ground of an aesthetic judgment just as much as what has pleased others. Granted even that the presence of an appetite *does* count against the aesthetic character of a judgment, there are still numerous occasions when we judge food or persons to be pleasing without our appetite being aroused. The wine taster who spits out the sample after tasting it affords only the clearest instance that experience gives us the distinctness of our desiring to satisfy an appetite and our appreciation of the taste of food and drink or the looks of people. That the two are distinct is not to deny that sometimes they are closely intermingled and hard to disentangle. Kant's error, perhaps, is in thinking that we can have a motive in appraising something or judging it to be pleasing or displeasing. Only actions can have motives. We do not judge for a reason, though we can have reasons for our judgments.

The case against erotic appraisals being aesthetic ones remains unproved. The difference between heterosexuality and homosexuality, it might therefore be suggested, amounts to no more than a matter of taste; some people happen to like or prefer the opposite, others the same sex, and others still happen to like both or have no decided preference. But the suggestion would be entirely unilluminating because it is tautological. What "heterosexual," for example, means is being sexually attracted to or having an erotic liking or preference for the opposite sex. What would be substantive is the suggestion that *the reason* why heterosexuals, for example, are sexually attracted to or have an erotic liking or preference for the opposite sex has to do with matters of taste rather than, say, their sex, glands, hormones, physical characteristics, upbringing or education, psychological development, experience with the opposite sex, moral rectitude, a striving to conform, etc., etc.. If the suggestion is correct it would explain not only why (predominantly or exclusively) heterosexual or homosexual people differ, but why some heterosexuals like or dislike certain types of members of the opposite sex or prefer them to other types; that is, it would explain the diversity of the likes, dislikes and preferences within heterosexuality. Since we have no hesitation in using terms for aesthetic qualities in our erotic appraisals the case for explaining the difference between heterosexual and homosexual attraction, likings or preferences as being due to differing aesthetic appraisals of other people, according to whether they belong to the opposite or same sex is powerful. That is, some people as a matter of taste are sexually attracted to, or like or prefer sexually, the one sex rather than the other; others, as a matter of taste are sexually attracted to and like sexually other people of both sexes and have no preference for one as against the other. And the reasons for being sexually attracted, liking or preferring sexually other people of the one sex rather than the other, or being sexually attracted to or liking sexually both, and preferring sexually neither as against the other, are aesthetic reasons based on aesthetic judgments and appraisals. Of course, being of one or the other sex is such a general feature of other people that knowledge that people have erotic likings or preferences for other people of the one or of the other sex tells little about their opinions of which people they find attractive or erotic; any more than knowledge that people like or prefer certain colors or vocal music tells much about their tastes in art or music. I suspect it is due to the sheer generality of this feature of other people, namely, that they have a sex, which largely explains why most people are blind to the obvious and have recourse to some causal psychological explanation of homosexual attraction; since where less general features of people are involved — the hackneyed example is blondes and brunnettes — nobody questions that sexual likings or preferences are due to taste or seeks some elaborate and implausible psychological explanation.

The objection which might be made to such an account is that heterosexual and homosexual appraisals should not be put on the same footing. If homosexuality were, say, a kind of impotence or a morbid fear of the opposite sex or a pathological craving — the sexual counterparts of a morbid abhorrence of food, hydrophobia, a jaundiced palate, drug addiction, or an irrational craving to consume something bizarre like soil — the objection would have some force. It has to be said that many people through ignorance take homosexuality to be like these things. What they lack is the personal experience which would demonstrate the absurdity of their notions; or if they have sexual feelings toward their own sex, the calmness of mind and freedom from prejudice — prejudice often nurtured by external sources — to interpret their own experience correctly. Homosexuality is frequently thought of as a symptom of some unknown and yet undiscovered disease. It does not seem to have occurred to those who think this that the absence of any evidence of invariable morbidity or of a pathological condition are grounds for thinking that it is not a symptom of any disease at all. It is fair to describe the situation in the recent past as being that the more such evidence was discovered to be lacking the more energetically theorists sought to discover an undiscoverable disease or malfunctioning. The fact that not all men and women are exclusively either heterosexual or homosexual disproves theories about impotence or fear of the opposite sex. [16] Such theories ignore the sexual feelings of the person and concentrate on the difficulties he or she has in coming to terms with a hetero-sexually dominated society. If homosexuality is a "complaint," it is not a "complaint" in the sense of a disease but in the sense that people seek help and complain about being homosexual. In the absence of medical evidence, the next step is to classify homosexuality as a "psychological" illness which is vague enough to cover any eccentricity of behavior. If the extent of homo-sexual feelings and behavior were better known, it would soon be realized how ridiculous it is to call homosexuality "abnormal." No abnormality can be pointed to using medical or biological criteria. If "abnormal" means "rare" or "unusual," however, homosexuality is slightly less common than hetero-sexuality.

My argument has been that the undeniable relativity of erotic appraisals confirms the doctrine of the relativity of all aesthetic judgments. Judgments with affective terms used according to the relative construction express merely empirical statements. Aesthetic qualities, whether named by affective terms used absolutely or by other terms, are relative to the autonomous judgments of people, but these autonomous aesthetic judgments are not merely empirical. This is the sense in which aesthetic qualities are relative. In short, aesthetic qualities are relative because aesthetic judgments are relative. This relativity of judgment must not be confused with the notion of the relativity of truth. Relativity of truth is certainly not supposed in the relative use of affective terms. And the predicates used in aesthetic judgments are not true of the things they are predicate of relative to *the persons* making the judgment, but relative to their judgments, which of course are autonomous. This can be seen by remembering that when people make judgments which use affective terms absolutely it does not follow that they judge empirically that the thing in question has the emotional effect on themselves. What I judge to be interesting, *tout court*, may not be interesting to me as a matter of fact. The claim to universal validity of aesthetic judgments is not a claim to truth, otherwise they could (in principle) be proved or established. Contrary opinions in matters of taste are not both true as the doctrine of the relativity of truth would have it. Such claims to the absolute truth of the opinions would only result in statements about the relation of those opinions to those who hold them, as Aristotle observed; and though these statements would themselves be true absolutely they would be distinct from the opinions which claim absolute truth. To claim or demand the agreement of everybody is not to say that everybody would agree with the judgment. if only they judged correctly, as a claim to truth would presuppose. I may be fully aware that other people are unlikely to agree with my judgment. Respect for the autonomy of judgment means being aware that others may also judge autonomously, but differently, from me. Kant's notion of the imputation of agreement *a priori* to everybody seems to me to be a confusion of the claim to universal validity with the claim to truth. Aesthetic judgments are relative then in the sense of being relative to the autonomous faculty of judgment: their validity is entirely dependent on the judgment people exercise.

An objection to my whole approach to erotic appraisals is that their relativity can easily be explained causally, analogous to the way in which a causal explanation can be given of why red objects look red to normally sighted people, namely by reference to the physiology of the eye and brain. This view shares with Sibley the mistake of thinking that mental and experiential conditions of discerning a quality do not make it less objective than physical conditions. The difference between erotic qualities and colors, of course, is that whereas half the human population belongs to the one sex, the other half to the other, most people happen to have (though it might not always be so) normal color vision. Being female or male is undoubtedly a physical, or rather an anatomical, physiological, and endocrinological matter. A judgment that somebody is pretty or sexually attractive, however, is not a plain report on what you observe. As Sibley points out, [17] you can observe, say the features of a person quite accurately and yet not notice the prettiness or attractiveness. Erotic appraisals involve the exercise of judgment. Appraisal and judgment can be exercised quite independently of parts of the body like eyesight, the other sense organs, genital organs, or glands.

What is wrong with a causal account of erotic appraisals in particular, and judgments and evaluations in general? The short answer is that it cannot do justice to Kant's points about autonomy of judgment and the claim to universal validity.

In "The Skeptic" Hume sketches a picture of the mind as though it were an organ like the eye. He states that the mind

> it is not content with merely surveying its objects, as they stand in themselves: It also feels a sentiment of delight or uneasiness, approbation or blame, consequent to that survey; and this sentiment determines it to affix the epithet *beautiful or deformed, desirable or odious*. Now, it is evident, that this sentiment must depend upon the particular fabric or structure of the mind, which enables such particular forms to operate in such a particular manner, and produces a sympathy or conformity between the mind and its objects. Vary the structure of the mind or inward organs, the sentiment no longer follows, though the form remains the same. The sentiment being different from the object, and arising from its operations upon the organs of the mind, an alteration upon the latter must vary the effect, nor can the same object, presented to a mind totally different, produce the same sentiment. (p. 218)

On this view contrary erotic appraisals could be explained by a causal mechanism between the object of appraisal and the mind: heterosexual men have a different fabric or structure of mind from heterosexual women, or heterosexual women a different mind from homosexual women, and so on. The objection to this theory is that a causal sequence of events is looked for to explain divergences of opinion. No allowance is made for the fact common experience attests to that people can, though perhaps do not always, judge for themselves and be responsible for arriving at their own opinions and beliefs. The theory reduces people to automata. Further, it takes no interest in the judgments themselves, only in how they come to be. It concentrates on the purely empirical matter that a person is judged to be good-looking or is attractive to somebody, and seeks to explain it. It ignores the validity of the judgments and the reasons that might be given in justification of them.

In saying this I am not denying the possibility of giving some explanation of people's opinions in matters of taste. Such explanations would be historical, that is, about the origins and development of people's tastes, rather than causal. Though you might argue that it is unlikely that somebody could arrive at an opinion without having come under certain influences or gone through a certain series of events or had a certain development, you cannot, except where specific items of knowledge are concerned, argue that the person could not have arrived at the opinion without these prior events occurring. Nor can you argue that a given sequence of events inexorably leads to the holding of certain opinions. Edward Bullough writes that "we certainly do account for taste in ordinary life often enough. We have a perfectly definite idea *why* X dislikes Chopin or Y paintings of the Dutch School . . . . The lack of consensus of opinion in aesthetic matters is consequently not unaccountable." This is perfectly true, but he is wrong to say that the *"efficient* causes are mostly known to us"; the "antecedants" of tastes are not efficient causes.[18] It might be that the opinion can be seen to be in character with the personality of the person. Or it may be that some past incident has stimulated development in a direction that may or may not have occurred if the incident had not. It is unfortunate that some gay apologists try to rebut the obvious, namely that adolescents with early sexual experience with the same sex may turn out in adult life to be predominantly attracted sexually to the same sex. It might well be that their subsequent development is not more likely to be homosexual than heterosexual having had these early experiences; but that early experience is formative of personality hardly needs saying, and it is useless to try to deny it. It is more than unfortunate if the nature of the apology against charges of "corruption" of youth is that all may turn out well in the end.

Explanation of people's tastes by reference to past experience and development, influences, personality, etc., are, however, mainly irrelevant to consideration of the claims of aesthetic judgments. Confusion readily arises between explaining an opinion in a matter of taste and explaining a like or dislike. Often it can be inferred from people's opinions that they like or dislike a thing, but "like, dislike, or indifferent" is too crude a classification to provide an instructive explanation of the opinion. To give an adequate explanation you must first understand what the opinion is; perhaps it does not fall definitely into any of the three classifications. In so far as explanations of the opinion throw light on the nature of the opinion itself, they are relevant to considering what is claimed by the aesthetic judgment. But explanations which refer to the person liking or disliking the thing (or person) judged do not.

That people have certain likes or dislikes can never be a justification of an aesthetic judgment. This is Kant's doctrine. Matters of taste are more than "merely matters of taste" since argument, Kant's "quarreling," about them is possible. Reasons for our aesthetic judgments can be given even though these reasons can never be conclusive nor binding on other parties to the argument. They can only be persuasive or compelling if the other parties see their force — herein lies the autonomy of judgment. But it is never a reason for somebody's aesthetic judgment that the person has certain likes or dislikes. At best it is a more or less adequate explanation of the person's judgment. Rather, it is the other way round: reasons for liking or disliking a thing (or person), where it is a matter of taste, express themselves in aesthetic judgments and appraisals.

The relativity of erotic appraisals, therefore, cannot be accounted for by giving a causal explanation of people's erotic preferences or likes or dislikes for other people. Rather, it is people's erotic appraisals which are cited as reasons for the preferences or likes or dislikes in question. A causal explanation of these preferences or likes or dislikes would not account for the relativity involved in erotic appraisals because it could not comment on their claims to universal validity. The alternative account is that erotic appraisals are aesthetic judgments, so their relativity is that involved in aesthetic judgments in general, namely, the relativity that arises from their autonomy and claim to universal validity. A consequence of this account is that it is wrong to suppose there must be a quota of heterosexual and homosexual people throughout different populations: one in twenty or whatever. Such a hypothesis would be reasonable if a causal explanation could be given for why some people are (predominantly or exclusively) heterosexual rather than homosexual. But if it is due to matters of taste there can be no quota, except by chance. It might so happen, for example, that the proportion of exclusively heterosexual to homosexual people in Saudi Arabia is the same as that in The Soviet Union and also in Bolivia. But this would be due to chance. On the account I have defended responsibility is left with people themselves. There remains the possibility, however, that certain people are capable of developing their tastes in areas they had not thought they were capable of so doing. Whether this is really so, I believe people are free to judge for themselves which people they find sexually attractive.

Support for the quota theory seems to be given by Hume's assertion in "The Skeptic" that the "fabric and constitution of our mind no more depends on our choice, than that of our body." It is not "in a man's power . . . to correct his temper" (pp. 221-2). Francis Hutcheson makes much the same point as Hume:

> In reflecting upon our *external senses*, we plainly see that our perceptions of pleasure or pain do not depend directly upon our will. Objects do not please us according as we incline they should. The presence of some objects necessarily pleases us, and the presence of others as necessarily displeases us. Nor can we by our will any otherwise procure pleasure or avoid pain than by procuring the former kind of objects and avoiding the latter. By the very frame of our nature the one is made the occasion of delight and the other of dissatisfaction.

The same observation will hold in all our other pleasures and pains.[19]

That we cannot choose what we find to our taste or pleasure does not derogate from the responsibility we have for our judgments of taste. We shall still be held responsible by others for all our judgments even if they are heteronomous, or if we are insincere in that we feign our feelings. This is a reason why, if possible, we should judge autonomously. That we cannot judge as we please is just what autonomy of judgment consists in: our judgments remain unaffected by what, if we could choose, we might wish them to be. "No man would ever be unhappy, could he alter his feelings," Hume argues. "PROTEUS-like, he would elude all attacks, by the continual alterations of his shape and form" (p. 221). If we could make things which did not please us, or we were indifferent to, please us we should become so unreasonably tolerant as to be thought to be in a state of idiocy and less than completely human. It is because we abrogate our responsibility that insincerity of judgment, the pretense to hold opinions we do not hold, makes us less than rational. This is an important point. It is often pointed out that a person cannot choose to be heterosexual or homosexual. It might appear to lend weight to attempts to give a causal account of our erotic appraisals; but on the contrary, it shows how any purely causal account must be inadequate as an explanation of our erotic appraisals since it denies responsibility in judgment.

Hume does add that "the mind is not altogether stubborn and inflexible, but will admit of many alterations from its original make and structure" (p. 223). There are "insensible" influences on the mind, such as education and habit, which act "in an indirect manner." Of course, we can cultivate likings for things and overcome an initial dislike for them. This is what the expression "an acquired taste" refers to. Possibly many people in adolescence acquire an enjoyment of smoking this way: by persevering until they lose their initial distaste; partly because they have heard how pleasurable smoking is supposed to be, so they expect that unless they are defective in some way they should enjoy it too; and partly because they imagine that the habit is a mark of maturity and being adult, so carries social prestige. It would be foolish to deny that something similar does not happen with erotic likings and preferences. Heterosexuality may well be for many an acquired taste rather than one which springs unsummoned from disposition or temperament. Nonetheless, the influence we can bring to bear on ourselves is limited, as Hume sees. He says of the affections:

These are of a very delicate nature, and cannot be forced or constrained by the utmost art or industry. A consideration, which we seek for on purpose, which we cannot retain without care and attention, will never produce those genuine and durable movements of passion, which are the result of nature, and the constitution of the mind. A man may as well pretend to cure himself of love, by viewing his mistress through the *artificial* medium of a microscope or prospect, and beholding there the coarseness of her skin, and monstrous disproportion of her features. . . (p. 225)

Kant's notions of the autonomy of judgment and speaking with a universal voice have great attraction, but I wonder if they do full justice to the relativity of our aesthetic judgments, including our erotic appraisals. Writing about judgment in general, not just aesthetic judgments, Kant says: "However small the extent and degree to which a person's natural gifts may reach, yet it indicates a man of *enlarged thought* if he sets aside the subjective private conditions of his judgment, by which so many others are confined, and reflects on his own judgment from a *universal standpoint* (which he can only determine by placing himself in the standpoint of others)" (40). Kant assumes that there is a universal standpoint which can be abstracted from the individual standpoints of everybody. Presumably it is the universal standpoint we reflect from when, in making a judgment of taste, we believe we speak with a universal voice. But is there a *single* universal voice? Kant says that this is all that the judgment of taste postulates, though the universal voice is only an idea — that is, it is not that we believe that everybody does speak with one voice; rather it is that we believe people should speak with one voice (8). It does not seem to me, however, that the claim to universal validity requires there be an ideal *universal* voice. That is, in reflecting from the universal standpoint we may be conscious that there is not one, but a plurality of voices, some of which may even be contrary to others.

This would help to resolve the difficulty I have mentioned about the absolute construction of affective terms, namely, that I can judge a thing to be interesting or a person to be (sexually) attractive without judging that it is interesting to me or the person (sexually) attractive to me. Erotic appraisals provide the clearest and most common illustration of the difficulty, perhaps because since people tend to be either inhibited from adopting, or unable to adopt the attitudes of others in matters of sex *as their own*, they can only imagine them. Of course, this is not easy to do. Differences in tastes always tend to puzzle us, which goes some way to explain why in matters of erotic tastes heterosexuals refer to gay people as "queer," and why they wonder what "makes" us "queer." But the differences with regard to erotic appraisals are so clear, even to heterosexuals, that people are compelled to rely on imagination, if, as is even more common, they are not to ignore all differences and blindly assume that there is just one, usually male heterosexual, standpoint. It is not that I judge the thing to be interesting or the person to be attractive but am not myself interested in the thing or attracted to the person, since this would suggest that given the right circumstances I might be interested or attracted; if it is interesting to me, or he or she attractive to me, it does not follow that I am interested or attracted, merely that the thing or person tends to interest or attract me. So, I judge the thing to be interesting though not interesting to me. I am certainly not judging that it is interesting to others for that would be a purely empirical statement based on experience of what happens to interest the people in question; which, of course, I could judge for myself, and so it would be an autonomous, besides an empirical, judgment. If anything is clear, it is that I am not basing my judgment on even the most cursory empirical research about what happens in fact to interest other people. Perhaps I am making a heteronomous judgment derived from the autonomous judgments of people the thing is interesting to. There does not seem to be any place in Kant's system for a judgment which claims universal validity, yet is heteronomous. Besides, how do I derive a heteronomous judgment from other people's autonomous judgments without relying on empirical judgments that these people have made certain autonomous judgments? If my judgment is autonomous and claims universal validity yet I dissociate myself from it, it must be because I imagine how others judge, and so appreciate the diversity of human nature.

Despite its materialistic aspects, Hume's essay "The Skeptic," can be read as a celebration of the diversity of human nature. As his title suggests, relativism has often been lumped together with skepticism. With some qualification, it is a mistake to think that relativism of values constitutes a denial of knowledge. On the contrary, it broadens knowledge by making us see the same thing in a variety of different lights. Read in this light "The Skeptic" is a reminder of the dignity and indominability, you could almost say, intransigence, of the human spirit.

Dennis Altman makes an interesting remark about tolerance: "The real mark of tolerance is its failure to imagine the experience of others. I am constantly made aware that even the most liberal of straights thinks of a world that is entirely heterosexual, rather as there are few whites who really comprehend that for millions of Americans this is not a white country." [20] Claims to universal validity might seem to be intolerant[21] in that they seem to discount any contrary claims. But if we adopt a universal standpoint we shall see that the relativity of aesthetic and erotic appraisals arises out of their claims to universal validity. Parochialism and provincialism are not merely an over-concern for matters that affect us as members of a particular kind or class of people rather than others; they exhibit a total lack of awareness that others may not share our concerns nor be affected by those matters, and are concerned and affected by different matters. To appreciate the relativity of our aesthetic and erotic appraisals, in turn, is to "enlarge our thought," in Kant's phrase, and to attempt to imagine the vastly different experience of others. So understood, aesthetic and sexual relativity does not concern "no more than mere matters of taste." As a philosophical doctrine, the relativism of aesthetic and erotic values transcends such mundane comments and can change our whole outlook toward our fellow human beings.

NOTES

[1]G. E. Moore, *Ethics* (1912), (London: Oxford University Press, 1963), chapter III, pp. 63-4. Compare also: "The Nature of Moral Philosophy," in *Philosophical Studies* (1922), (London: Routledge and Kegan Paul), pp. 333-4.

[2]Immanuel Kant, *Critique of Judgment* (1790), section 33. All further references to Kant to sections of this work. I have used the translations of both J.H. Bernard (New York: Hafner, 1961) and J.C. Meredith (Oxford: The Clarendon Press, 1911).

[3]Compare the remark of Peter Thomas Geach about sentences which express a relation, "we must not think that a sentence that has one subject-predicate analysis cannot have more than one," *Mind*, 59 (1950), p. 462.

[4]G.E. Moore, *Principia Ethica* (1903), (Cambridge: Cambridge University Press, 1960), section 50, pp. 83-5.

[5]I borrow the expression from Monroe C. Beardsley, *Aesthetics: Problems in the Philosophy of Criticism* (New York: Harcourt, Brace and World, Inc., 1958), p. 42.

[6]Compare Stanley Cavell, "Aesthetic Problems in Modern Philosophy" in *Philosophy in America* ed. Max Black (London: George Allen and Unwin Ltd., 1965), p. 91.

7The saying is mentioned by Aristotle, *Metaphysics XI* 6, 1062b12-13; see also IV 5, 1009a6-14.

8*Metaphysics*, IV 6, 1011b3-5, trans. by W.D. Ross (Oxford translation).

9Frank Sibley, "Aesthetic and Nonaesthetic," *The Philosophical Review*, 74 (1965), p. 137.

10David Hume, "Of the Standard of Taste" (1757) in *Essays, Moral, Political and Literary*, ed. T.H. Green and T.H. Grose (London: Longman, 1875), I, 272. All further references to Hume to page numbers of this volume.

11F.N. Sibley, "Objectivity and Aesthetics," *Proceedings of the Aristotelian Society* Supplementary Volume 42 (1968), p. 46.

12Michael Tanner, "Objectivity and Aesthetics," *Proceedings of the Aristotelian Society* Supplementary Volume 42 (1968), p. 63. I use Tanner's words as being merely illustrative and symptomatic of a pervasive but unthought-out point of view. I do not intend to ascribe this point of view to Tanner himself.

13Clive Bell, *Art* (1914), Ii (London: Arrow Books, 1961), pp. 27-8.

14This use of "we" betrays the poverty of imagination that is a symptom of blindness to the relativity of taste and values. See p. 299, note 20.

15R.G. Collingwood, *The Principles of Art* (Oxford: The Clarendon Press, 1938), pp. 38-40.

16Compare Roger Baker's argument that the attitude to homosexuality "that it is a sickness or mental aberration" receives "a severe shaking when confronted with an evident homosexual component in an otherwise heterosexual person." "Bisexuality," *Gay News*, 47 (May/June 1974), p. 10.

17"Aesthetic Concepts," *The Philosophical Review*, 68 (1959), p. 423.

18Edward Bullough, *Aesthetics, Lectures and Essays* ed. Elizabeth M. Wilkinson (London: Bowes and Bowes, 1957), p. 19.

19Francis Hutcheson, *An Inquiry Concerning Beauty, Order, Harmony,*

Design (1725), The Preface, ed. Peter Kivy (The Hague: Martinus Nijhoff, 1973), p. 24.

[20]Dennis Altman, *Homosexual Oppression and Liberation* (New York: Avon, 1973), p. 54.

[21]Compare Cavell's comments: "I think an air of dogmatism is indeed present in such claims; but if that is intolerant, that is because tolerance could only mean, as in liberals it often does, that the kind of claim in question is not taken seriously." ("Aesthetic Problems in Modern Philosophy," p. 97).

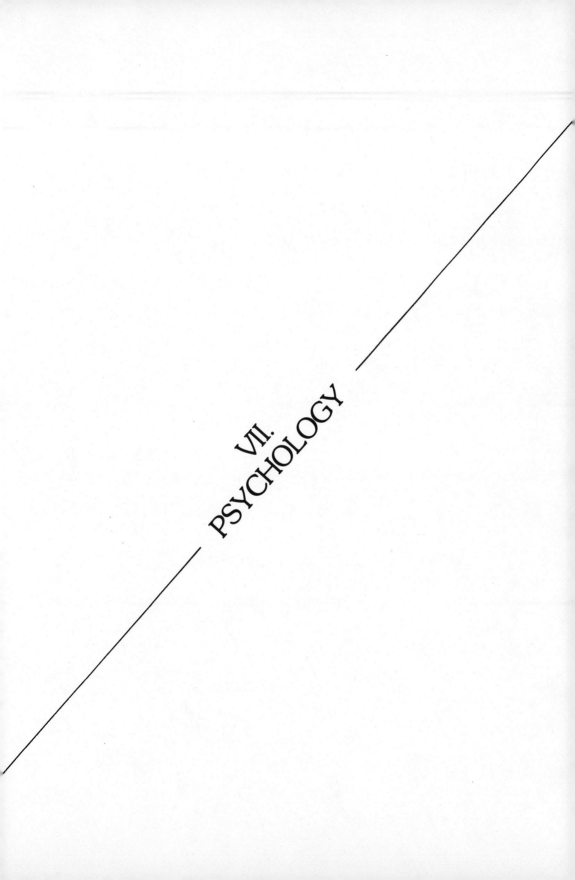

VII.
PSYCHOLOGY

❧

Conflicts Over Rights and Needs In Homosexual Relationships

By John P. De Cecco and Michael G. Shively

The study of the interpersonal relations of homosexual men with other men and of homosexual women with other women may reveal new capacities and choices in their relationships. Such studies are now possible since the dread of pathology, immorality, and criminality surrounding homosexual relationships is lessening. Two developments have lifted the spectre of pathology. One is the growing number of studies that show few if any significant differences in personality traits and social adaptations of nonclinical samples of homosexual and of heterosexual men and women (e.g.: Freedman, 1971; Hooker 1963; Minnigerode, 1975; and Siegelman, 1972a, 1972b; Weinberg and Williams, 1974). The other is the decision by the chief organizations of psychiatrists and psychologists to no longer consider homosexuality in itself as mental illness. The dread of immorality has been lessened by actions and policy statements of some religious groups at local, state, and national levels to admit publicly identified homosexuals to their congregations and clerical ranks. The weight of criminal sanctions has been lifted by legislation in seventeen states by August, 1976, allowing consenting adults of the same gender to have private sexual relations.

The purpose of this chapter is to explore how homosexual relationships can be made more democratic. The change to democratic relationships can be accomplished by using negotiation to resolve conflicts between rights and needs.

DEMOCRATIC RIGHTS

A democratic relationship is one in which both parties recognize and defend the democratic rights of each party. The concept of democratic rights used here is borrowed from previous research (De Cecco and Richards, 1974).

There are four basic rights. *Participation in Decision-Making* is the right of each party to make and implement decisions and rules that govern the relationship. *Equality* is the right to the same opportunities within the relationships — sexual, material, personal, and social. *Dissent* is the right to disagree, criticize, and protest. *Due Process* is the right to hear and answer charges of wrongdoing before punishment is considered or imposed.

PSYCHOLOGICAL NEEDS

Individuals do have rights but they also have needs. In a democratic relationship the satisfaction of one party's needs must respect the other party's rights. Democratic relationships can be maintained only when the parties respect both rights and needs and their interaction. Conflicts will inevitably arise in democratic relationships since needs constantly require accommodation to rights.

We are investigating four needs which have been identified in clinical research as important in homosexual relationships (Bieber and Associates, 1962; and Ovesey, 1963). We have defined these needs as follows: *Power* is the need to control the decisions, standards, and actions of another person. *Dependency* is the need to submit to the decisions, standards, and actions of another person. *Competition* is the need to attract more attention or win more favors than another person. *Sexuality* is the need to make sexual contact with another person.

Each need represents an inevitable source of conflict with each right. The right of decision-making, for example, conflicts with power needs when one party makes and implements all the decisions and rules for the relationship. It conflicts with dependency needs when one party abdicates to the other party all responsibility for making and implementing rules and decisions for governing the relationship. It conflicts with competition if one party makes unilateral decisions and breaks rules mutually agreed upon to win more attention and favors than the other party. It conflicts with sexuality when parties do not jointly make and implement decisions and rules governing their sexual behaviors.

DEFINITION OF CONFLICT

In our studies of interpersonal relationships of homosexual men and of homosexual women, we define *conflicts* as "specific incidents that have occurred between particular parties, at particular times and places, which have aroused anger that moved one or more parties to action." The term applies to situations with alternatives for action in the immediate future.

DEFINITION OF NEGOTIATION

In order to preserve democratic rights and satisfy psychological needs, all parties must participate in resolving conflicts. A model of conflict resolution as negotiation was established in previous research (De Cecco and Richards, 1974). The model now has four successive steps: (1) statements of issues by both sides made with direct, verbal expression of anger; (2) agreement by both sides on a common statement of issues; (3) bargaining by both sides, with each side gaining and making concessions; and (4) both sides agreeing to each party's responsibility for implementing agreements.

Democratic rights are protected in each step of the model. The right of decision-making is protected by each party's participating in all steps of negotiation. Dissent is protected by each party's having the opportunity to verbalize anger and state issues. Due process is protected by each party's having the chance to hear and answer charges made against it, to agree to the charges that will be the focus of the conflict, and to agree to a settlement of the conflict. Equality is protected by each party's gaining and sacrificing on a par.

Negotiation is a way for parties to create alternatives that neither party alone could create. Negotiating helps a person to learn about the rights and needs most important in a particular conflict. By avoiding negotiation, the individual also avoids learning how to shoulder the responsibilities of protecting rights and satisfying needs.

To protect the rights of each party, negotiation of conflicts must be attempted. Not all conflicts over rights and needs can be resolved through negotiation. However, conflicts that cannot be negotiated are often recognizable only after negotiation has been attempted.

CONFLICT RESEARCH

There are three sources of data on the interpersonal relationships of homosexual men and women. There are the clinical data on patients in treatment (e.g.: Bieber, 1962, 1965; Ovesey, 1963, 1965). There are data derived from administering personality tests to non-clinical samples of heterosexual and homosexual men and women. There are the social psychological data of our studies of conflict in the interpersonal relationships of homosexual men and of homosexual women (De Cecco and Shively, 1975).

The clinical data are limited to samples of homosexual men who voluntarily entered treatment to become practicing heterosexuals. Research using personality tests focuses on traits and not relationships. It cannot reveal conflicts in these relationships over rights and needs.

Our social psychological data are descriptions of particular incidents provided by self-identified homosexual men and women. Respondents were given a list of democratic rights with a definition for each right. Using this list, respondents were asked to do the following: (1) to assign ranks of 1 and 2 to the rights of the respondent which were most central to the conflict; (2) assign ranks in a similar fashion to the rights of the second party; and (3) give reasons for assigning each rank. Respondents were then given a list of psychological needs with a definition for each need. They were asked to assign ranks and explain their choices as they had done for the democratic rights. They were then asked whether the issues were primarily psychological needs, democratic rights, or both for each party and were asked to explain their choices. Finally, they were asked in what alternative ways could all parties have dealt with the conflict.

In the following section we will present two conflict incidents. The first was related by a homosexual man, the second by two homosexual women. By presenting and analyzing these incidents we will show how our theory and data can apply to the dynamics of conflict in homosexual relationships. The incidents will provide examples of how the violation of democratic rights is related to the expression of psychological needs. The incidents also show how the parties dealt with conflict; our analysis will show what the parties should have considered if they were to have used negotiation to resolve the conflict.

CONFLICT INCIDENT I

The following incident was chosen to illustrate how power and dependency needs can abridge the rights of decision-making and dissent. It was described by a twenty-five-year-old homosexual man:

The conflict happened about a year ago at the home of a friend whom I was spending time with (in *and* out of bed). Only he and I were involved. I had gone over to his house one evening knowing that I would probably be spending the night. The place was filthy as usual. He was an artist and used his entire apartment as a studio. Paint, sawdust, rotted food, cat hair, and just plain dirt covered everything in the place. Soon after going to bed I noticed that the cat's litter box smelled so bad that I couldn't even go to sleep. I said to him, "What is that awful smell?" He responded, "It's probably the cat's litter box." I asked him why he didn't change it. He said he couldn't afford to buy cat litter all the time. I asked him why in the hell he kept the cat if he couldn't afford to take care of it properly. He got outraged at my comment and starting yelling "Well what can I do with it? No one wants a cat and I don't want to take it to the humane society because they will kill it." One word led to another and before long I was criticizing him for how dirty his apartment was. He responded that he couldn't live the way *I* did (tidy, clean housekeeper). We stopped seeing each other.

The respondent ranked dissent as his only democratic right violated. He gave this reason: "As defined here only dissent. I feel I had a right to complain about something which physically disturbed me without being jumped on." The respondent ranked dissent first and due process second as the rights of his friend that were violated. He gave this reason: "I guess he had the right to refuse to clean up his apartment and live just the way he wanted to. Guess he had the right to live in filth if that's what he wanted."

We see decision-making as the primary democratic right violated. Both parties appeared to be imposing standards of cleanliness that had not been discussed and agreed to. We agree with the respondent that the right of each party to dissent was also violated. Instead of considering each other's criticisms, they attacked one another's standards of cleanliness. We do not agree that due process was violated in this conflict since both parties did have a chance to hear and answer charges without punishment.

The respondent saw the following psychological needs as unsatisfied in this conflict. He chose only power for himself. He gave this reason: "I wanted him to clean the place up so I didn't find it so offensive to be there." For his friend he chose only power. He gave this reason: "If any, he had the need, I think, to control how I felt about existing (sleeping, eating, etc., amidst all that dirt). He had to make me accept it or else. I chose the 'or else' path."

We agree that power needs were central to the conflict. Each party's power needs may have lead him to violate the other's right of decision-making. Each party appeared to need to control the decisions and actions of the other in order to impose his personal standard of cleanliness. The respondent did not recognize that dependency needs may have been unsatisfied in each party. The "outrage" expressed by the friend seems to indicate uncertainty about his own standard of cleanliness. The respondent's words "tidy, clean housekeeper" also may indicate uncertainty about his standard. Each party may have needed to submit to the other party's standard of cleanliness. The failure to acknowledge this dependency may have resulted in both parties' failure to listen to the criticisms of their present standards. This failure to listen violated the right of dissent.

The respondent saw only democratic rights as issues for himself and only psychological needs as issues for his friend. We see both rights and needs as equally important issues for both parties. By emphasizing his own rights and his friend's needs he did not perceive the conflict between rights and needs. Perceiving this conflict could have provided a basis for negotiation.

They dealt with the conflict by not seeing each other again. They used avoidance instead of negotiation to resolve the conflict. The way the conflict ended may show that their power needs were stronger than their dependency needs.

Within a framework respecting the rights of decision-making and dissent, each could partly have satisfied both his power and dependency needs by agreeing to new standards of cleanliness. The least that could result from an attempt at negotiation is that each party would recognize that the need to maintain his standard of cleanliness was more important to him than the need to continue the friendship. In that event, each party would have taken responsibility for his part in ending the relationship.

CONFLICT INCIDENT II

The following conflict incident was described by both parties in separate interviews. One party is Susan, a 25-year-old homosexual woman, and the other is Alice, a 23-year-old homosexual woman. They identified themselves as lovers. First we present Susan's description of the conflict:

When we first started living together — and first had oatmeal — one of us made it *her* own way. Which made the other one gag. My lover makes it *mushy*, it comes out really gooey . . . I remember we'd start to have oatmeal — I'd be in a good mood, I'd cook it and then (she would) complain about how awful it was. So now we don't have oatmeal together. We eat other stuff. I might cook it for myself once in a while but not for her. She might cook it but she cooks it *her* way. (And I cook it mine.) She likes it her way and I like it mine. She likes it mushy — yuk!

This is Alice's description of the same conflict:

The first time we ever had oatmeal, we had to decide how to do it. There are two ways to cook oatmeal. One way you boil the water first. The other way, you throw the oatmeal in while the water's cold. I like it when you start with the water cold (then it's creamy). We bought the oatmeal (we were already living together). I cooked it my way (the creamy way) and she said she didn't like it that way. I said "Oh." She said, "Let me do it my way next time." I said OK. Then, the next time we had oatmeal, whoever cooked it, cooked it the other person's way, the way the other person might have preferred it. So it's a compromise — whoever gets up first cooks it the other person's way. There's now no hassle about who cooks it or when. The only thing we notice is whoever doesn't get it her way gets up and says, "Oh, I hate it this way." But it works.

We accept the respondents' presentation of the incident. We are not trying to determine the facts, but only to analyze the perceptions. These descriptions show how the parties to a conflict can agree in their perceptions of issues while they differ in their perceptions of how the conflict is resolved.

Susan chose decision-making as her only democratic right violated. She gave this reason: "We had to decide which kind of oatmeal we wanted — we both had our preferences — I can still make my own separately." Susan chose decision-making as Alice's only right violated. She gave this reason: "The issue was one of decision-making."

Alice ranked due process first and dissent second as her rights violated. She gave this reason: "She criticized me before I had a chance to realize what her wishes were about oatmeal." She ranked dissent first and decision-making second as Susan's rights violated. She gave this reason: "I cooked it the first time without asking her how she liked it. She was the victim of the conflict, not me."

We see both women violating the right of decision-making. Susan decided to prepare and eat oatmeal by herself without consulting Alice. Alice decided to cook oatmeal Susan's way without consulting Susan.

Neither woman exercised her right to dissent. Neither said to the other "I don't like the way you're preparing the oatmeal." Each complained about the oatmeal as it was served but not about the issue — which was the way in which the other had prepared it. By complaining about the effect of the oatmeal on themselves, they avoided criticizing the actions of the other person. Complaining alone is not dissent because it is not clearly directed at the issue. We do not agree that due process was an issue because no specific charges were made by either party.

Susan chose power as her unsatisfied psychological need. She gave this reason: "She wouldn't give in." For Alice, she also chose only power. She gave this reason: "I wouldn't give in."

Alice ranked dependency first and power second as her psychological needs left unsatisfied. She gave the following reason: "She didn't tell me what she wanted so how could I 'submit' before I made the oatmeal." Alice ranked power first and dependency second as Susan's psychological needs left unsatisfied. She gave the following reason: "I didn't know or ask."

When Susan said that neither one would "give in," we assume that she meant that they would not give up their preferences for the consistency of the oatmeal. When Alice says "I didn't know or ask," we assume she is referring to the way in which Susan liked to have oatmeal prepared.

We see both women expressing dependency needs. Susan needed to eat the oatmeal the way Alice prepared it. Susan in this way submits to Alice's decision. Alice expressed her dependency needs by wanting to cook the oatmeal Susan's way regardless of her own preference.

We see both women expressing power needs. Each expressed her power needs initially by preparing the oatmeal her own way and expecting the other to eat it. Susan then expressed her power needs by deciding alone to prepare oatmeal only for herself. Alice then expressed her power needs by preparing oatmeal using Susan's method.

In this conflict we see a pattern in the interaction of the rights and needs of both women. Their power and dependency needs seem to be in conflict with the right of decision-making. They expressed power by avoiding joint decision-making. They expressed dependency by submitting to the preference of the other party. Their dependency needs seem to be in conflict with the right of dissent. They appear to act as if direct criticism would jeopardize their dependency on each other.

Susan saw democratic rights as the primary issue for herself. She gave this reason: "We had to decide — we had to compromise — neither of us wanted to force the other — just wanted to have it their own way." She saw democratic rights as the primary issue for Alice. She gave this reason: "We had to decide — she wasn't trying to shove the gooey stuff down my throat."

Alice saw democratic rights as the primary issue for herself. She gave this reason: "We were learning how to tell each other what we needed in advance — decided to talk things over." She also saw democratic rights as the primary issue for Susan. She gave the following reason: "pretty much the same as mine — learning to relate to each other."

We perceive both rights and needs as equally important for both parties. By emphasizing only democratic rights for both parties, they failed to consider what needs were left unsatisfied. The phrases "neither one of us wanted to force the other" and "we were learning how to tell each other what we needed in advance" indicate their dependency. Susan's words "just wanted to have it their own way" may be Susan's expression of her power needs.

According to Susan, they dealt with the conflict by no longer eating oatmeal together. According to Alice, they dealt with the conflict by reaching a compromise whereby one would prepare oatmeal in the other's way.

Each tried to resolve the conflict without the aid of the other. Their accounts of the way in which they handled the conflict are contradictory. Although both women use words indicating compromise, it appears they never mutually agreed to a resolution of the conflict.

When asked for alternative ways for dealing with the conflict, Susan replied, "if one of us had been on a power trip, we could have forced the other to have it our own way. Or we could have oatmeal all the time and each make in our own way." When asked for alternative ways of dealing with the conflict, Alice replied, "We could have never had oatmeal again. Or one of us could have forced the other to eat it one way all the time."

We see no suggestion by either woman for negotiation even in the alternatives they suggest. They simply propose more force or avoidance.

The first step of negotiation is the statement of issues by both sides made with direct, verbal expression of anger. They did not take this first step. Susan and Alice want to cook for each other. This may represent an expression of power needs. Each also wants to eat what the other cooks, and they want to eat it together. These may be expressions of their dependency needs. To satisfy those needs within the framework of democratic rights, each would have to express direct criticism about the way the other prepared oatmeal. By exercising the right of dissent, they take the first step of negotiation. By participating in making decisions about issues that affect the relationship, they open the way for taking the other steps of negotiation.

CONCLUSION

Our purpose in this chapter was to show how relationships can be made democratic by considering both rights and needs in resolving conflict. We propose the use of negotiation as a way to protect rights while satisfying needs.

Democratic rights were defined in the Declaration of Independence as belonging to individuals. Those participating in liberation movements have viewed them as civil rights applying to institutional conflicts. In this study we have treated them as human rights applying to interpersonal conflicts.

The two incidents we analyzed illustrate how important protecting democratic rights can be in resolving everyday conflicts. By recognizing the rights and needs of individuals in their conflicts, we may understand more about everyday conflicts. By using negotiation, we may understand better how to deal democratically with conflicts.

Further research may provide refinements of the concepts and the model we have presented.

REFERENCES

Bieber, Irving, and Harvey Dain, Paul Dince, Marvin Drellich, Henry Grand, Ralph Gundlack, Malvina Kremer, Alfred Rifkin, Cornelia Wilbur, and Tody Bieber, *Homosexuality, A Psychoanalytic Study of Male Homosexuals* (New York: Basic Books) 1962.

Bieber, Irving, "Clinical Aspects of Homosexuality," in *Sexual Inversion* ed. J. Marmor (New York: Basic Books) 1965, 234-257.

De Cecco, John and Arlene Richards, *Growing Pains: Uses of School Conflict* (New York: Aberdeen Press) 1974.

De Cecco, John and Michael G. Shively, "A Study of Perceptions of Rights and Needs in Interpersonal Conflicts in Homosexual Relationships," San Francisco State University: Center for Homosexual Education, Evaluation and Research, 1976.

Freedman, Mark, *Homosexuality and Psychological Functioning* (Belmont, CA: Brooks/Cole) 1971.

Hooker, Evelyn, "The Adjustment of the Male Overt Homosexual," in *The Problems of Homosexuality in Modern Society*, ed. H.M. Ruitenbeek (New York: E.P. Dutton & Co., Inc.) 1963, 141-161.

Minnigerode, Fred A., "Age Status Labeling in Homosexual Men," *Journal of Homosexuality*, Spring, 1976, *in press.*

Ovesey, Lionell, "The Homosexual Conflict: An Adaptational Analysis," in *The Problems of Homosexuality in Modern Society*, ed. H.M. Ruitenbeek (New York: E.P. Dutton & Co., Inc.) 1966, 127-140.

Ovesey, Lionel, "Pseudohomosexuality and Homosexuality in Men: Psychodynamic as a Guide to Treatment," in *Sexual Inversion*, ed. J. Marmor (New York: Basic Books) 1965, 211-233.

Siegelman, Marvin, "Adjustment of Male Homosexuals and Heterosexuals," *Archives of Sexual Behavior*, 1972, (2:1) 9-25.

Siegelman, Marvin, "Adjustment of Female Homosexuals and Heterosexuals," *British Journal of Psychiatry*, 1972.

Weinberg, Martin S. and Colin J. Williams, *Male Homosexuals: Their Problems and Adaptations* (New York: Oxford University Press) 1974.

Towards
A Gay Psychology

By Mark Freedman

Homosexuality was first studied by psychologists and psychiatrists as a deviation from the heterosexual norm. In most cases, "deviation" was equated with "defect." Case studies of disturbed homosexual men and women were reported in psychology journals in the hopes of shedding light on the "etiology" of this condition, as well as developing effective ways to treat it. Psychologists designed tests which contained "signs" to point to homosexual tendencies.

Today, we have some clues as to how the sickness notion of homosexuality emerged. These factors were surely crucial: The Biblical injunctions against homosexuality, the emphasis on the supposed superiority of men over women, and the need for separation of sex roles; Christian suppression of pagan religions which included homosexual practices; the rise of the medical model which extended the concept of illness to the realm of emotions and behavior; the labeling of deviant behavior as mental illness by psychiatrists; and the consequent silence of well-adjusted gay people who could have challenged the emerging stereotype of the sad, neurotic homosexual.

In the 1950's and 60's, a group of psychiatrists and psychologists emerged as "experts" on homosexuality. (Most of them — in the United States at least — were Jewish. One viewpoint holds that their fathers wanted them to be a doctor and their mothers wanted them to be a rabbi. Their solution was to become a psychiatrist, making pronouncements about sin and moral improvement in the guise of sickness and health.) These "experts" based their varied notions of homosexuality on either armchair speculation or analysis of homosexuals in therapy, a highly unrepresentative sample of gay people. (We certainly would not accept a description of heterosexuality based just on experience with heterosexual patients in therapy!) Actual comparative research on the adjustment question was never considered by these experts.

The first good research on the personal adjustment of gay men was done by a female psychologist, Evelyn Hooker of U.C.L.A., in the mid-fifties. In this study, she compared homosexual and heterosexual men who were not in therapy. All of the men — divided up into pairs of comparable age, intelligence and schooling — were given a battery of personality tests. These tests were then analyzed by expert clinical psychologists, who rated each person on a five-point scale of personality adjustment without knowing the subject's sexual orientation. The results indicated that the judges could not identify the sexual orientation at better than a chance level and that the ratings of the homosexual group were not significantly different from those of the heterosexual group. In other words, the homosexual men were rated as being no more disturbed than the heterosexual men. About two-thirds of both groups were rated as normal or better.

Dr. Hooker drew some tentative conclusions from her study: Homosexuality as a clinical entity does not exist — its forms are as varied as those of heterosexuality; homosexuality may be a deviation in sexual pattern that is within the normal range, psychologically; and the role of particular forms of sexual desire and expression in personality structure may be less important than has frequently been assumed. Most of the studies done in the following decade have confirmed her findings and conclusions. Unfortunately, most of the studies have used male subjects. There was a gap in our knowledge of Lesbians.

In 1967, I decided to do my doctoral research with female homosexuals. Groups of lesbians and heterosexual women were compared on several personality measures. My preliminary results show that the lesbians are no more neurotic or disturbed than the heterosexual women (only a small percentage of each group manifested disturbance), both groups functioned as well as most people in the general population, and on some attributes the lesbians functioned better than the control group.

These provocative findings led me to seek out more data on the ways that gay people might function better than non-gays. At this point, it appears that there may be at least four major areas in which gays often function better than non-gays: 1. Inner-Direction/Centering, 2. Sex Roles, 3. Sexuality, 4. Identity/Self-Disclosure.

Inner Direction/Centering

Many gay people have responded to social pressures against homosexuality by "centering" — discovering and living by their own values. This quest for identity, purpose, and meaning in life often begins early, as soon as they come to appreciate the tremendous pressure in society against homosexuality.

My own research with lesbians found them scoring higher than the control group on several scales of personality test designed to measure positive psychological functioning, including "inner-direction" (autonomy), "spontaniety," "feeling reactivity" (sensitivity to one's own needs and feelings) and "time competency" (orientation to the present as opposed to being obsessed with the past or anticipating the future). Likewise, June Hopkins (1969) compared lesbians and matched controls on Cattell's 16-Personality-Factor test. Among the adjectives with which she characterized the lesbian group were: independent, resilient, bohemian, and self-sufficient. Marvin Siegelman (1972) compared a non-clinical sample of lesbian and heterosexual subjects on personality inventories. The lesbians scored significantly higher than the controls on "goal direction" and "self-acceptance."

Studies with gay men have discovered similar patterns. For example, a Kinsey Institute sociological survey conducted by Martin Weinberg and Colin Williams in 1969 which questioned over 1,000 American gay men found that 52 percent rejected "conformity in general" as an important value.

I have met many gay people who have "centered." They do not reject all social conventions and mores. Rather, they choose which ones are right for them and evolve new patterns to substitute for the ones they reject. David is such a person:

> David is a 25-year-old gay man who works as a counselor in a private psychiatric hospital. He is also a doctoral candidate at a school of professional psychology in Los Angeles. He and his lover Roger have lived together for two years. They have an intimate, caring relationship, although one that is not sexually exclusive. (Their agreement: it is all right for either of them to have sex with others.) David is immersed in his work and his studies. He also finds time for movie going, dinner parties, tennis, and occasional trips to the baths. Eventually, he hopes to develop a private practice specializing in counseling gay couples.

For some gay people, feelings of separateness have led to creatively opposing the values and the institutions of the dominant society from which they feel alienated. This pattern has also occurred in intelligent, creative members of the other discriminated-against minority groups. The result of this creative opposition has been new social concepts and increased sensitivity to the value of the person in our society.

Sex Roles

The stereotype of gay people almost always includes deviation from conventional sex roles: the homosexual man is effeminate and the lesbian mannish. Of course, as with any stereotype, there is a grain of truth here. Gay men often show "feminine" emotions and characteristics; lesbians often exhibit "masculine" ones. Our sexist society denigrates this behavior. Recent research has shown that even educated persons disapprove of sex-role deviation, especially of males acting like "sissies." Most people, when questioned about desirable attributes of a mentally healthy person, devalue "feminine" traits; they do not consider most so-called female characteristics, such as *gentleness*, to be socially desirable or psychologically healthy for either sex. I would disagree: In some cases, deviation from stereotyped sex roles is a positive attribute.

Research and personal experience shows that many gays are able to show a wider range of emotional expression because they are not confined by stereotypes sex roles. Lesbians are more able to show "masculine" attributes (assertiveness, aggressiveness, etc.) than non-gay women. My research showed lesbians to be more accepting of their natural aggressive feelings and more like men in their motivational patterns of work satisfaction than the control group of heterosexual women. Many gay women are more able to express "feminine" emotions (tenderness, weakness, etc.) than most non-gay men. This is confirmed by the work of Siegelman (1972) who found that gay men scored higher on "tender-mindedness" and "submissiveness" than non-gay men although no difference was found with regard to "neuroticism."

The shared wisdom of the gay world is that two men or two women living together as mates quickly see the limitations of stereotyped sex role activities (breadwinner versus homemaker) and characteristics (dominance versus submission). This tends to encourage a transcendence of the sex roles and more sharing and mutuality.

One social psychologist who tape-recorded the conversation of a group of gay people at a small social gathering identified over thirty terms for nuances of relationships. He concluded that gay people probably have a more sophisticated knowledge of social interaction than nongays. This supports the contention that many gays transcend conventional roles and patterns of relating to others.

Sexuality

There is good evidence to believe that there are major differences between gay and non-gay sexuality: openness about sexual needs, ability to perform in group sex, and, of course, what happens in bed.

The social arrangements preparatory to a homosexual experience are often much more direct and honest than in heterosexual situations. Before having sex with a woman, a heterosexual man may have to wine and dine her and convince her that he is interested in her mind and personality and (sometimes) that he loves her. Among gay people, there is more often an understanding that, at least initially, there is to be "sex for sex's sake." The prospective partners typically do not have to feign love or any other emotion that would be manifestly false at this point in the relationship. Sometimes these arrangements continue and result in a meaningful relationship; othertimes, the arrangement is merely a one-time sexual experience, valid and enjoyable in itself.

Gay men are more comfortable in group sex situations than non-gay men. Gigl (1970) investigated a sample of 680 gay men. Fifty-five percent of them participate in group sex at least once a month. Probably most of them do this at a gay steam bath, a situation in which men can have casual sex. In contrast, two extensive studies of heterosexual group sex (Bartell, 1971; Paulson & Paulson, 1972) — a comparable self-selected situation — showed over three quarters of the men unable to perform sexually.

Finally, what happens in bed is also significant. Gay people may be better able to know what feels good to their partner: a man knows what feels good to another man because he knows what makes his own body feel good. Also, women can find qualities of nurturance, warmth, and tenderness from other women that many men are incapable of expressing.

Many gay people are able to eliminate sex roles in bed and can enjoy a variety of sexual activities. Weinberg and Williams (1974) found that 55 percent of their male sample have engaged in a variety of sexual practices (mutual masturbation, giving and receiving fellatio and anal intercourse). A poll by The Advocate, the national gay newspaper (1974), found that of 213 gay men responding, 40 percent engaged in a variety of sexual practices (oral, anal, masturbation); 73 percent took both "active" and "passive" roles in bed. Andrea Oberstone (1974) compared 25 lesbians and 25 heterosexual women between the ages of 20 and 45 years. Both groups were rated as well-adjusted and both reported playing mutual roles sexually most of the time. However, more lesbians stated that they play an active role while more heterosexual women reported playing a passive role. Lesbians also expressed greater satisfactions in their relationships — emotionally, sexually, in friendship and common interests — than their heterosexual counterparts. It seems that many gay people know how to focus on sex as an expression of warmth, tenderness, and sensuality; they can enjoy sex as recreation without being concerned about procreation.

Identity/Self-Disclosure

In our society, there have been severe sanctions against gay people. Many homosexuals have been rejected by their families, fired from their jobs, dishonorably discharged from the military, and even physically assaulted when their sexual orientation became known. As a consequence, most gays have been forced to hide behind the mask of heterosexuality in order to survive. Because of this hiding, gay people may be more sophisticated than most non-gays about the various masks people have to wear in our society as well as the relationship between identity and role playing.

Likewise, because "coming out" (openness about being gay) is a process of self-disclosure the person can control, many gays have a more complex understanding of the degrees of self-disclosure than most non-gays and they are often more candid and open. My study showed that the lesbian group had a lower lie score on the Eysenck Personality Inventory than the heterosexual control group, indicating that they were more candid and less defensive. Horstman (1972) matched two groups of 50 homosexual and 50 heterosexual men. The homosexual group had a lower L (lie) score on the Minnesota Multiphasic Personality Inventory, suggesting the same conclusion.

All of these characteristics suggest that, in certain psychological traits, gay people are different from nongays. I believe that we should now go beyond studies of comparative functioning to research of new areas. These probably should include homophobia, the gay experience and sub-culture, and how we can help other gay people to "actualize" themselves.

Homophobia

It is now becoming evident that homosexuality *per se* is no sickness or defect. Rather, *homophobia* — the irrational fear of homosexuals — is a severe disturbance which affects many people in our society. It has done incalculable damage to both heterosexuals and homosexuals: Homophobic feelings have stimulated beatings and killings of "obvious" homosexuals, made gay people feel defective, and made both gays and non-gays uncomfortable with certain feelings and traits in themselves which were not in accord with their designated sex role.

Homophobia has become the subject of research studies only recently. Preliminary findings indicate a positive correlation between homophobia and authoritarian attitudes, especially as they relate to sex role separation. After analyzing a national survey of social attitudes by the National Opinion Research Center of the University of Chicago, Ken Sherrill concluded that people who were uncomfortable with the idea of sexual relations between two adults of the same sex were also conservative on issues of civil dissent, sex role deviation, and the mixing of races socially. A.P. MacDonald found that those people who hold negative attitudes toward gays are more likely to support a double standard between the sexes, more cognitively rigid, more intolerant of ambiguity and more authoritarian than non-homophobic people. Data from this study and others support the notion that homophobic attitudes are mostly determined by the need to preserve masculine and feminine roles rather than by conservative sexual standards. (Few heterosexuals have a sophisticated idea of what gay people do in bed.) In keeping with the sex role explanation, another study had subjects rate heterosexual and homosexual men and women on the concept of "potency." Here is their ranking, from most to least potent: Heterosexual men, lesbians, heterosexual women, gay men.

The research on homophobia has just scratched the surface. More work on this and on improving attitudes towards gay people needs to be done.

The Gay Experience and Sub-culture

Up until recently, heterosexual behavior has been the standard for gay people to live by. In the last few years, a viable gay sub-culture has emerged with its own unique lifestyles and experiences. We need in-depth investigations of the social psychology of the gay world. This might include patterns of socializing among lesbians, the organization of bike clubs, different strategies people use in coming out, and the dynamics of *menage a trois*.

I shall focus on three aspects of the gay scene: the way gay people deal with conflict, with aging, and with sexual fantasies.

Conflict is a basic part of human interaction. In the gay world, there are many instances of conflicts among gay people and between gays and nongays. It would be useful to know more about these conflicts: Who was involved, what was the issue, what psychological needs were most related to the conflict, was there any violation of civil liberties, etc. A group of gay psychologists to which I belong has begun to study these issues. In a pilot study, we asked people we interviewed to tell us about a conflict over issues of homosexuality. Many of the conflicts were with other gay people (especially lovers); however, a significant number involved interactions with nongays (for example, fights with parents). Some of the conflicts were based on mostly psychological needs, while others were more related to civil liberties issues. Here is an example of the latter:

It happened this summer in a hospital emergency room. When I came to work this man was on a stretcher. The guy was facing the door and had a broken ankle. I'm squeamish about those things. At the point I saw him he had refused treatment and they called an ambulance to take him to the hospital and he was refusing that, too. He said, "Call my house-man!" to one of the nurses. It was an hour before anyone did this. In the meantime, the employees were passing around the rumor he was gay. He was a physician. The nurses pointed to "physician" on the admission sheet. Well, finally, they called this guy's houseman and the man who apparently was his lover pulled him up and set him in the car. For two weeks the staff entertained themselves with this story, including the night supervisory. It was disrespectful to him and to the public to have this man in public view with a compound fracture. He should have been put in a private place.

Obviously, the physician's right to equal treatment was abridged because he was gay.

A preliminary analysis of our data indicates that the most salient psychological needs in these conflicts were power and dependency. This reflects the fact that most of the conflicts reported to us were between lovers or friends and that the main civil liberty issue was decision-making. Almost none of the conficts was negotiated or constructively resolved. Previous research on heterosexuals has yielded similar findings: Our society does not teach us positive ways to handle interpersonal conflict. Even though gay people have been viewed as radically different from others, we are still products of the socialization practices of our culture.

Further research on conflict will explore antecedent conditions and consequent behavior. We are particularly interested in what aspects of a conflict situation are most likely to promote negotiation and conflict resolution.

❧

Another fascinating area for psychological study is aging. There are many myths in the gay world surrounding this area. For instance, many young men are terrified of getting old because they equate it with a sad, lonely, sexless existence. Likewise, many young lesbians are terrified of aging because they have never seen a lesbian older than forty — they unconsciously assume that you die before you're fifty if you are homosexual. Of course, gay novels and psychiatric case histories have fed into these fears as has the American cult of youth. There is now some empirical research on aging being conducted in the gay world. Some of the questions it seeks to answer are: "When do people begin to think of themselves as middle-aged or old? What is the relationship between the age at which the person came out in the gay world and his or her present social life? How do education, socio-economic status, and ethnicity relate to perceived happiness in middle and old age? Has the person's self-concept remained stable or has it fluctuated greatly as he or she has gotten older? What is the relationship between sexual activities in the person's youth and in old age?"

These questions should yield valuable insights into this important area and may help to quell fears of growing old.

✿

Gay sexuality is appreciably different from nongay sexuality in many ways. Some were mentioned: Honesty about sexual attraction to a prospective partner and ease of getting into a sexual relationship; flexibility of sexual practices; readiness to engage in group sex; etc. All of these require further research. For example, what is the relationship between taking a variety of roles in bed and stability of a lover relationship? Or in what ways is fist-fucking related to psychological needs like domination, submission, guilt, and humiliation?

One area that has been somewhat researched is gay sexual fantasies. *The Body Politic*, a Canadian gay liberation newspaper, included a questionnaire on sexual fantasies in one issue. Fifty gay men filled out and returned the questionnaire. Their average age was 24 years and they probably were more liberal politically than most gay men in the general population. Here are some of the results: 77 percent of the gay men reported having their first homoerotic fantasy before age thirteen; Only 30 percent of the reported "sexual" fantasies mentioned specific sexual acts (e.g., "Going out with very muscular men, but with a great deal of touching and caressing"); 60 percent of the gay men reported fantasies about a warm, loving relationship; only 6 percent of the fantasies reported by these gay men involved S & M; 80 percent of the fantasies of men over 25 were about younger men, generally 18-25 years old; two-thirds of the fantasies involved people known by the respondent. These data are provocative — they paint a different picture of gay men than the traditional one of the promiscuous, genitally-oriented homosexual. There is much territory still to be explored, including sexual fantasies of lesbians, the relationship between self-concept and idealized sexual partners, how sexual fantasies develop, etc.

Helping Gay People Actualize Themselves

This area illustrates the relationship between gay interests and mental health. There are several good ways of understanding the intentions and effectiveness of mental health activities. One of the best is the public health framework, which describes different types of prevention and treatment. This framework is especially applicable for conceptualizing mental health activities in the gay world.

Public health theory encompasses three levels of prevention: primary, secondary, and tertiary prevention.

Primary prevention involves changing factors in the environment which cause, or lay the foundation for, disease or disturbances. For example, primary prevention of mental retardation in children might include improving medical care and nutrition for pregnant mothers to help avoid birth difficulties which often result in brain damage or retardation in their children.

Secondary prevention is related to catching the disease or disturbance at an early state, before it gets severe. This is most properly regarded as treatment. Medically, this might include cobalt therapy for cancer when it is discovered in the early stages. Child guidance for emotionally disturbed children would be a good example of secondary prevention of psychological disorder.

Tertiary prevention encompasses working with the disease or disturbance after it has developed extensively to keep it from getting worse. This might involve sending a tubercular person to a sanitorium to recover, or briefly institutionalizing a person experiencing a psychotic episode. Tertiary prevention is essentially a form of rehabilitation.

Primary prevention in the gay world revolves around a variety of activities. One of them is eliminating the false image of homosexuality as a sickness or defect, to help people who are 'coming out' feel better about their sexual orientation.

This is implemented through dissemination of better informed literature on homosexuality; public talks, especially to students and to professional groups who are regarded as authorities on sex; gay pride activities, including parades, dances, and social, political, or cultural groups; and consciousness-raising groups to understand social oppression and to get in touch with the advantages of homosexuality.

Also included under this framework would be law reform activities which seek to decriminalize gay sexual behavior and job counseling services which help gay people get good jobs where they can be open about their sexual orientation. This prevents disturbance by eliminating one source of stress (not having an income) and promotes mental health by integrating the person's sexuality into his whole life.

Secondary prevention relates to early treatment. In the gay scene, this might involve crisis intervention — for example, setting up a telephone hotline for emergency calls such as ones for people contemplating suicide. A phone service might also provide information about available legal, medical, and psychological resources which are sympathetic to gay people.

Gay counseling services provide help with a variety of problems including guilt or shame about being gay; creative blocks; irrational fears; and difficulties with close relationships. Some of these problems are unique to the gay scene; others are basic human problems, but the person wants to see a gay counselor rather than a non-gay therapist who believes that homosexuality is a sickness or a defect. Gay counseling services might use one-to-one counseling, encounter groups, or psychotherapy groups to implement their goals.

Another perspective is radical therapy. The watchwords of radical therapy are, "Psychotherapy means change not adjustment." Underlying this is the belief that, more often than not, it is society that needs change, not the client. We are all aware of the distorted social attitude towards sexuality, yet many of us have blamed ourselves for our situation.

Radical gay therapists are now realizing that one cannot work only with the individual's psychological problems, but that social oppression must be confronted as well. One gay therapist I know encourages his clients to help the gay cause in some way as one aspect of their therapy. This might entail giving money to a gay group, helping gay organizations by lending a hand, or even being involved with a gay demonstration or picket line. The offshoots of this are a positive identity as a gay person and enhanced self-esteem, and it helps to produce social change.

Tertiary prevention involves rehabilitation techniques. In the gay scene, intensive counseling for alcoholics or drug abusers is especially needed. Also, help is needed for gay people whom society has written off — or, at least, not made provisions for — like parolees, ex-mental patients, and "delinquent" youths who are gay.

There are a variety of activities in the gay scene which directly or indirectly eliminate distress and mental disturbance or promote good functioning. The public health model provides a useful framework for understanding how our efforts help and whether they are likely to be effective in the long run.

Although rehabilitation is important, our major efforts should go toward prevention and early treatment of disorders. Perhaps in the near future these efforts will produce visible results.

Just as Black psychology and female psychology are now being developed out of the special experience of these groups, a gay psychology is also emerging which will help us better understand ourselves, the gay community, and the greater society. Hopefully, it will help to build a positive gay identity as well.

BIBLIOGRAPHY

Bartell, G.D., *Group Sex*, New York: Peter H. Wyden, 1971

The Body Politic, no. 14, July-August 1974, pp. 22-23

Freedman, Mark, *Homosexuality and Psychological Functioning*, Belmont, CA: Brooks/Cole, 1971

Gigl, J., "The Overt Male Homosexual," unpublished doctoral dissertation, U. of Oregon, 1970

Hooker, E., "The Adjustment of the Male Overt Homosexual," *Journal of Projective Techniques*, 21, 1957, 18-31

Hopkins, J., "The Lesbian Personality," *British Journal of Psychiatry*, 115, 529 (1969), 1433-1436

Horstman, W., "Homosexuality and Psychopathology", unpublished doctoral dissertation, U. of Oregon, 1972

Macdonald, A.P., "The Importance of Sex-Role to Gay Liberation," *Homosexual Counseling Journal*, Vol. 1, No. 4, Oct. 1974

Oberstone, A., "A Comparative Study of Psychological Adjustment and/ Aspects of Life Style in Gay and Non-Gay Women, unpublished doctoral dissertation, California School of Professional Psychology, 1974

Paulson, C., & Paulson, R., "Swinging in Wedlock," *Society*, February, 1972

Siegelman, M., "Adjustment of Male Homosexuals and Heterosexuals," *Archives of Sexual Behavior*, Vol. 2, No. 1, 1972

Weinberg, M., and Williams, C., *Male Homosexuals*, London and New York: Oxford University Press, 1974

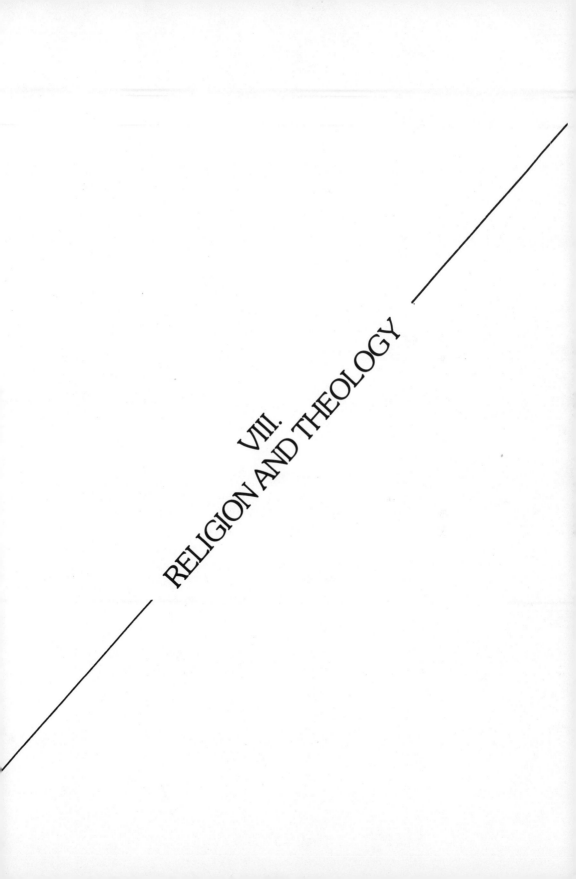

VIII.
RELIGION AND THEOLOGY

Gay People
And Moral Theology

By The Rev. Ellen M. Barrett

Camus said that "the welfare of the people . . . has always been an alibi of tyrants, and it provides the further advantage of giving the servants of tyranny a good conscience." If the welfare of the people is so powerful a pretext (and those who oppose the repeal of the sodomy laws certainly would have it so in the civil context), how much more so is "the will of God" in an ecclesiastical one. Too often both moral theology and ethics have been and are still used to perpetuate expediencies that have little to do with a serious consideration of the relationship of God and humankind, but much to do with a self-interested preservation of nearsighted and arbitrary cultural norms. Morality becomes "a test of our conformity rather than our integrity." There are, of course, a variety of alternatives available from the liberal ethicists and theologians, but too often they are manifestations of impotent good-will and fuzzy thinking. There is a tendency on the part of our friends, both the lukewarm and the ardent, to play fast and loose with the "queen of the sciences." Trying to define real problems out of existence only relegates them to a dangerous sort of logical invisibility from which their sharp corners proceed to bark unwary liberal shins.

What, then, *are* some of the problems? The traditional one is, of course, scripture. In 1955 Canon Bailey slew the dragon of the Sodom and Gomorrah story in Genesis 19 by proving that the verb "to know" was not the one specifically meaning homosexual acts, and was used in sexual contexts less than a dozen times out of over four hundred in the Old Testament, and in all those cases heterosexually. Finally we are reminded that the anti-homosexual exegesis of the story does not appear until later rabbinic times when both the chief Rabbis and Paul needed to reinforce warnings to their flocks to avoid assimilation into the surrounding Hellenistic (and Roman) culture whose easy tolerance of sexual plurality was linked in their minds with idolatry. So much, briefly, for Sodom. The remaining Old Testament passages, especially

Leviticus 18:22 and 20:13, link male homosexuality with the cultic excesses of the Hebrews' idolatrous neighbors, and with the inversion of the proper order of things that a Yahwist would see in polytheism. Paul, both in Romans 1:26-27 and in 1 Corinthians 6: 9-10 follows very much in the tradition of his Jewish forebearers. The anonymous author of 1 Timothy does the same, true to his characteristic tendency to make what is at least lively in Paul a platidinous lump. The idea of a gay identity or lifestyle is nowhere to be found in scripture. Only the heathen Greeks who could not understand the puritanical Hebrew barbarians could have evolved with such a notion. So much for specific references in scripture. Anyone can prooftext — either to support a point or explain it away. My favorite prooftexter is Troy Perry of the MCC, who points out such items as the liability to judgment of a long-haired man wearing wool pants and a cotton shirt and a short-haired woman in a red dress and gold earrings eating shrimp cocktails and rare steak. Which does not remove the problem of biblical literalism. Neither, in fact, does the scholarship of a Bailey or a Treese.

Can *any* approach penetrate such narrow thinking? If not, should we continue our vain attempts at reason or should we simply abandon the field? Certainly simplistic advocacy of gay life that dismisses the real presence of biblical condemnation with no attempt to examine the texts ignores the weight these few verses have lent to homophobic laws and church policies.

Next we come to the theological tradition begun in Paul and epitomized by Thomas Aquinas' pronouncement of homosexual behavior as "the crime against nature." Given his understanding of "nature," culturally conditioned as it was (as ours is) by a strict heterosexual party line inherited from the Old Testament, such a judgment is not surprising. No one much noticed in his day that when Paul speaks of man as the image of God and women being merely created from man, Paul is committing a vast exegetical error. Be that as it may, adherence to the Pauline order of creation does lead one to believe that the God-given norm is heterosexual, male dominant, female submissive. A modern exponent of this kind of polarization by sexes is Karl Barth, for whom the separateness of maleness and femaleness and their union in marriage is an essential part of humankind's fulfillment of its creation in the image of God. Homosexuality is for him idolatry because it puts creature ahead of creator in uniting with one's own image rather than the other half of God's proper order. Grace, for Barth, overcomes this and every other sin, but presumably change to heterosexuality would be one of the fruits by which one could recognize the operation of grace in the homosexual?

But back, for a moment, to "the abominable and detestable crime against nature not to be named among Christians." Is it against nature at all? Scientific research indicates homosexual behavior in every species, from fruit-fly to elephant to human. And some sixty-four percent of the seventy-six societies other than our own on which data is available at the Yale Human Relations Area Files have an acceptable place for homosexuals. Evidence indicates that homosexuality's most damning epithet is incorrect, unless the Bible tells us that isn't the way we were made to be, that that does violate the *imago Dei* in us. Let us look again at Genesis and its two accounts of creation. In Chapter 1, the older of the two, we read "and God created man (generic) in God's own image. Male and female (specific) God created them." Together they were given dominion over all things. In the Adam and Eve story, Eve is made from Adam's rib and when they are banished he is given dominion over her. No mention is made of anyone's being created in the image of God at all. St. Paul has pulled a fast one on us by conflating the two accounts to make it seem that man has in himself the image of God and woman is a mere appendage. He also conveniently forgets that Adam's overlordship over Eve is a result of the Fall, and this a *disorder* of proper creation which should have been remedied by Christ along with all of the rest.

But I digress. My point is this: the image of God in us has nothing to do with what is both technically and literally the accident of sex. The Fall involved the will, not sex which Genesis 1 properly places in a secondary phrase. We are like the divine Logos, Christ, who is the Supreme Image of God because of the Logos within us, that reasoning and willing capacity within us which is born for union with God and separates us from the beasts of the field.

Traditional Catholic theologians like John F. Harvey say our will should be used to train ourselves away from the indulgence of our unnatural desires. Having little sympathy for his idea of naturalness, I have even less for some of his other ideas. He says the guilt many of us have felt about being gay stems directly from its inherent unnaturalness and that society only reenforces this "natural" guilt. If this were so, then homosexuals in societies that approve of their way of life would also be guilt-ridden, and of this I see no evidence. What he counsels for the gay who will not or cannot change is a life of chaste celibacy more ascetic than that of most priests. Surely it is impractical to expect celibacy of most people. The value of celibate life as a freely accepted vocation is cheapened by making it obligatory for a whole class of people. Besides, virtue is only virtue, just as sin is only sin, if one's will consents to it. Being legislated or being forced into being virtuous is a contradiction in theological terms. Surely whether one removes free will by ecclesiastical fear tactics or by psychological conditioning, one is thereby violating the image of God more blasphemously than ever possible simply by loving another human being of the same sex. Then, too, refusing to allow one to act out the sexual dimension of love seems to be a violation of the incarnational tendency of love, the prime example of which is, of course, Jesus himself. We human beings are not just souls; we are bodies as well, and God himself participated in our bodily life, dignifying and sanctifying it forever as an instrument of love.

There are many liberal opinions, of course, that would oppose Harvey's party line. One of the strangest is put forth by the same Canon Bailey who saved us from Sodom. For him we are technically guilty of sin, but not in fact liable because of a species of invincible ignorance. For others we are sinners like everyone else, but . . . it is the one *but* I cannot buy. My sexuality is not the issue. How I use it, as how I use any of God's gifts, *is* the issue. But more on that in a moment. The most prevalent moral stand current in liberal Protestantism is rather that of our Episcopal Church — support the abolition of civil discrimination against gay people and continue to practice a quiet and unobtrusive version inside the Church.

This simply will not do. Scholarship and creative theologizing must be joined to action to change the de facto disabilities gay people suffer in the Church, particularly by addressing seriously a variety of hitherto ill-explored questions. Does the duration of a relationship necessarily have any bearing on its moral legitimacy? Can there be a morally acceptable one-night stand? Is monogamy the only acceptable pattern for gays as well as heterosexuals, and if so, how much other traditional baggage must we carry? Is there anything in our lifestyles (and they are varied) that might make life more human for heterosexuals? I am sure we all can think of questions that need to be addressed.

Most of this interrogatory effort will fall on the shoulders of gay men, and rightly so. The Church follows its Hebraic predecessors as a male hierarchy. Though our redemption in Christ should have overturned all the effects of the Fall, the subservience of women included, the Church still clings to an outmoded way of doing things based on the life of a small band of nomads for whom survival meant treating women like breeding stock. Now that the Messiah has come, there can be no excuse for saying that women's part of the priesthood of all believers is to be carried out only in motherhood.

But the Church does not listen to women yet; so it is my gay brothers who must speak loudest for our acceptance as gays. I have one fear, though, and that is when gay men are accepted (because though they are homosexual their sexuality affirms the virtues of maleness) and when heterosexual women are accepted (after all, they do relate to men closely), lesbians will still be out in the cold because our sexuality is a total and radical affirmation of woman-nature, which the Church has never allowed. Rather we have been told that we are "the gateway of the devil and because of us even the Son of

God had to die." The fate of the world's first "woman-identified-woman" warns me. Lilith, Adam's first wife in Jewish legend, left the Garden after saying "I too was made by God from the dust of the earth, and therefore we are equal. Why should I lie beneath you?" Last seen heading for Egypt, Lilith has been made into the mythical prototype of all witches and uppity women generally. I often think that she, more than Eve, is the mother and role model of lesbians. Be that as it may, her story is a good indication of what happens to self-affirming women in the institutional Church.

In the Body of Christ this is not so. Even Jesus the man, bound voluntarily as he was by his first-century Jewish context, was remarkably open and supportive of women. But there is still doubt in my mind as to whether some of us who are members of the Body of Christ can remain much longer as members of the institutional Church. I mean to stay as long as I can, but unless my gay brothers are an actively helpful leaven in the ecclesiastical lump, women, to survive as Christians at all, will have to find a less claustrophobic environment.

One of my hopes for the gay movement in the Church is that it will remove Paul's words to the Galatians from the realm of ideal and theory into practical and living theology: for as many of you have been baptized into Christ, have put on Christ. There is neither Jew nor Greek, there is neither bond nor free, there is neither male nor female: for you are all one in Christ Jesus. (Galatians 3:27-28). Nothing about heterosexual, white, or male — simply one in Christ . . . *all* of us.

BIBLIOGRAPHY

Bailey, Derrick Sherwin. *Homosexuality and the Western Christian Tradition.* London: Longmans, Green & Co., 1955. Reissued in 1975 in U.S.A. by Shoestring Press.

Gearhart, Sally Miller and William Reagan Johnson, Editors. *Loving Women/ Loving Men.* San Francisco: Glide, 1974.

Harvey, John F. "Pastoral Responses to Gay World Questions." *Is Gay Good?* Ed. W. Dwight Oberholtzer. Philadelphia: Westminster, 1971.

Nouwen, Henry J.M. "The Self-availability of the Homosexual." *Is Gay Good?* Ed. W. Dwight Oberholtzer. Philadelphia: Westminster, 1971.

Oberholtzer, W. Dwight., Editor. *Is Gay Good?* Philadelphia: Westminster, 1971.

Perry, Troy. "God Loves Me Too." *Is Gay Good?* Ed. W. Dwight Oberholtzer. Philadelphia, Westminster, 1971.

Pittenger, Norman. "The Homosexual Expression of Love." *Is Gay Good?*, q. v.

von Rorh, John. "Toward a Theology of Homosexuality." *Is Gay Good?* q. v.

Rule, Jane. *Lesbian Images*. Garden City, NY: Doubleday, 1975.

Secor, Neale A. "A Brief for a New Homosexual Ethic." *The Same Sex*. Ed. Ralph W. Weltge. Philadelphia: Pilgrim Press, 1969.

Shinn, Roger L. "Homosexuality: Christian Conviction and Inquiry." *The Same Sex*. Ed. Ralph W. Weltge, q.v.

Treese, Robert L. "Homosexuality: A Contemporary View of the Biblical Perspective." *Loving Women/Loving Men*. Eds. Sally Miller Gearhart and William Reagan Johnson, q.v.

Weltge, Ralph W., Editor. *The Same Sex*. Philadelphia: Pilgrim Press, 1969.

This paper was first delivered at a panel on "Modern Moral Theology" at the first national meeting in Chicago of INTEGRITY, an organization of Gay Episcopalians, in August 1975.

Gayness: A Radical Christian Approach

By Ara Dostourian

HUMAN SEXUALITY: THE PROBLEM POSED

We live in a sexually repressive society. We are taught that our sexuality must be kept under strict control, based on the assumption that it is part of our "animal" heritage and as such, can debase or destroy us if allowed unbridled sway over our lives. Such an assumption presupposes a dichotomy between sex and love, between the individual as an animal and the individual as a rational, loving human being. Our capacity to love some individuals is often counterposed to our sexual attraction to others. We are taught to feel complete and human when we love, but unwholesome and degenerate when we have sexual feelings, except under very special circumstances, such as marriage.

Our society has not cultivated in us the capacity to link sexuality and love, to relate caring for another to physical attraction for that person. It is indeed unfortunate that the Christian tradition has, in general, accepted this dichotomy and even imbued it with a divinely ordained aura. It is to the credit of Judaism that it has not gone to the extremes that Christianity has in dichotomizing sex and love (witness the references to sexuality throughout the Old Testament, e.g., The Song of Solomon). Nevertheless, the Hebraic Tradition cannot be considered a model for human behavior today, since its relative openness to sexuality had its limits, albeit less so than Christianity. The Christian church, because of its twisted attitude towards human sexuality, has done much harm to its members. Perhaps this attitude is understandable and forgivable within the context of pre-modern times since Christianity naturally adapted to, or more correctly, reacted against, the sexual mores of the time. However, it is very difficult to exonerate the Church for its stance on human sexuality today, since attempts are being made in contemporary life to link sex and love. It is symptomatic of Christianity's moral bankruptcy that it has either been incapable of coping or has refused to cope with the problem. This bankruptcy is especially glaring in light of the fact that a number of non-Christian groups have been in the forefront of attempting to relate sexuality to love.

The Church's refusal to deal with the problem of human sexuality has caused much anguish to many of its members, causing them to look elsewhere for direction and guidance. Most people are very conscious of their sexual feelings. Christians are no exception. Is the Church willing and prepared to meet their needs within the sexual realm? I think not! Can its ministers and priests deal with the sexual problems of their parishioners and members, such as masturbation, pre-marital sex, extra-marital sex, group sex, attraction to individuals of the same sex, etc., without outright condemnation at worst or moralistic platitudes at best? I think not! Appeals to biblical tradition or to canon law are no longer meaningful for many Christians. Quoting scripture or canonical texts is no substitute for thoroughgoing and in-depth struggling with the Christian tradition to see what it has to say about the sexual problems confronting people today. My purpose is to begin the process.

I will first delineate the historical process by which human sexuality has come to be more and more identified with love and relationships. Then I will attempt to deal with this new phenomenon from a Christian point of view. Finally, I will propose some general suggestions as to what I think the Church, together with its ministers and priests, can and should do in ministering to its members' sexual needs and problems. Since my main thrust is on gayness from a Christian point of view, I will be dealing with and emphasizing the gay aspect of human sexuality more heavily. However, it must not be forgotten that all sexuality is interrelated and that the basic sexual problem confronting our society as well as the Church is not a matter of sexual preference or sexual activities, but is the artificial dichotomy between sex and love, a dichotomy which is only now beginning to mend.

THE HISTORICAL CONTEXT OF SEXUALITY

Sexual urges have been part of human existence going back to the animal origins. However, what has set persons apart from other species is our capability to interact with our environment and change it for our own benefit. Indeed, persons are animals, but more. Persons can think, feel, love, reflect on their surroundings, make choices, etc. It is this aspect of persons which is brought out in the Adam and Eve story of the Judeo-Christian tradition. Hence, to refer to sexual urges as merely animalistic does a great disservice, for those urges must be seen within the context of human environment and human relations with others. This is the key to human sexuality. Human sexuality is quite different from animal sexuality, for it has the potential of going beyond the bounds of simple urges and needs. It has the potential for linking with human love and caring. Animals are incapable of doing this, for they cannot interact with their environment in such a way as to change it for their benefit, except perhaps in a very limited way. Animals can only survive and reproduce their kind. Persons can go further and build up a civilization with various institutions, thought patterns, values, etc. Therefore, unlike animals, persons are not limited by animal origins. They can go beyond them; how far depends upon the nature of one's environment and how he/she interacts with it. A person's attitude towards sexuality, like any other attitude or value he/she holds, depends on the nature of the environment and the way in which one relates to that environment.

From an historical point of view, it is interesting to see how attitudes towards sexuality, in the context of the environment, developed among the early Hebrews. The Hebrews were a nomadic people and as such were not numerous, at least as compared with the surrounding settled peoples against whom they had continuously to struggle in order to survive, as well as to preserve their religious and cultural heritage. Under these circumstances of a minority people with a rather heterodox view of the world (at least for that time) and surrounded by numerous hostile peoples, reproduction became very important for survival. Hence, the Hebrews developed rather open attitudes towards sexuality as long as it was confined to heterosexuality. In fact, sexual relations outside of marriage were permissible, since reproduction was essential for their survival. Witness the various passages in the Old Testament which permit and encourage sexual contact, even outside the marriage bond (Genesis 16:1-6, 19:30-38, 2 Samuel 11:2-5), and sometimes even go so far as to extol and eulogize the joys and pleasures of sexuality (Song of Solomon 7). However, none of their relative openness to sexuality should cloud the very strong injunctions against homosexuality which the Hebrews maintained. After all, if their survival as a people was threatened, any type of sexuality which worked against such a survival had to be unequivocally condemned (Genesis 19:1-11). Moreover, the "spilling of one's seed on the ground" (masturbation) was likewise condemned on the same grounds, as militating against the survival of their people. Thus, the attitude of the Hebrews towards sexuality was deeply colored by the environment and setting in which they lived and with which they interacted. Sexuality was good as long as it contributed to the survival of their people. Very little thought was given to linking sexuality with human relationships.

Turning to the attitudes of the early Christians towards sexuality, in some ways a more backward view existed compared with that of the Hebrews, one with a very strong anti-sexual bias. One has only to listen to St. Paul's dictum: "For it is better to marry than to be aflame with passion" (I Corinthians 7:9), as well as his unyielding stand on "unnatural relations" (Romans I:26-27), in order to understand the early Christian position on sexuality. Many Christians are quite disturbed by Paul's pronouncements concerning sexuality and women. How could a divinely-inspired man say such things? Does this invalidate Paul's other words which indeed witness to the working of the Holy Spirit in him? In dealing with Paul's view on sex and women, one must try to understand the environment with which he and other Christians had to cope. The Greco-Roman world in which early Christianity rose and developed was imbued with a very distorted and anti-human view of sexuality generally and of women in particular (at least from the modern point of view). In the first place, sexual contact was looked upon as having nothing to do with human relationships and love. The highest love one could have was a spiritual one between two men (love for a woman was looked down on as they were only considered a means of reproducing the species — "baby-making machines"). It is true that this love (Platonic love) could lead to a physical relationship, but that act usually placed the relationship on a lower level. When male poets, writers, and others talked of their amorous affairs with young boys, etc., such affairs were based more on infatuation and sexual hedonism than on solid person-to-person relationships. Under these circumstances, it is no wonder that St. Paul and the early Christians were disgusted with the sexual mores of the time. All they could see around them was a sexuality related to nothing except manipulation and hedonism, and since they had no other reference point for sexuality (which we do today in attempting to link sex and love), they unequivocally condemned it. The extent of their condemnation was such that St. Paul even opted for celibacy as the ideal state for the Christian.

As already stated, sexual attitudes, like all human attitudes, develop out of the environment in which people find themselves and with which they interact. This was true of the sexual attitudes of the Hebrews and early Christians. It is only in the modern period (since 1500) that the link between sex and love began to be forged, often very tenuously. Of course, the courtly love of the Middle Ages was in part a protest against husbands' property rights in wives and was a response to the need of persons to relate feelingfully (not just breedingly) towards their sexual partners. As all readers of Chaucer and the other medievalists know, the chivalric code in fact was not the careful expression of nonsexual matters and respect towards a beloved whom one intended to marry (as Sir Walter Scott and modern romancers would have children believe) but was rather an elaborately stylized ritual of adultery, always between a young unmarried knight and an older married woman, who became the knight's sensual mentor. The "honor" was in not telling rather than in abstinence, and each partner was expected to live a happier marriage with someone else for having had this spirited encounter by linking sexuality and feeling, as opposed to linking sexuality with property in the conventional marriage.

In a slightly less prestigious form, modern society has preserved the institution of the "mistress," by which married men are freed from the wives, whom they have devalued as housekeepers and child-bearers. The mistress becomes a more desirable person on whom to shower affections linked with feelings, especially as both share a fairly equal bit of independence so often missing from the role of wife in our culture.

With the advent of feminism and women's liberation has come a demand that marriage itself encourage the linking of sex with love, in a context of mutual respect for the full and equal personhood of both partners.

THE CONTRIBUTION OF THE WOMEN'S AND GAY MOVEMENTS

In the nineteenth century, with the accelerated industrialization of the European countries, the role of women began to change radically, albeit gradually. Women were needed as wage earners in the factories, and hence were wrenched out of their secluded and subordinate positions in the home. This development continued in the twentieth century and further accelerated. Women learned to be more and more independent of men. This process was aided by the creation of labor saving appliances for the home, as well as the development of birth control devices. The Women's Suffrage Movement of the nineteenth and early twentieth centuries and the present day Women's Liberation Movement can be understood only on the basis of the industrialization of Modern Europe. Freed from the limiting and stultifying environment of the home, women have been encouraged to be creative in ways other than child rearing and household management.

Now, what has all this to do with the link between sex and love? Before industrialization women were tied to the home and their husbands. Even if the husband maintained a love-sex relationship with his wife, she had to subordinate her feelings to his. Only her husband was to enjoy sex, she was not; she was merely to serve him in bed, as she did in the household, and as she did in bearing him children. Now freed from the constraints of the home and child rearing (to a certain extent), women have begun to define their lives from their own perspective as women, rather than from that of their husbands or other men. Thus, Women's Liberation is with us. The Women's Movement is not based on man-hating and the destruction of femininity; it is based on women defining their own roles independently of men. Through the movement, women have learned that the male and female roles imposed upon people by society are false, that they are destructive to human relations and development. A woman is still a woman if she plays baseball, wears pants, is strong, etc. A woman (or for that matter a man also) can perform all these acts and still rear children, take care of the house, be soft and gentle, etc. In effect, why divide up roles into masculine and feminine? Why not allow individuals to live as they please as long as they act humanly with one another? These attitudes are being fostered by the Women's Liberation movement.

The Gay Liberation and Women's Movements are obviously very closely linked. Both are in conflict with the dominant mores, by which a woman is to be subordinate to "her man." Society teaches that she is supposed to play a feminine role in every respect. She must learn to depend on "her man" for sexual satisfaction, protection, security, etc. Similarly, the gay individual, whether male or female, has been taught not to transgress the sanctity of his or her sexual role. If a man loves another man he is considered a pervert, since he is violating a taboo by rejecting the male role society has assigned to him. If a woman loves another woman, she also is condemned supposedly for undermining her role as a female. Many gays do not recognize this separation of male and female roles, considering the separation false and destructive. Some gay men show their contempt for the conventional separation of masculine and feminine roles by transvestism. Contrary to popular belief, in many cases these gay men do not want to be women: it's usually obvious that they are not); what they do want to show is that putting on a dress doesn't make one a woman, just as baking a cake or performing some other household task doesn't make a man a woman.

How has this rejection of the separation of male and female roles helped forge a closer link between sex and love? Let us take the Women's Movement first. Many women, reacting against the demeaning experiences they have had with men through sexual and social subordination, have banded together to struggle against what they have termed "male chauvinism" (the ideology that males, being the more rational and stronger of the sexes, should be the ones to dominate and direct society) and "sexism" (the ideology which discriminates against individuals on the basis of their sex or sexual preferences). As these women have united and struggled together, they have begun to develop strong ties with one another, both political and emotional. They have begun to realize that it is not essential to have men in their lives or to depend on males in order to feel that they are complete women. They have begun to feel that as women they are strong and able to lead fulfilling lives in whatever career they choose, irrespective of what society tells them is the "ideal" for their sex. It is within this context that the Women's Liberation slogan "sisterhood is powerful" is used. Now, traditionally speaking, one of the factors which has been the prime cause for the difficulty in linking sex and love has been the domination of male over female. If there is domination and subordination between two individuals, genuine love cannot flow between them, for love cannot be coerced or forced. Once the traditional roles of dominating male and submissive female have been destroyed, then the two persons have a much better chance of relating on a more equal, and hence more human, level. Herein lies the basis for forging a link between sex and love.

Turning to the Gay Liberation Movement, we can see similar developments, though perhaps from a different perspective. Gays in the movement have rejected the roles assigned to them by straight society and have affirmed their humanity irrespective of their sexual preferences: "loving men doesn't make me less of a man," "loving women doesn't make me less of a woman." In rejecting male and female roles, gays, like women, have also repudiated the domination-subordination syndrome which a male chauvinist and sexist society has imposed on all. In doing so, they have maintained that one's sexual preferences are incidental to one's being a human and a person. What is important is that individuals relate, since the male and female roles imposed by society have been destroyed. There is an interesting point relative to both the Women's and Gay Movements. Some women in the former, in the process of struggling together with their sisters, have developed very strong emotional ties with some, such that they have been able to relate to them sexually. Since most of these women have come out of basically heterosexual backgrounds, it is quite revealing to see what close bonds between individuals, coupled with the destruction of male and female roles, can effect. Kate Millet, one of the more respected leaders of the Women's Movement, has herself declared that she is capable of relating to women sexually as well as to men. This assertion was prompted by some anti-gay sentiment in the movement's early years, as a number of women were affirming their lesbianism.

Through the activities of the Women's and Gay Movements many people have learned to see sexuality within the context of loving and of affirming human relationships, rather than within the context of the male-female, dominant-submissive, reproductive, marriage syndrome imposed by traditional society. One important aspect of this change has been the realization that the traditional view encouraged possessiveness and jealousy on the part of individuals closely involved with one another, whether as friends or as lovers. Society has taught us to take one mate to whom we are to give our ultimate loyalty. We are to remain "faithful" to that person, both emotionally and sexually. As close as we get to others (and admittedly a certain degree of intimacy is allowed with them by traditional society), we must still reserve that "special" love for our mate. What this has resulted in (and naturally so, given the demands of society) is, in many cases, distorted relationships between individuals: "you are spending too much time with that other person," "if you love someone else, there won't be enough love for me," "since you are close to other friends, it is obvious that I am not taking care of all your needs — there must be some inadequacy in me," etc. These feelings of jealousy and inadequacy certainly do not help people's relationships with one another. There is no natural or binding law which says that persons must relate to one mate or lover in this limiting and exclusive way. One of the realities of life many people today are recognizing is the possibility of developing a number of intimate relationships, some of which can involve sexual contact. People are discovering that these intimate relationships in no way limit their capacity to give genuine love; in fact that capacity is enhanced rather than destroyed.

Sexuality now is seen less and less in the context of procreation, male-female roles, domination-subordination, possessiveness, the one ultimate mate or lover, and more and more in the context of intimate friendship, care and concern for others, non-demanding and free-flowing relationships, etc. In this matter, sexuality, has become more integrated into the lives of people. There are more and more individuals today who are developing a number of close and intimate relations, some of which are being expressed sexually, in some cases involving the same sex. These relationships are no less responsible than the traditional marriages. After all, why can't persons develop a number of close relations and maintain these in a very responsible way? Traditional society accepts responsible frienships; why not friends for whom one shows love and caring through sexuality? Thus, in this new approach to sexuality and human relationships (which some refer to as the Sexual Revolution, since our concepts of sex have been drastically changed and modified), sex no longer is a fetish (something unique and special, reserved only for one individual in one exclusive relationship and not to be given to anyone else), but becomes one of the many means open to express friendship, love, concern, care, etc. for others (other ways being giving of presents, inviting people to dinner, having intimate discussions, spending time in activities of common interest, etc.). Now, how do all these changes in people's attitudes towards human sexuality relate to Christianity and the Church? As mentioned earlier, the Christian tradition has never adequately dealt with the problem of sexuality. While this failure was due to the sexual climate in which Christianity arose and developed, this climate has now changed. Under these new circumstances it would be both rational and human for the Church to deal with the issue of sex anew, especially since it has a better chance of solving the problem now than in its early history (the Greco-Roman and Medieval periods), when sexuality was not in the least linked to love and human relationships.

MODERN CHRISTIANITY'S ATTITUDE TOWARDS SEXUALITY

Modern Christianity has made some efforts to deal with the problem of linking sexuality and love. The very fact that the Church, at least some of its branches, has, through ministers and priests, provided some counseling for its members on sexual matters shows a certain amount of progress. However, much of this counseling has been oriented towards marriage, while there has been rather strong disapproval, tacit or otherwise, of any sexuality outside the state of heterosexual matrimony. This stance shows that the Church is still very strongly committed to sex only within the context of procreation, male and female roles, and the one and only exclusive relationship. Anyone seeking counseling on sexual matters whose behavior does not conform with the official position (marriage as the ultimate and only means of expressing sexuality), is either unequivocally condemned for his/her feelings or at best discouraged from acting on them, while being encouraged to adopt the dominant heterosexual-marriage ideology. Even in rather open and free counseling situations individuals who have sexual experiences with a number of persons of the opposite sex, as well as those who have erotic feelings for persons of the same sex, are told that though these relationships are not "dirty" and "perverted," they nevertheless are not as wholesome as those within a marriage. Little thought on the part of these counseling ministers and priests is given even to the possibility that a sexual relation within a marriage might not necessarily be a loving and responsible one, much less to the possibility that such a relationship outside of marriage or with a person of the same sex might very well be based on love, care, and accountability.

It seems that the Church either is unable or refuses to see human beings as complex individuals, who have fundamental needs and emotions. It is in the very depths of our nature to desire relationships with others on various levels: we seek out one another, we enjoy each other's company, we spend time together, we participate in many activities together, etc. In the process of relating to others, we express our feelings and emotions for them in different ways: we try to be sensitive to their needs and wishes, we help them to the best of our ability, we express concern for their well-being, we are happy with them and sad with them, etc. The bonds between us and others become stronger and closer, and develop to an even greater extent when our love and concern are reciprocated. In some cases where there is a strong bond between friends, irrespective of their sex or society's impositions, it is both natural and human for them to relate sexually. We hold and hug one another to show our mutual intimacy. Why not in some cases express that intimacy sexually? The point is not that we should necessarily relate sexually with every intimate friend we have, but that with some friends it is very natural to do so. I have had a few close friends (some married and of the same sex) tell me that they would like to show their love for me sexually, but that they could not get themselves to do so because of their commitments in marriage (their mate would disapprove) or because society has taught them to relate sexually only with the opposite sex. I certainly understand their position and respect them for it. However, such an attitude shows the tremendous impact traditional society has had on our lives and on our relationships with one another. These friends have, in effect, admitted that they do consider it natural to relate sexually with me, but to have been unable to bring themselves to do so because of society's restrictions.

The Christian tradition, as I have already mentioned, has taken a very rigid attitude concerning human sexuality. Much of this, I believe, has been due to the inability of traditional society to integrate sex and love. In defending its position, the Church has frequently appealed to scripture and the tradition (canon law, theological works, pronouncements, etc.). In addressing myself to this issue, I will not try to criticize that position on the basis of scripture and tradition (as some apologists for open sexuality in the Church have done), for as I have already stated, the early Christians, having no reference point for a solid view of human sexuality (the Greco-Roman view debased and distorted sex), condemned it outright. Christians must refrain from wrenching quotes from scripture out of context to defend or criticize this or that position. One can use scripture equally to condemn sexual expression towards the same sex (Romans 1:27) or to uphold the opposite (I Samuel 20). When Christians struggle with a human problem, rather than looking at it from this or that written word in scripture or the tradition, we should try to view it within the context of the whole Faith. This I will try to do.

It seems to me that the basis of the Christian faith is love (" . . . You shall love your neighbor as yourself" — Matthew 22:39), not an abstract love, but a very specific and personal love. This love has many aspects and expressions: caring, concern, affirmation, non-abuse, affection, responsibility, acceptance, support, freedom, non-coerciveness, dignity, understanding, sympathy, giving, sensitivity, sharing, etc. This love also knows no bounds (Ephesians 3:19). It cannot be limited or circumscribed. It cannot be pigeonholed into one category or another. It can never be coerced or forced, but only freely given. Possessiveness and jealousy are not a part of it. It cannot be restricted by societal structures and mores. If according to the Christian tradition love has no bounds or limits, then, it can be given and received on various levels, even on the sexual. If I as a Christian develop an intimate, loving relationship with another person or a few other persons, what unChristian act would I be committing if I expressed that love sexually? Would it be correct to call that sexuality sinful since it is done outside marriage? If it is sinful, then the whole relationship should be called into question. But, if I am relating to an individual in a loving and responsible way, how then can my sexual expression of that love be condemned?

This is the crux of the issue facing many Christians today. Some in the Church will argue that marriage has been ordained by God as the only permissible channel through which sexual love can be expressed, adding that even society has conformed to this "divine will." This argument cannot hold up to historical analysis, for it was pagan, pre-Christian society which established the norms and mores for sexual relations between individuals and *not vice versa*. What the Church has done is to adopt these norms and then invest them with a divine aura, as if God Himself had ordained what society had established.

Arguments defending heterosexual marriage as the only Christian option are unimpressive. They raise more questions than they solve. Similar to this are the arguments ostensibly from biology and nature; individuals were meant to give themselves to only one person; it is natural for a man and a woman to be one and to be possessive and jealous of one another; men and women are not biologically equipped to relate physically with the same sex, etc. Once again, these arguments are questionable, because they reflect more of society's attitudes on human relationships, rather than either biological or natural necessity. A person may feel the need to have a number of intimate relationships, some of which are expressed sexually. This freer attitude can help overcome or counter feelings of possessiveness and jealousy, making a relationship more wholesome and loving. In fact, it is possessiveness and jealousy which are "unnatural," in that they destroy human relationships rather than develop or maintain them. Moreover, a close relationship in a traditional marriage limits anyone's capability of intimacy. Similarly, a person may meaningfully relate physically with a member of the same sex. Such action has been going on since time immemorial as a function in nature (hence "natural"), and there are many ways of relating sexually to persons other than the traditional "missionary position" (the male on top and the female on the bottom with the penis inserted into the vagina).

A RADICAL PROPOSAL
TO CHANGE THE CHURCH'S ATTITUDE TOWARDS SEXUALITY

If, on the basis of Christian love and responsibility, one can maintain, as I have, that for the individual a number of intimate relationships are possible, some of these being expressed sexually, then it is the responsibility of the Church, its members and leaders, to revise the traditional attitudes on sexuality and human relationships.

In the first place, the Church cannot continue to maintain the sacrosanct character of marriage as the sole channel for sexual expression open to the faithful. Let me not be misunderstood. I am not advocating that the sanctity of marriage should be done away with. What I am saying is that a number of other alternatives should be upheld as equally valid and sacred: marriage between individuals of the same sex, group marriage (communal living), or any other type of relationship or relationships based on love, intimacy, and responsibility. I well realize that this change of attitude will be a very difficult one for many Christians, not only because of the strong impact of socialization, but also because a good part of the faithful have been taught to link their particular sexual mores and attitudes with Christianity and the Gospel. Just as many contemporary Christians are beginning to revise their views concerning the secular state ("God and Country" are no longer being linked together in the traditional manner, but rather it seems that many Christians are now going back to the New Testament dictum: "Be not conformed to this world . . ." Romans 12:2), so also they need, I believe, to change and reformulate their attitudes on human sexuality.

One thing sorely lacking in the Church is adequate counseling on sexual matters. In many cases this is not due so much to the unwillingness of ministers and priests to deal with sexuality as to their lack of knowledge and understanding about the subject. They are especially ignorant about gayness and hold a number of misconceptions about gay people. There can be no adequate counseling of gays as long as ministers and priests persist in maintaining the various gay stereotypes. One stereotype is that a gay person is exclusively homosexual. Now, there are gays who are, but also there are many that might be considered bi-sexual, that is, attracted to both the same and the opposite sex in varying degrees. Modern psychology shows that most of us are basically bi-sexual, but that due to our socialization we tend to be attracted to one pole or the other. Related to the stereotype of the exclusive homosexual is the misconception that all gay males are effeminate, while gay females are masculine and tough. The truth is that most gay people cannot be distinguished from the rest of the population. There are many heterosexual men that are effeminate. The majority of transvestites are not homosexual but heterosexual. The truth might surprise a lot of people; if that is the case, then the impact of society's categorizing gay people into neat compartments has been quite strong on the thinking of the majority of the population.

Another very common misconception is that gays are promiscuous and unable to develop and maintain both strong and long-term relationships. This assertion is indeed surprising in a society where divorce among straights is well over twenty-five percent. Those supporting this view should perhaps spend more time looking honestly at our present society, rather than concentrating solely on the sexual preferences of a minority group. Perhaps in a highly individualized and mobile society like ours, it is very difficult for persons, gay or otherwise, to maintain exclusive and long term relationships, for the societal pressures of the past are no longer present. If the established family ties and institutionalized supports of the straight marriage cannot keep people together, what can we expect of disenfranchised gay marriages? Marriage is very complex. Individuals in our society who are able to make a long-term and exclusive marriage work are rare. One should not conclude that marriage is the only ideal because it is the most permanent and hence the most responsible relationship. Responsibility has many different levels. One does not have to live with another the rest of his or her life to act responsibly and lovingly. In fact, there are many cases of marriage where the partners have acted in the most unloving and irresponsive ways. The important factor is not the type of relationship but the spirit in which it is lived.

Perhaps one of the worst misconceptions about gay people, and one abetted by the psychiatric establishment, is that they are sick and unable to develop loving, lasting relationships because of a malfunction of their psyche. Actually, this misconception is grounded more in the male-female dichotomy we are all socialized into than in any psychological reality. Unfortunately, psychologists from Freud on have accepted this masculine-feminine separation. On this basis, psychology has maintained that the boy needs a man (his father) to identify with, while a girl needs a woman (her mother). If the proper identification does not take place, there develops a malfunction in the psyche which might lead one to be attracted to the same sex. This nonsense is based on the untested assumption that the male role and the female role as defined by our society are not only good but also necessary. If the roles themselves are imposed from without by society and if indeed they hinder the full development of the human being, then how valid are the psychological theories dealing with the cause of homosexuality? Moreover, it is now being shown that role identification does not necessarily establish one's sexual orientation. For example, there have been cases where boys have identified with their mothers and yet have developed a heterosexual orientation.

After all has been said and done about whether or not gays are more sick than straights, the overriding fact is that all people in our society have deep problems in relating to one another. Our society does not provide a healthy environment for individuals to relate to one another in a loving, intimate, and responsible way.

What can the Christian church, through its ministers and priests, do about all this? What can Christianity say to people who are finding it more and more difficult to relate to each other in a loving and caring way? This seems to me to be the problem, rather than sexual preference or style of life. The answer is for the Church to uphold a concept of human sexuality based on love and responsibility, irrespective of sexual orientation or way of life. To accomplish this, the Church must take a very open attitude to various sexual orientations and various forms of human relationships (marriage — gay and straight, communal living, single living, short term living, etc.), as long as these are conducted in a responsible and loving way. The Church cannot look upon one or another of these relationships as superior to the rest (as it has done traditionally and still does) for doing so perpetuates an injustice on those Christians who have developed alternatives to traditional marriage. Should Christians be relegated to second-class status as members of the Body of Christ? To do so, is to be both cruel and anti-Christian. God has created a multivaried world, made of individuals with different approaches to life. If one's life is lived in a Christian manner, that is, in a loving and human way, then God's purpose is being carried out, his creation is being affirmed.

Modern Christianity must break out of its heavily socialized past; it must develop the acumen to differentiate between what is of society and what is of the Gospel. Consider the current conflict in the Episcopal church concerning the acceptance of women into the priesthood, a problem raising a veritable storm in that Church. Those opposed to the ordination of women have tried to show that it is against scripture and tradition. But how much of the subordination of women is due to Christianity and how much to the socialization of the early Christians (the same, as pointed out above, can be said for the Church's attitude towards sexuality)? There can be no compromise on this issue: the Lord created men and women equal. To bar women from the priesthood, in effect makes them second-class members of the Body of Christ.

What I have proposed is revolutionary. I have no illusions about its being accepted and implemented in the near future. Nevertheless, I believe that it is in keeping with the revolutionary nature of Christianity and the Gospel, which seeks radically to transform the world and human relationships on the basis of love. The Church, in order to fulfill its function and sustain itself, has had continually to reinterpret the Faith to each generation. Whenever and wherever it has failed to do this, it has opened itself to irrelevance and self-destruction. Perhaps modern-day Christians may not choose to deal with the problem of human sexuality in the same manner as I have, but deal they must if the Gospel is going to have significance for contemporary people. For the Church to choose to ignore the issue and thus maintain its anachronistic approach means that the secular elements of society will monopolize the arena and impose their own solution, a solution which obviously will not be informed by the Christian faith. With such an abdication of responsibility by the Church, its position in society and the world will be further eroded, and perhaps then the passage will ring true:

> *"Even now the axe is laid to the root of the trees;*
> *every tree therefore that does not bear good fruit*
> *is cut down and thrown into the fire"*
> (Matthew 3:10).

Christopher Isherwood
And The
Religious Quest

By The Rev. Canon Clinton R. Jones

"Come to the Cabaret!" is a phrase from a popular tune being spun by many disk jockeys wherever Broadway show scores reach an appreciative audience. *"Cabaret"* both as play and movie stands out as one of the biggest hits of the past decade. It is the poignant story of pre-war Berlin in the early 1930's. Author Christopher Isherwood — novelist, essayist, playwright, biographer, translator, travel raconteur, and script writer — is a prolific, yet careful, contemporary man of letters who continues to win the respect of artists as well as the growing esteem of an ever-widening public.

But why choose for a theological discussion this author of *Goodbye to Berlin* from which the popular play *I am a Camera* evolved and from this the musical *Cabaret?* How could such a writer fit within the confines of "a religious quest"? An answer rests in the person of Isherwood himself. As Isherwood makes real the characters he draws, he not only draws deeply into the human heart, but also reflects with insight upon the social forces which mold those who play the roles he has set for them. Isherwood's own interest in theology and religion has long been explicit, as in his important study of his guru *Ramakrishna and His Disciples* (1959). Prof. Terence Dewsnap has already set a precedent for looking at the religious dimensions of Isherwood's fiction, as in "Isherwood Couchant," (*Critique*, 1971), 31-47. There may well be many reasons for Isherwood's spiritual insights, but the one I choose to emphasize is the fact that Isherwood is a homosexual. Isherwood openly acknowledges his homosexuality, as when he spoke explicitly as a homosexual writer at the 1974 MLA. In every novel he has written, one or more of his major characters is homosexual. His book *A Single Man* keeps its basic focus on the relationship between two homosexuals, one of whom is a middle-aged professor in a California University.

Those who are part of the vocal and often militant homophile movement would want the world to believe that the homosexual artist has more talent because of his homosexuality. It is not difficult to understand why militants would take such a position, for whenever a minority has been oppressed there is a vigorous effort to try to produce every possible evidence to support such an ameliorative premise. However, regarding alleged bonus talent in homosexuals, support also is issued by non-homosexual psychologists and sociologists. For example, practicing psychotherapist Hendrick M. Ruitenbeek of NYU provides in *Homosexuality and Creative Genius* evidence of bonus talent in the works of such men as Gide, Shelley, Saint-Pavin, Whitman, Radclyffe Hall, Symonds, Zola, Wilde, and Proust. In his introduction he quotes Antonia Wenkart: "Is a neurotic or psychotic patient creative? The answer is 'yes.' It is shown in the degree of destructiveness, which is proportionate to the magnitude of frustrating failure to exist."[1] Ruitenbeek also cites Abraham Maslow's concept of "peak experience," i.e., those moments in the lives of gifted people at high levels of maturation when they become "more whole and unified, more unique-alive and spontaneous, more perfectly expressive and uninhibited . . . more effortless and powerful, more daring and courageous . . . more ego transcending and self-forgetful."[2]

Ruitenbeek draws the conclusion that the work of the homosexual is "colored, molded, influenced, and directed by the fact of his homosexuality."[3] However, he believes that in the final analysis there is not sufficient proof of a definite association between creative genius and homosexuality. It is at this point I would agree with him. I am of the opinion that there are many great homosexual persons in the whole history of our culture who have excelled in music, in painting, in sculpture, in literature, and many other fields. Their attainments are not necessarily caused by their homosexuality; but the fact that specifically as homosexuals they have known pain, rejection, hostility, and social insecurity conditions the directions of their achievements and surely affects their attitude about people and the world in which they have had thus to suffer.

What has particularly impressed me about Isherwood is the way in which he presents and develops the homosexual characters which appear throughout his writings. While his homosexuals suffer, for the most part they are not destroyed by their suffering and do not become distorted, disturbed, embittered, unproductive persons. Rather they manage to function in society, to avoid destruction of themselves and others, and can hardly be described as psychotic, sick, twisted, or seriously neurotic. Such is not true of many other contemporary homosexual writers such as Tennessee Williams, Gore Vidal, and Jean Genet, who probe deep, involved problems either within the characters or in the society. These three constantly focus on bitterness, hate, disillusionment, perversion, cruelty, and unfulfillment. By contrast, in the work of Isherwood one senses, over and over again, his tenderness, his compassion, his understanding, even his love as he expresses what must be a healthy and deep concern for persons. While Isherwood does not champion a political movement, he sensitively celebrates and fully accepts homosexuals and their life styles. Perhaps in his own way, whether this is direct intention or not, he is doing more for the homosexual than others who are more militant. He is helping the reader to accept the homosexual and to have more understanding about homosexuality. In this quiet way he is winning for the homosexual what she or he needs more than anything else — acceptance.

Isherwood's life is not easy to sketch. While "Christopher" is one of the major characters in his novels and it seems that he is telling a great deal about himself, actually "Christopher" mainly tells about others — who *they* are, what *they* feel, why *they* may be doing what they do. He keeps himself and his feelings quite well hidden, a necessary consequence of his desire actually to be the camera.

It is true that he did write his autobiography *Lions and Shadows* and *Kathleen and Frank*, and often used fictitious names for his friends so, he stated, they would not be embarrassed by their association with him nor would feel incriminated by what he had to say. Isherwood hardly seems aggressive or boisterous.

High Lane, Cheshire, was Isherwood's English birthplace, on August 26, 1905. He was baptized as Christopher William Bradshaw Isherwood, but as soon as he began to publish he forsook both middle names and their initials. His early education was at St. Edmund's School, Hindhead, Surrey, where he and Auden first met. His delightful short story "Gems of Belgian Architecture" provides some realistic insights into English school-boy life in the early years of the first world war. His undergraduate days were spent at Corpus Christi in Cambridge and it is in *The Memorial* that we find reflections upon the way of life he knew on the banks of the Cam. Also in *Lions and Shadows* he notes, "Looking back, I think that those first two University terms have been amongst the most enjoyable parts of my whole life. I had sufficient money, and no worries as long as I could be together with Chalmers, which was all day and most of the night."[4] 'Chalmers' is later identified as Edward Upward, later author of *In the Thirties*. I single out this particular quote because it rather indicates Isherwood's early inclination to establish relationships which were apparently intense and long lasting. He also refers to his ties with Auden, who in the autobiography, is 'Hugh Weston': "Was the analyst-patient relationship between Weston and myself far more permanent and profound than either of us realized?"[5] Well, apparently, this was true enough for they ended up taking long journeys to far off places — even the Orient as well as working together as co-authors of three plays *On the Frontier, The Ascent of F6,* and *The Dog Beneath the Skin* along with the travel narrative *Journey to a War.*

After leaving Cambridge he became a tutor in London for a year then made a rather sudden decision to study medicine. His one year, at King's London was enough to convince him the world of microscopes and test tubes was not for him, and being fascinated by the stories reaching Britain about life in Berlin, he headed off for that politically turbulent city in 1930, where for the next three years he made a living, often meagre, as a teacher of English. It is from this period that he finds the material for perhaps his most popular novels *Goodbye to Berlin* and *The Last of Mr. Norris.* His visit to Greece during this period is recounted in one of the most charming stories contained in *Down There On a Visit.*

The ominous and threatening war clouds which began to gather upon the horizon sent him back to England, where between 1934 and 1936, he was involved in journalism and writing scripts for Gaumont-British films and it is about these movie assignments that he centers the theme of his *Prater Violet.* The trip to China with Auden was in 1938 and just prior to the United States entry into World War II, he took up residence in California to begin his association with Metro-Goldwyn-Mayer. The war found him working with the American Friends Service Committee and about this same time he developed a consuming interest in Hinduism. He edited a compilation of essays to which he also contributed *Vedanta and the West,* and later he went to India to emerge as a devoted disciple of Ramakrishna whose biography he published in 1959.

It was in 1946 that he became a U.S. citizen and the following year journeyed through South America later to relate these travels in *The Condor and the Cows.* Upon his return to California he became a professor at Los Angeles State College and the University of California at Santa Barbara. These associations surely served as the background for *A Single Man.* His recent novel, *A Meeting by the River* (1967), makes reference to his California film days but more particularly to his associations with the kind of life he knew briefly in a Hindu Monastery beside the Ganges. He presently lives in Santa Monica, California, and as all his biographical notes rather pointedly state, "remains unmarried."

There is much misunderstanding and misinformation (in some persons almost total ignorance) about homosexuality even in this so-called "enlightened" age. A focus on the homosexual characters developed by Isherwood demands a clear perspective. Many persist in saying that homosexuality is "unlawful," "immoral," "unnatural," "an abnormal sickness." Persons at all levels of society, even those within the Church, are all too ready thus to reject, to abhor, to ostracize, to isolate the homosexual. I disagree with each of these attempts to describe homosexuals. More positively, I believe that homosexuals are very little different in character or needs from most hetero-sexuals in society. Only the superficial details of a homosexual's behavior fail to conform to the patterns of the established heterosexual majority in our modern American culture. The basic needs of the homosexual are little different from those of the heterosexual. His or her hunger for love and acceptance, his or her drives for purpose, for discipline, and for fulfillment are ever present. Likewise, generally speaking, religious needs are the same; however, perhaps because of the social taboo, homosexuals have a few problems which do not confront the heterosexual. I am of the strong opinion that persons would not, if they had free will in the matter, elect to be homosexual. Given our present culture and its restrictive institutions (including the Church!), there are too many disadvantages to face. Surely the homosexual has some searching questions: Why did God make me this way? If He made me, and my lot is so difficult, how can He be called "good"? How can I accept myself when so many others, even the very members of my family, often reject me; yet I know I must accept myself since Jesus has said "Thou shalt love they neighbor as thyself"? Am I really a sinner if I act out my homosexuality? So many in the Church feel, "I sin and I may make my confession, but how can I ever control such a basic physical-emotional drive? How can I be an honest and open person when I have constantly to 'wear a mask' so that my family, my friends, my employers do not discover my sexual nature? How can I deal with others in my interpersonal relationships — how can I avoid using people? How, when the establishment of long-standing, meaningful homosexual relationships is made so difficult, can I cope with the loneliness that so often overtakes me?"

Earlier I stated that Isherwood speaks helpfully to the condition of the homosexual. In some direct, but usually in more indirect ways, he addresses himself to the questions raised in the last paragraph and in so doing helps interpret the homosexual to society and at the same time gives the homosexual some encouragement to accept himself. What follows attempts to illustrate this premise.

The World In the Evening revolves around the love and marriage of Stephen and Elizabeth. At one juncture of this relationship Stephen is involved homosexually with a younger man, Michael. Eventually Elizabeth who was already suspicious of the situation, hears the facts about Stephen. Her response is full of tenderness and understanding, Stephen questions: "When you found out, weren't you disgusted?" To this Elizabeth replies:

> Because it was a man? What difference does that make? You know, I had a friend, once, whose husband used to have affairs with men. I asked her if she minded that more than if it had been with women. And she said, "Neither more or less. What I grudge is the time he spends away from me. And that's the same in either case!" Elizabeth then goes on to say to Stephen that she feels he has been unkind to Michael by letting Michael believe that he loves him, and she gently admonishes him by saying "next time this happens I want you to promise that you won't let the other person believe all kinds of things that are impossible and untrue . . ."[6]

In this same novel there are two men who are making a real effort to establish a working relationship. They have known each other for four years. Charles is the doctor in a small Pennsylvania town and Bob is still finishing his time in the armed service. At one point of the story Charles has just put Bob on the train to go off for a long tour of duty and later a mutual friend Sarah, who is a Quaker, is visiting with Stephen, her nephew. She said that she wanted to say something to Charles but lacked the courage. When Stephen prodded her to verbalize what was in her mind she replied:

> I wanted to tell him — Oh, it's hard to express it without sounding presumptuous — not to mind too much if we haven't understood him as we should have. I mean I'm afraid we're all of us apt to be very cruel and stupid, in the presence of what we're not accustomed to. I fear that Charles feels cut off from us now, and bitterly lonely; and we refuse him any word of comfort. Oh dear, we're so dreadfully smug and arrogant, most of us; so very sure we know what's right and what's wrong. Sometimes, Stephen, this lack of charity — even among those of us who call ourselves Friends — it horrifies me![7]

Isherwood does not put a rosy glow on homosexual relationships. He shows that they can be real, full of joy as well as pock-marked with insecurity and pain. In his *Goodbye to Berlin* he tells of a summer affair between a basically neurotic Englishman, Peter, and a younger German boy, Otto. Peter says: "It seems funny to think now — when I first met Otto, I thought we should live together for the rest of our lives. But, oh my God! the vision of a life with

Otto opened before me like a comic inferno."[8] As "Christopher" in *Down there on a Visit* he tells of his relationship with Paul. "Paul and I had met because we needed each other. Yes, now I suddenly say that; I needed Paul every bit as much as he needed me. Our strength and our weakness were complementary. It would be much easier for us to go forward together than separately."[9] Again, "This was one of the happiest periods of my life. The longer I lived with Paul, the more I became aware of a kind of geisha quality in him; he really understood how to give pleasure, to make daily life more decorative and to create enjoyment of small occasions."[10]

The novel *A Meeting by the River* is the confrontation which takes place between two English brothers, Patrick, a successful movie producer, and the other, Oliver, about to take his final vows in a Hindu Monastery. There is a sub-plot about the homosexual relationship of Patrick, married with a family in England, and Tom, and handsome young man in Los Angeles. In one letter from India, Patrick tells Tom, "I need your love, terribly . . . Is that outrageous of me? Yes, of course it is. But I'm still asking for it, and I don't apologize."[11] "As for my being crazy, yes, I suppose many people would call it that, people who never felt as I do now and never will because they'd always stop themselves in time before it got out of control. Such people live in perpetual terror of what's inside themselves, they imagine it would destroy them."[12] Patrick writes again, "What I want to tell you tonight is this — as far as I'm concerned our relationship seems to keep on going stronger and deeper, although we're apart. I mean this literally! It's very strange, something I've never experienced before with anyone."[13] Although the relationship does not endure, both receive lasting values from it.

Isherwood's most expressive accounting of a homosexual relationship is *A Single Man*. The story is one day in the life of George, a fifty-eight year old professor who has lost his younger lover, Jim, through an automobile accident some months previous. This was a long, stable, deep relationship in which both men fulfilled their own purposes in life. George is bitter — bitter because he feels the world did not, does not, and will not accept the homosexual relationship. He reflects, "All are, in the last analysis, responsible for Jim's death; their words, their thoughts, their whole way of life willed it, even though they never knew he existed."[14] In his classroom he lectures:

> So, let's face it, minorities are people who probably look and act differently from us and have faults we don't have. We may dislike the way they look and act, and we may hate their faults. And it's better that we admit to disliking and hating them than if we try to smear our feelings over with pseudo-liberal sentimentality. If we're

frank about our feelings, we have a safety valve; and if have a safety valve we're actually less likely to start persecuting. I know that theory is unfashionable nowadays. We all keep trying to believe that if we ignore something long enough it'll just vanish . . . [15]

Surely with this passage, Isherwood is trying to tell us that it's time to discuss homosexuality openly, to air the prejudices, and to make some responsible decision how society should deal with it.

Possibly the most poignant paragraph in *A Single Man* comes as George reflects upon what his middle class neighbors felt about his relationship with Jim. Neighbor Mrs. Strunk is very inquisitive, and George thinks he would like to say to her: "But your book is wrong, Mrs. Strunk when it tells you that Jim is the substitute I found for a real son, a real kid brother, a real husband, a real wife. Jim wasn't a substitute for anything. And there is no substitute for Jim, if you'll forgive me for saying so, anywhere."[16]

Isherwood keeps trying to tell about the soul-searching which a homosexual undergoes as he or she tries to establish identity and finally moves the hard step of self-acceptance. At the end of *Prater Violet* when "Christopher" is expressing some doubts about the homosexual way of life which can be filled with so many "brief encounters" and such lack of satisfaction, he looks into himself and obviously is tempted by the thought of heterosexual marriage:

I see something else; the way that leads to safety. To where there is no fear, no loneliness, no need of J., K., or M. For a second, I glimpse it. For an instant, it is quite clear. Then the clouds shut down, and a breath off the glacier, icy with inhuman coldness of the peaks, touches my cheek. 'No!' I think! I could never do it. Rather the fear I know, the loneliness I know . . . For to take that other way would mean I would lose myself. I should no longer be a person. I should no longer be Christopher Isherwood. No. No. That's more terrible than the bombs. More terrible than having no lover. That I can never face![17]

It is a revelation such as this which may, in part, suggest some reason for Isherwood's interest in Hinduism. In preparing the introduction for the book edited on Vedanta he writes: "Vendanta teaches us that life has no other purpose than this — that we shall learn to know ourselves for wht we really are."[18] Apparently Isherwood found an acceptance of homosexuality in Hinduism which he never found in Christianity. In *Meeting by the River* Patrick observes in a letter to Tom: "I'm reasonably sure that a Hindu monk would not be disgusted, like some prudish Christian parson, at the mere mention of sex between two men. They are far more broad-minded here (India) than we in England or American can really ever be, even if we call ourselves sophisticated, because we've been trained since childhood to regard certain kinds of sex as wicked. To the Hindu monk, all sex is ultimately just sex." [19]

Isherwood says, "I myself am a devotee of Ramakrishna." This is certainly borne out by the fact that he has published the biography of this unusual nineteenth-century mystic. In the account of Ramakrishna's life, Isherwood says:

"Since childhood, Ramakrishna had shown from time to time an inclination to assume the character of a woman . . . So as he entered upon the sadhana of the madhura bhawa, he asked Mathur (his superior) for women's clothes. Mathur provided him with a beautiful and valuable sari from Benares, a gauze scarf, a skirt and bodice. To complete the transformation, Mathur brought him also a wig and a set of gold ornaments. Needless to say, Ramakrishna's latest sadhana caused a whole series of scandalous rumors. But he and Mathur ignored them."[20] Isherwood is making no homosexual connection here, but rather trying to say that such an unusual situation seemed natural to Ramakrishna, and his superiors were not disturbed. This was just a phase in Ramakrishna's life, and it was an honest acting out of his personality which Isherwood says is "now predominantly masculine, now feminine." [21]

What can one say in conclusion about Isherwood and the "religious quest"? Certainly one does not see a searching Camus, a religiously provocative Sartre, nor a make-religion-relevant Eliot. Rather one sees an artist truly eager to introduce us to a wide variety of characters as real as any people we might meet next door, or while travelling, or even within our own families. Without "beating the drum," he lets us come to know, to appreciate, to respect, even to admire and to relate to homosexuals, even without thus labelling them. Possibly in his own generally quiet, refined way and by avoiding some "blaring call to arms" to espouse and proclaim the "cause" of homosexuality, he has been winning more friends for homosexuals than many of the other so-called literary "champions of the cause." It is the Elizabeths, the Sarahs, the Pauls, the Patricks, the Georges, the "Christophers" who will help the world to know that the homosexual is a real person — needing love, knowing pain, striving for purpose, searching for ideals. These persons will help dispel the fears of those who may be frightened should the homosexual find a place of acceptance in Church and society and in turn will give some hope to those who would pray that the day of dignity may come when "the mask" might be removed and they know the acceptance which the Lord Christ has promised.

NOTES

[1]Antonia Wenkart, "Creativity and Freedom", *American Journal of Psychoanalysis,* XXIII, No. 2 (1963), 199.

[2]Abraham H. Maslow, "Creativity in Self-Actualizing People," in Harold H. Anderson (ed.) *Creativity and its Cultivation* (New York: Harper and Row, 1959).

[3]Hendrick M. Ruitenbeek, *Homosexuality and Creative Genius* (New York: Astor-Honor, Inc., 1967). XVIII.

[4]Christopher Isherwood, *Lions and Shadows* (New Directions, 1947), 72-73.

[5]Ibid., 217.

[6]Christopher Isherwood, *The World in the Evening* (New York: Random House, 1952), 213.

[7]Ibid., 289.

[8]_____ *Goodbye to Berlin* (New York: New Directions, 1935), 97.

[9]_____ *Down There on a Visit* (New York: Simon and Schuster, 1959), 245.

[10]Ibid., 254.

[11]_____ *A Meeting by the River* (New York: Simon and Schuster, 1967), 50.

[12]Ibid., 82.

[13]Ibid., 130.

[14]_____ *A Single Man* (Lancer Books, Inc., 1964), 32.

[15]Ibid., 59.

16Ibid., 24.

17_____ *Prater Violet* (New York: Ballantine Books, 1945), 158.

18_____ (Editor) *Vedanta for Modern Man* (London: George Allen and Unwin Ltd., 1952). IX.

19_____ *A Meeting by the River* (New York: Simon and Schuster, 1967), 134-135.

20_____ *Ramakrishna and His Disciples* (New York: Simon and Schuster, 1959), 113.

21Ibid., 112.

Evils and God —
From a 'Process' Perspective

By The Rev. Norman Pittenger

This chapter has for its subject the fact of evils in the world and the reality of God — this is, as viewed from the perspective of process theology. You will notice that it does not speak of the 'problem of evil,' since this would be required only if the God about whom we are concerning ourselves were an all-controlling, totally omnipotent, entirely self-contained being, responsible for anything and everything that happens in the creation, either directly or (as classical theology would say) 'permissively.' You will also note that I have spoken of the fact of *evils*, in the plural, since I am convinced that to lump many different facts together under the noun 'evil,' in the singular, is to indulge in a confusion of categories, to overlook the several sorts of 'thing' or 'happening' which we tend to classify as being 'evil,' and then to seek a solution of such a collection which will not inpugn the goodness of God nor diminish the usually understood type of power which has been styled 'divine.'

Attention is first directed to a variety of evils with an endeavor to show that when these are properly described (so far as we are able to do so), *and* when the concept of God is true to the basic affirmations both of Christian faith and of sound (if not 'classical') theistic teaching, we find ourselves confronted by a world which is by no means 'the best possible world' (in the sense of 'best conceivable'); but also is not a world about which only unmitigated pessimism is possible. Indeed, a sound view of the whole matter will permit neither proximate optimism nor ultimate pessimism, but rather a genuine realism which on the basis of Christian faith may lead to an *ultimate* optimism.

First, let us consider the variety of situations or occurrences which we commonly call by the adjective 'evil.' I assume that it is agreed that a general process view of the world is accepted: that the world is a world of change and development, not a static and fixed order; that its components are not *things* or substances but events, happenings, or occurrences — in my own phrase, 'energy-events'; that it is a societal world, in which each element in it is affected by, and affects, every other element; that coercive power is not the strongest power, despite appearances, but that what Whitehead called 'persuasion' and I as a Christian call 'love' *is* that strongest power; and finally, that God, who *is* Love (here I speak as a Christian, of course) is not the only causative agency, although he is the supreme such agency, while he is also the recipient of, hence influenced and affected by, whatever takes place in the creation. It is in that context and with those presuppositions that I wish, then, to distinguish among the various 'evils' with which we are familiar. Unless that context and those presuppositions are accepted, at least for the purposes of this discussion, there is no use in continuing the matter, since too much would be left unresolved by way of prior conceptions and convictions.

First of all, and obviously, there are disorders in the natural world — earthquakes, tidal-waves, volcanic eruptions, hurricanes, and the like. Let us clear these out of the way, for nobody calls them 'evil' until and unless there is life — usually, human life — which is imperiled, damaged, or destroyed through their happening. What is more, anyone who has read L.J. Henderson's classic of several generations ago, *The Fitness of the Environment*, or similar books published more recently, knows that for the most part, if not entirely, such natural disorders are tied in with the sort of world in which we live. I shall not dwell on the point, save to remark that the given-ness of a creation like ours is marked by phenomena of the natural order which make life a possibility, maintain the proper physical and chemical conditions, keep that world at a temperature and with graduations of cold and heat within tolerable limits; otherwise, there would be no human existence on this planet. Now unless it can be shown that the various physical laws which govern such planetary circumstances are alterable at will, we may conclude that the way in which things happen at *that* level must be part of the inevitable ordering of nature, but not the direct activity of God after the fashion of the insurance laws which speak of 'acts of God' — and somehow in thus speaking assume that any occurrence in which there is no human interference is by definition, and without question, done by a God who is supposed to behave in an arbitrary and meaningless fashion.

If God, however, is not a creator in that automatic sense but is 'with his creation,' moulding it from everlasting to everlasting and always working in and with *some* created state of affairs, then there is no 'problem' here. There is the *fact* of occurrences which under certain circumstances we may *describe* as evil. At the same time, there is sufficient independence in the created order for it to 'make itself,' provided that it continues as a cosmos and does not become simply chaotic. The exercise of divine power does not negate such independence; it accepts it and uses it for the potentiality of higher emerging forms, including human life itself as the highest such form known to us.

Second, there is suffering and pain at the level of sentient existence, whether this be lower biological structures or more sophisticated ones like animal life or human life. We must not commit the 'pathetic fallacy' at this point and take it for granted that, say, a crab whose claw has been torn off in struggle with another crab has the same high degree of sensitivity that we should have if our arm or leg were thus wrenched from our body. There are degrees of sensitivity; the higher the living organism, the more affected is the situation in respect to the nervous systems it possesses. I am not here speaking in a callous way; I am only warning against the sentimentality which is the absurd extreme of the genuine compassion anyone must feel at suffering however slight and insignificant. What is more, the very nervous systems which make pain possible at the human level also make pleasure possible. You cannot have the chance of the one without the chance of the other. So far, then, I believe that the adjective 'evil' is often misapplied here.

But there *is* a point when the adjective is appropriate. This is the point at which, for example, cancer cells proliferate without regard for their host. Where there is a faint analogue to purely self-assertive development or growth, then there is a denial of possible harmony and cooperation. Thus, in Whiteheadian terms, some of the countless actual events in the creation, in moving towards the achievement of their aim, pay no attention to the pattern of commonalty or social existence. Each such energy-event has its own degree of power and its own causative capacity; each seeks its own intensity in actualizing its potentiality. The power of God in this matter is exercised, once again, in preventing contrast, particular development, and fulfillment of aim, from becoming totally destructive conflict and hence arriving at anarchy, chaos, sheer and unrelieved disorder.

This is more patently the case with psychological anguish. "We look before and after / And pine for what is not." We suffer emotionally and mentally, both for ourselves and for others — perhaps more when others are thus affected than when we ourselves are in anguish. Yet here we have the inevitable accompaniment of our sociality, influencing and being influenced by others and more especially by other human agents. This works itself out as we, or others, among the innumerable centers of power (which are the actual events), fail to achieve proper self-actualization or to act in cooperation and harmonious working with other such centers or *foci*.

When we come to what we commonly style moral evil (and when a religious perspective is entertained, we call this 'sin') we are in the presence of false self-assertion, failure to move forward along the line of creative advance in association with others, rejection of the lures to better realization of possibilities. Responsibility rests with those agencies which 'decide' — in the profound sense of cutting off *this* possibility by choosing for *that*, whether with vivid awareness or perhaps with hardly any such awareness at all; and such responsibility presupposes the freedom of the individual along with accountability for choices made. The consequences of such choices, over many ages, is the horrifying evil we well know in the human situation.

The situation which results from this variety of 'wrongnesses,' failures to advance, backwaters, lack of cooperation and harmonious development, deviations and distortions, and the like — and at all levels, too — is nothing short of tragic. That is why no proximate optimism is possible for thoughtful people. Realistic appraisal of how things go in the world forces us to recognize and accept the fact that there *are* terrible evils, indeed appalling evils of different sorts and at different levels. What Unamuno called "the tragic sense of life" cannot be avoided by any civilized man or woman. In *that* sense there is what we might call a provisional pessimism in respect to the state of affairs in which we are immersed and which we know so well. And we are all of us caught up in this situation, since we are 'members one of another,' certainly at the human level . . . and also in our relationship with the animal realm as well as in the sheer physical-chemical basis of our existence as conscious, knowingly free, and plainly responsible creatures.

If reality is a process compound of countless actual events which have each of them power and a degree of decision, with the 'chanciness' which these events involve, the divine actuality we call God must himself be *one* of the causative agencies, but by no means the *only* one. If our model for God is sheer Love, as a Christian anyway must believe, the divine power is not omnipotence in the sense of absolute over-riding of all other agencies. God works ceaselessly to 'persuade' every creaturely agent to actualize itself in harmonious solidarity with others. But God is frustrated, in this concrete working, by the order upon which he is working. Save insofar as limits are set to prevent contrast from ending in utterly destructive conflict and hence on chaotic anarchy, God is not a primary coercive drive or thrust; he is characterized by Love and his working is towards what Teilhard de Chardin called 'amorization.' If this seems to point towards a 'finite God,' so be it; but I believe the phrase is inaccurate and misleading. This is because it wrongly portrays God as having some possibility of sheer omnipotent control and suggests that he does not, in fact, exemplify (in Whitehead's word) the principles which of necessity apply to any and every actuality as it works and as it is. But there is something more to be said.

From the perspective of process thought God is also from everlasting to everlasting; he is not eternal, as being outside succession, but he *is* eternal as being himself eminently temporal, which is to say successive (with a past from which he is and works, a present in which he is and works, and a future towards which he is and works) in a fashion which far exceeds our very limited and partial experience of the time-series. So we may say that God has 'all time' in which to accomplish his purpose of Love. We may also say more than that. In the process way of seeing things, God is the chief recipient of what happens in the world. He receives unto himself and uses for further activity in the creation, what in that creation has been 'determined, dared, and done.' The di-polar view of God, as both supreme (but not only) causative agent and supreme (but not only) recipient; or as 'primordial' and 'consequent' (in Whitehead's language); or as abstractly conceivable yet concretely actual and operative (in Hartshorne's words): this guarantees that his provision of initial aims which are to be subjectively realized by the creatures is complemented by his 'saving everything that can be saved.' Since this is the case, there is room for what was styled earlier an 'ultimate optimism' — provided, of course, that we do not make pretentious claims that we ourselves must have some conscious and self-acknowledged awareness of victory and refuse to play the creaturely game unless we have certainty of due rewards for our presumed goodness. All is ad maiorem Dei gloriam — and God's glory is not in his exhibition of coercive control but in his sharing of love. To have contributed to that love, to have shared in it, and to have been received into it, is or ought to be sufficient, at least for a Christian. We may rightly hope that we can have somehow such an awareness of this participation but we dare not demand it.

But what have these considerations got to do with the fact of evils in the world? The answer is that we are called to be 'fellow-workers' or 'co-creators' (St. Paul and Whitehead are here being quoted and I think they are saying the same thing) with God who is Love, in his eager, indefatigable and indefeasible concern for establishing the victory of good over evil, care over indifference, and love over hatred. In Jesus Christ this victory was placarded before humankind in the Cross, suffused with resurrection light. What Jesus is and what Jesus stood for are in Christian faith everlastingly present in the consequent nature of God. As thus in and of God, they provide for God new opportunity to work lovingly in the creation, as well as the disclosure of what God is and is always up to.

The multiplicity of creative agents, in a world of process, makes evils with all their horror practically inevitable, as R.C. Miller remarks in his American Spirit in Theology (p. 171); but as Miller goes on to say, "only through the same multiplicity could good become" a possibility and an actuality. When such good is accomplished, as supremely it is in the classical instance of divine self-disclosure in Jesus Christ, it is never lost. For the perfected actuality, says Whitehead (*Process and Reality*, p. 532), which is "what is done in the world," is "transformed into a reality in heaven, and the reality in heaven passes back into the world. By reason of this reciprocal relation, the love in the world passes into the love in heaven, and floods back again into the world. In this sense, God is the great companion — the fellow-sufferer who understands."

I wish to conclude with two comments. The first is that while we may properly describe *all* evils as deviations or distortions from the ongoing creative advance, we must not have a mistaken notion of what these words mean. In a world which is in process — a world of change and movement — there is always the possibility that things will 'go wrong,' largely because at all levels there is the reality of decision while at the *human* level that decision is made with conscious awareness. The trouble with the word 'deviation' in particular, is that it has often been regarded as appropriate for what are thought to be 'violations' of a given, fixed, and unchangeable order. Obviously no process thinker can speak in that manner. Above all, it is quite improper to use such a word to describe particular modes of sexual interest and behavior, like homosexuality, as a condition and a life-style. There is no difference from majority behavior in this area, to be sure; but that is not at all a matter of 'deviation.'

My second comment is the result of a remark by an acquaintance who had read the earlier part of this chapter. He tells me that to his mind my approach to evil is a 'trivialization' which reduces evil (and more particularly *sin*) to "backward drags, dangerous side paths, and hence distortions." For him — and he says for most people — evil is much more 'radical,' rooted in very nature of things and their way of 'going.' Much the same criticism was made of Pierre Teilhard's treatment of the subject; a *monitum* from the Vatican condemned his views as unduly rosy and optimistic. I hope that I have made it clear, however, that I see all evils, and particularly moral evil and sin, as serious, tragic, frighteningly prevalent, and always to be taken with deepest concern. Our difference is in the description of what evil *is*, rather than in the horror that it rightly awakens in us. But I cannot agree that evil and sin are *radical*, if we have regard for the correct meaning of that word. 'Radical' means 'at the roots'; and to talk about evil and sin as 'radical' is a denial of the great Jewish and Christian affirmation of the essential goodness of the created order, as God made and is making it. The evil in it and the sin which we know so well and share so horribly are defects of that good creation; or in modern idiom, they are existentially real and appalling but they are *not* 'of the essence' of creation as such. I do not see how any instructed Christian could think otherwise.

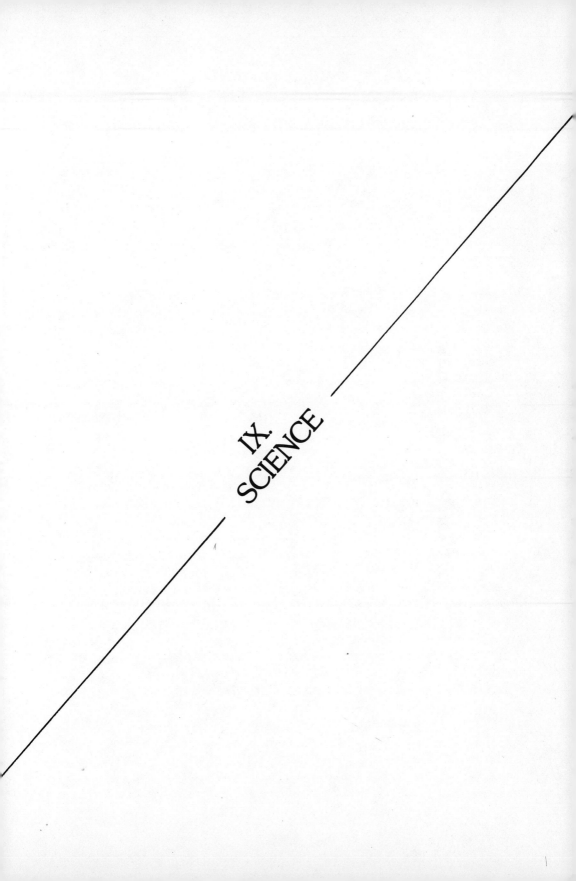

IX.
SCIENCE

Towards A Gay Analysis
Of Science and Education

By Stephen J. Risch

The gay movement must not be merely a movement of resistance. It must be a movement of liberation and social revolution. Resistance movements seek change by collectively *going outside* everyday life in an attempt to block external oppression. Liberation movements involve a collective redefinition of self, coupled with demands for new rights and entitlements. The gay person who assuages her or his guilt by radical chic evening activities while engaging in daily executive jet set activities, is resisting, and is at best a rebel. The gay person who refuses to accept the hierarchical structure of his or her work place and organizes coworkers into collective action to change that workplace, is liberating, and can be at best a revolutionary. Processes of resistance accept the legitimacy of everyday activities. Processes of liberation encompass a new awareness that certain everyday patterns previously thought to be legitimate are morally wrong or illegitimate — liberation activity must occur *within everyday life.*

Because sexuality is integral to our lives, both as individuals and in social interactions with others, sexual liberation cannot be divorced from a general reassessment and reevaluation of human relationships. Several authors, especially Marcuse[1] and Altman,[2] provide a general description of the effect of sexual liberation on our everyday lives. However, as yet, no one has provided such a description for specific occupations. I am concerned here specifically with a political gay analysis germane to academics within the sciences — an analysis concerning how we teach, how we do science, and what kind of science we do.

It is not popular within the academic community to suggest that an individual's personal-political lifestyle should influence his or her teaching and research methodology and objectives. Indeed, many scientists still labor under the myth that science is somehow neutral and value-free. I will argue that it is much more realistic to admit in general our work reflects our political ideology and that one should struggle toward bringing the two into harmony — in this case harmony between our work and our philosophy of sexual liberation.

A philosophy of sexual liberation has two aspects. First is a rejection of all sex negative and utilitarian views of sex. Sex is not dirty and should not be secretive and guilt ridden, nor should it be moored to the family and child rearing. The claim of Marcuse and Altman is that the human person is naturally polymorphously perverse: that we enjoy the ability to take sexual pleasure from all parts of the body, and that we are all inherently bisexual. Second, closely connected with straight society's denial of inherent bisexuality is the rigid sexual polarization into masculine and feminine genders, and the associated roles which can dominate our personal relations. In western society this polarization has resulted in the system of patriarchy in which "the cultural norm of male identity consists in power, prestige, privilege, and perogative *as over and against* the gender class of women."[3] Sexual liberation is inconsistent with any kind of relationship in which one individual's comfort and well being is contingent upon the labor of another, in which one individual refers exclusively to another for validation of his/her self worth, or in which one individual achieves some benefit by simultaneously denying the humanity of another. Such oppressive interactions currently occur not only in bed and between partners in personal relationships but also in job relationships. Ultimately, gays in the sciences will have to decide how this second aspect of sexual liberation should affect the way in which they teach and do research.

I do not mean to imply that there should be a philosophy of education or a way of doing science peculiar to gay people. A theory of sexual liberation should not lead to qualitatively different conclusions from theories of liberation that follow from other sources of oppression. A philosophy of human liberation must be holistic. The analysis of the contemporary role of science and education which will be presented here is very similar to that of the straight Left. In fact, many would argue that a gay analysis and a radical political analysis are one and the same. I will not argue here whether or not this is so. The important point is that gay people, having suffered a very personal and intense type of oppression, are in a good position to recognize the oppressive nature of current education techniques and science methodology. As a result, we should be in the vanguard in attempting to revolutionize the structure of education and science.

Oppressive Pedagogy in an Oppressive Society

The education system in the United States mirrors well the hierarchical and aggressive nature of our society — the same kind of society that gay people find so personally oppressive. Traditionally this country has employed a "banking" approach to education in that it has established a hierarchy of people, with those at the top making deposits of so-called facts into the heads of those at the bottom. Paulo Freire, a Brazilian educator, first used this banking metaphor to describe the educational system of western society and much of what follows is based on his analysis.[4]

In our system of education the teacher, who is the depositer and "active" agent, knows all, and the student who is the receiver and "passive" agent knows little or nothing. The process is one-way — morbid because it is static. Since the process requires a narrating subject and listening objects, the information is handed to students who thereby lose much of the excitement of initial discovery. The assumption that teaching can best be handled by one individual, the teacher, is naive. In attempting to understand reality, we try to gather as much information as possible. Why then do we rely on one judgment, one process, one person as a basis for education?[5]

A banking approach to education is not only an ineffective way to develop ideas, but necessitates the dehumanizing of students and teachers as well. At one end of the extreme, students are told essentially not to think, but rather to mechanically absorb a set of facts. At the better end of the extreme, the banking system involves a teacher addressing students about ideas, concepts, and his/her interpretation of facts. In either case, the student is a passive note-taker who goes home and studies what the professors have professed, rarely meeting with them in dialogue so that all can arrive at new perceptions about the world. Students are told that their business is to "study," and so come to believe that they are not capable of creativity and invention. Teachers are also oppressed by the very system in which they oppress their students. By refusing to participate in a dialogical process, they deny themselves the rewards which accrue to *all* participants in such a process.

The teacher-student relationship is based on dominance and subjugation and as such it builds a rigid "class" distinction (the teacher-student barrier). The teacher is considered a superior human being by virtue of possessing something — knowledge in this case. The student is considered inferior by virtue of not possessing that knowledge. Even more oppressive, this class distinction supports the idea that the most appropriate form of behavior for a have-not is silence, passivity, and a feeling of inferiority. An alternative, liberative concept of education must be based on the principles of equality between teacher and student, the dialogical method, and the notion that our ideas about reality are not fixed and final, but necessarily change and evolve over time. The purpose of education is to learn a process of comprehending reality, rather than to learn what someone else (an authority) believes that reality to be.

Freire suggests that the goal for each individual is the development of *conscientizacão*, the overt awareness not only of a process of analysis, but also of the liberating, humanizing effects of using such a process better to understand the world. People develop *conscientizacão* through two-way dialogue (the dialogical method) in which students and teacher together determine what questions and problems they wish to understand, and exactly how they should go about trying to investigate them. The ultimate goal of education by this method is freedom, for by answering cooperatively evolved questions the individual gains not only a deeper understanding of the material conditions of the world in which he or she is living in, but also a confidence in her or his ability to understand that reality. Such confidence is a crucial and necessary step toward freedom from oppression. It is not a step anyone can take for anyone else — and, thus, it cannot be taught by one person to another. Together, people can discover the process by exchanging ideas and experiences about the world. By this conception, reality is not composed of a set of rules or facts about the world so much as it is composed of a viewpoint consistent with the experience of many people. Only through common experiences and understanding can a whole people be free; otherwise, there is freedom only for some and oppression for the rest.

Common experiences can only occur when people regard themselves as being equal. The banking system is antithetical to understandings based on mutual experiences. In many ways the banking relationship reflects the structure of sexual relationships in our society as much as it does the traditional student-teacher relationship. Males have been the arbiters of human identity, wielding power and prerogative over women. Women are expected to be passive receptacles, not only for the hard cock, but also for advice and validation of self worth, all of which come from men. Unfortunately, many homosexual relationships resemble this traditional heterosexual pattern.

If sexual liberation is not to be artificially compartmentalized from a more holistic form of liberation, then the educational structure as well as the traditional relationship of "fucker" and "fuckee" will have to undergo revolutionary change. In particular, the climate of the classroom must begin to evolve away from what might be called the sexist norm: the active, dominant, expert, inserting cold hard facts into passive, ignorant novices.

Just as the banking system of education reflects aspects of sexist personal relationships, a liberative process of education such as that discussed by Freire incorporates the basic themes of sexual liberation. Gay people have refused to accept straight people's prescriptions about what we should do with our bodies. Can we then turn around and deny our students the liberating effect of defining their own reality, of determining what questions they want to understand, and exactly how they should go about investigating them? A comprehensive gay analysis also rejects the idea that there should be a dominant and subjugated partner in personal relationships. Rather it asserts that neither partner should consistently define the terms of the relationship, both being equally responsible for developing an attitude of mutual trust and respect. It is hardly consistent for teachers with a gay consciousness to willingly participate in a strongly hierarchical system of education in which students are systematically excluded from important decisions that affect their lives. Instead, we must reject traditional teaching methods and mold a new educational process, one based on communication between loving, committed and humble people whose respect for each other precludes the use of subjugation and ego-fulfillment as tools of education.

The Uses and Methodology of Scientific Research

The structure of science in western countries in many ways resembles our oppressive system of education. Such a resemblance is hardly surprising since both merely reflect the norms and ideology of the society they serve, one that is patriarchal and corporate-capitalist.

Given recent events, it is easy to see how the *use* of science oppresses individuals and groups of people. The electronic battlefield in South East Asia and the Race-IQ controversy here at home are just two of the more recent and flagrant examples of such abuse. However, the *methodology* of science is just as oppressive as its uses and is perhaps more relevant to a gay analysis. Like education, scientific methodology is elitist and dominated by individualistic expertise (and, of course, usually male expertise), despite the potential for communality in the way the scientific method might be practiced. Gay people who actively participate in science should ask to what extent they are supporting an institution whose values directly conflict with the goals of sexual liberation.

While gays in several other disciplines have organized caucuses, gays in the sciences have not yet organized or otherwise discussed how being gay affects their role as scientists. This is not surprising as so many scientiests (even more than other academics) attempt to compartmentalize their work from their personal lives. The myth that science is somehow politically neutral or value free is still a generally accepted axiom of most scientific workers, at least in the form that suggests a person's political beliefs should not affect his/her research methodology or choice of projects.

However, scientists acting within any social order will to some extent, internalize the ideological assumptions of that society. These assumptions affect: (1) the selection of facts to accumulate, 2) experiments to perform,

3) methodology of the experiments, and 4) the theoretical framework within which to set these facts. A comparison of science done in the United States and China will serve to clarify how different political ideologies result in radically different ways of doing science.

Science in the United States: An analysis of the scientific structure in the United States must begin with the realization that the United States is a corporate capitalist state and that a tiny minority of the population, through its wealth and power,controls the major decision-making institutions of our society. Both the goals and methodology of science in such a system are consistent with the long term strategy of the capitalist class.

The ruling class, through government, big corporations, and tax-exempt foundations, carefully controls the basic direction of reserach in the United States. For example, billions of dollars are spent on space research while pressing domestic needs are given lower priority. Money is funded for research on organ transplants, heart disease and strokes, major killers of middle and upper classes, rather than for studying the broad range of effects of malnutrition, which affects mainly the lower classes. Agricultural research emphasizes the development of high yield crop strains which are most profitable for large agribusinesses, rather than techniques of ecologically sound practices for peasant farmers. Development of energy systems emphasizes nuclear fission, profitable to the large energy corporations, rather than the, as yet unprofitable tapping of solar energy. Sociological studies are focused on individual aberrations, such as innate tendencies for criminality (XYY chromosome research), biologically determined lowered IQ and organic causes of "mental disease" (e.g., homosexuality), rather than on the effects of an oppressive society on individuals. How can such blatantly obvious contra-dictions exist?

Though a complete answer to this question is beyond the scope of this chapter, it will be useful to summarize, if a bit sketchily, how the servitude of science to the imperial capitalist system inevitably leads to such contradictions.[6]

The capitalist strategy consists of at least three basic parts. The first is the maintenance and strengthening of the international domination by United States capital. This is necessary to provide continually profitable opportunities for the export of capital so as to absorb the surplus product[7] constantly being generated both at home and abroad. This necessity leads to ever-increasing subjugation , especially over the Third World. Subjugation is inevitably reacted to, sometimes violently. With the growing revolt of oppressed peoples of the world, the United States ruling class is relying more and more on technological means of terrorization and control: anti-personnel bombs, napalm, poison gases, herbicides, geophysical warfare, etc. These abuses of science are well known and liberal scientists have already organized to stop them.

The second fundamental thrust of capitalist strategy is to insure a steady and predictable increase in the productivity of domestic labor. The ability to extract an increasingly better return on the wage investment by curtailment of the necessary labor time to produce a given product is crucial to the maintenance of the predictability of domestic industry, and its ability to compete in the international market. This increase in labor productivity is needed to maintain profits and at the same time sustain the living standard and employment of the working class. Otherwise it would be impossible to sustain the internal consumer market and curb domestic class struggle so necessary to the preservation of social control by the ruling class. The key to increasing the productivity of labor is the transformation and reorganization of our major industries through increased automation of the production process. This reorganization depends on *programmed* advances in technology such as the introduction of labor-saving machines and intense specialization of tasks. Increased return on labor investment also requires the development of whole new sciences specialized in gathering, organizating, and utilizing information. Hence we have seen the rise of systems analysis, cybernetics, management science, etc.[8]

The third aspect of the capitalist strategy is ideological control. As the fundamental contradictions of capitalism become more and more intensified, intellectuals of all sorts are called upon to utilize their expertise to justify the existence of those contradictions. The most obvious front is neoclassical economics. Though less obvious, equally important and insidious is science. Thus we see repeated attempts at resurrecting eugenics to justify the existence of deprived individuals. The so-called scientific analyses of Jensen and Herrnstein are only the most recent of such attempts.[9] The current emphasis on problems of overpopulation rather than distribution to explain apparent food and energy shortages is another in a long list of the uses of science to justify a bankrupt ideology.

These three aspects of the capitalist strategy for the use of science are largely concerned with what is frequently termed "applied science." Many scientists claim that they have escaped the possibly oppressive uses of applied research by pursuing so-called basic or pure problems. Two arguments are relevant here. First, even research without immediate or foreseeable practical applications serves to provide a more sophisticated background from which technology can be derived. In fact, our technological society has brought the processes of discovery and application so close together that in many instances they can no longer be separated. Only seven years passed between the recognition that the atomic bomb was theoretically possible and its detonation over Hiroshima and Nagasaki. The transistor went from invention to sales in three years. More recently, research on lasers was barely completed when engineers began using it to design new weapons for the government.

Second, the problem of evaluating basic research does not end with a critique of its applications. Scientific knowledge and products, like other products and services in our society, are marketed for profit. They are not equally distributed to, equally available to, or equally usable by all the people. Instead they are channeled through an organization and distribution of scarcity in such a way as to further define and produce the desired political or economic ends of those in power. For example, computers, satellites, and advertising, to name only a few, all rely on the findings of basic research. These technologies are not owned by, utilized by, or operated for the masses of the people, but instead function in the interests of the government and large corporations.

So far discussed is the way science serves corporate capitalism by emphasizing the *product* of research efforts. However the *methodology* of science is inextricably linked to its goals, and in the United States both reflect the same oppressive social system.

In institutions of basic research such as universities, the research laboratory is organized like a market place. Here research directors work for a "profit" measured in: 1) number of publications, 2) professional esteem, and 3) service to corporate capitalism. Such a profit motive results in a strongly hierarchical framework within the laboratory. The head of the lab usually designs all research projects and publishes all the papers, while the lab assistants are assigned to routine tasks associated with carrying out the experiments. Just as in our system of education, there are "experts" and "ignorant" novices. According to research directors this is the most efficient way of doing science. The professor does not have to "waste" time explaining the reasons for conducting certain experiments or their theoretical underpinnings, since the technicians do not need this information in order to do their assigned tasks.

This elitism within research laboratories mirrors a general mystification of science and technology observed in the rest of society. Most people feel that they lack the information necessary to understand how they are affected by, and how in turn they might affect, technological manipulations and basic science. Scientists have traditionally avoided making understandable information available to all those for whom it might be pertinent. Instead, we are told that it is better to let the professionals take care of things. As a result, our control over many important decisions has been relinquished to various experts. For instance, women are frequently not provided with basic medical information about their bodies, and control is thereby surrendered to drug company researchers and physicians. On a larger scale, the process of mystification insures that only the needs and interests of an elite class of academics will be represented in the funding of research.

Within the laboratory setting, the process of mystification inhibits the lab assistants from participating in important decisions. They are thus dehumanized because they are prevented from developing *conscientizacão* — from participating in the process of analysis and using such a process better to understand the world. The oppressive power structure within laboratories can only be transformed when we decide to maximize something other than a professor's academic prestige and service to corporate capitalism. How different would research methodology be if our goal was to involve everyone in a cooperative search for scientific principles and their application to the benefit of all people?

Science in China: While the power elite in the United States are diametrically opposed to a cooperative ideal, the Chinese seem to be actively forging a cooperative and non-elite science, with the goal of improving the material conditions of their whole society. Within the past few years a number of American scientists have visited China, observed their universities, and talked with Chinese scientists. Their reports indicate that the radically different way of doing science in China derive in part from their socialist political ideology.[10]

As might be expected, many of the principles which guide Chinese scientists are almost the negation of those which influence United States scientists. First, the Chinese believe that all human activity is political. Therefore, there can be no neutral or value free science. Rather than falsely attempting to divorce science from politics, the Chinese strive to devise a scientific methodology and research program consistent with their egalitarian ideology. Pursuant to this goal, the Chinese are attempting to make scientific knowledge and products equally distributed to, equally available to, and equally usable by all the people of their country.

One of the most profound changes instituted during the Cultural Revolution was the attempt to disestablish intellectuals and technical experts as a privileged, elite class. This was effected in part by democratizing the way research institutions are governed. Universities are no longer run by a group of elite professors but rather by elected committees that include ordinary workers, peasants, and students. Scientists are encouraged to do part of their research work at factories and agricultural communes, working with nonscientists on problems directly relevant to the needs of the people. Workers and peasants are invited into research laboratories where they are encouraged to become familiar with the theory and techniques involved in research and to criticize present practices and suggest research projects.

Partly from a political analysis of the negative effects of elitism and partly from a philosophy that values human life above profit, Chinese scientists make little attempt to differentiate between pure and applied science. All science is done in the service to the people, to the end of building a socialist state. Many traditionally "nonapplied" fields are currently finding new application (and sometimes new vigor) through such a political analysis. Ethan Signer, who visited China in 1971, reports that fossil and evolutionary botanists are now working on the geobotany of pollen grains, work useful in petroleum prospecting; bacterial geneticists formerly doing pure research are now developing new strains with better growth characteristics and higher yields for industry; entomologists have switched from esoteric entomology to combating plant pests.

This melding of pure and applied research *superficially* resembles the consulting process seen within United States universities. In this case, university-based researchers whose primary interest is usually in relatively esoteric questions, advise industries concerning particular applied problems. However, the efforts in China to combine pure and applied research differ both in motive and result from the consulting process in the United States. In the United States consulting occurs because the researcher wishes to make more money and the consulting industry wants to increase profits. In China, scientists visit farm communes in order to work on practical problems that will benefit all the people, not just a privileged elite. There are no bonuses for scientists or higher profits for the industry. Rather, the society as a whole benefits, first of all by increased industrial and agricultural production, and secondly by discouraging the development of a scientific elite which would inevitably look after its own interests at the expense of the rest of society.

The methodology and apparent objectives of science in China contrast sharply with that of science in the United States. While science in the United States serves the interests of a small elite class and only a privileged few enjoy the benefits of creative work, the Chinese are evolving a structure of science that serves the needs of their entire society while at the same time involving masses of people in the liberating activities of searching, recreating, and inventing.

Because it is well known that China does not recognize gayness as a valid lifestyle, it may seem contradictory that I would imply we should consider their method of doing science as a possible model. China is a society that still embodies important contradictions, and I believe one of the most significant to be the sex negative attitude which appears to pervade personal relationships. While the Chinese have made significant progress in eliminating the institutionalized sexism which characterized their feudal past, they have yet to recognize the *second* goal of sexual liberation — the recognition of the essential polymorphic perversity of human nature. Nevertheless, I do not believe that their incomplete analysis of sexual liberation should prevent gay people from recognizing and emulating those aspects of their society that do reflect a liberative philosophy. Furthermore, it seems to me that the exhortation of Mao, "Let a hundred flowers bloom, let a hundred schools of thought dispute," will eventually lead the Chinese to a realization that alienation *within* as well as between the sexes inhibits us from realizing our full human potential.

Towards a gay analysis: If the concept of liberation is holistic, thus encompassing sexual liberation as well, gay people in the sciences should consider the implications of a gay analysis for the kind of science they do. I have argued that sexual liberation is inconsistent with those human relationships in which some individuals achieve benefits by subjugating others. With what type of science is sexual liberation most consistent?

A gay analysis implies at least three imperatives for the practice of science. First, and hardly an imperative unique to a gay analysis, the products of science must not be used against human beings. That this is necessary to avoid oppression of some humans by others is tautological. Had science been practiced according to a gay perspective, technology would never have had such a large input into the obscene war crimes perpetrated on the Vietnamese people by the United States government, psychology and genetics would not be used to justify the oppression of black people, and medical mumbo jumbo would not even attempt to deny homosexuals their personal freedom.

Second, absolute priorities must be given to formation of products of scientific work that benefit those involved directly or indirectly in their production. Scientific goals must negate the practice of synthesizing a product from the labors of others in order to exclusively benefit the elite. For example, research resources in the area of transportation technology would be allocated to the development of adequate mass transportation before the development of supersonic transports and lunar landing systems. In the latter cases, the benefits primarily accrue to the owners and managers of large corporations in the form of bloated profits and faster jet travel for executives. Research on mass transit, however, would directly benefit all those who contributed their labor and/or taxes.

Third, a scientific methodology consistent with a gay analysis would include all scientific workers in important decisions as to what research projects are initiated and how they are carried out. More experienced researchers would work collectively with novices, realizing that both groups can make creative contributions while at the same time learning from each other. This collective attitude, in addition to generating a more materially productive science, would likely lead to the development of *conscientizacão* among all participants — the overt awareness not only of a process of analysis, but also of the liberating, humanizing effects of using a process to better understand the world.

These three imperatives are virtual antitheses of the way science is practiced in the United States. Paradoxically, one of the most homophobic societies in the world, China, exhibits a science which appears to be in close accordance with what I have considered to be a correct gay analysis. Yet the emulation of China should not be our goal; its system is not perfect and is embedded in a totally different socio-cultural background than that of the United States. Rather we must forge our own system of doing science, a system which might take its inspiration from a gay analysis. What China has done is to show us that an alternative to the oppressive United States system is a real, practical possibility.

As gay people, people with a fully developed and holistic gay analysis, we must forge ahead to build a gay science. We should seek to develop research projects and a methodology that reflect our goal of human liberation. We should organize to oppose all aspects of the scientific establishment which are counter to our gay analysis.

Developing valid research goals and methodology, as well as organizing opposition to the current scientific establishment, are difficult tasks within the present university structure. Nevertheless, at least one national organization in the United States, Science for the People has been actively organizing scientists in an attempt to expose and counter the elitist and technocratic biases that permeate the scientific and academic establishments. One vehicle for doing this has been the publication of a bimonthly magazine called *Science for the People* (16 Union Sq., Somerville, MA 02143) by a collective of scientific workers. While many gay people have avoided (for good reasons) working with so-called straight left organizations, Science for the People has taken a strong anti-sexist stand in its analysis of the United States scientific establishment. Rather than splinter into all-gay science collectives, it would seem more productive for gay people in science to work with others, both straight and gay, towards what should be our common goal — a radical reorientation of research methods and objectives in the United States.

Conclusion

In the last few years many of the legal restrictions aimed at gays have been abolished in western countries. This trend will likely continue in the future. Superficially one might conclude that this would make it easier for gay people to integrate their analysis of sexual liberation into their everyday lives, making it seem less necessary to drop out in order to live a less oppressive lifestyle. However, as Marcuse and Altman have both pointed out, rather than a reduction in oppression, we are observing a move toward sexual permissiveness without a concomitant increase in the acceptance of our goal of human liberation — greater apparent freedom but freedom manipulated into channels dictated by the norms of corporate capitalism. Sexuality is increasingly becoming a marketable commodity used openly in the advertising media. Thus the oppressive stigmas directed at gays are merely relocated from the courts to Madison Avenue. As Altman puts it, the barely concealed message of contemporary advertisements is, "If you work hard and earn lots of money, you too can have a beautiful man/woman." This repressive "tolerance" hardly produces a climate wherein gays in academia might restructure their careers to fit a liberative model.

What is particularly unfortunate is that many gays seem to have comfortably adjusted to the change in oppressors, partly, it seems, because our new "freedom" has allowed gays to assume more power over others, to become the oppressors of the oppressor. Gay people have internalized the guidelines of the oppressor in a variety of ways. As a reviewer in Milwaukee's GPU News noted, the object change from "chick" to "trick" does not suggest a diminution of sexual exploitation." Similarly, a gay person who continues to teach in an authoritarian way or to participate in a hierarchical and competitive science structure is not integrating a revised and liberated notion of human behavior, but is merely mimicing the old oppressive one. As the stigma attached to being a known homosexual decreases, more and more we can "proudly" take our places on the boards of large corporations and in the front of lecture halls. Stoltenberg has even suggested that this is why male homosexuals have been in the forefront of the gay civil rights movement, since civil rights for gays means primarily that *male* homosexuals will be able to assume all the rights, privileges, and powers belonging to the male gender class in our society.

Hopefully, gays will realize that we cannot assume the "right" and "privilege" to oppress others without at the same time denying our own freedom. Still, it is very difficult to surrender power once offered; as oppressed people, we suffer from a duality which has established itself in our innermost being. We are at one and the same time ourselves and the oppressor whose consciousness we have internalized. The conflict, then, lies in the choice between being wholly ourselves or divided, between ejecting the oppressor or not ejecting the oppressor, between being domesticated by straight society or transforming it.

ACKNOWLEDGEMENTS

I wish to thank Jean Stout, John Vandermeer, Marlene Palmer, Dave Newton, Bruce Steinberg, Vicki Sork, Gayle Ruben, and Doug Futuyma for their collective criticism of the manuscript and for their many helpful suggestions.

NOTES

[1]H. Marcuse, *Eros and Civilization* (Boston: Beacon Press, 1955).

[2]D. Altman, *Homosexuality, Oppression and Liberation* (New York: Avon Books, 1971).

[3]J. Stoltenberg, "Toward Gender Justice." *Win*, Vol. XI, No. 10 (1975), 6-9.

[4]P. Freire, *Pedagogy of the Oppressed* (New York: Herder and Herder, 1968). Two excellent reviews of the book were also consulted: 1) G.A., *Science for the People*, Nov. 1972, 22-24. 2) M. Palmer, V. Sork, and J. Stout, unpublished ms.

[5]For an analysis of why the educational system exists as it does, see: S. Bowles, "Unequal Education and the Reproduction of the Social Division of Labor," *Review of Radical Political Economics*, Vol. 3, No. 2 (Fall/Winter 1971), 1-30.

[6]B. Zimmerman, L. Radinsky, M. Rothenberg, and B. Meyers," Science for the People," 1971. Available from *Science for the People*, 16 Union Sq., Somerville, Ma. 02143. V.I. Lenin, *Imperialism: The Highest Stage of Capitalism,* (New York: International Publishers, 1939).

[7]Surplus product is here used in the Marxian sense of the excess labor time which is expropriated from the worker by the capitalist.

[8]H. Braverman, *Labor and Monopoly Capital* (New York: Monthly Review Press, 1974).

[9]G. Allen, "A History of Eugenics in the Class Struggle," *Science for the People* (March, 1974).

[10]E. Signer, "Biological Science in China." *Science for the People*, Vol. 3, No. 4, Sept. 1971, 3-5, 15-19. See also their report in *Science: China Walks on Two Legs* (New York: Avon, 1974).

[11]*G.P.U. News*, (November, 1974), 11.

X.
SOCIOLOGY
AND POLITICAL SCIENCE

Coming Out:
Toward a Social Analysis[1]

By John Kyper

To be homosexual has traditionally meant an invisibility no less destructive for its being, in part, self-imposed. My most humiliating memory is of feeling forced to laugh at a fag joke, because I didn't dare to expose my homosexuality by objecting to it. Denying one's own reality is a universal gay experience in our culture, and thus the cycle of invisibility, alienation, and superstition feeds on itself.

Affirming my homosexuality was a lonely struggle, against a pervasive social lie. Only recently has this cycle become the object of a political movement. Gay liberation begins with self-affirmation, expanding to an analysis of oppressive myths and of the larger society that stigmatizes homosexual expression.

I

Coming Out: A Significant Individual Choice

No concept is as vital to understanding the gay liberation movement as that of "coming out." This is the name for the process by which an individual discovers his/her homosexuaity, and then integrates it as part of the personality.

Depending upon personal values, outlook on life, and social environment, coming out can be either to one's betterment or detriment. To an earlier generation of homosexuals, the taunt that echoes throughout *The Boys in the Band* — "Show me a happy homosexual and I'll show you a gay corpse!" — had the ring of truth. Many still think of their homosexuality as a burden. To gay liberationists, however, coming out is an emotional catharsis resembling the evangelical experience of being "saved." It is a turning point marking the revolt against years of indoctrination and discarding the sham of pretended heterosexuality.

"Come out" is a traditional term of the homosexual subculture that dates back indefinitely. Its origin is subject to speculation, for homosexual history is difficult to document.

Our problem, then, comes back to this, that we have been denied a history because we were not supposed to exist. The history books have been written by those who shared the white, American, heterosexual male consciousness, defining everything in terms of this model. Blacks and women, at least, were too obvious to be ignored, but their role has been minimized and their heroes largely ridiculed or forgotten.

Gays lack even this token presence. We are a non-people, denied heroes. Historical and literary figures have been sanitized, to obscure the stigma of "deviancy." I did not know until nine years after his death that Dag Hamiskjold was homosexual. E.M. Forster did not feel it safe to publish his novel *Maurice* or his other homosexual stories during his lifetime. And those who have been long dead, like Willa Cather or Horatio Alger, evoke sensation upon their discovery.[2] Accepted reality ignored them.

This lack of heroes (role models) has had disastrous consequences for an incalculable number of homosexual women and men. Denied positive images of homosexuality as they were growing up, they despised their feelings and thus themselves. Cultural propaganda about the "unnaturalness" of homosexuality — whether in the form of religious hysteria, political innuendo, or patronizing tolerance — insures that most will encounter deep feelings of guilt while exploring this forbidden path, seeing only the sleazy/grotesque stereotypes of the "typical homosexual."

Societal pressures discourage coming out. It is much easier to pass as a member of "straight society" — truly a silent majority of the homosexual population! The state of personal/sexual repression is commonly called "being in the closet." Its manifestations can include complete sexual denial, or engaging in homosexual acts but lying to friends and perhaps even rationalizing to oneself.

The fear of losing one's job forces most homosexuals to be discrete. A friend who resented having to lie once referred to the syndrome of the "Monday morning pronouns," i.e., changing the gender of his sexual partner when talking to fellow workers. Thus the homosexual population is assumed negligible because it is largely invisible.

A generation later, it is difficult for us to imagine the uproar that greeted the publication of Alfred Kinsey's *Sexual Behavior in the Human Male*. Most Americans could accept, reluctantly, the realization that their heterosexual mores bore little resemblance to their professed morality. But the big shocker was the revelation that 37 percent of the white adult male population had had some homosexual experience. Of all the statistics contained in the "Kinsey Report," those detailing the prevalence of homosexual behavior were among the most violently attacked; for if it could be shown that this kind of activity was so common, how could it be dismissed as "abnormal" any longer?[3]

Among homosexuals, too, Kinsey was sensational — and some saw a potential constituency in these statistics. The German Scientific Humanitarian movement, beginning in the 1860's, was the first attempt to organize homosexuals as a political force. In America, however, the first faltering attempts date only from the 1920's. A number of short-lived groups were formed in the following decades, some of them with colorful names like "Legion of the Damned" and "Knights of the Clocks."[4]

What was to be known as the "homophile movement," and later as gay liberation, evolved from these modest beginnings. In 1950-51 two events of decisive importance occurred: Using the pseudonym of Donald Webster Cory, Edward Sagarin published *The Homosexual in America*, the first book to view homosexuals as a minority group. And in Los Angeles the first Mattachine Society was formed as a secret society.[5] Legend has it that it was formed in a closed room, with the blinds drawn, and lookouts posted at the door.

The early 1950's, an era when Joseph McCarthy was routing the "Communist homosexuals" from the State Department, was not an opportune time to start a movement. As a result, the Mattachine was defensively anti-Communist, seeking accommodation with middle class respectability.[6] Growth was slow for the first dozen years. With the first gay picketings in the mid-1960's — of the White House, the Pentagon, the Civil Service Commission, and Independence Hall — "gay pride" was first defined. At a time when the conservative homophile leaders were passing on to be replaced by militant activists, "coming out" was acquiring its present political connotations.

The symbolic turning point in gay history was the now-mythologized Christopher Street rebellion in New York in June, 1969. The event is celebrated annually by gay liberationists. It began innocously, with an early morning raid on the Stonewall Inn, a popular Greenwich Village gay bar. For years homosexuals in New York had been resigned to such raids, but this time it was different. Instead of fleeing or submitting to arrest, the patrons fought the police, and they were joined by their brothers and sisters from neighboring bars. Rioting continued for two nights.

Christopher Street was of course not as much a cause as a consequence of the new militancy. It was a catalytic event, like Rosa Parks' refusal to sit in the back of the bus, which touched off a decade of black civil rights protests. The new consciousness had been transformed from an elite to the mass of the gay community. As Allen Ginsberg exulted shortly after the riot, "They've lost that wounded look that fags all had ten years ago."[7]

To learn about the Stonewall — four months later in a *Newsweek* article "Police and the third sex" — was the knowledge I needed to come out. I realized I was neither alone nor different. To come out, at 22, was one of the most important personal decisions I have ever made. While no one person's experience is "typical," a personal account has value as a summary of some of the aspects of oppression and the decision to act against it.

My homosexuality was something I was never supposed to acknowledge as a part of myself. Instead, I was brought up with the expectation that I would eventually marry and have children. No adult I knew could admit the possibility that I should differ; that I might desire other males was never a plausible alternative. Certainly there was nothing that my parents could have less wanted me to become — except, perhaps, a murderer or a thief. And so I was told tales of dirty old men who might want to molest me: "Never accept a ride from a stranger."

Throughout my adolescence I received similarly undesirable images of homosexuality. I grew up in New Hampshire and Vermont, where as far as I knew, there were no homosexuals. Once I had an erection in the shower after gym class, and the ridicule was painful. That I was different from my contemporaries was a realization I desperately wished to evade. "Queer," I learned, is an epithet as vicious as "nigger," but I could find no one who shared my subversive passion. My queerness was a badge of shame that I alone felt, and I suffered alone, in secrecy.

Not until I was twenty did I begin to face the truth. During a brief psychiatric hospitalization, I was able to admit to myself the reality of my long-repressed feelings. The problem of what to do continued to bedevil me for two more years.

As I matured, I found that my most difficult obstacle was my alienation. I was told that I was not alone — but I could not believe it. That there were millions of "normal" looking people who were also gay meant little to me. How could I relate to people I could not recognize? I saw only the stereotype of the "limpwristed fairy" and the cruel bitchery of *The Boys in the Band* (presented to the public as an enlightened view of its subject). Neither of these suggested a lifestyle that I wanted to emulate.

My anomie was aggravated by the near-invisibility of the institutions of the homosexual subculture. The gay bars proved hard to find, even in large cities. I saw in their deliberate obscurity the judgment of society and that I had no right to explore this way of life. Its shame and secretiveness were apparent after several unpleasant incidents of being propositioned, while hitchhiking and in bus stations, as well as a couple of bad sexual experiences in YMCA's. If homosexual activity occurred in anonymity, as I assumed, how could individuals who had such impersonal contacts maintain their self respect?

In my confusion I allowed myself to be influenced by the prevailing psychiatric opinion, which declared that I would be happier and healthier were I to become heterosexual. I made the mistake of reading Albert Ellis' pretentious "definitive" book, *Homosexuality: Its Causes and Cure* — and taking it seriously. His arguments provided the prop for my self doubts that I had to repudiate before I could come out.

Albert Ellis is a former Chief Psychologist for the State of New Jersey, who has gone into private practice and has written numerous books on sexual behavior. In the 1950's he was controversial for advocating the repeal of laws against homosexuality, as well as the abolition of nearly all sexual taboos. Liberal though he may have been, his understanding of homosexuality is limited. Like other practitioners of the "gay is sick" school, his observations are largely confined to his patients. A few years ago at a zap organized by members of the Rutgers Student Homophile League, he admitted that he knew only "four or five" gays outside a therapeutic environment.[8]

Ellis condemns homosexuality with slippery, circular logic. He cites the polymorphousness of human sexuality and blames exclusive homosexuals (though *not* exclusive heterosexuals) for limiting themselves to one kind of sexual outlet. Furthermore, they are biased because they "never gave heterosexuality a full chance" and are therefore unqualified to decide for themselves — as witnessed by their unwillingness to submit to treatment. Most curiously, Ellis maintains that gays are childish and self-defeating because their sexual activities are against the law![9]

In other words, it's sick because it's sick, because it's sick. Ellis' dogmatism is thinly veiled beneath a superstructure of nonsequiturs and unsupported generalizations. But at the time I read this I was intimidated by his arrogance and by his professional qualifications. It did not occur to me that he, too, was biased, by his heterosexuality.

Living in a society that condemned my feelings, hearing all manner of authorities pontificate upon my "deviation" — naturally, I was inclined to think myself sick because I could find no opposing view. But I could not suppress my homosexuality. I was experiencing a personal struggle that became, at times, nearly unbearable: What did I really want to do? Were the opinions I held about my sexuality *my* opinions, or had they been imposed upon me by society? Was I "sick" only because I believed I was? The influence of my upbringing was still so strong that I felt incapable of answering these questions for myself.

When at last I accepted my homosexuality, I was affirming my integrity to live my own life. I had decided to stop rationalizing because, at the deepest level of my consciousness, I knew that I did not want to change. Thus, I reasoned, if these were my feelings, why should I deny them? Certainly by expressing my love for other men, I would be harming no one else. Who possessed the authority to tell me I would be harming myself? Such an explanation of my "disease" was a pseudoscientific rationalization of popular superstition.

No longer having to pretend was an immediate relief. My first act of coming out was to walk into a gay bar, something I had never dared to do before. To discover that gay people were more than a stereotype — they were fellow human beings who felt like me and had known the humiliation of being "queer" — was a liberating experience. Once I saw that I was neither alone nor exceptional, I began to realize that my sexual orientation was not the most important fact of my existence. I remained free to develop my own lifestyle for myself.

I came out at the end of 1969, a year when I was making other decisions crucial for the direction of my adulthood: trying marijuana for the first time, dropping out of the University of Vermont and moving to Boston, becoming a conscientious objector. For over five years I have been involved in Boston's gay movement. Whatever difficulties I have encountered for my outspokenness, I have never regretted my initial decision to come out. The price of my outspokenness has never equaled the pain of denying myself.

II

Gay Mythology

Coming out is gradual and ongoing. It encompasses not only the realization of one's homosexuality and consequent proclamation of friends, but also a long-term education. In this gay education, the pervasive American myths about homosexuality must be continually challenged.

The "pansy" and the "dyke," for many, still represent the entirety of gay existence. These individuals, it is assumed, had dominating mothers, they lead wretched lives, they hate themselves, and they despise the opposite sex. Sometimes people express surprise upon learning that I am homosexual. I do not look or act "like one of *them*," and my life's pattern does not follow the stereotype of how deviates are supposed to deviate from normal heterosexual development.

Mircea Eliade has defined several characteristics of preliterate myth that I want to adapt for my definition of "myth": It is considered absolutely true and sacred. Adherents believe because they believe. Empirical evidence is used only to bolster myth, never to contradict it. In addition, it attempts to explain how something came into existence, in this case a pattern of behavior that reflects the mysteriousness of human sexuality. Adherents "live" myth by internalizing it, and they believe that homosexuality can be prevented once its origin is known. [10]

The key assumption underlying such myth is that homosexuality is an aberration caused by something that went wrong in childhood, that no one would have freely chosen it as a way of life. Conventional psychiatric theory and popular belief both have begun with this assumption. There has been little corresponding speculation about the "cause" of heterosexuality, the desired form of sexual functioning.

Perhaps the most dangerous and intractable myth about gays — especially gay males — is that we are "child molesters" or at least a bad influence to have around children and adolescents. The belief that we "pervert" the innocent young is a carryover from traditional myths linking homosexuality and witchcraft. [11] The irrationality with which it is held reflects public ignorance about how individuals "become" homosexual, and is thus a misunderstanding of both homosexuality and child/adolescent sexuality.

This is a myth whose repercussions I have experienced since the first time I was warned against taking rides from strangers. (That old admonition, sure enough, still finds a response when I am propositioned while hitchhiking.) Twenty years later, in 1972, I was refused a job as an aide at a Boston state hospital, judged "not suitable to work with young people." I had become one of the people my parents had warned me against.

I attempted to reason with the nursing supervisor who had disciminated against me. A lawyer and a psychiatrist called her on my behalf, to be told, "We can't have them around our young patients." That there were probably dozens of homosexuals employed at her hospital had not occurred to her. Like several friends who are tenured teachers of the Boston School Department, these employees would be subject to immediate dismissal were their homosexuality known.

One of the classic literary expositions of the myth is the episode "Hands" from Sherwood Anderson's 1919 novel *Winesburg, Ohio*. It is the moving tale of Wing Biddlebaum, a small town school teacher. He loves his students and is devoted to them. "And then the tragedy. A half-witted boy of the school became enamored of the young teacher. In his bed at night he imagined unspeakable things and in the morning went forth to tell his dreams as facts.

Strange, hideous accusations fell from his loose-hung lips. Through the Pennsylvania town went a shiver. Hidden, shadowy doubts that had been in men's minds . . . were galvanized into beliefs." [12] The men of the town beat the teacher, attempted to lynch him, and he fled.

In 1955-56 Boise, Idaho, experienced this tragedy on a more sophis- ticated and widespread scale. This scandal began with the arrest of three men — a freight line worker, a shoe repairman, and a clothing store clerk — on morals charges, lewd and lascivious conduct with minors, and infamous crimes against nature. The Boise *Statesman* quoted the county probation officer that "about 100 boys" were involved in a homosexual ring. [13]

The hysteria had just begun. One of those arrested pled guilty in the hope of receiving psychiatric care —and was sentenced to life imprisonment. Then a prominent local banker was arrested. The *Statesman* editorialized:

> The decent foundations of the Boise community were jolted beyond description recently with the arrest of three local men on morals charges involving young boys. It did not seem possible that this community ever harbored homosexuals to ravage our youth . . . It might not be a bad idea for Boise parents to keep an eye on the whereabouts of their off springs. To date a number of boys have been victimized by these perverts. The greatest tragedy of all is the fact that young boys so involved grow into manhood with the same inclinations of those who are called homosexuals. [14]

Over the next month a dozen more men were arrested. Most were eventually convicted and given sentences ranging from six months to 15 years.

Before it ran its course, the witchhunt perpetrated more injustices: A local teacher panicked and left immediately for San Francisco when he read that the prosecutor had promised to "eliminate" all homosexuals: "Enemies of society — that's what we were called. I remember very well. So I asked myself, where will this stop? I've never had any kind of relations except with consenting adults. But is Boise going to be calm enough to draw the difference? Will they *look* for the difference? No, I knew they'd go after anybody who wears a ring on their pinky." [15] Bearing out his logic, four of the men were arrested for committing homosexual acts with other adults.

The boys themselves were not as innocent as the city fathers wanted to believe. A psychiatrist who was later able to interview 32 of them remarked:

> I don't think that there was one among them who grew up to be a homosexual. Most of the kids who had participated had done so for

a combination of kicks and rebellion against parental authority. Some did it for money . . . others did it for power. That's right, power! I remember very well one child telling me how it made him feel important to stand there, with his arms crossed, while an "old man" as he called him got down on his knees in order — as the boys put it — "to blow me."[16]

To complete the hypocrisy of the whole affair, one of the defendants named as a partner the son of a city councilman who had been clamoring for more prosecutions.[17]

Seventeen years later the discovery of the murder of the 28 boys in Houston demonstrated how little public understanding has changed. Homosexuality and pederasty were both commonly confused with homicide. To many, I am sure, Dean Corll was an object lesson of the dirty old man who lusts after boys. Misquoting a Baylor University clinical psychologist in a telephone interview, United Press laid it all to "the syndrome of homosexuality, sexual abuse, and eventual homicide."[18]

Dallas police soon announced the uncovering of a nationwide "boy prostitution ring." *Newsweek* rhapsodized about the "possible links to Corll [that] added one last layer of depravity to the whole case." Only toward the end did the article admit, deviously, that the two stories were unconnected! [19]

Only a year after the Houston mass murders, ABC television scheduled a "Marcus Welby, M.D." episode featuring the rape of a fourteen year old boy by his science teacher. The good Dr. Welby spends the bulk of the show reassuring the boy that his "manhood" has not been lost. Gay liberationists around the country demanded that the show not be aired because it perpetuated a dangerous sterotype. Although ABC decided to air the episode as scheduled, gay pressure persuaded affiliates in seven cities, including Boston and Philadelphia, not to show it; and eleven national sponsors cancelled off the program.

In a front page editorial, "See Marcus Welby on T.V. Tonight," Editor William Loeb of the Manchester, New Hampshire, *Union-Leader* declared that the show "presents the perfect answer to those people who say that homosexuals are just innocent people trying to 'do their own thing.' This shows the terrible consequences of allowing such individuals to be in contact with young people."[20]

Not surprisingly, the gay liberation movement has become the object of such wrath, and the myth of the "homosexual child molester" has been embellished into a conspiracy to subvert the youth of America. The behavior of William Loeb is an excellent case in point. Although his extreme invective puts him in a class by himself as a publisher, the *Union-Leader* has considerable influence upon New Hampshire thought and politics. The extensive "Letters" page demonstrates that his views on homosexuality are widely shared (and disputed).

For several years Loeb had slandered homosexuals from time to time. But with the establishment of a Gay Students Organization (GSO) at the University of New Hampshire, he escalated his attack. (The morality of UNH students has been a preoccupation of his for years. Once he reprinted in full an offending poem from a student publication, to demonstrate how "obscene" it was.) When the Student Senate recognized the GSO in the spring of 1973, Loeb replied with an editorial entitled "Pansies at Durham." Joining in the attack was Governor Meldrim Thomson, a man whose repressive politics resemble Loeb's.[21]

In November, after a GSO-sponsored dance, Thomson had the University administration cancel the Organization's right to hold social functions. The GSO responded by sponsoring on campus the Boston production of the play *Coming Out*. During the play copies of the Boston publication *Fag Rag* were distributed, which contained a satirical article, "How to Proselytize."

The *Union-Leader* viewed the article in another light. Confusing GSO and *Fag Rag* for its readers, a banner news story read:

> The apparent aim of the "Gay Students" at the University of New Hampshire, to entice and corrupt other students and males of surrounding communities to engage in homosexual activities, came to light last week on the Durham campus . . . Homosexual students passed out a newspaper called the "Fag Rag" which had articles encouraging the "Gay Students" to corrupt other males, not so inclined, to participate in homosexual acts.[22]

Governor Thomson sought to ban *Fag Rag*, and Loeb followed with another front page editorial: "As revealed by the unspeakably filthy publications distributed by homosexuals at the University of New Hampshire, their purpose is to seduce as many of their fellow students as they can. Like any diseased bacteria, they want to spread through healthy bodies."[23]

The theme of homosexuals "perverting" innocent children and adolescents ran through the *Union-Leader's* coverage of the controversy it had helped to start. When United States Judge Hugh Bownes ruled that the GSO had all the rights and privilege of any other student organization, Loeb countered with a front page banner: "Perverts Will Flock to UNH," and an editorial, "Judicial Madness": "It has been one devil of a bad week for the decent people of New Hampshire who are trying to protect their children and themselves, but especially their children, from the corruption of those who would try to turn New Hampshire and the rest of the United States into a Sodom and Gomorrah."[24]

The GSO controversy generated numerous letters to the editor of the *Union-Leader* (which boasts that it "publishes more Letters to the Editors than any other newspaper in the United States"). Most of them were hostile to the GSO, as the following:

> I read three papers every day . . . and very seldom does a day go by when I don't read something about the depredation of boys and young men by homosexuals. Have you [Judge Bownes] forgotten the mass murders of 27 boys and young men in the Houston, Texas, area last year? Have you forgotten the homosexual ring in Times Square in New York City that lured run away boys into their net and sold them into male prostitution? The cases of abuse of young boys by homosexuals is endless . . .[25]

William Loeb and Meldrim Thomson could not stop the GSO, but they had exploited popular prejudice for their own benefit.[26]

The myth was exploited again, more successfully, a few months later in New York City. After several years of gay lobbying, a bill that would have prohibited discimination on the basis of sexual preference was finally voted out of the City Council's General Welfare Committee. Approval by the entire Council is considered a formality for bills voted out of committee. But then the Uniformed Fire Officers' Association, AFL-CIO, ran a full-page ad in the *Daily News*, claiming that the bill would, among other things, corrupt the young. The Catholic Archdiocese of New York responded with the allegation that the bill would fatally weaken family life. Most of the Council members were up for reelection in 1974, and the Fire Officers and the Archdiocese were able to stir up enough hysteria to cause the bill's narrow defeat.[27]

In March, 1975, Ottawa, Ontario, experienced a witchhunt reminiscent of the Boise affair. City police began by issuing sensationalized reports of a "homosexual vice ring" involving youths aged 11 to 17. Although police insisted they were out to end prostitution, only two of the 18 men they arrested — the organizer of the "ring" and his assistant — were charged with anything connected with prostitution. Of the 16 customers arrested, 13 were charged with having sex with persons between 16 and 21, and no one was charged with any acts with anyone under 14. Ottawa newspapers published names, addresses, and occupations of those arrested. One was a civil servant, who jumped 13 stories to his death the day his name appeared.[28]

Demonstrating the changes in the two decades since Boise, Gays of Ottawa picketed the police and the newspapers to protest the disciminatory treatment of the case; and they were able to enlist support from outside the gay community. One of their targets was the Canadian Criminal Code, which stipulates 21 as its age of consent for homosexual acts — and 14 for heterosexual acts.[29]

The idea that children and adolescents have any right to sexual exploration is bitterly resisted. In July, 1972, a Toronto gay liberation newspaper *The Body Politic* published an article making just such a suggestion. Entitled "Of Men and Little Boys," it stated in conclusion that "if the child is to cease being property, if it is to attain to full civil liberties, if it is to achieve economic independence, if it is to relate meaningfully to society as a whole, then of necessity it must move away from the family unity of the Christian West. Anyone who leads the child into sexual awareness and exploration is helping to do just that."[30]

All three Toronto dailies attacked the article. One writer editorialized: "The homosexual seduction of a child is a loathsome, pernicious thing" and suggested that *The Body Politic* be prosecuted for counseling a crime. In the following issue the author replied that the press hysteria had confirmed his argument:

> No one commented on the topic of child sexuality, though full acceptance of the child as a sexual being was essential to the development of my arguments. I think this was partly because the press was more interested in defaming the homosexual population than in giving any serious thought to the topic of children's rights; however, we must face the fact that the contemporary mind in general refuses to accept the reality of the horny, hard-pricked 4 year old boy, or the 6 year old girl rocking blissfully on the arm of a chair. It is still the innocence = purity and purity = chastity equation which orders our thinking in these matters.[31]

Two years later the Toronto *Star* cited the article in refusing to accept a classified advertisement from *The Body Politic*.

Pre-1969 homophile groups had condemned all sexual activity with minors. Their goal had been to legitimize homosexuality only between consenting adults — then a seemingly hopeless goal. Their position was a tactical necessity at that stage of the struggle.[32]

What justification has the myth of the "homosexual child molester"? In their 1965 study *Sex Offenders*, members of the Institute for Sex Research concluded that homosexuality per se bore no more correlation to offenses vs. children than did heterosexuality. Of the categories of homosexual offenders studied, "the homosexual offender vs. children is the least oriented toward his own sex." Furthermore, physical force was seldom used (as opposed to heterosexual offenses vs. children); the boy was likely as not a friend of his adult partner; and in half of the cases studied the boys encouraged the offenders.[33] Dr. Wardell Pomeroy, a co-author of the study, elaborated that "many children sixteen, or even fourteen, or twelve, are adult enough to know exactly what they are doing."[34]

Alfred Kinsey ascertained that sexual play frequently begins early in children, and homosexual play is not uncommon.[35] The belief that childhood seduction will cause an individual to become homosexual later on in life is an oversimplification.

> Boys who have already acquired homosexual tendencies are of course likely to seek homosexual contacts with others of their own age. Quite frequently also they seek sexual contacts with older youths and men; indeed, in many cases involving the "seduction" of a youth by an older man it is very difficult to specify which of the two is really the seducer. But it is certain that when a boy actively seeks the sexual attentions of another younger or older male the resulting experience is the *effect* of his homosexual tendencies, not the *cause* of them. It is not too much to imagine that in those cases in which a boy has actually been seduced by an older male, it is the boy's compliance that makes the seduction possible. Most youths who have not already developed homosexual tendencies probably fail to respond to seduction and either remain entirely indifferent to homosexual advances or respond with aggression and hostility.[36]

The enduring potency of the myth is traceable to the mysterious fascination that homosexuality holds to those who know little about it. The process of coming out, how an individual realizes his/her homosexuality, is the least understood aspect of gay life. Ignorance encourages people to view the homosexual community as a sinister "fraternity," which becomes a self-fulfilling prophecy by the ostracism and persecution that such an attitude encourages.

Once during a police interrogation, the officer questioning me asked awkwardly how long I had "been homosexual." I believe that I said I had come out a few years before. Had I taken his question literally, I would have made the absurd (to him) reply that I had "been homosexual" since my earliest childhood fantasies of other little boys.

III
Straight Pathology

Until recently, few had challenged the anti-gay prejudice that pervades American society. Psychiatric and legal evaluations of homosexuality, which were almost uniformly negative, are now slowly changing due to pressure from gay liberationists.

Homosexuality has traditionally been the subject of scientific (and pseudo-scientific) study, but the same has not been held true for the prejudice against homosexuality. There has been little examination of the motives behind "queer bashing," a popular sport of urban gangs. Or behind Joseph McCarthy's crusade against the "communist homosexuals" in the State Department. Only a few years ago did Dr. George Weinberg coin the term "homophobia":

> I am describing a clear-cut but prevalent form of phobia. It has not been identified as such by the experts because the sufferer's viewpoint jives with most experts' opinions that homosexuals are disturbed . . .
> What causes homophobia — the dread of being in close quarters with homosexuals — and in the case of homosexuals themselves, self loathing? Volumes have been written — by psychologists, sexologists, anthropologists, sociologists, and physiologists — on homosexuality, its origins and its development. This is because in most western civilizations, homosexuality is itself considered a problem; our unwarranted distress over homosexuality is not classified as a problem because it is still a majority point of view. Homophobia is still part of the conventional American attitude. [37]

Weinberg traced its causes to five different sources: the Judaeo-Christian condemnation of homosexuality, the secret fear of being homosexual, repressed envy of homosexuals' supposed greater freedom. They are considered a threat to societal values, and they lack the vicarious immortality of children and family. [38]

It was appropriate that copies of *Society and the Healthy Homosexual* should be presented to members of the Massachusetts Legislature during the

Commerce and Labor Committee's February, 1974, hearing on bills that would have prohibited discrimination against homosexuals in employment, housing, credit, mortgages, and insurance. Two months later the Senate sent S. 1585 to amost certain death in the Senate Rules Committee. Taking a cue from the book, reporter Jeffrey Allen of the Boston *Globe* commented upon the defeat of the 1974 gay rights bill with a column entitled, "Homophobia bars path of bills to help gays."[39]

Since 1970 members and supporters of Boston's gay movement (and gay groups from throughout the state) have annually testified before legislative committees on behalf of a set of bills that would decriminalize consensual homosexual (and heterosexual) acts and would extend existing civil rights laws. (I have been a participant in several of these hearings, testifying three times.) Their first efforts went almost unnoticed, but their lobbying has become increasingly effective. While not successful enough to push through these bills, they were able to influence the 1974 election campaign and help defeat several anti-gay candidates. The "gay vote," hitherto a nebulous concept, was coming into its own; and the 1975 session saw these bills come yet closer to passage.

The most consistent target of gay lobbying has been Chapter 272 of the Massachusetts General Laws, entitled "Crimes Against Chastity, Morality, Decency and Good Order." Section 34 punishes with twenty years' imprisonment "the abominable and detestable crime against nature" (commonly defined as sodomy, or anal intercourse). This law has been in its present form since 1836, and its antecedents date to 1641. Section 35, enacted in 1887, prescribes five years or a $1000 fine for undefined "unnatural and lascivious acts."[40] A companion, 35a, gives a stiffer penalty for acts performed "with a child of sixteen or under." Also outlawed in Chapter 272 (though with less severe penalties): fornication, adultery, lascivious cohabitation — and blasphemy.

Such laws would be laughable were it not for their tragic implications. Traditionally in Massachusetts, the only legal form of sexual activity has been intercourse between a married husband and wife, without contraceptives. It would be impossible and undesirable to apprehend the multitudes of people who have violated 272. Whatever enforcement is made will necessarily be discriminatory, against those few who were unlucky enough to get caught.

The best known victim of these laws was Edward Rastellini. In June, 1968, he was arrested under Sections 34 and 35a for (supposedly) performing sodomy on a 16-year-old hustler with whom he was friends. He spent two years without trial in Charles Street Jail and was finally discovered by Bill Baird, the birth control advocate. Baird arranged for his bail, but Rastellini was found guilty and sentenced to five-to-fifteen years at Massachusetts Correctional Institute Walpole. He was the victim of other inmates because of his homosexual offense and the mistaken belief (spread by the guards) that he was in prison for child rape. On November 7, 1973, Edward Rastellini was stabbed to death at MCI Bridgewater.[41]

Few cases are as extreme or as sensational. More commonplace in Massachusetts are arrests by police entrapment, at Interstate highway rest areas and in public toilets. (Throughout 1974 there was a series of arrests at Jordan Marsh's downtown Boston store.) Rather than actual imprisonment, victims of entrapment face the more realistic prospect of public ridicule and loss of job. In September, 1973, eleven men were arrested in a single day in a State Police stakeout in Brockton. The local *Enterprise* published the names and occupations of the eleven, including two high school teachers. When telephoned, a spokesman for the newspaper replied that "they were criminals and should be treated as such," and hung up.[42]

Unnatural and lascivious acts, Section 35, is a statute commonly used in such arrests, although violators are often charged with other, or additional, felonies and misdemeanors, including open and gross lewdness, soliciting and disorderly conduct. Richard Rubino is a Boston attorney who has handled numerous homosexual-related cases over the last five years. He represented Rastellini before he was killed, but the bulk of his gay caseload has been entrapment arrests. He estimates that these arrests occur "at least two or three times a week" in Jordan Marsh and on the Interstates.[43]

On November 1, 1974, the Supreme Judicial Court of the Commonwealth ruled that Section 35 could not be enforced against sexual acts performed in private between consenting adults. Ironically, the unanimous decision was made while upholding the conviction of a man who had forced a woman to perform fellatio upon him. The defendant had argued that "unnatural and lascivious acts" was unconstitutionally vague, and the Court restricted its application to cases of force.[44]

The full scope of this ruling is not yet clear. Elaine Noble (who four days later became the first acknowledged homosexual to win an election, to the Massachusetts House) felt that the ruling was not directly applicable to gays, using the narrowest, heterosexual interpretation of the Court's action. But she saw it as a stepping stone that can help get rid of the law, which can be cited in a possible test case and in future repeal attempts.[45] In the case of an entrapment arrest since the ruling, Richard Rubino won acquittal for a client who had been charged with soliciting to perform an unnatural act.[46]

Reportedly, the first attempts to change the sex laws occurred in the 1950's, with the singlehanded lobbying of Prescott Townsend (who, despite his eccentricities, is commonly credited as Boston's first gay liberationist). [47] But the movement's active lobbying dates back only five years, to a February, 1970 hearing in front of the Judiciary Committee. Representatives of the Homophile Union of Boston (HUB), the Daughters of Bilitis (DOB), and the Student Homophile League (SHL) appeared to testify on behalf of bills submitted by Bill Baird to repeal sections 34, 35, 18 (fornication), and 36 (blasphemy). Their efforts rated one sentence in the Boston *Globe*, and the bills were quietly tabled. [48]

In the next two years Baird's petitions suffered a similar fate. This was a time of slow growth for Boston's gay movement, when many local activists (myself included) felt frustrated and discouraged by the activities of gay liberationists in smaller cities, like Minneapolis and Rochester, and of course in New York.

By 1972 the situation had begun to change. There developed a new self-confidence among the gay community, reflected in growing political activism and the growth of institutions like the Homophile Community Health Service. In November, Barney Frank, a former aid to Mayor Kevin White and U.S. Congressman Michael Harrington, was elected a state Representative, from the heavily gay district of Beacon Hill and the Back Bay, on a platform that included the pledge to introduce gay rights legislation.

Rep. Frank kept his word and introduced three bills: One would have repealed various sex laws, and the others would have extended existing anti-discrimination statutes to include "sexual preference." The latter two were the first gay antidiscrimination bills introduced in Massachusetts, and their February, 1973 hearing in the Commerce and Labor Committee received sympathetic coverage in the Boston *Globe* and on WNAC-TV. Although none of these bills got beyond committee,the gay cause was attracting increasing support and sympathy, especially from liberal-activist groups like Citizens for Participation in Political Action (CPPAX), the National Organization for Women, and the Civil Liberties Union of Massachusetts.

Until this time legislators simply ignored gay demands. In September, 1973 Elaine Noble, HUB, and DOB organized Gay Americans Day. Gays from all over Massachusetts converged on the State House to lobby among their senators and representatives. A few sentaors and representatives were openly hostile: Sen. Francis X. McCann (D-Cambridge) snapped, "I voted against it in the past and also will in the future. Get lost!" Another one remarked: "If I were a landlord, I wouldn't rent to homosexuals for fear of my children." But most listened politely, and a few soon announced their support for gay rights. [49]

In 1974 a package of gay bills was again introduced by Barney Frank and by several other sympathetic legislators. This was a gubernatorial election year, and gays eagerly took on the task of lobbying for legislative support — aided by the improved communication of the weekly *Gay Community News,* and by the psychological boost of Elaine Noble's candidacy for Representative from Boston's Fenway neighborhood, another heavily gay district. But the increased visibility also meant a more vocal opposition and more blatant attempts to dodge the issue.

The Commerce and Labor Committee approved the antidiscrimination bills after a hearing in which witnesses (including myself) documented examples of discrimination, sending the bills to the Senate floor. The Judiciary Committee, however, was openly hostile to H. 2601, which would have been decriminalized various consensual sexual acts. Some legislators at the March 20, 1974 hearing were concerned about the effect of legalization upon children and felt that repeal was unnecessary because the law was so seldom enforced (even though Richard Rubino testified about the Rastellini case). One Committee member, Rep. Charles Robert Doyle (D-West Roxbury), told Barney Frank that he was "proud to say I had a proper Jesuit education." Not surprisingly, the bill received an adverse report. The Committee that day was much more sympathetic toward Attorney General Robert Quinn's testimony on behalf of a toughened pornography law.[50]

After the Commerce and Labor Committee hearings, the antidiscrimination bills were consolidated into S. 1585, then voted into the Senate Rules Committee, where it died. H. 5863, which would have prohibited discrimination in the Civil Service, had a more interesting history: On May 8th the Bill was passed by the House on a voice vote because of its inconspicuous title, "An act to prohibit discrimination on certain preferences under the Civil Service Law." Immediately Rep. William Carey (D-Mission Hill, Boston) moved to reconsider, saying that it was "up to us to save the morals of the Commonwealth, or we may as well close up shop." The bill was reconsidered and defeated, but the 139-79 margin was considerably closer than gay rights advocates had expected.[51]

Until recently the Legislature had refused to take gay rights bills seriously. The opposition can be attributed to homophobia and a related fear of constituent reprisals. The heavy influence of the Roman Catholic Church in Massachusetts has resulted in similar frustrations for proponents of birth control and abortion legislation. Although Cardinal Medeiros took no stand against legalization of homosexual acts (and even gave oblique endorsement to antidiscrimination efforts), members of the Judiciary Committee were sympathetic to representatives of Catholic churches who testified against homosexual law reform. (One Church member cited Edward Gibbon's *Decline and Fall of the Roman Empire* to support his arguments, though the book also blames the fall on the spread of the Roman Church — and has consequently been on the Prohibited Books Index for two centuries.)

The 1974 elections demonstrated that support of gay legislation was not the political liability many legislators had feared. Most of the pro-gay legislators were re-elected, and several opponents, including Doyle and Carey, were defeated in the primaries. The most spectacular defeat of all was that of Attorney General Robert Quinn, who was running for Governor. In a letter the preceding winter to the president of HUB, Quinn declared, "I am more concerned with protecting the family than I am with endorsing a license for deviant sexual conduct."[52] Gays appeared more sympathetic to his Democratic primary opponent, Michael Dukakis, who had endorsed gay rights legislation. In the closing week of the campaign, Quinn, badly trailing in the polls, lashed out against Dukakis' "liberal" positions on gay rights, abortion, pornography, marijuana, and busing — a desperate ploy that failed.

In five years gays have grown from a position of no political influence, to become a minority strong enough to receive support from others: the League of Women Voters, the American Bar Association, and other organizations, as well as from a growing number of legislators, including the Black Caucus. As Barney Frank put it, "The gay rights issue is no longer just a concern of the gay community . . . it's a litmus test of liberalism." But this new prominence also brings the dubious benefit that politicians will now lie about their gay record when speaking in front of liberal groups. Frank cites a CPPAX-sponsored Candidates' Night in May, when an aide for Governor Francis Sargent and the Republican candidate for Secretary of State, Sen. John Quinlan (Norwood), both claimed that they had supported gay rights bills.[53]

The case of Sargent is an interesting example of political expediency. Throughout the 1974 session of the Legislature, there were rumors that he might endorse the gay bills. Gays wrote urging him to make a public stand, but the most Rep. Frank was finally able to get from him was the pledge that he would sign the bills if they were passed — a meaningless promise because by then the bills were already dead. Only after the September primary did Sargent endorse gay rights, because he had defeated his anti-gay opponent, Carroll Sheehan, and he no longer had to worry about facing Quinn in the general election. So desperate was he for gay support that he sent a congratulatory telegram to the WCAS-AM program "Closet Space" after the Supreme Judicial Court struck down Section 35, four days before the election. Now that Michael Dukakis was his opponent and gay rights was no longer a "radical" issue, Sargent could endorse it in his losing bid for re-election.

The Gay Legislation '75 Committee began organizing for the upcoming session a few days after the election. Three bills were again filed. The

Massachusetts Bar Association gave special support to the repeal of the sex laws because of the Supreme Judicial Court's decision, and the antidiscrimination bills were given additional impetus by Federal court rulings requiring a connection between job performance and sexual orientation to justify dismissal. But Rep. Frank warned the Committee against premature optimism. He expected that opposition would also be more organized after the surprise showing of the Civil Service bill in the previous session, and that passage would require several more years of effort.[54]

Once again gays testified before legislative committee hearings, and in March 150 came to lobby at the State House in the second Gay Americans Day. Attorney General Francis X. Bellotti announced his support for all three bills. During his campaign for election to succeed Quinn, Bellotti had taken no stand, and many expected him to remain neutral throughout the session. Both the Commerce and Labor Committee and the Public Service Committee reported their bills favorably out of committee with unanimous votes.[55]

Frank's warning was borne out by the history of the Civil Service bill. On April 29, the House passed H. 5868; but two days later it adopted an amendment striking out section 2, which would have prohibited a state agency from dismissing an employee on the basis of sexual orientation — in effect, gutting the bill. Five of the fifteen who switched to weaken the bill were Boston Representatives angry at Rep. Noble for voting against an anti-busing bill.[56] In the floor debate Rep. William Connell (D-Weymouth) charged that the bill "would give these people the right to recruit. These people are predatory. These dykes, faggots and queers are after your sons and daughters."

A motion for reconsideration failed several days later, and the bill was sent, as amended, to the Senate. Prior to the House debate, a group called the National Alliance — Western Massachusetts Branch, believed to be affiilated with the John Birch Society, passed out a statement condemning gay legislation: "Any acceptance of homosexual activity as 'normal' is, among other things, a negation of the community as it must be constituted if the race is not to perish."[58] The bill was later narrowly killed in the Senate.

Judiciary quietly shelved the decriminalization bill. Commerce and Labor again approved the general antidiscrimination bill, but soon the entire Legislature was embroiled in a budget crisis reminiscent of New York City's. Exacerbated by Dukakis' poor leadership, the Legislature drastically cut social service spending and increased taxes to cover the state's deficit, finally approving a budget in November — over four months after the 1976 fiscal year had begun.

Indicative of its priorities, it slashed 34.5 per cent from the budget of the Massachusetts Commission Against Discrimination, which would enforce the antidiscrimination bill. Already, the Commission had a backlog of 2000 cases, which was almost certain to grow.[59] In the closing weeks of the 1975 session, the Legislature hurried to consider its backlog of remaining bills, finally adjourning 11 hours before the beginning of the 1976 session. The antidiscrimination bill was among the many to expire with the session, but all three bills had again been introduced and the process begun again.

The 1975 session brought the gay bills yet closer to passage. After years of struggle, gay liberationists have begun to realize their goals: The American Psychiatric Association finally took homosexuality off its "sick list" (though slyly replacing it with "Sexual Orientation Disturbance" as a loophole for anti-gay psychiatrists). Increasingly, states are striking down their barbaric sex laws, and employers are announcing they will not discriminate. It is probable that Massachusetts will soon enact antidiscrimination legislation, as will other states, and possibly even the Federal government. All of these moves are important, but as blacks discovered a decade ago, they are only a beginning. Liberation is still a long way off.

NOTES

1Portions of this essay have appeared in abbreviated form in the following issues of the *Gay Community News:* II, Nos. 33 & 34, and are here used with the editor's permission.

2The stories of Willa Cather and Horatio Alger are told in Jonathan Katz's documentary play, *Coming Out* (1972).

3D. W. Cory, *The Homosexual in America,* p. 88. A more recent, and unconvincing, attack on the validity of Kinsey's statistics and on the inferences drawn from them is contained in the Wydens' *Growing Up Straight,* pp. 33, 174-75.

4R.E.L. Masters, *The Homosexual Revolution,* pp. 45-7.

5Ibid., pp. 65-6.

6Ibid., pp. 68-9.

[7]Quoted, Lige Clarke and Jack Nichols, "Remember the Stonewall!" *Gay*, June 29, 1970, p. 5. In fall, 1969, *Come Out!* was founded in New York as one of the first gay militant publications.

[8]Telephone conversation July 22, 1974, with Lionel Cuffie, founder of Rutgers Student Homophile League.

[9]Ellis, *Homosexuality*, pp. 79-84.

[10]Mircea Eliade, *Myth and Reality*, pp. 18-19.

[11]See Arthur Evans' continuing series on "Gays and Witchcraft" in the two issues of *Out* magazine and beginning in Fag Rag #11.

[12]Reprinted in the homosexual anthology *Different*, p. 229.

[13]John Gerassi, *The Boys of Boise*, pp. 1-4.

[14]Quoted, Ibid., pp. 11-13.

[15]Quoted, Ibid., pp. 14-15.

[16]Quoted, Ibid., pp. 35-36.

[17]Ibid., pp. 119-20.

[18]"Mass Killers Lack Consciences," Boston *Herald-American*, August 12, 1973, p. 13.

[19]"Fly Now, Pay Later," *Newsweek*, August 27, 1973, pp. 22-25. "The police found some tenuous links between Corll and Norman [the head of the 'ring'] but they were not sure what they added up to. Besides Norman's arrest record in Houston, there was the further coincidence that Dean Corll had mentioned a homosexual club in Dallas to one of his young accomplices . . . Most jolting of all was a strip of photos in Norman's apartment with the word 'kill' scrawled across the pictures of several young men — but this turned out to mean only that their photos were to be deleted from the next catalog."

[20]*Union-Leader*, October 8, 1974.

21It also turns out that Loeb has had undue influence upon Thomson's administration. During the 1974 gubernatorial campaign, the Concord *Monitor's* statehouse reporter discovered that Thomson had made 138 phone calls from the Governor's office to Loeb's Massachusetts and Nevada homes in the first 18 months of his term. The reporter was able to correlate the calls to important decisions the Governor had made. An additional 116 calls to the *Union-Leader* were later revealed. — *More*, IV: 12 (Dec. '74), . 4.

22"Apparent Goal of 'Gay Students' at UNH Revealed," *Union-Leader*, Dec. 14, 1973. (*Fag Rag #6*).

23"Sodom and Gomorrah at Durham," *Union-Leader*, Dec. 18, 1973. The uproar resulted in international publicity for *Fag Rag*, which returned the compliment by reprinting in full both the article and the editorial, in the following issue (#7&8).

24*Union-Leader*, Jan. 18, 1974.

25*Union-Leader*, Feb. 5, 1974.

26The GSO controversy is just one example of the *Union-Leader's* disproportionate influence on New Hampshire politics in the three decades that Loeb has been its editor. In *The Boys of Boise*, John Gerassi reveals how the Boise scandal was engineered by the local power elite for its own ends (pp. 20-27).

27George Whitmore, "Gay Rights Bill Defeated in New York," *Win*, X:24 (July 4, 1974), pp. 6-7.

28"Homosexual Witchhunt," *GO Info*, II:2 (April-May '75), pp. 1, 4; and Ron Dayman, "Police and Press Lies End in Death," *The Body Politic* #18 (May-June '75), pp. 1, 6.

29Ibid. Many Americans and Canadians naively assume that gay oppression does not exist in Canada because the 1969 Omnibus Act legalized consensual adult homosexual acts. Actually, the situation is not much different from the United States. There is no antidiscrimination or other human rights legislation for gays, the Immigration Act still discriminates, and the police in many cities harass gays routinely.

[30]Gerald Hannon, "Of Men and Little Boys," *The Body Politic* #5 (Summer '72), p. 3.

[31]Hannon, "Children and Sex," *The Body Politic* #6 (Fall '72), p. 3.

[32]Gerassi, op. cit., p. 111. One work contemporary to the Boise scandal that attempted to give psychiatric substantiation to the myth of the "homosexual child molester" is Hervey Clecky's *The Caricature of Love* (1957), but its shrillness belies its scientific aspirations. The insinuations of Albert Ellis' logic are equally dangerous:

> Although many heterosexuals would love having intercourse with teenage girls, they sanely accept the fact that their benighted society will incarcerate them for statutory rape if they seek out such young partners; so they keep their hands to themselves when they are in the presence of "jail bait," and they thereby keep out of trouble. Homosexuals in our antisexual culture fail to calmly accept in practice, while vigorously fighting in theory [by trying to change the laws, or striving for social acceptance?], the restrictions of this culture; and they thereby *almost always* get themselves into various legal, social, and vocational difficulties. —— Ellis, op. cit., p. 79, italics added.

[33]Gebhard, et. al., *Sex Offenders*, pp. 283-85, 292-94.

[34]Quoted in Gerassi, op. cit., p. 112.

[35]Kinsey, et. al., *Sexual Behavior in the Human Male*, pp. 163-68.

[36]Wainwright Churchill, *Homosexual Behavior Among Males*, p. 214.

[37]George Weinberg, *Society and the Healthy Homosexual*, p. 4.

[38]Ibid., pp. 8-17.

[39]Boston *Globe*, May 14, 1974.

[40]This term is commonly used for such acts as fellatio and cunnilingus. Commentary on Sect. 35 in *Mass. General Laws Annotated*: "The words

'unnatural and lascivious act' are words of common usage with a well defined, well understood, and generally accepted meaning, signifying irregular indulgence in sexual behavior, illicit sexual relations, and infamous conduct which is hateful, obscene, and in deviation of accepted customs and manners." Quoted from Jacquith v. Commonwealth, 1954.

41"Gay dies in Bridgewater," *Gay Community News* (*GCN*), I:22 (Nov. 17, 1973), p. 1. Bill Baird was serving a ten day sentence at Charles Street for giving a birth control device to a Boston University student in a 1967 demonstration. State law prohibited the sale of prophylactics, even though they were openly sold in drugstores and the state collected a sales tax on them! Baird's notoriety did not help Rastellini. The Homophile Union of Boston (one of four local gay groups at the time) had no facilities for legal aid, the Civil Liberties Union of Massachusetts refused to take the case, and his public defender did nothing to expose the contradictions in police testimony. *Fag Rag* #7&8 (Spring '74) has published the transcript of Rastellini's trial.

42"The Brockton 11," *GCN*, I:16 (Oct. 6, 1973), p. 1; "More arrests," *GCN*, I:18 (Oct. 20, 1973), p. 1.

43Conversations with Richard Rubino: May 31, 1974, and Dec. 4, 1974. Rubino has represented clients in Boston Municipal and in various suburban district courts. "Each case, no matter how similar they are in fact, has to be treated individually. The most important thing I deal with is an individual's future." Variables include: the judge and the prosecutor, the client's consciousness (whether in the closet or out), what job he has, whether or not he has a previous criminal record, whether he was entrapped with a codefendant or a policeman. In each case Rubino's aim is to prevent his client from getting a criminal record.
His strategy varies accordingly: He may advise his client to plead "not guilty" and try for an acquittal. He may try to convince the judge (as he did for two of the Brockton defendants) that the charges should be dismissed because of what the client has already gone through. Or he may have his client admit to a "finding of fact," sealing his arrest record after six months.

44Court relaxes state sex laws," *Globe*, Nov. 2, 1974, p. 1.

45Conversation with Elaine Noble: Nov. 21, 1974.

46Conversation with Rubino: May 29, 1975.

[47]Conversation with Tony Roberts, Jan. 19, 1974. Townsend was a member of a Brahman Bostonian family, who graduated from Harvard shortly after World War I. He had been arrested numerous times for sexual involvements with boys, and he once served a prison term. He harbored runaways, some of them junkies who took advantage of his generosity. In time, both of his Beacon Hill townhouses burned. In the late 1950's he founded the Boston Mattachine, which eventually broke up over his egocentric behavior. His notoriety helped to stunt Boston's gay movement. HUB was the first permanent organization, founded in 1969, a comparatively late date. He died in 1973 at the age of 78.

[48]Those testifying had no illusions, for no one had bothered to oppose their testimony. The bills were introduced "by request" (i.e. at the behest of a constituent) by Michael Dukakis, then a representative from Bookline. — *Massachusetts Legislative Documents*, 1970.

[49]"State House winces," *GCN* I:16 (Oct. 6, 1973), p. 1.

[50]I also attended the Judiciary hearing. Accounts of the two hearings appear in *GCN* I:37 (March 9, 1974) and *GCN* I:40 (March 30, 1974).

[51]"Gay bill sent to dead end," *GCN*, I:44 (April 27, 1974); "Anatomy of a defeat," *GCN*, I:47 (May 18, 1974).

[52]Quoted from Rachelle Patterson, "Politics wins out over civil rights," Boston *Globe*, March 17, 1974.

[53]Conversation with Barney Frank: Nov. 25, 1974.

[54]"Legislation plans ready," *GCN*, II:22 (Nov. 23, 1974), p. 1.

[55]*GCN*, II:34, 35, 37, 38, 43, 45 (Feb.-May, 1975).

[56]Gay rights, like the feminist issues of abortion and the Equal Rights Amendment, have been affected by the political and social turmoil in Boston in the wake of court-ordered busing in the autumn of 1974. Gangs of South Boston youths have attacked gays, blacks, and Puerto Ricans in nearby Bay Village; and racist politicians have indulged in gay-baiting to discredit integration.

57David Brill, "Mass. bill bounced around," *GCN*, II:46 (May 10, 1975), p. 1. Connell's outrageousness is reminiscent of William Loeb's. In 1973 he attempted to bar Mel King (D-South End, Boston) from taking his seat because King was wearing a dashiki. At the beginning of 1975, after Gov. Dukakis had appointed two Jewish women as department heads, Connell complained that the Commonwealth was being ruled by a "Jewish matriarchy."

58Brill, "Amended bill passes," *GCN*, II:47 (May 17, 1975), p. 3.

59Ronald Rowland, "MCAD cuts staff, faces backlogs," *The Bay State Banner*, XI:9 (Dec. 11, 1975), pp. 1, 24.

BIBLIOGRAPHY
I. Books

Churchill, Wainwright. *Homosexual Behavior Among Males*. Englewood Cliffs, NJ: Prentice-Hall, 1967.

Cory, Donald Webster (pseud. for Edward Sagarin). *The Homosexual in America*. New York: Greenberg, 1951.

Eliade, Mircea. *Myth and Reality*. New York: Harper & Row, 1963.

Ellis, Albert. *Homosexuality: Its Causes and Cure*. New York: Lyle Stuart, 1965.

Gebhard, Paul H., John H. Gagnon, Wardell B. Pomeroy, Cornelia V. Christenson. *Sex Offenders: An Analysis of Types*. New York: Harper & Row, 1965.

Gerassi, John. *The Boys of Boise*. New York: Collier, 1968.

Kinsey, Alfred C., Wardell B. Pomeroy, Clyde E. Martin. *Sexual Behavior in the Human Male*. Philadelphia: W.B. Saunders, 2948.

Massachusetts General Laws Annotated.

Massachusetts Legislative Documents.

Masters, R.E.L. *The Homosexual Revolution*. New York: Julian Press, 1962.

Weinberg, George. *Society and the Healthy Homosexual*. Garden City, NY: Anchor, 1973.

Wright, Stephen, ed. *Different: An Anthology of Homosexual Short Stories*. New York: Bantam, 1974.

II. Periodicals

Bay State Banner, Boston, Black community weekly.

The Body Politic. Toronto, bi-monthly.

Boston *Globe*. Boston, daily.

Boston *Herald-American*. Boston, daily.
Fag Rag. Boston, gay male quarterly.
Gay. New York, weekly, defunct.
Gay Community News. Boston, weekly.
GO Info. Ottawa, bi-monthly newspaper of Gays of Ottawa.
Manchester *Union-Leader*. Manchester, NH, daily.
More. New York, monthly, journalism review.
Newsweek. New York, weekly.
Out. New York, monthly, defunct.
Win. Brooklyn, NY, weekly, associated with War Registers League.

III. Persons Interviewed

Lionel Cuffie, founder and president of Rutgers Student Homophile League, 1970-72.
Barney Frank, Mass. House of Representatives, 1973—.
Loretta Lotman, founder and director of Gay Media Action (Boston), 1973-74; media director of National Gay Task Force, 1975. She co-ordinated the "Marcus Welby" boycott (p. 395).
Laura McMurray, lesbian activist, 1969—. She was a founder of the local DOB and has coordinated the legislative efforts for several years.
Elaine Noble, Mass. House of Representatives, 1975—. She was also a founder of the local DOB and a longtime feminist activist.
Tony Roberts, member of the Boston Mattachine, 1960-61.
Richard Rubino, Boston attorney, member of the law firm Rook, Roth & Rubino.

Meeting Males
By Mail

By John Alan Lee

A recent sociological study of Toronto, Canada, (population two million), concluded that one of the most pervasive social problems in the city was the difficulty single adults experienced in meeting suitable partners.[1] Of course the survey was referring to heterosexuals. The problem of being single and happy in the big city is a frequent topic in Toronto's daily newspapers. For example, a full page was devoted to "ways singles can meet in Toronto."[2]

Ways of meeting ranged from "Walk a dog" to "Take in crowd scenes at City Hall" to "Visit the Art Gallery more often." Less obvious suggestions included purchasing a bicycle to roam the city, and combining with other singles to rent a downtown apartment exclusively for the purpose of holding singles parties.[3]

It's a trifle ironic that heterosexuals should have problems meeting each other in a city with a famous "sin strip" (Yonge Street) amply provided with bars, body rubs, and burlesque halls; with swinging singles bars such as Standing Room Only at the Hyatt Hotel; and even with Singles Festivals. The most recent festival attracted an estimated 10,000 men and women! Yet it is true that single adults are "Toronto's largest minority." A decade ago, only nine percent of the housing units in the city proper, were of single occupancy. Today the proportion is 23 percent.[4]

Within the singles minority is a group with special problems which are the subject of this chapter: homosexual males without partners. With a greater population than San Francisco, Toronto affords its gay males a choice among only four gay bars. These are all located in the downtown ghetto, and rather rigidly stratified by social class. There are no neighborhood gay bars.

Worse, Toronto is a weekend town. The bars are jammed to overflowing on Friday and Saturday nights, and near-vacated on week nights. Under Ontario's blue liquor laws, bars are not open on Sundays. The gay dance clubs are also weekend activities. (There are three, and they are unlicensed, and cater only to males. In addition the Toronto homophile association holds weekend dances for men and women). Of course the baths "never ever close" but you're wasting your money on weeknights unless you're either very lucky or not at all fussy.

It's not surprising, then, to frequently hear Toronto gays express that favorite line, "Tired of the bar scene." The more conventional simply hibernate in winter, confining themselves to accustomed friends, and burst forth in a veritable madness of cruising in the summer. The more imaginative (or is it the more desperate?) resort to newspaper advertising.

One favored technique is the use of Shared Accommodation ads in the daily papers. Some gays don't have a room to share — but they advertise one anyway, and encounter some interesting people that way. Or they reply to advertisements placed by others, when they are not looking for a place to live at all. This meeting game is sufficiently common to have forced many hetero-sexuals to include a reference to their sexual orientation in their Shared Accommodation ads. The newspapers have contributed to the problem by refusing to include terms of homosexual orientation in the ads of those bold enough to admit it.

Sorting one's way through the vague insinuations and covert references ("Where do you drink?") must be a difficult chore for those who are genuinely advertising rooms to rent. Recently I was in this position myself, and definitely not looking for sex partners. Among the callers were those who asked right out "Are you gay?" and some even blunter: "How many inches have you got?" "What do you like to do in bed?"

A more customary classification for advertisements of those seeking com-panionship, is the Personal column. This also has the advantage of an opportunity to use a postal box, which, as we shall see, opens whole new worlds of contacts.

One disadvantage of the Personal column is the refusal of the daily news-papers, which pride themselves on "family readership," to print any adjectives which apply to the companion being sought. The advertiser may describe himself or herself in tasteful detail, including the term "heterosexual," but not the terms "homosexual" or "gay." Hence it is becoming a reasonable assump-tion that an ad which does not specify heterosexuality either directly, or by such phrases as "loves children," is quite likely to be gay.

I recently place a Personal ad which read:

Dominant, masculine, handsome male seeks cheerful companion. Post Box . . .

The newspaper refused to accept this formulation, not because of the term "dominant," but because I had applied an adjective to "companion." Even cheerful adjectives are ruled out! However, the ad was printed when I reworded it to read:

Dominant, masculine, handsome, cheerful male seeks companion.
Post Box . . .

Of course the responses included both men and women. In fact the female responses were more interesting, and included one specifying an interest in "oriental bondage" — whatever that might be. The point is that certain key words have more than obvious meanings for those wise to the art of personal advertising. One amusing recent example which the "family readership" editors obviously didn't fathom, was this:

Docile male, 38, interested in leather craft, seeks companion.
Write to Post Box . . .

The Postal Box

Renting a box at a local post office accomplishes more than the mere acquiring of an anonymous address. It taps a unique constituency of people looking for partners. A post box has distinct advantages over listing your telephone number in an advertisement. It also enables you to answer other people's ads anonymously, by directing replies to the box. Besides, most people like to get mail. There's a moment of excitement when you open the box to see if any letters have arrived.

Responses to your ad can be controlled and disposed of, at your own timing, without intrusions into your home life. There are no chances of 4 a.m. calls, or troublemakers calling weeks after your ad appeared. There is much less likelihood of friends and workmates recognizing your post box in an ad (many people read the Personal column out of curiosity) than would recognize your telephone number. Changing a phone number is expensive, but a postal box is cheap — only eight dollars a year in Canada.

I have operated a postal box for two years now, placing test advertisements of various specifications in the daily papers and the gay media, and replying as well to the advertisements of others through my post box address. I have accumulated more than one hundred correspondents, both heterosexual and homosexual, including some married women looking for a discreet affair. I have arranged about thirty personal encounters with correspondents. As a result, some of the patterns of types of users of post boxes and meetings by mail, have begun to emerge.

Since I have accumulated more data on homosexual males than on any other category, my analysis is devoted to this category of advertisers and box users.

Users of Personal Ads

Typical users of personal ads and post box correspondence seem to fall into two classes — the desperate and the discreet, with some people in both. The majority, in their letters, express difficulty in meeting people, or at least, the right person. Judging from personal follow-ups, many of them have good reason to be shy. They are less physically attractive than the average at gay bars, and would not stand a good chance in the meat rack competition.

Compensating for this disadvantage, however, is the fact that a majority of my correspondents were of a higher socio-economic status than I encounter in Toronto's gay bars and dance clubs. For many, discretion seemed quite warranted. They occupied prestigious positions in the community. High government officials, prominent businessmen and educators, and even a church leader have been among my correspondents. Of course it requires several exchanges by letter and/or telephone, as well as personal encounters, before these statuses are divulged. Homosexual acts between consenting adults in private are legal in Canada, but many persons would still prefer to remain in the closet. To walk into a public bar, or even a private gay dance club, is to take the chance of being recognized by someone to whom you do not wish to reveal yourself.

The hide-and-seek games of mailbox meetings can produce some amusing encounters. Some of your own best friends may unwittingly apply to be your lover. The very qualities which make you good friends, are likely to suggest a compatible partnership, except for that elusive factor of physical attraction whose absence has always confined your relationship to friendship.

You may also find yourself corresponding with the same person several times over, should he or you change the wording of the ad or the post box number. The inclusion of a first name in the ad itself is a fairly common means of avoiding this.

A personal ad combined with a postal box may produce the most surprising revelations about people you thought you knew well. I received a boldly honest reply (considering he was writing to a perfect stranger) from the 70-year old father of one of my lifelong heterosexual colleagues. This man had already survived two wives, and now, for the first time, was admitting to himself a long-repressed attraction. Of course I contacted him, and we have since had several pleasant and helpful discussions.

Follow-up

After the first exchange of letters — or several rounds later in a cautious correspondence — a conversation by telephone is usually advisable, as an intermediate stage before a personal encounter. It provides another opportunity to select carefully before fully revealing oneself or becoming entangled in an embarrassing relationship. Disclosure of one's phone number is usually still a step short of revealing one's address.

A phone conversation can add important data in a process of immediate feedback, but it can also prove misleading. When conversing with someone we have never seen in person, we often produce mental/visual images of the other's appearance, based on the suggestive elements of vocal pitch, tone, accent, and nasal quality. The concept of the "sexy voice" is familiar to all, but the effect of voices on us goes much further. "The medium is the message" in many cases, but it may be a false message leading to disillusionment when people meet face to face.

Even a telephone conversation does not facilitate the asking of certain questions which may be relevant, and not yet discussed by mail. Is he balding? Photographs may not reveal this. What does his skin feel like? Tactile and olfactory qualities are vitally important to most people's sexual attraction, and are not satisfactorily revealed by photo or phone.[5]

A neutral territory is the best for a first personal encounter. That way, neither party has the advantage of being on home territory, or the disadvantage, if the visitor is slow to depart after you have decided you're not interested. Public places such as subway stations or street corners should be avoided, however, because one party will almost inevitably arrive before the other, and a period of waiting may be uncomfortable. There's always the possibility of being "stood up" so a meeting in a small, quiet bar or restaurant is preferable. Don't forget to agree on specific means of recognizing each other — people don't always look like their photographs.

Typical Advertisers and Their
Sought-For Partners

At some point in his work, the sociologist is likely to start counting things and producing statistics. That point has now arrived. The techniques of content analysis enable us to make at least some tentative conclusions about gay male users of personal advertisements, using two familiar media: *The Advocate*, a twice-monthly paper originating in San Mateo but widely read and advertised in, throughout North America, and *The Body Politic*, a gay liberation paper issued every two months from San Mateo and read by about 5000, mostly young gay liberation types, in Canada and the United States.

Both papers are predominantly oriented to gay males, and carry few female personal advertisements; hence my analysis is exclusively about males. Personal ads in each paper may relate to a variety of concerns other than the meeting of a partner or lover. I have eliminated all ads promoting sales of products, of course. In addition I have eliminated all ads designed for mere sexual contact, with no further relationship. ("Horny tonite? Phone . . ." "Hot and ready for action." "Male model to satisfy your desires," etc.).

In addition, I am excluding all ads relating to master and slave relationships. This does not imply any moral judgment on such relationships, and I am certainly not suggesting that they are devoid of love. However, the specifications in these ads are so distinctly different from the general "seeks companion" or "seeks lover" ads, that I prefer to make a separate analysis of them elsewhere.

The following statistics and comments are based on analysis of three randomly selected issues of *The Advocate* for the past year, and five issues of *The Body Politic*. In the three *Advocate* issues, there were a total of 876 personal advertisements, of which 248 (28%) qualified for inclusion in my analysis. In the five *Body Politic* issues, there were 74 such advertisements.

Personal ads can range all the way from those specifying a highly defined (and probably statistically rare) ideal partner, to those seeking a practical and compasionate arrangement of like-minded persons, to those who are so desperate it appears almost anyone will do. Examples:

A special someone

I'm a trim, attractive guy, 33, 5'11", 151, very straight appearance, quiet and intelligent. I'd like the almost Platonic friendship of a masc. man, 22-44, who must be w/blt & muscular, straight appr. and have clean habits; one who could be thoroughly turned on by the simple joys of affectionate fondling, touching, kissing, & gen. body contact, but who'd be turned off by Fr., Gr., S & M or anything far out. One who'd enjoy the likes of music, conversation, quiet moments, TV ball games; one who'd be discreet, sincere and a friend most of all. I'd appreciate a photo. Please write Jack . . .

W/m, 36, stable, educ., butch, seeks W/m, 18-30, who is warm, sincere and affectionate. Someone, please reply! Box . . .

San Diego physician seeks intimate friend or lover. If interested, send picture, personality description and your requirements for a mate to Box . . . My ideal is: Cauc. 25-35, butch, gdlkg, endowed and Gr act. No fats, dopers.

Since advertisers vary somewhat from issue to issue, there is no assurance that the patterns described below will be true of every issue of either newspaper. However, analysis over several years shows a fairly stable pattern of the most frequent characteristics.[6]

Characteristics of Advertisers

As the examples suggest, advertisers vary widely in the details of their own self-description. Only four characteristics occur with sufficient frequency through most ads, to be worth statistical summary. These are age, race, preferred sex role, and socio-economic status.

Of the 248 eligible ads from the three *Advocate* issues, 218, or about 87 percent, included a statement of the advertiser's (claimed) age. Whether truthful or not, the pattern of distribution of ages at least indicates what advertisers perceive to be acceptable self-disclosures. In the five *Body Politic* issues, 90 percent stated their age. Table 1 below shows the distributions.

TABLE 1 — AGE OF ADVERTISER		
	Percentage stating in	
Stated Age	Advocate	Body Politic
Up to 25 years	24%	27%
26 to 34	47%	49%
35 to 44	20%	24%
45 and over	9%	nil

"W/m" or white male, is the single most frequent datum in *The Advocate* personal ads. Of the 248 eligible ads, 63 percent indicate the race of the advertiser, and of these advertisers, 92 percent are white. Orientals account for five percent and blacks the remainder. In the *Body Politic* race is rarely indicated, no doubt a reflection of the much smaller proportion of non-Caucasians in Canada.

Thirty percent of the 248 *Advocate* ads include a statement of the advertiser's preferred sex role. Greek passive leads slightly. Greek active and passive and French active and passive account for more than three quarters of the preferred sex roles. Other alternatives of less common mention include j/o (jerk off, or masturbation) and "versatile." Again, sex role preference is less often included in *Body Politic* ads, and those who do state it are about evenly divided between active, passive, and versatile.

Finally, and least reliably (since distortion of status is probably even greater than that of age), a proportion of advertisers indicate their socio-economic status. In *The Advocate* sample, about 23 percent indicate a status, with "professional" and "businessman" the two most common, and "student" a poor third. In *The Body Politic*, by contrast, and reflecting its different readership, 23 percent of the advertisers describe themselves as students.

The Sought-For Partner(s)

Advertisers naturally vary in the extent of detail of specifications for partners. There were twenty-two categories of specifications which occurred in more than five percent of *The Advocate* and/or *The Body Politic* ads. These are listed in rank order for *The Advocate*, in Table 2. The somewhat varying rank order of specifications for *The Body Politic* is also shown.

Advertisers in both countries agree on the importance of specifying three characteristics of sought partners: age, willingness for a singular, lasting relationship, and a straight or masculine appearance. "Ageism" and the trend to "virility" in male homosexuals in North America have both already been commented on by social scientists. [7]

Beyond this point, however, the two samples diverge. For Canadians, it appears that "handsome is as handsome does." Canada is a less erotically-preoccupied society, especially compared to California, where many of the *Advocate* ads originate. The much greater proportion of gay liberation supporters among *The Body Politic* readership would also make a difference. Gay liberation ideology has generally deplored the overemphasis on stereo-typed beauty in interpersonal relationships.

Interests, hobbies and similar activities of the individual are ranked second only to age range in the *Body Politic* sample, while being handsome is mentioned so little it does not appear in the table. There is also less emphasis on sex organs than in *The Advocate*. While the analysis may suggest that liberated gays are different in their concerns than the "unliberated," I doubt that it indicates a widespread Canadian gay indifference to physical appearance in suitable partners. It may, however, indicate that Canadians are less convinced that considerations of physical appearance can be usefully defined in words in an ad.

Perhaps the familiar Canadian parsimoniousness is at work here too.

Table 2
SPECIFICATIONS OF SOUGHT-FOR PARTNER(S)

| Rank order: * Specification | Percentage of mention in ads in | | (Rank) |
	The Advocate	The Body Politic	
1. age range desired	73%	50%	[1]
2. singular, lasting relation wanted	53%	30%	[4]
3. straight - appearing, masculine, not "fem".	45%	31%	[3]
4. a specified physique	42%	27%	[6]
5. sincere, serious	40%	25%	[7]
6. of specified interests or hobbies or sports	33%	48%	[2]
7. warm, affectionate	31%	17%	[10]
8. specified race	23%	–––	
9. preferred sex role for partner sought	22%	22%	[8]
10. handsome, goodlooking	20%	–––	
11. other personality char. (sensitive, stable etc.)	19%	16%	[11]
12. not a drug user not into S and M	18% 18%	10% –––	[14]
13. intelligent, educated not fat	16% 16%	28% –––	[5]
14. size or type of organ (eg – "uncut")	15%	–––	
15. discreet	14%	8%	[15]
16. smooth, or hairy preferred social status	12% 12%	14% –––	[12]
17. not frequently at bars	10%	12%	[13]
18. preferred hair color	9%	–––	
19. non-smoker	–––	19%	[9]

* Rank order in *The Advocate,* The rank order in *Body Politic* is shown in brackets on the right side.

(The same attitude which enables American capital to dominate Canadian investment). For example, it will be noted that the Canadian advertisers mention the partner's preferred sex role as often as their American brothers (22%), but as we noted earlier, do not state their own orientation as often as American advertisers. Since both data are hardly necessary, words and expense are spared.

Probably the most startling contrast between the two samples is the much greater emphasis on intelligence or education in *The Body Politic*. A note of greater non-conformity is also struck, in the emphasis on non-smoking. Absence of references to "no S and M" may simply reflect the lack of an organized S and M or "leather" subculture in Canada.

One other interesting finding of my analysis, not indicated in the tables, is the absence of any frequent age gap between advertiser and sought partner(s). Lehne, in his sample of 50 gay males, found considerable evidence of such gaps, with older men frequently seeking much younger mates.[8] In my *Advocate* sample, 77 percent of the ads state *both* advertiser's age and preferred age range of partner, and in all but 17 percent of these, the advertiser's age is *within* the partner's range.

Interpersonal Competence By Mail

It is obvious from even a casual reading of personal advertising in either of the gay papers analyzed, that many advertisers do not put much faith or hope in this method of meeting a partner. For many, it is a "last resort" despite the fact that "this is a first ad." There are constant requests that only serious persons reply.

The presentation of one's self as "not really looking" for love or intimate relationship, is at least as common among gays as among heterosexuals in North America. "It's ages since I've been here" and "I don't go out very often" are often heard in the bar. It is permissible to admit that one is bored, or angry, or even unhappy, but hardly ever admissible that one is lonely. Indeed, we are likely to be frightened off by any advertiser who makes his need for intimacy too obvious.

Of more than 60 gay correspondents with whom I have been in contact through personal advertising, I would conclude that the great majority are sincerely looking for a partner, and certainly *lonely*, in the sense of feeling an anxiety-provoking absence of a trusted intimate with whom to share the private self.

An ad typical of those I have placed, read:

Possible dream?
Serious-minded, good-natured, young-looking professional man, 35, slim, smooth, attractive, 6 ft., 150, masculine but versatile, seeks compatible, emotionally mature mate, 25-35, to share life's many joys — home, garden, books, classical music, plays, art, films, travel affectionate sex. Photo please. Box . . .

This ad produced numerous resonses, most of which I followed up. Several led to brief affairs, but none to a "lasting relationship." Advertisers should not despair, however. I do know of those who have found a long-term mate this way. Certainly my experience in Toronto is that advertising — both placing and responding to others — brings contacts with individuals one has never met before and is unlikely to meet in the usual meeting places — the bars, dance clubs, gay liberation meetings, Metropolitan Community Church, beaches and parks, and so forth.

Since an apparently sincere and serious ad like my own cited above, will certainly produce more responses than the average advertiser (who is not doing a survey that requires him to follow up most leads) will want to pursue, some method of sorting the promising from the sterile is essential. With some experience, the user of personal advertising can develop the "interpersonal competence" for meetings by mail.

For example, the failure of a correspondent to reveal or discuss some specification which you have emphasized in your ad, (such as age), is a probable indication that he does not conform to your expectations, not only in this but in other important matters. When a correspondent openly ignores a specification (for example, mentioning that he has a beard, when you specify "clean-shaven") you can be almost certain of wasting your time with a follow-up. The correspondent is simply not taking you seriously.

Another clue worth watching is the grammar and syntax of the reply letter (assuming, like most Canadian advertisers at least, that intelligence and/or education are important). Can the respondent construct a complete sentence including words of more than two syllables? Also, it doesn't require a handwriting analysis to notice that some writers have an aesthetic sense of a page of writing or typing, which will serve as a clue to a wider aesthetic sensitivity, as well as neatness.

One of the most desirable qualities in personal advertising correspondence is a sense of humor. After all, no one should take this method of finding a lover *too* seriously! Among the examples I have received are letters in which the author rewites my advertisement so as to describe himself, thus demonstrating the complementarity of our qualities. In one case, the correspondent pasted my ad to a sheet of paper, and linked cartoon balloons with various phrases in it. It is not too extreme to suggest that if you're going to bother with this means of meeting people anyway, it is worth some trouble. A letter to a prospective employer who has never met you may be your first and only introduction, so you try to present a favorable image. Replies to personal ads should do the same.

Lastly (but not finally, for there are always new things to learn about meeting people), I pay careful attention to the topics which the correspondent gives priority and discusses at length. What does he think is important? Has he a clear and definitive idea of his own physical appearance which can be succinctly stated without being gross or pornographic? Is he in touch with his own mental processes, and able to sum up his major concerns or thoughts? Is he good at characterizing himself briefly and descriptively? Has he a wide range of interests and activities which would make him an interesting person to meet?

Some of these considerations can be applied, of course, to the problem of composing an ad in the first place. What to say about yourself and your sought-for ideal, considering the cost per word? If you know yourself, and know what you're looking for, then you should be able to express this clearly in an ad. If you don't, you're probably wasting time and money by placing ads. However, the experience of advertising, and answering ads, can be a growth experience. Who knows, you may even meet someone nice!

NOTES

[1] Leon Kumove Social Planning Ltd., Toronto; 1975 Social Survey.

[2] Toronto Daily Star, July 13, 1973, page 61.

[3] See also Maclean's Magazine, "The Meeting Game," Toronto, July, 1967.

[4] Metropolitan Toronto Social Planning Report, 1974 public brochure.

[5] The role of touch, often underestimated in intimacy, is discussed in detail in Ashley Montagu, Touching, The Human Significance of the Skin, (Harper, New York, 1972).

[6] Compare Table 2 here with Table 1, page 14, in John A. Lee, "Forbidden Colours of Love," papers of the Grove Conference on the Family, 1974 Annual Meetings, Hot Springs, Arkansas.

7See Gregory Lehne, "Gay Male Fantasies and Realities," papers of the Grove Conference on the Family, 1974 Annual Meetings; also reproduced in *The Body Politic*, no. 14 and 15, July-Sept. 1974. See also Laud Humphreys, "New Styles in Homosexual Manliness," in J. McCaffery, *The Homosexual Dialectic*, (Prentice Hall, New York, 1972), pp. 65-84; and "Dirty Old Men Need Love Too" in Humphreys, *Out of the Closets*, (Prentice Hall, New York, 1972), p. 115.

8The Lehne study, cited in footnote 7, was based on 50 gay male respondents to a *Body Politic* questionnaire. He found that while 64 percent of men under 25 fantasized partners of about the same age, as the respondent's age rose above 25, the age of fantasized partners tended to remain lower, so that the older the respondent, the greater the gap between own age and preferred partner's age. Lehne also found a surprising emphasis on warm, affectionate relationships in fantasies, considering that he specifically emphasized *sexual* fantasy. These findings probably reflect the predominantly gay liberationist orientation of the younger readership of *The Body Politic*, with his older respondents more likely to read the paper for its news and ads, but less likely to be liberated. Note in my Table 1, here, that there are no *Body Politic* advertisers over a stated age of 45, but there are obviously readers over this age, looking for younger partners. In the 74 *Body Politic* ads in my analysis, very few show an age gap between advertiser's stated age, and preferred age range of partner. *The Advocate*, however, is similar, yet much less liberated. Moreover, both papers have a definite majority of advertisers over the age of 25, and while Lehne found that his respondents over this age fantasized about much younger partners in 80 percent of cases, my advertisers show this tendency in only 17 percent of the cases in *The Advocate*, and less in *The Body Politic*. A possible explanation for this disagreement, rather than a difference of samples, may be the function of advertising itself, in contrast to responding to an anonymous mailed questionnaire. Advertisers may perceive it as socially disapproved to be "dirty old men" (see Humphreys, footnote 7) in search of younger partners. Hence they would either a) advertise the preferred age range of sought partner so as to include their own age, but have no intention of actually accepting respondents from the upper end of the stated range, or b) lie about their own age, if they thought they could get away with it. Some support for the second alternative is found in the frequent phrase in advertisements, "X years old, but looks younger," or "a youthful 45" and so forth. "Ageism" is a fascinating aspect of the homosexual search for a partner; however, it is essentially tangential to the main concerns of this study.

Index

Bowles, S. 383
Bownes, Judge Hugh, 396f
boy-love, 212
Boyette, Purvis E., 32
boys, 93, 96-97, 99, 233
The Boys in the Band, 387, 390
The Boys of Boise, 409, 413
Braham, Brahmanism, 259-260, 276-277
Braverman, H., 382
Brée, Germaine, 150
The Bridge, 193-199
Brill, David, 413
Brillon, P.J., 83
Britton, 83
Broadway shows, 350f
Brockton, Mass. *Enterprise*, 402
Brodie, Fawn, 100-101
Brogan, James E., 152-163
brothels, male, 92-93, 96
Brown, Norman O., 137
Brown, Rita Mae, 158
Brown Shirts (Nazi), 79
Browning, Robert, 182-185
Bucke, R.M., 197, 199
Buddha, Buddhism, 244, 261-262, 276-277
buggery, 69-70
Bullough, Edward, 295, 301
burial alive of homosexuals, 70
burning of homosexuals, 69, 70, 72, 75, 77,
    86, 88, 89, 90, 91
Burroughs, William, 144, 158
Burton, Sir Richard Francis, 92-103
busing (Boston), 405, 406, 412
Button, John, 180, 190
Byzantine empire, 70

Cabaret, 350
Cajus, Count, 98-99
Calendar of Dutch Historical Manuscripts, 84
California State University, Sacramento, 155
Cambridge, 201-202
Cambridge University, 352
camp, 181, 182
Campo di Fiori (Rome), 84
Camus, Albert, 329, 358
Canaanites, 85, 269-270, 280
Canada, 398, 409
Canadian advertisers for lovers, 422
Candide, 361
candor, 319
canon law, 336
Capitalism, 165, 166, 167, 173, 374
Carey, William, 404f
The Caricature of Love, 410
Cashdan, Sheldon, 123
Casper, Johann Ludwig, 98-99, 102
castration of homosexuals, 70
casual sex, 319
Catalonia, 72
catamite, 280; see prostitution, male
Cather, Willa, 388, 407
Catholics, Roman, 68
Cattell's Personality Factor Test, 317
caucuses, 373
causal explanations, 293-296
Cavafy, Constantin, 111, 140, 158
Cavel, Stanley, 284, 299, 300, 302
celibacy, 50ff, 331, 338
centering, 316f

Ch'an, see Zen
The Challenge, 211
character development, 351
The Charioteer, 158
Charles II of Parma, 99
Charles III of Parma, 99
Charles V (Holy Roman Empire), 70
*Charter to William Penn and Laws of the
    Province of Pennsylvania*, 83
chastity, 54
Chaucer, 338
chauvinism, 168-169
chauvinist, 156, 157
"child molesters," 390, 393-400, 402, 406,
    410, 412
child sexuality, 398-400
children, see also "School"
    —"The Children's Hour," 113, 117
    —gay bibliography for youngsters, 114
    —Gay Guidelines, 114, 118
    —gay primer, 111
    —gay themes in children's books, 111,
    113, 114
        —gay youngsters, 111, 116
    —teenage gay novels, 113-114, 118
"The Children's Hour: Must Gay Be Grim
    for Jane and Jim?" 113, 117
China, 96, 374f, 377-379, 380
chivaliric code, 338
choice, 287, 289, 296-297
Christ, 358
Christian, 335, 336, 338
Christian Church, 335, 348
Christian faith, 344, 349
Christian Science, 259-260
Christian Tradition, 335, 336, 342, 344,
    345
Christianity, 67, 68, 69, 71, 72, 75, 146,
    269-270, 273, 276, 335, 338, 342,
    343, 346, 348
Christians, 336, 337, 338, 344, 345, 346,
    348, 349
Christopher Street Rebellion (NYC), 389f;
    see Stonewall Riots
Chronographia, 83
Chu Hsi (Neo-Confucian), 281
Chuang-tse, 276-277
The Church, 5f, 332, 333, 335, 336, 342,
    343, 344, 345, 346, 348, 349, 354,
    358
Church of England, 72, 73
Church Fathers, 69
Churchill, Wainwright, 146, 149, 151,
    410, 413
The City and the Pillar, 174-175
Citizens for Participation in Political Action,
    403, 405
civil liberties, 321
Civil Liberties Union of Mass., 403, 411
Civil Service Commission, 389
civilization, 337
civilization and homosexuality, 210f
Clarke, Lige, 408
Clarus, Julius, 84
class structure and sexual liberation, 143-144
class system, 165-166
classification, in libraries, 109, 111
cleanliness, 308f
Clecky, Hervey, 410

fictional techniques, 352
Field, Edward, 178
Fiévée, Joseph, 100
Fire Island (Cherry Grove), 271-272
Fishman, Israel, 108, 109, 110
fist-fucking, 322
The Fitness of the Environment, 362
"The Flamingo," 244
Fleta, 70, 83
Fone, Byrne R.S., 200-215
formal cause, 265, 271-273, 281
formalism, literary, 135, 136, 147-148
Forster, E.M., 55, 135, 136, 143-144, 151,
      158, 187, 388
Fort Valley State College, 3, 39, 41
Foster, Jeannette, 112
Foster, Stephen Wayne, 92-103
France (death penalty), 69, 70, 72, 73
Frank, Barney, 403-406, 414
Frank, Bernhard, 244-251
Fraxi, Pisanus; see Ashbee, Henry S.
Free Briton, 76
free will, 331
Freedman, Mark, 117, 305, 314, 316-326
freedom, 296
Freeman, H., 82
Freire, Paulo, 371, 372, 382
French active, 421f
French passive, 421
Freud, Sigmund, 137, 180, 347
Friedenberg, Edgar Z., 49-56
Friedman, Sandford, 187, 190, 191
The Frontrunner, 158
fucking, 55
fugitives, Dutch, 87
fulfillment, 352
Fullerton, Morton, 191
Fung, Yu-lan (historian), 281
Fun With Our Gay Friends, 111
Futuyma, Doug, 382

Gallatin, James Francis, Count de, 201, 205
Ganymede, 279
Garde, Noel I., 99-100
garrotting of homosexuals, 73, 77, 88, 89, 90
Gautier, Théophile, 140
gay, 340, 341, 346, 347
Gay (NYC newspaper), 414
Gay Academic Union, 49, 61, 62, 178, 188
Gay Americans Day (Mass.), 403, 406
gay apologists, 295
gay bars, 389, 390, 392, 415
gay behaviors, 17-18, 33f, 46-47
Gay Bibliography, 108-112, 114, 115, 117,
      118
Gay Book Award, 108, 110-113, 116
gay cause as therapy, 325
gay chairpersons, 12-15, 42
Gay Community News (Boston), 404, 407,
      414
The Gay Crusaders (Tobin), 118
Gay Day, 58, 61
gay females, see lesbians
Gay Guidelines, 114, 118
Gay Legislation '75 (Mass.), 405f
gay liberation movement, 50ff, 108, 111,
      115, 116, 121-122, 128, 286, 339,
      340-341, 387, 389f, 395, 398, 401-
      406, 411, 412, 414, 422

gay liberationists, 203
gay literature, 35-37, 43
gay males, 216-243, 246-250, 308-310,
      316, 317, 319, 323, 332, 415-427
gay marriages, 21-22
The Gay Mystique, 111
Gay News (London), 292, 301
gay people, 115, 287, 298
Gay People's Union of University of
      Missouri, Kansas City, 68
gay self-definitions, 13-15
gay stereotypes, 392-400, 410
      see stereotypes
gay student-gay faculty relations, 61-63
gay student groups, 57, 59-61
      see students
Gay Students Organization (Univ. of N.H.),
      396f, 409
Gay Students at Temple, 58
gay studies, 35-37, 44-45, 61, 62, 113, 124,
      152-163
gay superiority, 274-275
gay vote, 401, 405
gay women: see lesbians
gay writers, 23, 24
gayness, 335-345
Gays of Ottawa (Ontario), 398, 414
Geach, Peter Thomas, 283, 300
Gebhard, Paul, 413
gender, 372
gender-reversal, linguistic, 231
Genet, Jean, 137, 140, 143, 145, 146, 158,
      190, 352
The Geneva School, 135
genocide, 56, 67, 70, 71, 82
Gerassi, John, 409, 413
Germany (Nazis), 67, 79-82
Gestapo, 81
Gibbon, Edward, 404f
Gide, André, 137, 140, 141, 143, 144,
      149, 190, 216-217, 224-243, 351
Gigl, J., 319, 326
Gilliatt, Penelope, 159
Ginsberg, Allen, 144, 178, 390
Gittings, Barbara, 107-118
GO Info, 414
God, 72, 82, 85, 86, 175, 268-269, 273-274,
      361-366
Goldman, Eric, 164, 177
Gomez, Antonio, 84
Gomorrah, 69, 74, 86; see Sodom
Good (in idealism), 260-261
good and bad (in materialism), 257
Goodbye to Berlin, 353, 359
Goodman, Paul, 50, 178
Gordon, Stephen, 107
The Gospel, 346, 348, 349
GPU News, 381
Graham, Martha, 181-182
Grahn, Judy, 124
grammatical construction, form, 283-284,
      285, 286, 287, 292-293, 300
Grand Canyon, 209
Greco-Roman, 338, 343, 344
Greece, 68, 69, 93-94
Greek active, 421f
Greek Love, see Boys
Greek passive, 421f
Groningen (executions), 88

group marriage, 346
group sex, 319, 335
groups, 324
Growing Up Straight, 407
guilt, 203, 234, 266-267, 273, 331, 370
Gulab Singh, 95-96
Gunn, Thom, 178, 190

Haarlem (executions), 88
Hadrian, 247-248
Hague (executions), 77, 87, 88
Hall, Lynn, 113, 118
Hall, Radclyffe, 351
Hamiskjold, Dag, 388
Hanckel, Frances, 111, 113, 117, 118
"Hands," 393f
hanging of homosexuals, 73, 88, 91
Hanon, Gerald, 410
Harmodius, 68
Hart Crane: A Biographical and Critical Study, 194, 198
Hart Crane: An Introduction and Interpretation, 194, 195, 198
Hart Crane's Sanskrit Charge, 195, 199
The Hart Crane Voyages, 198
Hartshorne, 365
Harvey, John F., 331, 332
hate, 352
hatred, 222
Hazo, Samuel, 194, 195, 198
Hebraic tradition, 335
Hebrew religion, 269-270, 273, 276
Hebrews, 337, 338
hedonism, 257-158
Hegel, 260, 263, 278
Henderson, J.L., 362
henotheism, 269
Henry VIII's law, 71
heresy, 68, 69, 71, 72, 78
hermaphrodite, 238
Herodotus, 94
heroes, heroines (spirits), 268, 273
Herrnstein, 375
Hess, Dame Myra, 52
heteroïsic, 262-263
heterophilic, 262, 275
heterosexual, 262-263, 265, 343, 347
heterosexual bias, 217
heterosexual men, 320
heterosexual marriage, 168, 170, 345
heterosexual patterns, 372
heterosexual women, 319
heterosexuals, 331ff
heterosexuality, 115, 286-288, 290-292, 294, 296, 297, 298, 299, 337
Heusden (executions), 89
hide-and-seek games, 418
hiding, 217-218, 320
        see closet, concealment
Himmler, Heinrich, 81
Hinduism, 353, 357
Hine, Daryl, 178
hinjras, 93, 101
hiring, 62
Hirschfield, Magnus, 80
Hisamatsu, Shin-ichi (Zen aesthetician), 278
historical, 336, 337
history, 67-103
History of the Inquisition of Spain, 72, 84

Hitler, 53, 79-82, 166
Hitler-Stalin Pact, 169
Hobbes, 257-258, 263
Hoffman, Martin, 149
Hölderlin, Friedrick, 179, 183
Holiness Code, 68
Holland (executions), 73-78, 85-91
        deportation of homosexuals by Nazis, 81
Holland, Isabelle, 118
Holland, Norman, 137
Hollywood, 287
holoscopic systems, 279
Holy Roman Empire, 201
Holy Spirit, 338
Home, Daniel Dunglas, 99
Homer, Winslow, 111
homoeroticism, 275
homoïsic, 255-257, 259, 261-264, 266, 271-276, 280
Homophile Community Health Service (Boston), 403
homophile movement, 389, 398
Homophile Union of Boston, 403, 411
homophilic, 255, 262-264, 267-277, 279
homophobia, 125, 220-221, 250, 320ff, 330, 400f, 404-406
        —females as more hostile, 15-17
        —objective measures of, 4ff
        —religious influences, 5-6, 9
        —regional influences, 5-8, 17, 22
        —school size influences, 8-9
        —size of department influences, 9f
        —taboo, 18-24
homophobic, 255, 264, 268-276, 279
homosexual, 346
homosexual aesthetics, 351
Homosexual Behavior Among Males, 410, 413
Homosexual Emancipation Movement in Germany, 84
homosexual imagination, 204, 208, 108
The Homosexual in America, 108, 389, 413
homosexual insight, 350
homosexual intellect, 205
"The Homosexual Literary Tradition," 123-124
homosexual literature, 201
Homosexual Oppression and Liberation, 158
homosexual relationships, 305
The Homosexual Revolution, 413
Homosexualität und Strafrecht, 85
homosexuality, 275, 288, 290-292, 294, 296, 297, 337, 366
homosexuality, cross-species
        incidence of, 331
        —Christopher Isherwood on, 200, 212-214
Homosexuality and Creative Genius, 351
Homosexuality: Its Causes and Cure, 391, 410, 413
homosexuality, J. R. Ackerly on, 202, 203
homosexuality and language, 145-146
Homosexuality: Lesbians and Gay Men in Society, History, and Literature, 113
homosexuality, psychological research, 307-308

homosexuality as substitute, 357
homosexuality, Vita Sackville-West on, 200, 209, 210-211
Homosexuality and the Western Christian Tradition, 71, 83
homosexuals, see gay males, gay people, lesbians
"Homosexuals and the Dealth Penalty in Colonial America," 83
homosexuals as symbols, 168ff
honesty, 319
Hooker, Evelyn, 305, 314, 316, 325
Hopkins, June, 317, 326
Horstman, W., 320, 326
Horton, Philip, 194, 197
hostility, 351
The Hot Season, 173
hotlines, 60, 61
Houston, Texas, mass murders, 395, 408
Howard, Richard, 178-192
hug-a-homosexual (gay kissing booth), 109, 110
Hugh-Smith, John, 192
human relations, 336
human sexuality, 335, 336, 344, 346, 349
Hume, David, 285, 294, 296, 297-298, 299, 301
humor, 220, 225ff, 425
Humphries, Laud, 123, 281, 427
Hutcheson, Francis, 296-297, 301-302
Huxley, Aldous, 278
Hyde, Montgomery, 84
Hyperboreans, 97
hypnotism, 260
hypocrite (in materialism), 257

I Am a Camera, 350
idealism, 259-264, 272, 274-275
identity, 200f, 320ff
idealogy, 171, 370
idolatry, 71, 330
If It Die, 143, 144
ignorance, 353
I'll Get There, It Better Be Worth the Trip, 118
illness, 219; see sickness
image of God, 330, 331
imagination, 298-299, 300, 301
The Immoralist, 140
The Impuritans, 217, 239
In the Thirties, 352
In a Yellow Mood, 174
inauthenticity, 53
incarnation, 332
incrimination, 352
independence, 362-363
Independence Hall, 389
India, 95-96
Indians, American, 67, 97
industrialization, 339
inner-direction, 316f
Inquisition, in England, 70; in Spain, 70, 72, 76; in Portugal, 72
insecurity, 351
Institute for Sex Research, 399, 413
Institutes au droit criminel, 84
Institutes of the Laws of England, 70, 83
insurance, 23, 46
INTEGRITY: Gay Episcopal Forum, 30

Intellectual Freedom Committee of American Library Association, 109
interpersonal competence in meeting my mail, 424
intimacy, 162
intra-sexuality, 267
intuition (in idealism), 261, 263, 272
I.Q., 373
Is Gay Good? 84
Isabella, Queen of Spain, 70
Isherwood, Christopher, 113, 158, 159, 181, 190, 200, 211-214, 350-360
Israel, ancient, 95

Jacquemont, Victor, 95-96
Jahrbuch für sexuelle Zwischenstufen, 83, 84, 85, 87
James, Henry, 55, 124, 179, 185-186, 191-192, 204
Jameson, Fredric, 138, 149
Jay, Karla, 15-16, 216-243
jealousy, 220ff, 236
Jensen, 375
Jesus, 270, 332, 333, 365
Jewish family, 168, 169
Jews, 52, 67, 68, 69, 70, 71, 80, 227, 315
job counseling services, 324
job discrimination, 109, 111, 116
job security, 3-48, 320, 324
John (Apostle), 270
John Birch Society, 406
jokes, 220, 225ff
Jonathan, 248-250; see David
Jones, Clinton R., 350-360
Jordan Marsh Co. (Boston), 402
Journal of Abnormal Psychology, 128
Journal of Homosexuality, 83
Journals of Christopher Columbus, First Voyage, 193
Journey to a War, 353
Jousse, Daniel, 72
Joyce, James, 55
Judeo-Christian tradition, 336
Judaism, 335; see Hebrew Religion
judgment, 174, 285, 286, 289, 293, 294, 296, 298
  —autonomy of, 284, 286, 292-293, 294, 295, 297, 298, 299
  —heteronomy of, 284, 297, 299
judgments, a priori, 283, 284, 286, 292-293, 294, 299
Judiciary Committee (Mass. legislature), 403, 404, 406
Justinian, 70, 85

Kadesh (goddess), 269
Kampen (execution), 89
Kant, Immanuel, 282-285, 286, 287, 289-290, 293, 294, 295, 298, 300
  —doctrine of universal voice, 284-285, 298
Karachi, 92, 93
Karlen, Arno, 149
Kathleen and Frank, 200, 211-214, 352
Katz, Jonathan, 113, 407
King Lear, 20
Kinsey, Alfred, 388f, 399, 413
Kinsey Institute, 317
Kinsey Report, 165, 177

Neue Gedichte, 244, 245, 247, 249, 250
neurosis, 351
neurotic, 315
New Amsterdam (executions), 73
New Criticism, 135
New Hampshire, 71 (death penalty), 390, 395-397, 409
New Haven (death penalty), 71
New Jersey (death penalty), 71
New Testament, 270, 346; see bible
New York City, 389f, 397
New York City Council, 397
New York State (death penalty), 71
New York Times, 213
Newbery-Caldecott Awards (for children's books), 111
newsletters, 60
newspapers, 416ff
Newsweek, 390, 395, 408, 414
Newton, Dave, 382
Nicholas V, Pope, 72
Nichols, F.M., 83
Nichols, Jack, 160, 408
Nicholson, Harold, 207, 209
Nicholson, Nigel, 200, 206, 207
Night of the Long Knives, 81
Nijinski, Waslaw, 186
Nile, 248
Nirvana, 261
Noble, Elaine, 402-404, 406, 414
nonaesthetic, 288-290
normality, abnormality, 272, 285, 288, 292, 293, 296, 298, 301, 316
Northwestern University, 107, 117
Norton, Rictor, 24, 123-124, 136, 138, 145, 149, 151, 192
Nouvelle Critique, 135

Oberholtzer, W.., 84
Oberstone, Andrea, 319, 326
obsessive sexuality, 204
O'Callaghan, E.B., 84
"Of Men and Little Boys", 398, 410
Ogden, C.K., 84
O'Hara, Frank, 178
The Ohio Review, 190, 191
Old Testament, 68, 71, 269-270, 335, 337; see bible, scripture, etc.
Om (personal name), 273-274)
On the Frontier, 353
One Reality (in idealism), 260-263, 274-275, 277
Ong, Walter, J., 148, 151
Oosterdeel-Langewoldt, 77
openness, 319
oppression, 52, 67-91, 230, 370, 381
optimism, 361
oral sex, 319; see cunnilingus
organs, genital, 293
organs, sense, 285, 293, 294, 296
orientals, 421
Orpheus, 140, 150
Orpheus, 140
Orlando, 140, 208, 209, 211
Ortleb, Chuck, 181, 191
Oscar Wilde Memorial Players, 112
Other Face of Love, 84
Ottawa, Ontario, 397f
Ouspensky, P.D., 195, 198

Out (magazine), 393, 414
Out: The Gay Perspective, 178, 191
Ovesey, Lionel, 306, 307, 314
Ovid, 94, 150

pagan religions, 315
pain, 351
Palestine, 68, 85
Pallavicino, Ferrante, 94
Palmer, Marlene, 382
pamphlet file in libraries, 115
pansexuality, 262
"The Panther," 244
Papon, Jean, 84
parades, 324
Paragraphy 175 (of German Criminal Code), 80, 81
parents, 321
Paris (executions), 72
Paris, 202f
Parks, Rosa, 389f
Parliament (British), 70, 73
Parmenides, 259
Parnassus: Poetry in Review, 190
participation in decision-making, right of, 306, 308, 309, 311, 312
Partisan Review, 181
passing, 139, 140, 150
passive roles, 319
passivity, 371
passwords, 321
Patanjali, 277
pathetic fallacy, 363
pathology, 51
Patience and Sarah, 110, 158
patriarchy, 370
Patterson, Rochelle, 412
Paulson, C., 319, 326
Paulson, R., 319, 326
peak experience, 351
pedagogy, 370f
Pedagogy of the Oppressed, 382
pederasty, 233ff, 279; see boys
pederasty, Burton's essay on, 92-103
pedophilia, see boys
Penitent Death of . . . John Atherton, 84
Penn, William, 71
Pennsylvania (death penalty), 71
Pentagon, 389
Penthesilea, 279
periodicals, gay, 109, 113, 115, 117
permissively, 361
Perry, Troy, 330
persecution, 227
Persia, 95
"Persian Heliotrope," 244
personal ads, 416, 418
personalities (in dualism), 264, 270-271
Persse, Jocelyn, 192
perversion, 54, 352
perversity, polymorphous, 370
perverts, 227
pessimism, 361
phallism, 280-281
phallus, 246, 250
Philistines, 248
philosophers, philosophy, 284, 286, 300
philosophy, 253-302
philosophy of sexual liberation, 370

sex negative, 370-379
Sex Offenders, 399, 413
sex role preference of advertisers, 421
sex-role stereotyping, 125-127
sex roles, transcendence, 318
"Sex and the Single Cataloguer: New Thoughts on Some Unthinkable Subjects," 108
Sex Variant Women in Literature, 112, 118
sexism, 122-129, 340
sexual aberrations (subject heading), 109
sexual attractiveness, 286-288, 290-291, 293, 295, 296, 298
Sexual Behavior in the Human Male, 388f, 413
Sexual Deviation (subject heading), 115
sexual interest, 366
Sexuality Morality, 110
"Sexual Orientation Disturbance," 407
Sexual Perversion (subject heading), 115; see perversion
sexual problems, 336, 342
sexual revolution, 342
sexuality, 287, 288-290, 292, 306, 336, 337, 338, 339, 342, 346, 391, 393, 399f, 401, 410f
Schachter, J., 82
Shakespeare, 18-20, 26, 31-32, 46, 55, 187
Shamans, 268, 269, 280
Shankara, 277
shared accommodation ads, 416
Shaykh Nasr, 95
Shelley, P.B., 351
Shennandoah, 190
Sherrill, Ken, 321
Shively, Michael G., 305, 307, 314, 305-314
Sibley, Frank N., 284, 285, 288, 293, 301
sickness model, 315, 354, 391f, 393, 395, 400, 407, 410
Siegilman, Marvin, 305, 314, 317, 318, 326
Signer, Ethan, 378
sin, 354, 363f, 366
A Single Man, 350, 356-357, 359-360
Sir Walter Scott, 338
sissies, 318
Sissinghurst, Castle, 206
Sixtus IV, 98
skepticism, 296, 297, 298, 299
slang, 145, 231
Smith, Henry Justin, 191
Smith, Joseph, 274
smoking, 297
social contract, 258-259
Social Democrats (German), 79, 82
social functions, 225
social hours, 59
social oppression, 325; see oppression
social prestige, 297; see respectability
Social Responsibilities Round Table of American Library Association, 108, 109, 112
society, 340, 343, 344, 345, 347, 348
Society and the Healthy Homosexual, 125, 160, 400f, 413
socio-economic status, 421f
sociology, 3-48, 385-427
Socrates, Intro., 146
Sodom, 69, 70, 74, 86, 237, 329, 332
Sodome et Gomorrhe, 217, 222, 237

sodomites, see prostitutes (temple/cult)
sodomy, 98-99, 401
—executions for, 70, 73, 74, 80, 85, 89
—statutes, 29
Soleinne, Martineau de, 99-100
solipsism, 263-264, 273-274
Somerville, James W.F., 282-302
Songs of Bilitis, 124
"Song of Myself," 197, 199
Sonnets to Orpheus, 244
Sonnini de Manoncour, Charles, 95
Sontag, Susan, 181, 190, 191
Sork, Vicki, 382
Sotadic Zone, 93
South Boston, Mass., 412
Southern Belles, 54
space, literary — as a homosexual motif, 142-145
Spain, 70, 72
Spanish Inquisition, 72, 76
speakers' bureaus, 60
Spears, Monroe K., 190
spies, 170-173
Spinoza, 260, 277
spirits, 264-270
Stanley, Julia P., 121-131
state (in materialism), 258-259
State Department, U.S., 389, 400
status (in dualisms), 270-271, 273
Statutes at Large of Pennsylvania from 1682 to 1801, 83
Stein, Gertrude, 111
Steakley, James D., 84-85
Steinberg, Bruce, 382
stereotypes, 174, 315, 318; see roles and sexual stereotypes
sterility, 237
Stevens, Wallace, 187
Sticks and Stones, 118
stigma, 271, 281, 381; see homophobia
Stirner, Max, 278
Stockinger, Jacob, 135-151, esp. 147, 151
Stoics, 259, 261, 277
Stoltenberg, J., 370, 381, 382
Stonewall Riots, 52, 110, 238, 389; see Christopher Street Riots
stoning of homosexuals, 68-69, 70
Stout, jean, 382
straight(s), 347; see heterosexuals
Strength through Joy, 85
structuralism, 147, 151
The Strumpet Wind, 170, 172
student-faculty relations, 61-63
student groups, 57, 59-61
Student Homophile League, Boston, 403
Student Homophile League, Rutgers University, 58, 61, 121, 391, 414
students, 10, 31f, 35, 41f, 111, 115, 117, 152ff
Sturgis, Howard Overing, 192
style, 200, 212
sub-culture, 321ff
subject headings in libraries, 108, 112, 115
subjectivity and objectivity, 283, 284, 288, 293, 298, 301
subjugation, 373
submission, 330
submissiveness, 318
subservience, 166

suffering, 351, 355; see genocide
Sufism, 260, 262, 278
suicide, 247
Sunday Bloody Sunday, 159
"The Sundial," 244
Supreme Judicial Court (Mass.), 402, 405, 406
surrealism, 146
suspension of judgment, 174
Susse, Aaron, Baron de la, 99
"The Swan," 244
Switzerland, 70
symbol, homosexuals as, 168
symbolism, 146
Symonds, John Addington, 92, 99-100, 107, 182, 351
sympathy, 274
The Symposium, 187
systems analysis, 375
Szasz, Thomas, 72

Tables . . . of Criminal Offenders (England, 1837), 72
taboo, 265-266; see homophobia
Tagett, Richard, 198
talent, 351
Talmud, 68, 82, 270
Tanner, Michael, 288, 301
Tao, Taoism, 259-260, 262, 276-277
Task Force on Gay Liberation of American Library Association, 105-118
taste, 282-285, 289-291, 294-296, 297, 298, 300
Tate, Allen, 188, 195, 198
teaching, 371
teenagers. See young people
technology, 374ff
Teilhard, Pierre de Chardin, 364, 366
Tel Quel critics, 146
Telos, 246
Temple University, 58
"Temporal Punishments Depicted," 74
tender-mindedness, 318
Tennyson, Alfred, 179, 183
tenure, 62
Terminal Essay, Burton's, 92-103
terms
    bisexual, 12-16
    bull-dyke, 126, 127-129
    drag queen, 126, 127-129
    effeminate, 125-126
    female, 125-126
    feminine, 125-126
    gay, 12-16, 124
    genocide, 67
    homosexuality, 123-124
    man-hater, 122, 127
    manly, 125-126
    mannish, 126
    masculine, 125-127
    nonblack, 16
    nonfemale, 16
    nongay, 12-16
    sissy, 125, 127
    tomboy, 125, 127
    woman-hater, 122, 127
    womanlike, 126
    womanly, 125-126
terrorization, 374

tertiary prevention, 324
Tertium Organum, 195, 198
textbook selection, 18, 43
textbooks, 24-27, 44-45, 116
theism, 361
Theodosius, 69
theology, 329
Theophanes, 70, 83
Theory of Legislation, 84
therapy, 315
Thessalonika, 69
Third World, 374ff
Thirwall, Connop, 93
Thomson, Governor Meldrim, 396f, 409
Thrasymachus, 257
Tobin, Kay, 117
Todd, Williams, 278
tolerance, 299, 302
Torée, Olof, 96
Toronto, Ontario, 398, 415ff
torture, 76, 82
Townsend, Prescott, 402f, 412
traditional marriage, 345; see marriage
"tragic sense of life," 364
Traité de la justice criminel, 72
transcendentalism, 259-260
transistors, 376
transsexuality, 280
transvestism, 18, 279-280, 340, 358
transvestites, 95-96, 346
Traubel, Horace, 191
Treese, Robert L., 330
Trefusis, Violet Keppel, 200, 207ff
tricks, 381
Trotsykism, 165
True-Blue Laws of Connecticut and New Haven, 83
Trumbull, J.H., 83
trust, 161
Trying Hard to Hear You, 118
Twain, Mark, 28
Two-Part Inventions, 179, 183-188
tyranny, 329
Tysens, G., 74

ulitarianism, 370
Ulrichs, Karl Heinrich, 92, 182
Ulysses, 55
Unamuno, Miguel, 364
Uniformed Fire Officers' Association, AFL-CIO, 397
United Press International, 395
universal standpoint, 298, 299-300
University of Chicago, 51
University of Missouri-Kansas City, 58
University of Paris, 72
University of Wisconsin, 59
unnatural, 210, 354
"Unnatural Crime," 84
unspeakableness, 67, 82
Unterecker, John, 199
Untitled Subjects, 179, 182-183, 185
Upward, Edward, 352
userers, 70
Utrecht (arrests), 74

Valencia, 72
Valerius Maximus, 94
Valéry, Paul, 145, 151